THE NINE LIVES OF JOHN OGILBY

Britain's Master Map Maker and His Secrets

———

Alan Ereira

DUCKWORTH

This edition first published in the United Kingdom by
Duckworth in 2019

Duckworth, an imprint of Prelude Books Ltd
13 Carrington Road, Richmond
TW10 5AA United Kingdom
www.preludebooks.co.uk

For bulk and special sales please contact
info@preludebooks.co.uk

A catalogue record for this book is available from the British Library Text design
and typesetting by Fakenham Prepress Solutions

Printed and bound in Great Britain by Clays

9780715652268

Contents

List of Illustrations

Introduction

On the evening of Monday, 8 February 1619, the eighteen-year-old John Ogilby stepped onto a stage in front of the entire court in the Great Hall of Whitehall Palace. This was a night of magic, the Shrove Monday masque organised by the Marquess of Buckingham, and Ogilby was the lead professional dancer. The masque had already been performed in the Banqueting House five weeks earlier, on Twelfth Night, but the show had not much pleased the King, and workmen clearing the scenery afterwards managed to burn the building down.[1] It had been erected for James but he had never liked it anyway. Now the entire stage and its machinery had been redesigned to fit into the Great Hall, which was less than half its size.[2]

Buckingham's reputation was at risk. The previous year's Shrove Tuesday masque had been written by Ben Jonson, and was detested by the King. The writer was now on an extended walking tour of Scotland and Buckingham had taken over. He and the set designer Inigo Jones knew they now had to demonstrate something brilliantly entrancing. So did the performers. John Ogilby would have to astonish the King.

Buckingham was twenty-six years old and the King was in love with him. He was James I's favourite courtier and the most celebrated dance performer of his time. When he was plain

George Villiers, the King had plucked him from obscurity, knighted him, promoted him to Baron, Viscount, Earl and then, on New Year's Day 1618, Marquess of Buckingham. The Marquess had found Ogilby dancing in a theatrical show and recognised him as an extraordinary talent. Now it was Ogilby who was the dancing commoner at court. Eight years before he had been a child pedlar working the streets to feed his parents in a debtor's prison. This was the night when he might leap right out of obscurity, to fame, wealth, even, perhaps, power.

Outside there was a winter chill, but the Hall was crammed. Last year some six hundred had attended, impossible in this small space. The Hall was jammed with elaborately dressed and overheated noble spectators, their lavish jewels sparkling in the candlelight, the ladies' feathered head-dresses and fans already smelling of the fug of smoke from the torches. Enthroned in front of the stage, looking at him expectantly, were King James and Queen Anne.

The masque had begun, as they always did, with grotesque low-life comedy, and then Inigo Jones' stage machinery began its work as the orchestra played: spheres and moons containing pages and torch-bearers descended, a heart-fortress opened to release Beauty, and then on came John Ogilby, fantastically dressed as Prognostication, the capering teller of the fortune of the year. He was the manifestation of an astronomical phenomenon that was the talk of the season, the comet that had appeared in November and taken over the sky in a most alarming way. It had hung over Britain for a month, visible even by day, its tail extending until it reached across more than half the sky.[3] England had been filled with prognostications, few of them encouraging.

The most eminent sky-watchers, including Galileo and Kepler, had more sense than to suggest that the comet was a prognostication of the fall of the mighty. What good would it do them to say it? James certainly disliked doom-laden prophecies, and wrote a poem to say that since no one had the faintest idea how to interpret the portent they would do better to say nothing. In private, he said it was "Venus with a firebrand in her arse."[4] John Ogilby, the best high-leaping professional dancer of the age, now manifested before him as the living embodiment and meaning of Venus with a firebrand up her arse.

Perhaps, as the astrologer John Bainbridge said, this comet heralded nothing but good.[5] Bainbridge would soon be Professor of Astronomy at Oxford, and that was the kind of prognostication that Ogilby was supposed to convey in his dance. He was a professional performer, and alone of the speaking cast had no script but was free to improvise. He capered up to the thrones and gave his poetical prognostication.

He then turned to excel himself with an astonishing leap into the dark. That must have been when he realised that it was the wrong move on this new, smaller stage, and he needed to twist in the air. His ligament popped. Crash.

At that moment, the musicians started up, the curtain at the back dropped, and a torch-lit scene appeared in mid-air with the lords and ladies of the masque – including Buckingham and Prince Charles – all in position. As the audience gasped and clapped, the set descended gracefully to reveal another illuminated perspective fantasy landscape in the air above them. It was a theatrical triumph. Ogilby crawled off unnoticed.

He would never dance again. He was crippled. This would be the story of his life – the firebrand up the arse, the leap, the ruinous crash. [6] But the comet did not only herald a crash for John Ogilby. It was recalled many times over the next decades as the harbinger of a great continent-spanning disaster that had been triggered in 1618 and grew like a long-lived whirlpool. It became the Thirty Years' War, which sucked all of Europe into its destructive maw, killing millions. New landscapes emerged, and in Britain that eventually led to Ogilby, a lame man in his seventies, creating a completely new way of seeing the land, a road-atlas. It was designed to presage a new future for the King and his Kingdom. Prognostication was still at work, setting out the future, in the 1670s.

*

John Ogilby was born in mysterious circumstances in Scotland in 1600, and was raised in poverty. He died seventy-six years later in London as the King's Cosmographer. He had made his reputation as a dancer, theatrical impresario, creator of public spectacle, translator, poet, publisher and finally as the man who quite literally put the new Britain on the map. There were other parts of his life for which he has never, until now, been known at all, including soldier, sailor and government agent. The world he was born into was profoundly medieval, the one he died in was recognisably modern. His work became to delineate this new world as the Cosmographer Royal responsible for scientifically determining its spatial structure so that it could be managed and governed by a new kind of state. He lived through the most deadly years Britain ever experienced.[7]

He survived one catastrophe after another to eventually bring the transformed country's portrait to birth, in a book called *Britannia*. This is not just a work of science and of reference: it is now clear that it formed part of a plot that reached to the very highest levels of power and was meant to re-shape the country.

During his lifetime, European civilisation was swept by an all-embracing change. Medieval philosophy, rooted in the religious thought of monastic learning, was replaced by new ways of thinking that challenged even the possibility of knowing anything. The old science, rooted in the confidence that we know the world through our senses and learn from tradition, was replaced by the new science of measurement and experiment. The old political order, based on hierarchic and dynastic power, was overthrown by a murderous tide of uprisings, rebellions and revolutions. The map of Europe was utterly changed, from a patchwork of medieval dynastic inheritances to a web of states and frontiers. Between Ogilby's thirtieth and seventieth birthdays, a combination of insurrection, famine and disease killed about a third of the continent's population. The survivors had to build a new kind of life in a new landscape.

I first came across John Ogilby when he was already over seventy, a man of spectacular energy and confidence, embarked on the project of measuring 26,000 miles of roads in England and Wales. I was following him on his Welsh roads, some 325 years after he had traced them, making a TV series on how things had been back in those days. That is when I realised that he was making something more than just a simple guidebook. It was designed as an instrument of conquest and of government, with a secret agenda that went to the very heart of what was being changed.

The transformation of Ogilby's world changed our understanding of heaven and earth in a way that has now come to threaten the future of the planet. Dramatic upheavals of thought and power 350 years ago created new political and commercial structures that launched the organised, systematised exploitation of nature that we now struggle to control.

The traditional understanding was clearly stated by Kepler in 1619. He was the discoverer of the laws that govern the movements of the planets, but he explained that, although these laws are entirely mathematical, the Earth must be understood as a living being. It is an integral whole, whose liquid flows and mineral contents are as important to its life as are the fluids and solids in a human being. He argued that the planet has a soul, intelligence and the capacity to experience and suffer, and spoke of "sympathy" between heaven and earth.[8] In the same year, René Descartes began the intellectual journey that would lead to a rejection of such assertions about the world, insisting that whatever cannot be known with certainty must be regarded as untrue. That argument, finally published in 1637 as the *Discourse on the Method of Rightly Conducting one's Reason and Seeking Truth in the Sciences*, is the foundation of the modern world.

I wanted to understand how and why we have changed. The life of a man who began in one world as a dance master, and ended in another as a scientific measurer and enumerator, became my key.

PART 1

The Journey to John Ogilby

Life 1. Beginning

The mysterious man

John Ogilby did not look like a secret man. His whole life, before and after he wrecked his leg, seemed to be a public performance. He was a dancer and theatrical performer who became an impresario and Master of the Revels in Ireland. He translated and published the classics in some of the most beautiful illustrated books ever produced, he flamboyantly wrote and orchestrated the public celebration of Charles II's coronation, and built the first Restoration theatre. With no experience of astronomy, mathematics or surveying, he was then appointed Cosmographer Royal, responsible for delineating the whole world. But somehow he managed to do all this while being mentioned in just a handful of surviving private letters and hardly any official documents. He pops up in the diaries of Ashmole, Hooke and Pepys, but just as a name, without reference to him doing or saying anything. He was never granted any honours. When he stops being on display, he disappears, a chimera, a vanishing act of smoke and mirrors. The truth is, he was not a simple or innocent man. Much of his life was spent in a grim world of spies, secret agents, indiscriminate slaughter and very discriminate execution.

Britannia is a product of the world of secrets.

Hidden origins

Britannia is the first road atlas ever made, a detailed and very beautiful scientific survey of the principal roads of England and Wales. It was commissioned by Charles II's principal minister, and there was a great deal of money behind it. It has a hidden agenda which has simply passed unnoticed. Some of the roads it shows were not actually in use, and represent journeys that no one wanted to make. It leaves out some important commercial routes, and the road to Liverpool is hidden. It was really designed as the handbook for a conspiracy, yet is flamboyant and extravagant. That is how it hides its secrets. The same is true of its author. The book was created after a quite fantastic personal journey through a landscape of catastrophic upheavals, and he needed to conceal the shape of his own life.

1. Cartouche on the first road in *Britannia*.

Historians speak of a mid-seventeenth-century "general crisis". The political philosopher James Harrington roared his way through a survey of his world in 1656: "What is become of the Princes of Germany? Blown up. Where are the Estates or the power of the people in France? Blown up. Where is that of the people of Aragon and the rest of the Spanish kingdoms? Blown up. On the other side, where is the king of Spain's power in Holland? Blown up. Where is that of the Austrian princes in Switz? Blown up."[1] By then Ogilby too had been blown up, as well as being washed up in a shipwreck and locked up in Dunkirk. The English had chopped the head off their king. Instead of living under the stable authority of an eternal divinely-ordained order, people experienced the world in a state of chaotic flux. Old confidence was replaced by new and fundamental doubt. Revolution, a word which had once represented the calm order of perfect heavenly movement, was brought to earth to represent a bloody overthrow of order. Traditional mathematics measured things that would be the same tomorrow as they had been yesterday. Now a new kind of mathematics was being created to measure rates of change, where nothing would be the same again.

Through all this upheaval, Ogilby, a man without position or resources, never lost his bearings or his vision of how the past would shape the future. But how it was supposed to do that was the secret of the book. It can only be understood by understanding the man. He was not who he is supposed to have been.

The tailor's material

Every account of the man relies on a single source for Ogilby's early life. That source is a set of notes in *"Brief Lives", chiefly of*

Contemporaries, set down by John Aubrey, between the Years 1669 and 1696. In 1672, when John Ogilby was seventy-one years old and preparing *Britannia*, he hired the forty-six-year-old Aubrey, a Fellow of the Royal Society, as an assistant. Aubrey had been ruined by unfortunate lawsuits, and his friend Christopher Wren had arranged for Ogilby to give him work. He was a remorseless collector of information about places and people. His confusing collection of notes, a bundle of corrected and rewritten manuscripts, is what is known as *Brief Lives*. His work is more honest than any biography because it was never turned into a story, and we can see Aubrey scrabbling for and striving to assess scraps of unreliable information. In Ogilby's case that was not easy. For some reason his employer kept the details of his origins secret. Aubrey reported that he said "drollingly that he would have as great contests hereafter for the place of his birth as of Homer's; but he made this cypher".[2] What follows is a scrawl where the second line is struck out and the last line is obscured by crossing out and ink blots. It seems to say:

At ... cleare
ther did I well fere
where ... man ... the father

The blots are deliberate, and appear to have been smeared on. They were made after the writing had dried, and with a different ink. It is possible to use that difference to enhance the writing a little, but it does not help much.

Who made this unreadable? Why should a man in his seventies, engaged on a project sanctioned by the King and the Privy Council, be hiding his origins? All Aubrey knew was that Ogilby had told an astrologer, John Gadbury, that he was born in or near Edinburgh in 1600, and Aubrey did not seem confident that he had this straight. There is no evidence that

2. Aubrey's notebook, MS. Aubr. 8, fol. 45, Bodleian Library, Oxford; below: with blotting reduced.

Ogilby ever asked Gadbury for a horoscope. Aubrey made a note to check further. All Ogilby would reveal was that "He was of a Gentleman's family, and bred to his Grammar". "Grammar" at this time simply meant speaking well and correctly, and indicates that he was brought up to speak like an Englishman, not a Scot. "Of a Gentleman's family" is an odd expression: he was not saying that his father was a gentleman, but that he was well connected. But his lips were sealed.

Aubrey goes on to say that Ogilby's father became a bankrupt and his parents were put in the King's Bench prison, where they became dependent on the boy: "His son relieved by his own Industry (Spangles, needles), being then but about the age of 12 or 13 yeares."

Aubrey was being invited to believe that Ogilby's father was an Edinburgh tailor. So why say he was "of a gentleman's family"? "Spangles" were sequins: the man was a craftsman as highly skilled as a jeweller or sword-maker. In an age before cars, effective heating and mechanical weaving, clothing was of universal importance. From the early Middle Ages until the late eighteenth century, the entire commercial life of northern Europe was rooted in the cloth trade. There was an incredible number of tailors, including, in 1600, half the craftsmen of Edinburgh. Clothes were also ways of expressing personal identity, wealth and status to an extent that we can barely understand. The clothes of ordinary people were their greatest expense, and a gentleman's outfit could require a fortune. The shimmering, spangled, embroidered creations worn by the masque audience who watched Prognostication perform cost truly fantastic sums. The days when a great lord could demonstrate his status by extravagant hospitality in his own castle were over: he and his lady now had to make that demonstration at royal palaces, so their riches had to be displayed on their bodies. That display was not just of costly materials and accoutrements, but also of the craftsmanship that served its wearer. Three hundred tailors worked on the wedding dress of King James' bride, Anne of Denmark.

Medieval clothing had been loose and all-concealing, owing more to the weaver' than the tailor, but men's dress now had to be cut and shaped to display and flatter the noble body. A successful tailor would be a prosperous man, and would be literate. The King himself petitioned the Edinburgh Incorporation to accept one of his personal tailors as a member. The use of quantities of spangles shows that John the tailor was a high-class outfitter. Spangles were used only on the most expensive and flamboyant garments. They were small discs cut from a sheet of silver or silver gilt, usually with an off-centre hole so that when sewn onto clothing they would catch the light, especially candlelight. He was evidently decorating the costumes of the aristocracy. He made his living serving the ladies and gentlemen of an elegant and cosmopolitan court ruled by an intellectual, reserved, rather effeminate King.

And there he would presumably have stayed, had Elizabeth of England had an heir. But she did not, and when she died in 1603 the Scottish King James VI was proclaimed James I of England. He rode to London, and so did most of his Court. England and Scotland had been fighting each other for centuries: there had been at least seven major battles between them in the previous hundred years. Now, in a bloodless triumph, the Scottish King took over England. His Progress made its stately way south, with James showering gifts and honours as he went.

James said that he would come back to Scotland in three years, but in fact he took fourteen years to return (and then did not stay long). In the meantime, tradesmen who had stayed in Edinburgh lost their livings and the city decayed. The position of the two hundred and fifty Edinburgh tailors was obviously rather grim once so many of their wealthy customers had left and the city's economy collapsed. John and his wife bundled up their possessions and set off with the five-year-old on a four-hundred-mile trek south.

It was a dramatic event for them, emigration with all the fabrics and tools of their trade. They must have spent about a month on the road to a new life, a road which had already been travelled by thousands of their fellow-Scots whose livelihoods were tied to the court. The Ogilbys could afford to make the journey relatively comfortably, and would have put their trunks in a wagon, but that would not have meant they had a coach. Coaches were aristocratic urban novelties. When the English Ambassador brought one to Scotland in 1598, "it was counted a great marvel".[3] It was an unsprung box. When the French Ambassador travelled from Edinburgh to London in 1603, his wife was carried the whole way in a chair with slings, by two alternating teams of four porters.[4]

We know that Ogilby's father was in London by June 1606, because there is a record of John Ogilby, tailor, being admitted into the Worshipful Company of Merchant Taylors there at a ceremony that involved swearing an oath of loyalty to the Crown and the Company.[5] The records of the Edinburgh guilds are not coherent enough to identify tailor John Ogilby, but the fact that he was admitted to the Merchant Taylors "by redemption" shows that he was established and successful. There were plenty of tailors in the Scottish countryside, but only an Edinburgh tailor could stand a chance of acceptance in the London Livery Company.

He would not have made the journey much before this ceremony, because without being admitted he would be barred from working. To enter it in this way, without having served an apprenticeship ("servitude") or being the son of a Freeman of the Company ("patrimony"), required good contacts and a deep purse. An invitation had to be offered, and a financial arrangement made that was enticing enough to overcome the Merchant Taylors reluctance to further dilute their large membership. Later the same year the merchant companies of London formally petitioned against a proposal to force them to accept "Scotchmen" as members.[6] This Scotchman's entry had been carefully prepared, by someone with serious influence. Aubrey would never discover the secret of John Ogilby's birth.

The debtor's prison

London would have been a shock to the Ogilbys. Edinburgh was a compact stone-built city with less than 20,000 inhabitants which had been dominated by the Court until 1603 and was now rather a hollow shell. London was over ten times as big, a rough, tough, bustling heap of mostly wooden buildings, people and dirt. The Court was not even part of this city, it was over two miles away in Westminster. According to Aubrey, things did not go well.

The tailor from Scotland never really stood a chance. His experience was in serving the Edinburgh Court, which looked to the Continent for its style and manners and had no connection to England. More precisely, as a member of the wealthy Clan Ogilvie, whose lands were in the fertile glens to the east, his main customers in Scotland had probably been the 5th Lord Ogilvie of Airlie and his sons. The eldest of them, the Master of Ogilvie, had been given a magnificent court wedding in 1581 and had been a Gentleman of the Bedchamber. Court fashions at Holyrood were quite different from Whitehall. The King's mother, Mary Stuart, had been married to the French Dauphin, and James' Queen was Anne of Denmark. Male courtiers followed French fashion, and ladies, German. Those Scottish nobles who had gone to London now wanted to be dressed in the English fashion and desperately needed a real London tailor. If the Ogilbys did not arrive until 1606, they had already missed the boat. Even if John's father could deliver the goods, he would obviously lose the commission the moment he opened his mouth.

Tailors working at this level of society needed huge sums for the materials to make lavish costumes with masses of gold and silver decoration. It was common to find wills where the value of clothes far outstripped everything else in the estate – sometimes because the dead man had sold off land to buy the wardrobe. A Thames waterman and poet named John Taylor wrote angrily of the kind of man who would

Wear a farm in shoe-strings edged with gold
And spangled garters worth a copy-hold;
A hose and doublet which a lordship cost;
A gaudy cloak three mansions price almost.

It seems that the infant John Ogilby imbibed with his mother's milk an understanding of the importance of showing extravagant luxury as the key to claiming a place in the public arena. This would shape his productions on stage, in ceremonies and in print. But he also learned that this carried huge financial risks. His father, looking to build a clientele from scratch in this city, had to have fabrics and decorations to display. If he did win a commission he could not expect money in advance, and would have to exercise great patience waiting to be paid while holding off his own suppliers. Looking for aristocratic clients meant he also had to have prestigious premises. None of this was cheap.

By 1606 the Edinburgh tailors in London had already started to starve. Their wealthier countrymen set up a fund to help them out, the "Scots Box", but still did not offer them work. John's father seems to have had enough reserves to keep going for a few years, but to do that he must have been spending his capital and then selling his stock. With insufficient commissions, he ended up bankrupt and became a prisoner of the Court of the King's Bench.

He was held under the Statute Against Bankrupts, Tudor legislation based on the firm belief that debtors are swindlers, liable to run off with goods they have not paid for. The object was to seize them and sell all they had for their creditors.

Having failed to keep the creditors off his back the tailor was in a grim place. The King's Bench prison in Borough

High Street, Southwark was filthy, overcrowded with around 400 inmates (mostly debtors) and had frequent outbreaks of typhus fever. The playwright Thomas Dekker was imprisoned there for a debt of £40 in 1612, and wrote in a letter that "I live amongst the Goths and Vandals, where Barbarousness is predominant". The prison was effectively a walled-in street with dwellings and some open space. It was ruled by laws imposed by the inmates, erratically overseen by their few gaolers. Dekker seems to have become particularly concerned for the prison keeper, living in a tumult of continuous violence: "I think he cannot sleep: for his pillow is not stuffed with feathers but with fears. Every prisoner sinks under the weight of his own debts, but the keeper feels the burden of all."[7]

The prison keeper and gaolers consoled themselves by charging prisoners for their keep, and for a large enough sum would let a man serve his sentence within a three mile radius outside the prison walls. Those who could not pay depended on money provided by a central fund, but they got little from it and in 1624 eighty inmates starved to death.[8] We do not know where Ogilby senior had his bed, but he was certainly better off than Dekker. Any tailor worth hiring could quickly insert secret pockets in hems and linings where small high-value objects could be stashed away. The only problem was to find some way of selling them without the creditors noticing.

That, as Aubrey evidently realised, would explain how the young John Ogilby came to be quietly selling high-value clothing decoration, a little at a time, and bringing back food for his parents. He must, Aubrey is suggesting, have been quite adept at concealing what he was up to. Little John, around nine years old, had been ducking and diving among the tailors of Southwark, which was a centre of the trade. Aubrey suggests he was twelve or thirteen, but his account describes

John's father being released in 1612, when the boy was eleven, so we can assume that he was in the King's Bench prison from around 1610.

The dance of the law

The King's Bench was, like all London prisons, a public space. During the day it was just as open to gossip, political intelligence, trade and free conversation as anywhere else in the city. It was inevitably particularly alive to scandals concerning lawyers and that may well be how young John Ogilby became aware of the importance of dance for the Common Law.

In 1610, the judges declared that they had the power to strike down an Act of the King in Parliament. The lawyers of Lincoln's Inn did not agree and were alarmed. They decided that judges were overstepping their power and they acted decisively and dramatically. On 2 February 1610, when the judges visited the Inn, the whole of the Bar refused to dance.

Dancing was at the heart of the law. Every Saturday through the winter until Candlemas, the Inns of Court held their Revels. Members of an Inn who did not dance could be fined. 2 February was Candlemas and the benchers of Lincoln's Inn, its senior members, had invited the judges to their Revels. The magnificent Great Hall was cleared of its long oak dining tables and benches to make space and the stately music began. But the lawyers would not dance.

This challenged authority at its core. The ritual of dancing the Old Measures was how lawyers physically participated in the inner law of the world which governed men and nature. The Common Law was not invented by Kings or Parliaments. It was the law inherent in the world from time immemorial, which lawyers learned to understand and interpret. The laws that kept the stars in their courses gave power to Princes and meaning to agreements. The Commonwealth and common sense, the common man and the Commons of England, formed a harmony with the heavens themselves and the Courts of Kings and Courts of Justice stepped together to the tune of the music of the spheres.

But the majority of the members of Lincoln's Inn had not been called to the Bar and never would be. They were young gentlemen completing an education that would fit them for life at court. Now the judges had set themselves above King and Parliament, and these gentlemen profoundly disapproved. They would not dance.

The most senior judge embarrassed that night was the Chief Justice of the Common Pleas, Edward Coke, himself a member of Lincoln's Inn. His court was a savage place, where men judged to have threatened the established order could be sentenced to having their guts torn out of their living bodies. It had now set its own power and its understanding of natural law above King and Parliament. A Dr Bonham had been imprisoned by the Royal College of Physicians because he was practising without their licence. Their power was based on two Acts of Parliament and a royal warrant. The King had told Parliament, a few months before, that a monarch is the most supreme power on Earth: "kings are not only God's lieutenants upon earth, and sit upon God's throne, but even by God himself they are called gods". But now the Chief Justice and his fellow judges declared that they were striking down these Acts of Parliament because they made the College a judge in its own cause. This, the judges declared, was contrary to natural law and so to Common Law, and would not be allowed. Even an Act of the King in Parliament must be judged and can be overthrown by the law.[9] No man and no power can be above the Law.

The King was furious. The members of the Inn, courtly men, were profoundly alarmed about where this would lead. So they dared to challenge the judges, and refused to dance.

When the benchers, the governing body of the Inn, met the next day to decide how to punish this mutiny, the word spoken was "decimation", the old Roman system for expunging shame from a legion by killing one in ten, chosen by lot. But the benchers were lenient to their brethren. It was the unqualified Under Barristers who were punished "for example sake". They were "put out of commons", refused admission to the dining privileges of the Inn, and told they would be fined if they ever again refused to dance in the Revels. And if any full barrister refused in future, he would be disbarred.[10]

The barristers' demonstration must have been widely known among the prisoners of the King's Bench, who had every reason to be interested in challenges to judges. This was the first skirmish in the coming battle over who ruled supreme, King, Law or Parliament, and it would grow in power and scale until it brought down the whole of England. But by the time the story had filtered down through gossip, young Ogilby would have understood something else from it; that lawyers must dance. This would be his life – not the dull Law, but the glamorous Dance. But as an urchin at the very bottom of London society, there must have seemed no way for him to enter that world of elegant revels his father had once helped to costume.

School

John may have learned about the importance of dance from hearing about the barristers. He would have learned about the practice of dance at school, which is where his talent first blossomed. As the son of a Freeman, he would have been enrolled as a pupil at the Merchant Taylors school. [11] At the time he was there, it was teaching its students how to display courtly graces to the very highest standard.

Merchant Taylors was founded as an Elizabethan grammar school in Suffolk Lane, about 150 yards from the north end of London Bridge. The largest school in the country, it had 250 pupils, around 100 of whom were charity cases. After his father's bankruptcy John would have been studying for free. The full fees were five shillings a term. There were six forms and boys normally went on to university at around sixteen. To get in he would have been tested on his catechism (in English) and needed to show that he could "read perfectly & write competently".[12] His home also had to be within easy reach; the school had its own catchment area.

There were only four men on the teaching staff, including the headmaster, but there was nothing unusual in that. Those seeking economies in education today may be tempted by this model, which depended on older pupils doing most of the teaching in this huge open-plan academy. Typical too was the school day, which usually began in the dark, at 6 a.m. in summer and 7 a.m. in winter, and ended at 5 p.m. with lunch from 11 a.m. to 1 p.m. Pupils knelt for prayer three times a day. There was no school on Sunday, but of course there was church. Any grammar school was a place of hard discipline: birching was common, casual brutality the norm. Violence was universally accepted as the right way to discipline children at home and at school, and it was the standard way of imposing law in a country with no police. Public executions for crime, burnings for heresy and mutilations for annoying authority were commonplace, and this very rough justice was swift and summary. School had to teach boys what was needed to survive: obedience, deference and manners as well as logic for disputation, how to sing prayers, compose poetry and speak the catechism. Neither pupils nor teachers would know anything about arcane mathematics such as multiplication tables. Not even Isaac Newton learned his tables. A gentleman or merchant could look them up in a book.

The school was also meant to teach its pupils to read and write in English and Latin and to debate in Latin, though it seems Ogilby did not get very far with that.[13] But there was another side to what may sound a very bleak education, one which explains the extraordinary number of playwrights and poets whose lives were shaped by the Merchant Taylors school when John was there. Its first headmaster had a remarkable educational philosophy for the period. As well as insisting on the importance of sport, he put music and drama on the curriculum. The school became famous for its theatrical productions, and for some years presented a play annually at court. When James came to the throne, the school had to learn a new way of performing before him.

The school was not doing this just for itself, but to advance the interests of the Company. Virtually all the foreign trade of England was controlled by some two hundred men in the "Worshipful Companies" of the City of London, and they were determined to build as close a connection to the new king as they possibly could. This was hard when James first came south, as the city was in the grip of a plague which took over 30,000 lives. All fairs were forbidden within fifty miles of London and James stayed well clear. The city had to make its significance evident to him by gestures rather than entertainment and the gesture they decided on was a loan of £60,000 to a monarch desperate for money. It was about half the value of the city's trade.

By 1607 James had settled in Whitehall and the Merchant Taylors invited him to attend the inauguration of their new Master. He accepted. They then tried to figure out what to do when he came. James was obviously very interested in performances on a large scale; he was constructing a huge Banqueting House at Whitehall for entertainments. The King would need some grand spectacle and they had no expertise in these courtly matters. So they hired instructors "by reason that the Company doubt that their Schoolmaster and Scholars be not acquainted with such kind of Entertainments",[14] and turned over £1,000 of their funds to food, drink and lavish performances in the school hall. Using, of course, their own pupils. This would have been young John's first year in the school, which accepted boys at six or seven. It must have created a powerful impression on him.

The King was placed on a throne at the end of the hall, in which hung a small theatrical ship, elaborately decorated. A boy dressed as an angel, holding a burning taper of frankincense, delivered what the record described as a "short" speech of eighteen verses "devised by Mr Ben Jonson the Poet, which pleased his Majesty marvellously well". Possibly so; he was easily bored. Galleries had been built for lute players, and three singers appeared in the ship wearing silk versions of seamen's dress, but they were all drowned out by a simultaneous performance of "cornets and loud music ... (the) noise was so great that the lutes nor songs could hardly be heard or understood". After this rather dubious performance the King went into a specially built dining room overlooking the hall where he could eat in privacy, except for the presence of two organs "whereupon Mr John Bull, Doctor of Music, and a Brother of this Company, did play during all the dinner time" accompanied by singing men and children from the King's

Chapel. It sounds a bit of a disaster, but the situation seems to have been saved by the three men in the ship, who sang a farewell song which the King liked so much he had them sing it three times. It was apparently a new composition by Dr Bull called "God Save the King".

The sixteenth century had seen England's rulers transformed into Renaissance Princes, whose courts were a world apart. They were not just sumptuous exhibitions of luxury and art, but also stages where courtiers had to display bodily grace. Being a courtier meant a constant performance of flattery of the Prince delivered with wit, agility and beauty. Until James arrived the Court had lived as a select community in an elevated world of royal palaces, and there was no royal palace in the City of London. The royal residence was in a far more exclusive enclave at Whitehall. When Elizabeth I appeared in the City, as when she opened the Royal Exchange in 1571, it was a calculated display of pageantry, almost a visitation from another planet. The boys of the school might perform a play at her Court, but they were visitors allowed in for the day. Now, however, Whitehall had enlarged itself and was embracing and absorbing the city. In March, James opened Parliament in Westminster saying that "*London* must bee the Seate of your King".[15] He was beginning the reshaping of England by integrating himself into this city of merchants.

Every livery company obviously wanted to hook James as a patron. The Clothworkers did it first, in 1606, with a magnificent entertainment at which he was enrolled as a Clothworker. Now his thirteen-year-old son and heir Prince Henry became an unusually young Freeman of the Merchant Taylors. The Livery Companies may have felt they were landing great royal fish in their golden nets, but the reality was the other way round. The royal family were not going into trade; the City

Corporations were being sucked into the Court. Westminster had not come to visit London, but to begin the slow process of swallowing it.

Having been trained in courtly entertainment, Merchant Taylors School now had some new survival skills to teach its pupils. The English court was a place of physical performance where men were expected to display grace in their movement. Courtiers were trained in a theatre of the body, which achieved its most flamboyant presentation in masques and revels (dances). A court masque was a uniquely English extravagant spectacle of theatre, music and dance for the delight of the king and queen. There was no clear distinction between stage and audience. Revels were part of the masque and the whole court was expected to perform. It was clear that a man who could dance might vault over such handicaps as a lack of aristocratic blood, and now that the Court had embraced the City, a new set of rules was appearing to measure attainment at Merchant Taylors.

Dance was as powerful a medium for education as any other. Queen Elizabeth's tutor, Thomas Elyot, had written a *Boke named The Governour* in which he pointed out that for Plato it was a way to describe the movement of the planets. He explained that dance is an expression of harmony and virtue, and analysed the steps of dances to make the point in detail.[16] The ritual of dance was described as a mirror of the dance of the heavens, and so could be seen as a proper pedagogic study. One phrase summarised how the movement of stars and planets in the sky was connected to earthly events, "As above, so below." It also applied to the patterns of dance. They mirrored the movement of the spheres, and so integrated humans with heavenly harmony and love. The brilliance of the dance of a masque, with magically ethereal spangled costumes shimmering in the candle-light, placed the court itself in the heavenly dance among the music of the spheres.

This was, of course, a world which young John had heard of. It was the world for which his father worked, but he could hardly hope to enter it. He must certainly have dreamed of it, but for it to actually happen he would need an incredible stroke of luck.

The lottery

On 29 June 1612, a large crowd of men and boys gathered at a newly built, brightly painted wooden shed in front of the great west door of St Paul's cathedral. This was the Virginia Company's Lottery House. It had cost around £700 and most of the expense had gone on hangings and banners to make it as striking as possible.[17] They displayed examples of the prizes, which were silver tableware, and exotic images of Virginia, especially of the natives. It was a display designed to catch passing trade, and that did not mean worshippers. It meant the whole throng of London, including schoolboys like Ogilby. There were titled gentlemen in colourful doublets with lace cuffs and large collars, wearing embroidered cloaks, some in great boots, others wearing expensive silver buckled shoes. Contrasting with these brightly-coloured lords, there were merchants – lots of merchants, Freemen of the livery companies who called themselves Fishmongers and Bakers, Dyers and Brewers, but who did not smell of fish or have flour in their hair. These were the men who ran the City. They wore discreet black coats, large breeches and stockings, with carefully placed badges, gold chains and expensive accessories designed to impress. There were other men who did have traces of fish and flour about them, taking time off from their shops, tradesmen in their weatherproof topcoats and beggars in whatever they could find. It was a busy heap of sightseers, many sporting impressive beards and moustaches and with a fine assortment of wigs and hats.

Around them were the stalls of dozens of booksellers. St Paul's Churchyard was the home of the publishing trade, and it was a good opportunity for them. John Davis' new book on the war in Ireland was competing with Heywood's *Apology for Actors* and the first translation of *Don Quixote*, while Gefferie Neue's *Almanac & Prognostication* was there to help gamblers decide whether to risk two shillings and sixpence on a ticket.

St Paul's was a vast crumbling monument to a disappearing age. It had once been the tallest building in England, but the spire had been felled by lightning in 1549. The nave, over 100 yards long, was an unofficial fruit and meat market and a hang-out for prostitutes. Pack-animals passed through it, the walls were plastered with advertisements, and it was popular with labourers and servants seeking their next job. The middle aisle, "St Paul's Walk", was also a daily gossip centre. It was a place of constant noise and rolling news. The West door was the perfect place for a lottery house.

Similar wooden structures had been set up there for two lotteries under Queen Elizabeth, in 1569 and 1586.[18] The first was to raise money to help strengthen ports and harbours. At a time when Spain could borrow money against future gold from America, Elizabeth needed to borrow by more ingenious methods. This lottery was a way of collecting a loan; the money was kept for three years and then every penny went into the draw. The second, just two years before the Spanish Armada arrived to invade, seems to have spoken more directly to people's fears and had prizes of armour. The West door had also served more recently as an extraordinary execution site. The Chief

Justice, Edward Coke, had given four of the Gunpowder Plotters the unique privilege of being hanged, drawn, and quartered there. A large crowd gathered to enjoy the spectacle of them being taken down from the scaffold while still alive, then disembowelled and their hearts cut out before their bodies were hacked into pieces. Part of the ritual was for the executioner to hold up each beating heart and proclaim "Here is the heart of a traitor!" According to popular report, one of the corpses shouted back "Thou liest." The next day's executions of the remaining plotters were performed at Whitehall, well away from the comedy ventriloquists of St Paul's.

John's school supported the objectives of the Virginia lottery as an act of loyalty. From a commercial perspective, the Merchant Taylors were unenthusiastic about America. James had granted a Royal Charter to the Virginia Company in 1606 with the sole stated purpose of civilising North America's savages. The cause of their savagery was, the Charter explained, that they lived "in Darkness and miserable Ignorance of the true Knowledge and Worship of God", and the Company would solve that problem for them.

The settlers who had disembarked the following year were not ideal missionaries. They were more interested in the Charter's grant that the Company should "HAVE and enjoy the Gold, Silver, and Copper, to be gotten thereof". The Crown would, as it happened, be entitled to 20% of any precious metal. The fact that it was all the property of the savages did not get mentioned.

In Ben Jonson's play *Eastward Ho*, which was put on in 1605, a character was persuaded to run off to Virginia because

gold is more plentiful there than copper is with us; …Why, man, all their dripping-pans and their chamber pots are pure gold; and all their chains with which they chain up their streets are massy gold; all the prisoners they take are fettered in gold; and, for rubies and diamonds, they go forth on holidays and gather 'em by the seashore, to hang on their children's coats, and stick in their caps.[19]

A third of the 150 colonists that had set out in 1607 died on the way. Most of the survivors described themselves as "gentlemen", and only eight had a useful trade. They constructed a ramshackle settlement, Jamestown, on the edge of a disease-ridden swamp. One week after their ships went back, only ten of them were fit enough to stand.[20]

Failure was not an option for the Virginia Company. It did not have the legal protection a modern company expects. There was no such thing as limited liability. If the Company failed all the investors would be personally liable. They might be bankrupted, and bankruptcy law was there to protect creditors, not debtors. To avoid collapse they had to send out a steady flow of new colonists to replace the dead, so more, equally useless settlers were lured on the Company's false prospectus. By 1610 about 600 colonists had fetched up in Jamestown, and some 540 of them were dead. Two years later around 300 more settlers had been brought, 130 of whom were already dead and buried.

As it could produce no income the Company had to be kept afloat by a fund-raising campaign supported by a public relations effort. That was the lottery. A leading member of the Company published a pamphlet claiming that Jamestown was now home to at least seven hundred healthy and well-housed men full of industry, that an eighty-bed hospital was being built, and American gold, "the undoubted certainty of minerals", was just around the corner. A ballad promoting the lottery mentioned gold five times.[21] The lottery's declared aim was to invest in the "plantation", but many knew that it was really to pay off the Company's debt and rescue its directors. It was said that the real problem was that the gentlemen who had gone there considered themselves too refined to do any work, evidence of "the extreme beastly idleness of our nation, which (notwithstanding any cost or diligence used to support them) will rather die and starve than be brought to any labour or industry to maintain themselves".[22]

By the end of May, when the draw was supposed to happen, the bulk of the tickets were unsold. It was obvious that either the prizes would have to be reduced, which would have made further lotteries impossible, or the draw would have to be postponed while a huge sales push was made. That happened, and a new date for the draw was set for 29 June. As things stood, with far fewer ticket-holders chasing the same prizes, the odds on a winning ticket were at least double what had been intended and of course people saw it in a better light. At this point the Merchant Taylors, who had refused to buy tickets, were finally persuaded to cough up £30. A number of individual tailors seem to have become aware of the improved odds, as did multitudes of others who now decided to chance a single ticket, including young John. It was almost a rational choice. When the draw opened, 60,000 unsold tickets were thrown away, including 240 supposedly bought by the Merchant Taylors Company but never actually paid for.

The "colonists" in Virginia, of course, gained nothing from the lottery. But while it was being drawn, they started experimentally planting sweet tobacco smuggled from the Spanish colony of Trinidad. The leaf had already been introduced into England from the West Indies decades earlier and there was a thriving market for it; King James denounced it as harmful and disgusting in 1604. The stolen seeds grew well. The colony would be saved by tobacco, not the lottery, and eventually the Virginia plantation would kill far more people elsewhere in the world than in Virginia. By the time Ogilby started work on *Britannia*, Virginia tobacco was being imported through Liverpool.

In 1612 the process of finding the lottery winners would hold London's attention for weeks. The previous winter had been harsh, and now there had been no rain all summer.[23] Everyone knew that crops and animals were dying, it would be a bad harvest, and food was getting expensive. The draw was entertainment for all and perhaps even offered hope to some. The crowd was there every day of the draw to cheer or boo the results and watch the pageant.[24] Over 60,000 half-crown tickets had been sold. They were pretty expensive but the story Ogilby told, as reported in *Brief Lives*, was that as an eleven-year-old he had decided this was a gamble worth taking. He had been selling off the family stock of embroidery decorations and used some of the money to buy a single lot in his father's name. He said that he had John senior inscribed in the lottery book with the words:

I am a poor prisoner, God wot,
God send me a good lot,
I'll come out of prison, and pay all my debt.

Names were written on slips of paper in one sealed barrel, prizes on slips in another. At the draw, an official sat between the barrels. He placed his right hand into a slot in one barrel, his left into a slot in the other, and read out the result. This blind marriage of gamblers and prizes was performed day after day for three weeks. The whole affair was an entertainment. The top prize, £1,000 worth of silver, went to a tailor and was carried to his house in a stately procession. In terms of the status conferred by wealth, it could be worth £5 million in our terms.[25]

John Ogilby had left his parents in the utter misery of the King's Bench, with only scraps to eat. Did they know what he had done with the money he had scraped together? He was supposed to be a charity scholar at Merchant Taylors school, not hanging around St Paul's. But one hot July evening, it seems young John came back to the King's Bench carrying a small fortune. It was enough to get his father out of prison and pay his debt. And there was enough left over to buy his own place in the world of dancing.

Believe it or not

The lottery's grand prize was carried to the house of the winner in a stately procession. That was probably the final event, the climax of the show. By then, the lesser prizes had already been awarded. Ogilby was one of the winners, and his world was transformed. John senior was indeed released from debtor's prison, and young John had the chance to buy an apprenticeship to a dancing master. It was a remarkable choice, but he was obviously pretty, showed promise, and was eager to escape from the world of tailoring.

We do not know the size of the prize or of the debt that had to be paid, but it must have been a huge win. Apprenticeships were too expensive for poor families, and this very limited profession with its wealthy clientele was never going to be cheap to enter. Dance lessons were surprisingly expensive, fifteen or twenty shillings a month. It was only six shillings to learn to play the viol.[26] A more ordinary apprenticeship would cost around £15 plus the money for seven years' food and clothing,[27] so probably £50; this one could have cost double, around £100,000 in modern money.

The story of this miraculous win has always been taken at face value because it comes from John Aubrey. That means it comes from a tale told by Ogilby himself in his seventies. Aubrey never said what the lottery was, but there were no others so far as we know. We can be sure that Ogilby became apprentice to a dancing master, and that meant there was a dramatic alteration in the family fortunes, but we cannot be quite so sure that the money came from a lottery. A gambling win has always been a fine way of explaining the source of money that has a more secret origin, and Ogilby was more interested in concealing his origins than confiding in gossips. But if John wanted to hide his origins, the real story needed to be replaced with another, both outlandish and satisfying. It is true that the words said by Aubrey to have been inscribed for his father's lottery ticket seem compellingly authentic: "I am a poor prisoner, God wot" – but a poor prisoner? The lottery ticket would have bought twelve pounds of meat, or seven dozen eggs. This was a very dramatic purchase, if it happened. Would a bankrupt watched by his creditors be able to blow a large sum of money on a lottery ticket, and do so with a public declaration of what he was up to? We have no record of the lottery book to verify it. We do have a record of the lots purchased for an earlier lottery, that of 1567. Ogilby, who became a leading practitioner in the lottery business, can be expected to have known this volume and others, now lost. It contains a few expressions of hope that are similar to the one which he says was written for his own ticket:

We Brewers God send us
A good lot to mend us

Their ticket cost 10 shillings. John Banks and his brewer mates won 1s. 3d. Edward Tibbet wrote:

> I was begotten in Calais and born to Kent
> God send me a good lot to pay my rent.

He won 1s. 9d. A consortium from the Spread Eagle in Gray's Inn Lane, where Ogilby would live and teach when his apprenticeship ended, finished up with just 1s. 2d.

> The spred eagle spred
> Hopeth for a good lot to be red.[28]

Ogilby would have been familiar with all this by the time he told his tale, sufficiently familiar that it looks as if his final, non-rhyming, line – "I'll come out of prison, and pay all my debt" – was not part of the supposed entry but a gloss to interpret a couplet pastiched from a standard model. Is the story true? Despite this apparent lesson in luck, he grew up into a man who ran lotteries, not one who bought tickets. He knew that the house always wins. That was what the Spread Eagle consortium had learned, and probably remembered.

The fact, of course, is that we can't be sure. We are assembling fragments of a life that was carefully obscured. Ogilby shrouded himself in secrecy while working on a public stage. He was a master conspirator, and nothing he said or did can be taken at face value. It may be that he could not tell the truth about his windfall without revealing his origins, and that he would not do. But as we will see later, he confided in one man who made a note after Ogilby's death, and that note has survived.

Life 2. The Dancer

John senior's release from prison may have left him with cash to live on but did not set him back on his feet. London in 1612 was not a comfortable place for a Scot. A ballad suggested that the purpose of the lottery should be to finance their expulsion to the plantation:

If either lotteries or lots
Could rid us of these rascal Scots;
Who would not venture then with thanks;
Although he drew nothing but blanks?

Perhaps this verse may have inspired Ogilby to attribute the family's windfall to the lottery. The next verse suggested that London only had room for the immigrants because the Virginia Company was emptying the city of true-born Englishmen:

But since Virginia made the tomb
For us, to make these rogues more room;
Let them be gulled that list to be;
Virginia gets no more of me.[1]

At the level of the court and aristocracy there was considerable friction between recently arrived Scots and English lords, which led in the first half of 1612 to some pretty nasty episodes of physical violence, accompanied by popular anti-Scots manifestations in the streets. Ben Jonson's *Eastward Ho* had annoyed King James (a Scot, after all) by having a character say that he wished a hundred thousand Scots could be sent to Virginia: "we should find ten times more comfort of them there than we do here". Another verse at the time listed the current scandals involving Scots – "They beg our goods, our lands, and our lives, they whip our Nobles and lie with their wives,/they pinch our Gentry ...", and ended with the threat to "make you as poor as when you came to us".[2]

A discharged bankrupt tailor from Scotland had no way to make a living in this city. Much of its life went on outside the walls, in the new shanty-towns that had sprung up away from the eyes and ears of the elite whose letters, plays and literature we rely on for information about Jacobean London. While the lottery was under way there was a mass exodus of Scots from the city; we only know this because of stories circulating in central London that three hundred frightened refugees had been seen fleeing home through Ware in Hertfordshire, twenty-two miles from the city on the main road to Scotland.[3] What riots and killings lay behind that we do not know, but it was evidently enough to lend credibility to a speech in Parliament in 1614 warning of massacres if the Scots were not cleared out.[4]

John Ogilby's parents did not join the exodus. Prison and poverty are not good for the health, and within five years of leaving prison John's father was dead.

Apprenticeship

Ogilby was a very pretty and graceful boy, and a natural dancer. At eleven he was just old enough to be apprenticed, and there were evidently some people who had their eye on him and were prepared to help him find a place that could profit from his abilities. Membership of a Livery Company was like membership of a family; it was for life, and bankruptcy did not change that. It was also hereditary, so young John could hope to be eligible for membership "by Patrimony" in due course. The Company was there to help its members. It seems likely that the Merchant Taylors school, recognising this boy's talent and his need for a home, helped him find a master. Thomas Draper, who happened to be an investor in the Virginia Company, had been admitted as a Freeman Merchant Taylor in 1603.[5] His brother Henry, "citizen and brewer" of the City, owned considerable quantities of London and suburban property.[6] Henry's son John was a bachelor dancing instructor of Gray's Inn Lane, and took the boy into his home. It was normal for an apprentice to live in his master's house. John's mother Katherine was very close by, in the same parish, and remarried in 1618.[7] Young Ogilby was by then well established in his chosen profession.

John Draper was a busy man. There was a huge community of people who needed to learn to dance in the right way. Many of them were pupil barristers, "under barristers" at the Inns of Court. The word "Court" meant just what it said – not simply a place of justice, but a place of courtliness, courtesie, requiring the manners of a courtier. Gray's Inn Lane was the right place for a dancing master. In 1574 the Crown granted three dancing masters a monopoly of dance teaching in London, with a savage penalty for unlicensed dance mastering: a fine of two pounds plus ten days in prison without bail.[8] Unlicensed dance masters were evidently a serious threat to social order.

John's apprenticeship would have begun at the start of the legal year, in October 1612, when Gray's Inn was beginning to prepare for its most ambitious masque presentation. This was its first entertainment for the King, to celebrate the first royal wedding in London for over a hundred years. On St Valentine's Day 1613, James' daughter Elizabeth would marry Frederick V, the Elector of the Palatinate, Germany's largest Protestant state. This was a lavish and exuberant triumph, and Gray's Inn was combining with the Inner Temple to put on a masque of spectacular glamour and theatricality. It was a big enough event to mean that Draper needed extra apprentices. The crowds at the Banqueting House were so great that the performance had to be postponed for four days. With costumes costing £60 for each masquer, this may even have meant that Ogilby's father, the newly freed court tailor, got some work from it.

The celebrations were themed around the union of the Thames and Rhine and the creation of a great European Protestant alliance to confront the Habsburg juggernaut.[9] That probably went over the head of eleven-year-old John. However lowly his place, though, the event was unforgettable, and in future years he would certainly be reminded of that message and be caught up by it. But for now he was plunged into the world of dance, performance and the Inn.

Today, Gray's Inn Lane is called Gray's Inn Road and is as urban as a street could possibly be, running from Chancery Lane to Kings Cross. When Ogilby went to live there it was surrounded by fields. All the Inns of Court were outside the city walls in the countryside to the west, and Gray's Inn, north of Holborn, was the most northerly. According to Stow's map of 1591, Gray's Inn Lane had dwellings from Holborn to the Inn itself, a distance of some 175 yards. Stow described it as "furnished with fair buildings, and many tenements on both the sides, leading to the fields, towards Highgate and

Hamsted".[10] Comparing that map with the ground plan which Ogilby himself drew in the 1670s, it seems that in 1612 there were fewer than fifty houses there, and there was open country behind those houses and beyond the Inn. But it was not exactly bucolic. These wooden buildings probably housed at least 350 people, including tradesmen, their families, servants, apprentices and lodgers,[11] and they were crammed with trouble. Court records show that forty-six individuals from that short street, maybe one in eight of its population, appeared before the justices of the Middlesex Sessions during Ogilby's first year in the Lane.[12]

His education was now taking place in an intense little world. The two hundred barristers of Gray's Inn had over five hundred students, but only about eighty of them would ever practise law. The Inns of Court were a kind of finishing school to prepare young gentlemen for life at court or in other genteel pursuits. The average age at which students entered the Inns was seventeen, after they had graduated from Oxford or Cambridge, or from one of the Inns of Chancery.[13] Gray's Inn was famous for its masques and revels. For the Christmas of 1594, Shakespeare's *Comedy of Errors* had been attempted by the Lord Chamberlain's Men, (probably including Shakespeare himself) in Gray's Inn but the crowd was totally out of control and took over the stage. It became known as the Night of Errors and a mock trial was held afterwards at which a "sorcerer" was acquitted of causing the trouble.[14] The Inn was swarming with what we would consider student-aged boys who fully intended to enjoy themselves, and the Lane was there to help them do it.

Of those forty-six inhabitants named in the Sessions for the year from February 1613, just seven were yeomen, presumably farming the open land around. Twenty-six were prostitutes or artisans of one sort or another, who seem to have been able to service an entire town in just a few yards of road frontage – tailors, haberdashers, chandlers, saddlers, bakers, locksmiths, victuallers, carpenters and, of course, vintners. There was even a stonemason in case you ended up needing a monument. There was inevitably an inn of the commercial sort, the Spread Eagle, which was the focus of quite a bit of trouble. Eighteen of the Gray's Inn Lane citizens were charged with crimes that year, including thefts of large sums in cash and fine clothing, and some serious violence. The innkeeper would take on prosecution himself if necessary, while ten of the inhabitants were standing surety (providing bail) for their friends. Seven men who lived in the lane are listed as "gentleman" or "esquire". "Esquire" is synonymous, in court records for Gray's Inn Lane, with "victim of theft".

A Stuart dancing master was a rather grave entertainer with expertise in "grammar, rhetoric, logic, philosophy, history, music, mathematics and in other arts".[15] This catalogue of studies associated with dance was written by Sir George Buck of the Middle Temple at exactly the time Ogilby was signing his indentures. Buck was arguing that the Inns of Court were as much a university as Oxford or Cambridge, and it was dancing masters who were playing the part of dons. Buck was the Master of the Revels. The Revels were serious stuff.

Being a student at one of the Inns of Court was not a question of preparing for legal examinations. There were none. If you wanted to practise law you simply watched and learned what went on and took part in mock trials, but that was only one part of the education. A student was there to experience living in a closely supervised community and to eat dinner in Hall for several years. It remains true today that only one in eight Inns of Court students become barristers, and though the number of dinners that must be eaten has been cut down, the ritual survives as the main lesson that an Inn has to teach; unless its pupils have become familiar with good cutlery and table manners, and know how to pass the port, they are regarded by the English judiciary as unfit to plead a case. In the seventeenth century, only "gentlemen of blood" were admitted, and it was compulsory to attend chapel, shave "at least once in three weeks", and wear a gown in public. At meals in Hall, hats, boots and spurs were prohibited as was loud farting ("any rude noise").[16] The student in those days had more to learn in Hall than just how to dine: he was being schooled to behave as a gentleman, which might mean learning how to practise the Law but certainly meant learning to sing, to fence and especially to dance. To be accepted as a member of the community of the Inn it was necessary to participate in its life, and for three months a year, from November until February, that meant attending revels every Saturday night, "it being accounted a shame for any inns of court man not to have learned to dance".[17]

That vision of the law has disappeared utterly. To us, law is contained in books, not in the steps of dances. But the Common Law, which was the only law practised in the Inns of Court, was understood not as book-learned but innate and natural: "The common law be no written law but depends wholly upon reason and custom."[18] Of course this was quite untrue – Common Law was a vast and obscure collection of arcane procedures – but this was the way lawyers spoke about it. Common Law was, they insisted, natural law, inspired by God, shaped by reason and matured by time and by learned judges. There was every reason to require a lawyer to join the dance.

Dancing was more admired at court than any intellectual or artistic gift. It was associated with beauty, and also with morality and with being in harmony with the world. The intimate connection between dancing, morality and law meant that it also provided a foundation for political authority. This has much to do with the vague concept of "Englishness"; there was a cultural sub-structure based on a connection between natural law and the word "common" – common law, common people, common sense, commonwealth, common land and the commons of England. This is too visceral and inarticulate an understanding to be called a political philosophy. Even at the height of the Puritan Revolution, when the King had been executed and Cromwell had disposed of Parliament and made himself dictator by force of arms, Common Law remained. The judges refused to conduct trials brought under an ordinance of the Lord Protector, they would only pay regard to Common Law. They were threatened and bullied, but Cromwell could not destroy them without undermining his own authority in a country that believed in the innate validity of tradition.[19] Lawyers even insisted that there was a date by which the tradition of commonality was fully formed: the coronation of Richard I on 3 September 1189. That is the marker of "time immemorial". This bedrock remains buried to this day in the heart of English identity, more deeply than St Crispin's Day or Firework Night. 750 years later, this was the date on which Britain committed itself to war to the death against Nazi Germany.

In 1596, the year after he was called to the Bar, John Davis from Wiltshire wrote a poem, *Orchestra*, about the meaning of the dance. The word "orchestra" did not mean a group of musicians; that meaning did not appear for another century. In Tudor and Stuart times "orchestra" meant simply "dancing". Davis' point was that there is only one orchestra, just one dance, and that is the dance of the entire cosmos and the law. His purpose was "Judicially proving the true observation of time and measure, in the Authentical and laudable use of Dancing". The Greeks had said that the planets and stars were fixed to invisible revolving spheres, whose movement filled the heavens with sound. The music of the spheres resonated with those in tune with cosmic harmony. This was the music of the cosmic dance, which provided a heavenly pattern for the harmony which human societies ought to imitate.[20]

The poet sets out to persuade a reluctant Penelope, the wife of Ulysses, to dance, because that is participating in the very structure of being, imitating heaven itself:

> … whose beauties excellent
> Are in continual motion day and night …

In place of the voice of God proclaiming the creation of the world over six days, the poem tells of an original chaos being ordered by Love, which imposed a cosmic pattern of motion. In this stately vision all natural order is set out in the movements of the elements, the stars and the planets, which move according to inviolable laws that rule heaven and the earth:

> Since when they still are carried in a round,
> And changing come one in another's place,
> Yet do they neither mingle nor confound,
> But every one doth keep the bounded space
> Wherein the dance doth bid it turn or trace:
>   This wondrous miracle did Love devise
>   For Dancing is Love's proper exercise.
>
> The turning vault of heaven framed was:
> Whose starry wheels he hath so made to pass,
>   As that their movings do a music frame
>   And they themselves, still dance unto the same.[21]

In this understanding, law was not a set of divine orders but an organic totality with a structure which was replicated, mirrored and traced on every level of being. "They err therefore who think that of the will of God to do this or that there is no reason besides his will."[22] Nature, God and humanity were bound by the same law, and while humans had the power to disrupt it, it would always prevail in the end. This was the understanding of law and polity which young Ogilby imbibed as the basis and the meaning of dance and of life, and it remained with him for the rest of his life. In truth, this was his religion.

In old age, working with members of the Royal Society, he inhabited a very different country, where nature was interrogated by logic and experiment, and lawyers had no reason or reasoning that would make them dance. But he became Britain's first Cosmographer Royal, and used this new scientific understanding in the service of the old cosmic vision which modernity was abandoning. Thomas Elyot's *The Governour* had taught in 1531 that men and women dancing complementary parts were engaged in the rhythms and laws set out in the heavens, dense with meaning. That was what Ogilby learned and would teach. Lines of men and women stepping through the circulating patterns of the measures, so many steps one way, so many reverse, were a conscious echo of the movements of the planets, with the cycles and epicycles that were used to explain the cosmos of Ptolemy and Aristotle.

What we know of the actual dances comes from the notes made by bar students trying to master the teachings of their dancing masters. The dancing master's primary work was to teach a set group of eight dances which started off every night's Revels. These were the "Old Measures", and they seem to have been formalised quite early in the sixteenth century, when the concept of dance as a reflection of cosmic order was being developed. Elyot analysed the steps of the measures to make the point in detail.

Ogilby's chosen profession of dancing master was, it seems, almost priestly in the eyes of courtly gentlemen. This was not a world in which women played much part; John Draper was and would remain unmarried. It obviously helped that as Ogilby grew up he was recognised as a remarkable athletic performer, of grace and beauty, with a charm that made him attractive in courtly company. Whatever talent had made Draper want him as an apprentice flowered in the company of the young landed gentry of Gray's Inn and was obviously helped along by his ability to endear himself to them. In a few years he was evidently regarded as highly capable – capable enough to be a teacher himself. That was just as well, because he was about to face a new challenge.

The young master

Aubrey says that "in short time (he) arrived to so great excellency in that art, that he found means to purchase his time of his master and set up for himself". Apprentices were not allowed to charge fees, and although he had learned very young how to make some money by quiet trading, there may be a bit more to the story. It has been suggested that Draper's pupils made Ogilby gifts,[23] but perhaps Draper himself was making Ogilby independent.

It seems likely that John Draper's life changed in 1615; when his father died he became the owner of a fine house and nineteen acres of Kentish Town, near Highgate. In 1617 we find a John Draper becoming a barrister of Gray's Inn. It looks as if the dancing master had given up trade and joined the landed gentry, which would obviously mean freeing Ogilby from his indenture (due to have run for another two or three years). Any payment by Ogilby may have been minimal.

Just around this time, the whole poetic edifice that tied together Law and the Dance began to crumble. The notion that the Common Law was mystically endowed with supreme authority was disintegrating in the face of its pedantry and capacity for staggering injustice. In 1615 the issue came to a head in a case concerning land that had been bought by the Earl of Oxford. It had emerged that the Cambridge college that previously owned this land still had a right to it and could recover it without paying compensation. That, Coke said, was the letter of the law. There was another court, the Court of Chancery, run by the Lord Chancellor, which did not apply Common Law but "equity", a law of fairness. It had the power to issue injunctions blocking people from taking actions that it disapproved. Now the Court of Chancery stepped in with an injunction to protect the Earl from this manifest injustice, invoking the royal prerogative of mercy. Coke insisted there was no royal prerogative to act against the Common Law. At this point King James demoted the Common Law from its place as the sole bedrock of English authority. He took that place himself, and removed Coke from his position as Lord Chief Justice. After 1616, Common Law judgements that were obviously unfair could be set aside by the Court of Chancery, "the keeper of the King's conscience".[24] Its own version of law, the law of Equity, became supreme. England was no longer ruled only by a system of natural law that extended through the universe, but additionally by the royal conscience. The Chancery men who practised this law of Equity had their own Inns, and were not necessarily the kind of men who were permitted to join the Inns of Court, or take part in the Revels. These lawyers had less need of dancing masters.

Ogilby began enlarging his horizon beyond the Inns, teaching stage performers, and he must have also been performing himself. It is clear that he was acquiring a remarkable reputation, and since he would not have had an opportunity to display his talents at revels (not being a member of an Inn of Court), he must have been visible on stage at a theatre. The closest theatre to Gray's Inn, a short walk away at Clerkenwell, was the Red Bull. It happened to be owned by John Draper's aunt Ann, which probably helped.

Theatre and masque

Today, Red Bull is associated with high energy, entertaining thrill-seeking and a drink; things were much the same at the Red Bull Inn in Ogilby's day. Ann Draper inherited the land from her father when she was sixteen. By 1605 she was widowed, and the theatre, a cheap inn-yard stage, was established on her property.[25] The company there was the Queen's Players.[26] They staged popular drama for a noisy audience: Webster's *The White Devil* was put on in 1611 and seems to have been booed off stage. They tried to move to a more expensive indoor theatre, a converted cock-fighting ring called the Cockpit where they could charge higher prices and better control access, but it was burned down by a mob of apprentices on Shrove Tuesday, 1617. By then Ogilby was no longer an apprentice. He was very likely involved with the troupe. Theatre companies were constantly changing names, venues and personnel. There was always room for talent, and Ogilby was clearly a talented physical performer.

Plays needed dancers. Dancers performed before plays, after plays and in the course of plays. The Red Bull was the stage for the boisterous farces of Thomas Heywood, some of which had dances built into the drama.[27] And somehow the sight of his performances, his physical beauty and his evidently growing reputation meant that by 1619 John Ogilby was dancing for the most courtly of all courtiers, the Marquess of Buckingham, in front of the King.

To have captured the attention of Buckingham and been given a significant role in his masque was a huge achievement. One contemporary observed that the King's favourite, "being an excellent Dancer, brought that Pastime into the greater Request. ... everything he doth is admired for the doers sake. No man dances better, no man runs, or jumps better; and indeed he jumped higher than ever Englishman did in so short a time, from a private Gentleman to a Dukedom".[28]

Quite how closely the King and his favourite were linked has been a matter of speculation for the last four hundred years.[29] In 1622 a French writer, Théophile de Viau, who had been in England, wrote a plea to "The Marquis of Boukingquam" asking him in the bluntest terms to fulfil a vow of sodomy:

Let me have what you promised me.

...

You have screwed Mr le Grand
You fucked the Count of Tonnerre.
And this learned King of England
Didn't he fuck Boukinquan?[30]

That is, as news reports now say, "unconfirmed", and James frequently insisted that sodomy was an unpardonable criminal offence. De Viau's writing was considered a threat to public morals in Paris and he was solemnly burned in effigy in front of

Notre Dame Cathedral. But James did call Buckingham "my child and wife", and they were often seen petting.

John Ogilby was now enrolled in a much more stellar place than Gray's Inn or a London stage. He was in the world of the richest and most powerful people in Britain, great aristocrats and royalty. The court masque was a ritualised dance-drama, visually brilliant, extravagant and spectacular, whose narrative demonstrated that the King was the fount of order and well-being on a cosmic scale. It began with an "antimasque", a dramatic presentation filled with carefully choreographed chaos and disorder, and then in a theatrical device which came to involve elaborate stage machinery, great lords and ladies would emerge costumed as gods, goddesses and heroes, admiring servants of King James, who would by his own divinely endowed authority bring order and harmony, peace and plenty. Although the narrative was expounded in a spoken text (for which professional actors were employed), what was being carried was a musical dance spectacle. At the end the whole court would dance and become participants in this world of imagined perfection. And now Ogilby was part of it.

The high-minded artistic concept of the masque was rather undermined by the enthusiasm of the court for having a really good time. The shift from the matronly court of the old virgin Elizabeth to one where lavish shows were performed by a very attractive Queen and her ladies shocked some people, especially as their dress was less than modest. In the year of James' accession, the rather priggish thirteen-year-old Anne Clifford recorded disapproval of the new Queen's masque at Winchester, "and how all the ladies about the court had gotten such ill names that it was grown a scandalous place".[31] That attitude seems to have inspired a wonderful, though perhaps unreliable account by Sir John Harrington of a masque of

Solomon and the Queen of Sheba that was presented for King James and Christian IV of Denmark, the Queen's brother, in July 1606. By the time the show started he claimed everyone was drunk. Harrington described how the Queen of Sheba, trying to make a presentation to the Danish King, tripped on the steps to his throne, fell on top of him and covered him in wine, cream, jelly and cakes. He took it all in good part and, having been mopped down, tried to dance with her, collapsed in a heap and had to be carried off to bed. "The entertainment and show went forward, and most of the presenters went backward, or fell down, wine did so occupy their upper chambers. Now did appear in rich dress, Hope, Faith, and Charity." Hope tried to speak, but was too drunk and left the stage, and Faith "left the Court in a staggering condition". Charity did manage to get on stage and make a speech and presentation to James. "She then returned to Hope and Faith, who were both sick and spewing in the lower hall." The final presentation was from Peace, whose attendants tried to keep her away from the scene for her own protection. She beat them up on set with her olive branch.[32] Harrington was undoubtedly an inventive man (he invented the flushing toilet), and the whole account may have been a work of fiction by an elderly, scurrilous and disappointed godson of Elizabeth, but it rang true to some.

The date of Ogilby's disastrous masque performance, February 1619, has been unknown until now. Aubrey refers to the event simply as "the Duke of Buckingham's great masque", without saying when it happened or what it was. Buckingham (at this stage a Marquess) was its creator and star, and evidently took the credit for it, as the author's name was not revealed. Ben Jonson wrote every other court masque of the period, but not this one, because his effort the year before had been such a failure. It was Prince Charles' debut in a masque, and this would always be a challenge as he had some deformity in his legs. As a child he had been given special rigid boots. The dances he and his companions were given to perform were gentle and disappointing. A Venetian reported that the show had bored and annoyed James, who shouted, "Why don't they dance? What did they make me come here for? Devil take you all, dance!"

The situation was rescued by the Marquess of Buckingham. He was a "high dancer", who could perform the "lofty Gallyards that were danced in the dayes of old, when men capered in the air like wanton kids ... and turned above ground as if they had been compact of Fire or a purer element".[33] He leapt into action and began performing extraordinary feats of balletic agility. James was entranced. He regarded Buckingham as his substitute son; he kissed the Marquess, stroked his face and left. The tired, overheated and ravenous crowd then fell on the feast that had been laid out for them, overturning the tables, trampling the food and smashing the glass dishes. The noise reminded the Venetian of a violent storm breaking windows.[34]

When it came to the next year's masque, there was a set and costume designer, Inigo Jones, but no playwright. Everyone was depending on Buckingham. One central problem was that Prince Charles would have to be given more interesting dance steps and far better preparation. Buckingham would dance as Charles' partner, so the Prince and he would shine together. Charles could do more than had been asked of him the year before; he put huge effort into strengthening his legs, working at riding and tennis. Buckingham could give some instruction, but he needed the right dancing master as well. Ogilby, who was Charles' exact contemporary, fitted the bill. He could also give a brilliant performance himself which would delight the King and not compete with the Prince.

Inigo Jones thought that masques were all about sets and costumes and did not need writers at all. He would not have minded that no author was given for "the Duke of Buckingham's great masque". Aubrey says "vide Ben Jonson" as a heavy-handed clue to the man he thought was behind it. He didn't believe for a moment that Buckingham wrote it himself. The real author has only recently been identified. It was George Chapman, the translator of Homer, who Ben Jonson had said was the best person to take on the job.[35] Chapman was in hiding, pursued for a debt of £100 and wanted to earn his fee in secret. His identity was kept quiet, and the text was not published until the nineteenth century.

There is no sign that Ogilby's accident spoiled the show for the spectators, or even that they were aware that anything had gone wrong. They were watching the spectacular entrance of the Prince and the Marquess. For Ogilby it was a catastrophe, his last dance, but the King was a happy man. The Duke of Savoy's agent was present and told James that "most impressive was to have seen his highness the Prince of Wales dance with such majesty and grace that he was honoured above all the rest; and next to him the Marquis of Buckingham (whom he loves like his own soul) having done better than the others; all of which he confirmed to me with tokens of great love for the one and for the other."[36]

Ogilby had done his job well and Buckingham would take care to repay the debt. There were now men at the highest level who trusted him as a delightful and capable teacher and would recommend him. He had learned how to survive in the company of Kings, Princes and Dukes, and even earn their confidence.

The evidence deciphered

It has been hard to identify when and where this happened because the basic contemporary text for Ogilby's biography is barely a text at all.

Aubrey says: "When the duke of Buckingham's great masque was represented at court (vide Ben Jonson) ... he was chosen (among the rest) to perform some extra-ordinary part in it, and high-dancing, i.e. vaulting and cutting capers, being then in fashion, he, endeavouring to do something extraordinary, by misfortune of a false step when he came to the ground, did sprain a vein on the inside of his leg."[37] But no one could figure out which masque this was.[38] The evidence has been missed.

It is encoded in a horoscope drawn up by Elias Ashmole. Ashmole spent many years trying to establish the empirical validity of astrology. He sought a scientific proof using reverse engineering. If astrology could predict the future, it must also provide a guide to the past. A "natal" chart shows the position of the planets at the moment of birth, and supposedly provides insights into the subject's future. So he decided to look at a number of natal charts for births long ago to see whether events "foretold" actually took place. He bought a little leather-bound volume of nearly four hundred pre-printed blank horoscope forms. He filled it with charts where he could use hindsight as a test of his craft. He filled in a natal chart for the City of London, followed by one for the fourteenth-century condottiere Muzio Sforza, and then for his own second wife and one for their marriage (which was disastrous). There follow the horoscopes of a series of dead celebrities (Henrietta Maria, Gustavus Adolphus, Richelieu, Cromwell and so on) and then, immediately after Charles X of Sweden, comes Mr John Ogilby. It was probably drawn soon after Ogilby's death in 1676.

At the bottom of the page is a list of six crucial moments in Ogilby's life, presumably originally provided by the man himself when he had consulted Ashmole. These are obviously the events Ashmole knows happened, and were significant enough to be represented in some way in the horoscope, if astrology has any meaning. Ashmole wrote his notes in his own cipher, a mixture of phonetic shorthand and invented symbols, appropriate to the mysteries of an astrologer. They are an important addition to Aubrey's mini-biography, but have never been correctly deciphered. The first line means "Broke his leg in Feb, at 18 years old". That is how we know that the masque in question was in February 1619.

This has not been realised up to now, because the original code-breaker made a mistake. Ashmole's cypher remained unbroken until 1949, when the impressively-named Conrad Hermann Hubertus Maria Apollinaris Josten created a dictionary of the symbols in a small address-book. Josten published his meticulous transcription of thousands of pages of Ashmole's notes in five volumes in 1966. He wrote that Ashmole's notes on Ogilby read:

> Broke his leg in Feb. at his 8 year(s) old
> Married in London in Feb. 1650
> 1642 upon his birthday he scaped blowing up with pounder
> 1633 in August he went to the Earl of Strafford's services
> 1644 he went to the Earl of Ormond's services
> 1625 a double quotodian ague for 18 weeks/all summer[39]

Josten knew nothing about Ogilby apart from describing him as "a bad poet", and so did not know that his translation of the first line could not possibly have been correct. No child

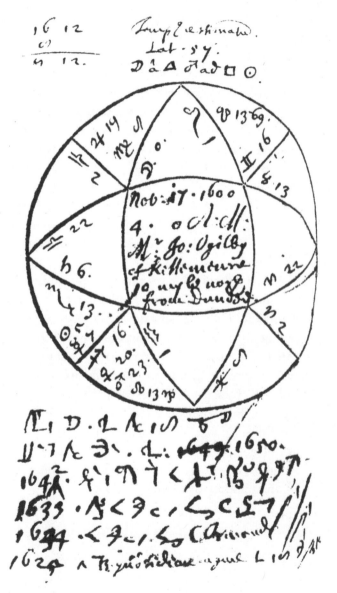

3. Ashmole's horoscope for Ogilby, Ms Ashm. 332, f.35°.

who broke his leg at eight would have been accepted as an apprentice to a dancing master at eleven unless the damage was inconsequential; there is no reason why Ashmole would have a note of a trivial injury and ignore his grave injury in the masque. The transcription makes no sense. But no one re-visited this cypher and Josten did not publish the key.[40]

He is quite inconsistent in according meanings to signs. His transliteration of the first line is "Broke his leg in Feb, at his 8 year(s) old", because he has read *ı ♫* as "his 8". But that is a mistake: it means "18". The same pair of symbols appear in the last line, which he correctly transcribes as "1625 a double quotodian ague for 18 weeks/all summer". The first line really says "Broke his leg in Feb. at 18 years old". Buckingham's great masque is finally revealed.

The whole of Ogilby's life has to be pieced together in this way, from fragmentary references and inferences, cyphers, hints and sudden shafts of reflected light that reveal what was happening on stage from a viewpoint behind the scenes. And even then, the "answer" can turn out to lead to a further mystery. In the centre of this horoscope is the information that Aubrey could never uncover. To make the horoscope, Ashmole had to know Ogilby's time and place of birth. He gives it, in plain English script, as "Killemeure 10 myles north from Dundee", at 4 a.m. So that was the secret that Ogilby was hiding even in his seventies. There must be a reason, but that will require the solution of another cypher.

Galileo and the dance

Although he was now permanently lamed, Ogilby could still teach. But the meaning of dance was changing. The next Twelfth Night masque at court, when Ben Jonson had returned to work, pulled out the rug from under the thesis that dancers were engaging with "The turning vault of heaven". Heaven, it had been shown, did not actually turn at all. That masque was *News from the New World Discovered in the Moon*, a comical presentation of two revolutions that would really change the world: Galileo's discoveries in astronomy, and the birth of newspapers. It is, so far as I can see, the first work of science fiction in English.[41] This masque undermined dance as an expression of cosmic harmony, because it danced itself into a new cosmos.

It is written for an audience who may be interested above all in fashion, luxury, power and status, but who are also able to chat about the most up-to-date developments in science and philosophy, and to enjoy them being played with in a light satire. It is a report of a visit to the moon made through a telescope, a word which did not yet exist in English so it is called a "trunk, a thing no bigger than a flute-case". The title is a reference to Galileo's Latin text *Sidereus Nuncius* ("The Starry Messenger") which created a sensation when it was published in 1610. The moon, like all heavenly bodies, had been supposed to be perfect: perfectly smooth and spherical, its dark markings caused by variations in light. The telescope revealed a detailed view of the moon as a physical body like the Earth, which fatally undermined the notion of a fundamental difference between the eternal firmament and the corruptible earth. Galileo also reported the existence of moons circling Jupiter. That obviously demolished the notion that all heavenly bodies orbit the Earth. Suddenly the idea proposed by Copernicus almost a hundred years earlier, that the Earth and other planets really orbit the sun, became entirely credible.

Copernicus had actually been scientifically discredited. Before Galileo, the only evidence that could have existed to support his argument was to see the planets being apparently displaced by parallax. If you look at the world through one eye, and then switch to the other, nearby objects appear to have moved against the background. That is a parallax effect caused by changing your viewpoint by a few inches. If the Earth orbits the sun our viewpoint must change by a huge distance between midsummer and midwinter, and so planets, which are relatively close, should appear to shift against the background of "fixed stars" in the same way. Tycho Brahe investigated and found that there was no sign of any parallax shift. He decided that there were only two possible explanations: either the Earth remains stationary or the parallax effect is too small to be seen – and that would mean that the distance between the planets and the fixed stars must be thousands of billions of miles. Since that would be absurd, Copernicus must be wrong.[42]

The logic was perfect, until it came to deciding what is absurd. The closest star is about twenty-five thousand billion miles away.

After *The Starry Messenger* the sky looked very different. The moons of Jupiter circle that planet and not the Earth. Our own moon is a place of corruptible geography like the Earth. The ancients did not know what we know. The cosmos must be immeasurably more vast than anyone had dared imagine. It was immediately clear that if Galileo had really seen these things, the entire ancient understanding of the cosmic order was undermined. The English Ambassador in Venice sent a copy of *The Starry Messenger* to James the day after it was published, saying Galileo was either going to be extremely famous or extremely ridiculous.[43]

The conflict with the Bible was more obvious. Galileo was told by the Vatican in 1616 that the notion of a moving

Earth was philosophically absurd and theologically mistaken or worse. The English court, though, was more relaxed. The Vatican's enemy was automatically their friend, and once Rome condemned Galileo they were quite cheery about him. They were entertained, not threatened, by the new vision of the Earth and Moon as very similar worlds. Ben Jonson's jolly masque reveals the delightful news that what was once an ethereal sphere "is now found to be an earth inhabited ... Variety of nations, polities, laws ... cities, boroughs, hamlets, fairs and markets. Hundreds and wapentakes! ... But differing from ours".

Those who believed in the mantra "as above, so below" had not meant it quite so literally. The ordered structure of the Earth-centred cosmos was being dismantled, but that did not mean that the idea of cosmic order had collapsed. Astrologers saw no reason to abandon their work, and Ogilby retained his understanding of cosmic law. But the pattern of dance no longer reflected the pattern of the sky. Galileo's telescope had undermined the whole concept of a universe dancing a pretty round centred on the Earth, and the vision of dance as a participation in cosmic order began to lose its meaning as the cosmic order itself lost its footing. Of course dancing continued as a social and courtly activity, but the Old Measures were losing their moral and pedagogic meaning. The basis of authority itself had been shown to be false. In 1611, one year after Galileo's revelation, John Donne wrote *An Anatomie of the World: the first Anniversarie.*

> ...new Philosophy calls all in doubt,
> The Element of fire is quite put out;
> The Sun is lost, and th'earth, and no mans wit
> Can well direct him where to looke for it.

...

Tis all in peeces, all cohaerence gone;
All just supply, and all Relation:
Prince, Subject, Father, Sonne, are things forgot,
For every man alone thinkes he hath got
To be a Phoenix, and that then can bee
None of that kinde, of which he is, but hee.

Donne had seen clearly how the new cosmology undermined earthly authority. That process was now on the march, and it moved to the beat of a military drum. A new dance had begun, and everyone would have to take part in its revels. Including Ogilby.

Life 3. The Soldier

The hidden life

Four years after dancing at court, Ogilby was with a company
of soldiers on the far side of the North Sea. It was the start of
many years of military experience, and it was one more part
of his life that he kept hidden. His first expedition was the
result of a post in the household of Britain's most fashionable
and romantic military hero. He was there thanks to his new
connections at court.

The material we have to work with to construct this period
of his life is as follows:

1 Aubrey's information that he had military training.
2 A reference in his horoscope noting a long illness in 1625.
3 The records of a claim for back pay in 1626 from John
   Ogilby, ex-prisoner of war.
4 A note from a judge of the Admiralty protesting about
   John Ogilby being given captaincy of a ship in 1628.
5 A case in the Privy Council in May 1633 in which John
   Ogilby claims redress from two assailants in Gray's Inn.
6 Ogilby's entry into the service of Wentworth, Lord Deputy
   of Ireland.

His military adventure began after he had recovered from his
accident, when he was engaged to teach two ladies how to

dance. "After he was lamed," Aubrey says, "He taught 2 of the lord Hopton's (then Sir Ralph) sisters to dance, then at Witham in Somersetshire; and Sir Ralph taught him to handle the pike and musket, scil. [namely] all the postures."[1]

Ogilby had been hired by an authentic hero, one of the most celebrated figures in England. To understand his new milieu, we have to understand Ralph Hopton, who would play a large part in Ogilby's life. He was from Somerset, four years older than Ogilby, the son of a very wealthy Member of Parliament, educated at the Middle Temple and Oxford. But he had walked away from the law and did not get a degree. He preferred a life of adventure, and it seemed that he and Ogilby could hardly be more different. On Saturday 28 October 1620, when Ogilby's pupils at the Inns were dancing in the revels, Ralph Hopton, escapee from the bar, was in Prague. He was one of 2,000 English Protestant gentleman volunteers who were there to defend King James' daughter Elizabeth against an invasion force of some 27,000 Catholic troops. The battle would begin on Sunday morning, and everyone knew that it would decide the fate of Europe. They also knew what was likely to happen.

The war that began that weekend would devastate central Europe. It is estimated that Germany lost up to 40% of its population, and the total death toll through slaughter, disease and starvation may have been 7.5 million. It produced Harrington's litany of Princes of Germany, Estates of France, Spanish kingdoms, power in Holland and Austrian princes, all blown up. Not to mention the collateral damage of the English Civil War. When the Thirty Years' War ended, in 1648, the map of Europe had changed from a shifting pattern of dynastic lordships into a defined jigsaw of countries and frontiers, the map we recognise. No one knew that this would happen, of course, but it was quite obvious in 1620 that Prague was where the future was to be forged. Ever since the start of the Reformation, Europe had been rumbling towards an epic and catastrophic religious war and this was the starting shot.

Prague was the capital of Bohemia, the largest city in central Europe and a home for Europe's Protestant intelligentsia. In 1617 the Bohemian crown was taken over by a Jesuit-trained Habsburg from Vienna determined to enforce Catholicism and Prague had exploded.

The Winter Queen

The Bohemian Estates – the representatives of the people – rejected the Habsburg and offered their crown to Germany's most powerful Protestant, Frederick V, the Elector Palatine, who was married to James' daughter Elizabeth. That was the wedding that had given John Ogilby his first work in the world of dance. Its celebration had invoked a mystical anti-Habsburg alliance of the Thames and the Rhine, and now that was coming to life in the city of magicians, painters, astrologists and alchemists. Frederick was crowned in Prague on 25 October 1619, and Elizabeth became Queen of Bohemia three days later.

Frederic and Elizabeth were already expecting an assault on the Palatinate from Madrid. The Spanish Habsburgs had their sights fixed on the Protestant Estates of Holland, with whom Spain had been forced to conclude a twelve-year truce that would expire in 1621. Then Spain would undoubtedly attack the Netherlands, and as its armies could not go through France, they would march through Germany. If the Palatinate was held by a Protestant he would have to be pushed out of the way, even if he was married to the King of England's daughter. Now Austria would also attack them, in Bohemia. A great many young and idealistic English gentlemen had been eager to help the romantic couple and travelled abroad to train as soldiers.

James had never intended to get involved in this sort of a war and refused to do so now, but he allowed the Palatine envoy, his daughter's ambassador, to raise volunteers in Britain. They had been ready and waiting ever since the Prague coronation: "With what great and general love Britain burned towards Frederick and Queen Elizabeth I can scarcely describe. There was not a soldier, an officer, or a knight, that did not beg to be allowed to go to the help of Bohemia."[2] Hopton was one of Elizabeth's courtiers and guards.

The imperial army reached Prague a year after Frederick's coronation. The assault on that Sunday morning, the Battle of the White Mountain, is one of the iconic battles of European history, but it was hardly epic: it lasted an hour before the Bohemians ran, leaving 4,000 dead and injured. Hopton saw the chaotic disintegration of Frederick's army.

Hopton the hero

Frederick was taken completely by surprise at his military collapse. As Prague fell, he and Elizabeth escaped. It was a dreadful flight of over 170 miles: Cossack riders were close behind and her own attendants pillaged several of the Queen's baggage wagons. She was in a coach, heavily pregnant, with Hopton among her bodyguard. As the roads deteriorated he lifted the Queen of Bohemia onto the back of his horse and carried her the last 40 miles to the temporary safety of Breslau (now Wroclaw in south-west Poland).[3]

Hopton returned to England as a popular hero, but more importantly he was a hero at court. He was adopted as a protégée by William Herbert, Earl of Pembroke, who had once been Shakespeare's patron and was one of the richest and most powerful figures in England. When James teased him by putting a frog down his neck, Pembroke's revenge was a pig in the royal privy. Everyone had a good laugh.[4] He had been instrumental in Buckingham's rise and wielded enormous power. He was also Lord Chancellor, in charge of all theatres and entertainments, which would have been rather relevant to Ogilby. The Earl decided to install Ralph Hopton in Parliament, and the seat he picked was Shaftesbury, close to his own family home. The elections had been in November, around the time when Hopton was saving the Winter Queen, so there was a sitting MP already, but what a Herbert wanted he tended to get rather fast. In February 1621, after being in session for less than a month, Parliament decided that the elected member for Shaftesbury was simply too annoying to tolerate, and Ralph was in London two days later. The by-election that followed had him installed in the Commons inside a week, without opposition. His predecessor, Thomas Sheppard, had offended by what was seen as pettifogging objections to a bill for enforcing the keeping of the Sabbath by, among other things, forbidding dancing. Sheppard, Sabbath dancing and freedom of speech were out, Hopton was in.

Hopton's contribution to the Parliament was to further weaken freedom of speech by denouncing Edward Floyd, a Catholic barrister who was said to have spoken scornfully of Frederick and Elizabeth. He was condemned to be branded, whipped at the cart's tail, fined £5,000 and imprisoned for life. The whipping was commuted and he was released after six weeks, but he was forbidden to call himself a gentleman ever again and he lost the right to give evidence in court. At his branding, which was in public at Cheapside, Floyd offered to pay £1,000 to be hanged and made a martyr.

The marriage

Parliament was adjourned in June and Hopton went back to the continent, probably to take part in the defence of Heidelberg. Prague was now desolate, a place of executions, its population in flight. The defence of Heidelberg was the last stand of the English volunteers, organised by one of Pembroke's distant cousins, Sir Gerard Herbert.[5] The city fell and was plundered at the end of September; Sir Gerard was among the dead. Hopton came home. It seems that his bachelor status now had to end and his sisters would have to dance at his wedding. That was his excuse for engaging Ogilby, who seems to have been recommended to Hopton by his commanding officer, Colonel Sir Charles Rich. Ogilby lived in the sexually ambivalent world of dance and theatre, and Sir Charles was a confirmed bachelor who had been one of the courtly gentlemen dancing in the masque where Ogilby was injured.[6] They were evidently well acquainted. Ralph Hopton was, like Sir Charles, a romantic soldier who seemed to enjoy ladies most if they were glamorous and untouchable. He had no enthusiasm for family life, and friends help each other as much as they can. Ogilby was now well known and trusted in a dense network of stylish gentlemen. And Ogilby understood what Hopton had been fighting for.

Hopton's new wife came by way of the Earl. Pembroke was one of the Gentlemen of the Privy Chamber, the King's personal friends and companions. One of them, Sir Justinian Lewin, had died in 1620. Lewin's monument in Otterden,

Kent, indicates just how much wealth you needed to be in the King's inner circle. Carved by the finest funerary sculptor in England in glorious life-coloured marble, it shows the elegant Justinian in courtly, gold-decorated armour. At his side, on the floor, kneels his grieving widow and wretched child in what was a very modern display of baroque emotion. That daughter was Justinian's sole heir, and now, somehow, Ralph was to marry her mother. It was organised before the end of 1622.

Hopton's new wife was in her late thirties and considered to be past child-bearing.[7] The marriage seems to have been arranged by Pembroke to ensure his friend's widow's future, as Sir Justinian had bequeathed his entire estate to their daughter, and his widow only had the income from it until the child grew up.[8] Once the wedding had been performed, in March 1624, Hopton would leave her alone and go straight back to the wars. Nevertheless, he benefited greatly. This marriage catapulted him into an altogether different league of company from anything his family had known: he was now properly connected. Of course he needed to acquire some courtly graces, and so did his family. He had four sisters; two were married, but the younger two, aged thirteen and fifteen, were not. These two young ladies needed a proper education, which meant learning to dance.

The first link in our chain of evidence is this connection between Hopton, Sir Charles Rich and Ogilby. It has been unclear when Ogilby was engaged by Hopton, and Aubrey's reference to him (many years later) as Sir Ralph at the time has created confusion. Hopton was knighted in 1626, but by then he did not have care of any of his four sisters. The two eldest, Catherine and Rachel, were married before him, and Mary and Margaret very shortly afterwards. So we can be confident that if Ogilby taught two of the sisters at the Hopton house, it was in the months before Ralph's wedding. That is significant in understanding what Ogilby did next.

Pike and musket

After the marriage in 1624, Ogilby the dancing master vanishes from view until 1631. The likeliest explanation is that he had stopped doing much dancing, and was busy at something else. One of the notes in the horoscope drawn up by Ashmole provides our second link in the chain of evidence for Ogilby the soldier. It records that he spent eighteen weeks of the following year, the whole summer, laid up with "a double quotidian ague".[9] This was a form of malaria with regular daily bursts of fits and fever producing aches, pains, vomiting, feverishness, an upset stomach and boils.[10] It was a most unlikely disease to contract around Gray's Inn. In England it was a disease of marshlands, especially in Kent, Essex and the Fens (Cromwell would suffer from it), but Ogilby had no reason to hang about in marshes. There was malaria around Bridgwater in Somerset, the low-lying Somerset Levels, but that was over twenty-five miles from Hopton's estate. The only marshlands with infectious mosquitoes near London were in the area around what is now Waterloo,[11] and so far as we know he would have no reason to go there. But it was endemic in the Low Countries, especially on the coast, where it is reckoned to have been responsible for one death in every four.[12]

Soon after the nuptials, Lt-Colonel Hopton was travelling back to war. It looks as though he took Ogilby in his regiment, the 4th Regiment of Foot commanded by Colonel Sir Charles Rich. That seems to be the explanation of Ogilby's illness and the context for Aubrey's report that Sir Ralph taught him to handle the pike and musket. Frederick and Elizabeth had become exiles in The Hague, so a new force was being assembled to rescue the Palatinate. Hopton would be part of it. He had raised two hundred men in Somerset and was training and drilling them while Ogilby was there. The dancing master had been caught up in his enthusiasm and friendship, and persuaded to sign up. That is why he was taught the use of arms.

"Pike and musket" was the new, modern warfare. There was a time when a gentleman's fighting expertise would involve being trained from childhood in swordsmanship and horse-manship, but that belonged to the old chivalric days when infantry consisted of archers, crossbowmen and peasants with sharpened agricultural implements. The war in the Low Countries had been fought by a new kind of army, a large body of men who had been given a crash course in the efficient use of weapons that could penetrate armour and dispatch cavalry. In England they were drilled in "trained bands", and there was no shortage of text-books for them. The basic work, published in a rather cumbersome and expensive edition in 1607, was *Wapenhandelinge* ('weapon handling') by Jacques de Gheyn. It was published in Dutch, French, German and English and republished over many years.[13] Its truly original feature was to show inexperienced soldiers how to handle weapons on the battlefield in engravings of 117 precise movements. The reference to Ogilby learning "all the postures" indicates that his training was based on this manual.

This is de Gheyns' ninth movement of handling the musket. To Ogilby it must have been perfectly clear that this is teaching soldiering as a dance which was learned as the Old Measures were learned, step by step in a matter of weeks. This novice musketeer is a creature of delicate movements,

4. Ninth movement of handling the musket, from Jacques de Gheyn, *Wapenhandelinge*.

with a fine turned out leg and well-developed calves. Instead of boots and armour, he wears soft shoes and ribbons. He has no helmet, but a huge feather on his embroidered hat, and is being taught to handle his weapon like a musical instrument. This was the image of soldiering that Hopton presented, together with the courage, dash and thrill of his actions. The art of war and the company of such soldiers must have seemed irresistible. Ogilby and Hopton evidently got on marvellously well. Hopton, the golden hero of England, had a military dance to teach the dancing-master, one that could be stepped through perfectly well by a man with a bad leg.

A dance that was designed not to end in a leap, but in glory. Or at least in the rescue of the shattered ruins of Heidelberg, the rebuilding of the romance of Elizabeth Stuart's court and the rescue of Prague from the dark oppression of Jesuit intolerance. The dance of pike and musket could sustain dreams, until you actually experienced it.

Pike and musket were pretty much the whole of an infantry force on the march, and they were weapons of military stalemate. Cities were so fortified that they could only be taken by siege, and with armies having such massive defensive power, Europe was being pulled further and further into a grim endless destruction that would not be seen again until the war of the trenches, 1914–18. This one would last nearly eight times as long, but in 1624 there was still room for optimism. Ogilby, who later wrote a comical verse about the life of a cavalry trooper, must have been given a horse because of his bad leg.

The whole business of drilling indicated that war was no longer a matter of individual dashing heroics. It was a matter of raising and keeping huge armies. Military forces had always been run by the nobility, but Europe's aristocrats, whether from the old chivalry or the new courts, were not the men for this work. A new kind of war-master was appearing, the professional war-lord, and Colonel Rich, Lt-Col. Hopton and Trooper Ogilby were now under the command of the first and greatest. His name was Ernst, Graf von Mansfield, the bastard son of a leading Habsburg warrior aristocrat from Luxembourg. Mansfield was the man to whom sovereigns could sub-contract their wars. He would deal with logistics, taxation, strategy and tactics. In the process, he would obviously become a diplomatic and military power in his own right, with shifting territory and allegiance. War was now not just a profession but a commercial enterprise, and Mansfield's enterprise was spoken of as a "military republic" in its own right.[14] The cost of this new warfare would impose strains on rulers and their finances that would themselves bring down governments, give birth to revolutions and shape the world that Ogilby inhabited.

Expeditions

In 1622 Mansfield had hired himself to the Dutch Republic and took over Frisia as his base, but ran out of funds and had to disband. Since war was his business, he now had to suck another country into the struggle, and Britain was his obvious target. Mansfield was fêted by London's crowd, royally entertained, and empowered to raise a force of 12,000 men and 200 horse. Most of these were not trained at all: they were pressed into service from the poor-houses. It seemed like a great way to deal with benefits scroungers until you actually saw thousands of raw conscripts marching towards Dover with weapons in their hands, under the guidance of local officials ("conductors") who simply wanted to hand them over to the army officers and be rid of them. The scale of robbery, rape and looting was sufficiently bad to scar the memories of the kingdom.

One of the regiments waiting for this rabble at Dover was Hopton's.[15] They were put onto ships for Calais. The voyage is very short, so the ships were not well provisioned. It was normal to expect to be on board for a few days at Dover if the winds were unsuitable, but the ships would be very crowded. When they arrived at Calais, though, the French did not let them disembark. Conditions on board soon became grim.

When it became clear that the French were being deliberately unhelpful the ships moved up the coast to Zealand, expecting a more sympathetic welcome. After all, they were there to help, and they were now suffering and starting to die. But someone had brought plague on board one ship, and the contagion was slowly spreading through the fleet. That settled their fate. No one wanted to let these violent, infested men anywhere near their towns, their farms or their families. According to Arthur Wilson, an English soldier at winter quarters close by, thousands upon thousands of bodies were thrown overboard to bloat and drift and slowly wash into the shallow waters where "(after the crows & dogs had their fill, & the air sufficiently tainted) they were thrown into great pits by hundreds".[16] Only a third of Mansfield's army made it back alive. The pikes and muskets were still packed away, untouched.

In July 1625, Wilson came back to England. So did Hopton. It was not a happy return. King James had died in March, and there was a plague epidemic raging. At Dartford, Wilson was ordered by his commander to go to London to see if it was safe. It was not. "I found nothing but death & horror: the very air was putrefied with the contagion of the dead." More than a fifth of Londoners were dropping dead. There were those who thought that this time the pestilence might rage until there were no survivors.

Hopton had been elected MP for Bath before he got back, and he said nothing in debates. He was evidently quite traumatised. He was urgently pressed to go on another expedition but refused because "the miseries we suffered in the last journey (though I could hazard myself willingly enough) make me afraid to have charge of men where I have any doubt of the means to support them".[17] He then withdrew from Mansfield's service. He recovered, and in 1626 was made a Knight of the

Bath in King Charles' Coronation honours list. But what had happened to Ogilby?

It seems he was considerably delayed. Our next piece of evidence is an assertion from the "commissary of the musters" in Portsmouth, a Frenchman called Dulbier,[18] that around May 1626 Ogilby was "Lieutenant of a Scottish company in the service of Count Mansfield".[19] The man had an astonishing capacity to take advantage of every disaster that struck him. There certainly were such companies. Large numbers of men were raised in Scotland for the war,[20] especially from prisons; in the years 1625–27 over 14,000 Scots left the kingdom. There is no reason to doubt that there were Scottish companies on board the fleet. But how he came to be a lieutenant of one of them is a mystery to us and was, it seems, equally baffling to the government.

The claim was put to Dulbier in June 1627, when Ogilby arrived in Portsmouth and requested his back pay, saying that he had spent the previous eleven months as a prisoner of war, having been captured at Dunkirk.

Ogilby had been lucky and fallen into hands that were content to wait for a ransom. He was, after all, a charming and persuasive man. He also had entertainment value, able to play the fiddle and even, if required, give dancing lessons. Somehow he must have managed to communicate with his friends – probably Hopton and Rich, and very possibly Buckingham, and been ransomed. The back pay was very possibly needed to refund his benefactor. But his military career was as much a mystery to the authorities as it is to us. Dulbier gave him a warrant for his pay, addressed to the King's Secretary, Conway. A lieutenant was a junior commissioned officer, responsible, under the captain, for the discipline and order of a company. Conway, a practical man who joked about his own illiteracy, could find no trace of a commission and would not pay without proof. So far as the government was concerned, there was no such lieutenant. Was it possible to become a commissioned officer in the field without a commission being issued? The answer is clearly "yes", once the commissioned officers are dead, and there were an awful lot of dead officers in this force. Ogilby's complete lack of military experience was irrelevant; he was a man of courtly bearing, and that was quite sufficient. One military historian has observed that "the concept of selecting a military officer or commander on the basis of competence, experience, or even seniority was still regarded as novel in England" by English Royalists twenty years later.[21] Dulbier certainly believed Ogilby but when pressed seems to have been unable to come up with a satisfactory document and stalled, saying his papers were in Hamburg.[22] Conway paid up on 19 June, awarding "Lieutenant Ogleby" the substantial sum of £88 "for his entertainment under Count Mansfeldt".[23] He had given in and agreed the payment one day before Dulbier wrote to him refusing to provide evidence. That suggests that Conway had been instructed to pay Ogilby by someone who was more powerful and in a hurry.

The great lord in question was almost certainly Buckingham, now in charge of the navy. He was in Portsmouth preparing to mount another catastrophic expedition, this time against the French, and Ogilby was part of it. It set sail on 27 June. There were 100 ships and over 7,000 men in the expedition, but given Ogilby's talent for retaining contact with his patrons and Buckingham's appreciation of his qualities, he may well have been given a place on the Duke's flagship, along with his beautifully dressed musicians.[24] The great cabin was laid out for music and dance, and Buckingham chose as his companions on board men who embraced an elegant bachelor life, such as Robert Herrick (who wrote sensuous poem such as "To the Virgins, to Make Much of Time", but never directed his verses at any specific woman and never married), and John Donne's son George. The expedition represented a vision of chivalrous military elegance. Its commander wore exceptionally large collars and a huge feather on the finest hat. Colonel Sir Charles Rich was also on the expedition. But not Hopton. The target was the French fortress of the Île de Ré, which they were to besiege and capture. It was a disaster from start to finish. The start was trying to land. Conditions were so difficult that all the siege engineers drowned trying to get ashore. The finish, three months later, was a glorious final assault in which it turned out the scaling ladders were smaller than the walls. The Mansfield expedition had only lost two-thirds of its men. Buckingham lost over 70%. 7,000 went out, 2,000 came back. Sir Charles Rich was among the dead. There were too few survivors to manage the ships, and it looks as though Ogilby was appointed captain of a storm-battered supply vessel to get people home. It was an odd appointment, which may be explained by his personal connection to Buckingham. He was no seaman, but the captain did not need to be. That was the master's job. He just needed to be a safe pair of hands who would make sensible decisions.

He was clearly delighted to have a ship of his own, and saw this as a very interesting career move. Being Ogilby, by the time he brought his ship safely to Portsmouth in November he would have learned a great deal about managing a vessel. But the ship was promptly commandeered by a Judge of the Admiralty, Sir Henry Martyn, who handed it over to a Naval captain whose vessel had been wrecked. Ogilby was outraged, no doubt politely, and set off immediately for London to have a word with the Lord High Admiral, further evidence of their personal link. On 31 January 1628 Sir Henry Martyn sent a cross note to Buckingham about "a land man, one Ogleby, a scot" who his Lordship had apparently sent back to Portsmouth to resume his captaincy of the now-repaired ship. Martyn was furious at the challenge to his authority, saying that Ogilby was no seaman and nobody in Plymouth had heard of him. Besides, he had arrived without a written warrant.[25] As with Ogilby's back pay, it seems lack of paperwork was fatal in war. The pen is mightier than the pike or the musket, a lesson which Ogilby seems to have learned very thoroughly for his later careers.

Ogilby the soldier/sea-captain seems hard to reconcile with Ogilby the dancing master; it might be easier to suppose there are two John Ogilbys on parallel paths. There actually was a soldier called John Ogleby, who was one of the 12,000 or so Scots fighting for Gustavus Adolphus in this period. He became a colonel, retired to Yorkshire and popped up in 1645 as a cavalry trooper in a Scottish battle.[26] There is no record of him in Britain in the 1630s or having any connection to Buckingham. There was only one John Ogilby/Ogleby who could walk straight in on the Duke and have his unequivocal support.

He evidently returned for a while to teaching dance. He needed to remake his civilian connections, and in July 1629 was granted admittance to the Merchant Taylors Company as "John Ogleby" by virtue of his late father's membership.[27] He may have been given some help in having the rules bent, because to be eligible he should have been born after his father's admittance, which was not the case. According to Aubrey he also took an apprentice, John Lacy. Lacy was to become the most celebrated comic actor of his time (and one of Nell

Gwynn's lovers). The apprenticeship must have begun in 1631, when Lacy first came to London. It is interesting that the actor also had a military career, becoming the Earl of Macclesfield's lieutenant and quartermaster.[28] By an odd coincidence, Ogilby already knew an army quartermaster, who generated the next piece of evidence of his military experience.

The brawler

Quartermastering would have come naturally enough to Ogilby. He displayed a flair for logistics and managing others. If Ogilby had not been in military service in the war it is unlikely that he would have had a close relationship with a serving quartermaster. If he had not shown a fighting courage, he would not have stepped into a brawl to try to protect that man, without concern for his personal safety. This case in the Privy Council in 1633 is a really fascinating and quite unequivocal piece of evidence that John Ogilby the dancer was also John Ogilby the fighter.

As a Scot by birth, Ogilby had no right to sue in an English court. But he could, and did, appeal to the Privy Council when he wanted redress from men who had beaten him up:

> 1633 May 31. Petition of John Ogilby to the Council. On Wednesday last petitioner was in the Inner Temple with Robert Abercromby, quartermaster, who has long served in the wars of Bohemia and the Palatinate, and saw one Best, a pragmatic (interfering) youth, and one Hodges, an old man, with others, set upon Abercromby, and tear his cloak from his back and ruff from his neck, endeavouring to drag him to prison without showing him any warrant, whereupon petitioner interfering, Best and Hodges beat and abused him.[29]

It takes great courage for a bystander to step into a brawl where he is outnumbered. Ogilby was no superman – he was beaten up. But he had no hesitation in going into the fight. As much soldier as dancer. But his final redress was not by fisticuffs.

The Solicitor General, asked to sort this out, said six weeks later that he had hoped to arrange for Ogilby to accept a settlement "but finds the petitioner upon such high terms that no moderate sum will content him".

Why was Ogilby being so proud? Any connection he had once had with Buckingham had expired with the Duke himself, who was stabbed to death by a survivor of the Île de Ré expedition. The assassin was executed but widely applauded. But Ogilby had a new connection, a man at the very centre of power, Thomas Wentworth. Wentworth was in effect a viceroy. After the assassination of Buckingham, Wentworth had become the President of the Council of the North, based in York. His acceptance speech was a declaration of the principles of cosmic harmony and the integrity of the order binding subject, sovereign and nature itself: "For whatever he be which ravels forth into questions the right of a King and a people, shall never be able to wrap them up again into the comeliness and order he found them."[30] He exercised power on behalf of the King and was a central figure in helping Charles establish his dominance over Parliament. In 1632, while retaining his power in northern England, he was appointed Lord Chief Deputy in Ireland. He left London for Ireland in June. According to another note on the horoscope drawn by Ashmole, Ogilby entered his service, arriving in August. This had obviously been previously arranged. That may have made him feel he could get more from the Council. He had certainly moved to a new level on the social ladder of the kingdom. He went to the new Lord Deputy as a "gentleman of the household", dancing master to his wife and children, and also as a member of the troop of guards.[31] That was not a job that Wentworth would have given to anyone without military experience, who could not be trusted to perform with well-drilled precision. John Ogilby was a soldier, and wrote a satire on the whole business, *Character of a Trooper*, which no one could find when Aubrey went looking for it.

Now aged thirty-two, he was too old to think of life as a fighting man; besides, the war in Europe was clearly an endless horror. Teaching dance by itself was no longer the priestly role it had once been, so finding more John Lacys to teach would not be very satisfying. But he was John Ogilby, and could always see which way to jump next. He could see a way to use his military experience, dance training and knowledge of the theatre to create a new career. In fact he could create a new life, in an exciting new world. He could have a hand in really shaping the future. So that is what he did.

Life 4. The Impresario

Ogilby was joining the most powerful household in Britain, as England was in the process of dividing. Would the King dominate Parliament or Parliament dominate the King? Charles had dismissed Parliament in 1629 and begun to rule without it, resurrecting forgotten levies that he could use to replace Parliament's grants. Wentworth, a Yorkshireman, had used his Presidency of the Council of the North to subjugate protesting northern gentlemen. His approach was ruthless, using the Star Chamber and imprisonment. Now he was to impose the authority of the Crown on Ireland, and every member of his household was part of the new order to be established there.

The power of spectacle

Wentworth did not need Ogilby just as a dancing master and trooper. His authority in Ireland was going to have to be established from a very weak base, and he had no connection with the place. A new basis had to be invented for exercising the power of government, and that basis, in Wentworth's view, was essentially one of public performance.

The Tudor system for subduing Ireland had been one of "plantation", importing Protestant settlers (the "New English"), giving them confiscated land and brutally applying English armies against what were seen as primitive savages. In 1596 an English settler, Edmund Spenser, wrote *A View of The Present State of Ireland* advocating genocide through starvation. In 1600 that became official policy for dealing with Ulster, the most Gaelic part of the island: "When the plough and breeding of cattle shall cease, then will the rebellion end."[1] By 1602 Ulster had been reduced to cannibalism, and the then Lord Deputy's secretary "saw a most horrible spectacle of three children (whereof the eldest was not above ten years old) all eating and gnawing with their teeth the entrails of their dead mother, upon whose flesh they had fed twenty days past …".[2]

Gaelic military resistance was totally crushed in 1601. The era of rule by slaughter was, Wentworth believed, now over. The new Lord Chief Deputy needed to establish the authority of his court there by appearing overwhelming and impregnable, impressive and unchallengeable. When Aubrey writes that Ogilby rode in Wentworth's troop of guards, we are being given a hint of his education in ceremony. Aubrey would certainly have known that these were no ordinary guards.

They were more about display than brute force. Wentworth was not happy about the "strange neglect" of the official military guard when the viceroy appeared in public "before the eyes of a wild and rude people".[3] He believed that he could make the Irish accept English rule by a kind of conversion through theatre.

Civic ceremony was of vital importance to the Lord Deputy, and he complained that it was not understood at all by the Irish administration. At the heart of his newly-invented public spectacle was this personal military entourage, created for the purpose. Ogilby was evidently one of his newly formed body of troopers, who wore black armour, rode black horses and had a plume of black feathers.[4] Surrounded by his Dark Riders, Wentworth was visibly established as no ordinary man.

The Stuarts had a very good grasp of the power of spectacle. There is no record of who organised Wentworth's public spectacles, but we can deduce from his later career that Ogilby was involved. In 1660, when King Charles II returned to England, he required a coronation procession to create a new vision of legitimacy, and Ogilby would direct the public appearance of royalty, aristocracy, military and civic power. He was trusted to make the restoration unforgettable and unchallengeable, defining the country's image of itself through the power of spectacle. We have no information at all about how he came to be in that position, but we can make some extrapolations. No one in Britain could have learned anything about royal spectacle during the Commonwealth, but something like this had been achieved by Wentworth in Ireland. That would have been when Ogilby was seen to have acquired expertise in grand ceremonies.

Getting to Ireland

Ireland was a long way from Whitehall, far enough for Wentworth's experiments in grandeur and spectacle not to immediately trouble the King. His own journey there had been a lesson in travel time. He had written a letter from Whitehall on 20 May saying that as soon as his ship had a favourable wind he "would not stay an hour".[5] Between snuffing his candle and arriving in Dublin, 360 miles away, two months passed. It was not an easy journey.

Wentworth sent his sumptuous robes and £500 worth of linen on ahead, by boat from Liverpool. To his great alarm, the cargo was seized outside Dublin by a pirate ship, the cheekily-named *Pick-Pocket of Dover*. There were at least three professional pirate ships patrolling the Irish Sea, and Wentworth claimed that they brought seaborne trade to a standstill. He realised that he was lucky not to have sent his gold and silver plate with his clothes.

It was possible for Wentworth himself to sail from Chester to Ireland, but even without pirates it was impractical because Chester is not on the sea. The city is on the River Dee, and the town quay had largely silted up by the seventeenth century. Ships had to moor some miles downstream, where there was no quay. Once people and cargo had been rowed out to their vessel and manoeuvred on board, they had to wait for a favourable wind to take them north to the sea. A sailing vessel cannot steer into the wind, but modern sails will at least allow a boat to steer to within 45 degrees of where the wind is coming from. That means that even if the wind is blowing from the vessel's destination, it can get there by tacking, zig-zagging towards its goal. Seventeenth-century ships could not tack at all unless the wind was strong.[6] They could not be in a hurry. They simply waited for a wind to blow in the right direction. The trouble with Chester was that the wind that would blow a ship out of the Dee might not blow it west to Ireland, but north, up the English coast. So having waited to find a south wind to leave Chester, the vessel would sometimes still have to anchor and wait for an east wind for Ireland. It could take weeks, and no one wanted to spend weeks imprisoned on a pitching, rolling, yawing ship at anchor within tantalising sight of land. Sometimes passenger vessels foundered waiting out storms in the Dee before they even raised their anchors. In any case Wentworth would not trust himself and his goods to an unknown captain. He insisted on sailing on board the *Dreadnought*, the King's own 32-gun warship commanded by a redoubtable naval hero.[7] When it had a favourable wind it could work its way from its base in Rochester to the Dee estuary where it could pick him up. He finally left London by road on 6 July. Ten days later he was in Chester (presumably picking up his plate and other goods). From there it took but a week to be ferried out to the waiting ship and finish the journey under the security of its guns. On 23 July an Irish planter, Sir Edward Denny, noted in his diary "The Lord Viscount Wentworth came to Ireland to govern the kingdom. Many men fear."[8]

Ogilby was not on the *Dreadnought*. He was stuck in London waiting for the Star Chamber to make a decision on his case against his assailants.[9] He must have arrived in Chester too late and missed the boat, so he had to risk the crossing by a more conventional route. *Britannia* shows the journey. It went overland from Chester to Holyhead to cross the Irish Sea. This was not easy: with fast riding and changes of horses Chester could be reached in two days, at a high price. Most people were likely to take twice as long. Then came the start of the adventure. Crossing Wales was, in English eyes, a journey through a savage land whose inhabitants had little care for law and spoke a barbarous tongue (we call it Welsh now but it was "British" then). The road passed through the cattle market town of Denbigh, where a court record of 1570 says it was foul and dangerous, and heavy laden horses struggled and fell in the deep muck. That was the easy bit. The journey continued to Conway, and then the traveller had to reach the island of Anglesey. Until Telford built a bridge over the Menai Strait, that meant walking or riding over ten miles of tidal sand.

This was not the end of the journey. Ten miles on from Beaumaris *Britannia* shows the traveller passing a gibbet, a reassuring sign of the authority of the castle, and then they would arrive in the port of Holyhead, reputed to have the greatest concentration of inns in Britain. The only reason anyone had to be in Holyhead was that they were waiting for a boat, as passenger or crew, or that they were offering services of some kind to ships or passengers. The inns were not particularly comfortable, but better than the boat. Once the wind was right the passengers boarded and the 24-hour crossing was possible. Not many boats were wrecked on the way over, though more were on the way back, and of course there were the pirates waiting if your ship looked Dutch or stuffed with valuables.

Teaching civilisation

Aubrey reports that Ogilby said he was employed to teach the Lord Deputy's wife and children to dance. Wentworth's children, by his previous wife, were a boy of seven and two girls aged six and three. The boy and elder girl would expect dancing lessons from a professional. A memoir by the daughter of the Keeper of the Tower of London recalls how she had seven or eight specialist teachers including a dancing master when she was about seven years old (which would have been in 1628).[10]

The children's stepmother, Lady Wentworth, would also need lessons. This was a very new marriage, his third. Up to now his wives had been the daughters of Earls, used to ceremonial living, but Elizabeth was about eighteen and the daughter of a strict Puritan gentleman from Yorkshire. She was extremely deferential to Wentworth and other important people. That would not do in her new position. She needed tutoring and Ogilby was recommended by his aristocratic contacts as a good choice. He was also discreet. This could mean that he was tutoring Elizabeth before she left England, before the marriage was made public. Wentworth had spent two years preparing for his mission to Ireland, and it seems clear that Ogilby's services were included in his planning. That may explain Ogilby's confidence in demanding a large settlement from his assailants when he pleaded his case with the Privy Council in July 1632.

Dancing seems to have been an important part of Wentworth's vision for Ireland. Not that he envisaged a dancing Ireland: that would have been altogether too Irish. His vision was of a courtly life, mirroring the court in England. Wentworth intended to seduce the population, or at least the most powerful part of it, into submission to his rule by the manifest demonstration of the luxury and civilised manners of English high culture. His household must obviously be perfectly prepared.

Ireland in the mid-sixteenth century had been populated by Gaelic clans with both native and Norman overlords. The Norman families, who quite often also spoke Gaelic, were now called the Old English. The people imported and given land under the Tudor plantation policy were the New English. By the time Wentworth arrived the monstrous Tudor policy of mass murder had served its purpose. It was now time to win hearts and minds.

New settlers in Ireland were now obliged to build proper stone houses to show an example of a better way of life. Cities were encouraged to grow for the same reason, and Irish dress was disappearing from them, except for the useful mantle. The English would have liked that to vanish too, as they felt it concealed too much. Wentworth's demonstration of English civilisation began with his new home, Dublin Castle, which he needed to transform from a decaying medieval heap (one tower collapsed while his children were playing below) into a stately palace. This meant not just extensive building and decorative work, but also the institution of regal etiquette. Ordinary gentlemen were now barred from the Presence Chamber. Only noblemen were now allowed past the Drawing-Chamber, and only the Council could enter the Gallery. Servants had to wait in the Great Chamber, and no one was to wear a hat.

He was promoting the virtues of English civilisation by providing a vision of royal splendour. Three weeks after delivering the new viceroy to Dublin, the captain of the *Dreadnought* chased a pirate ship off the coast, captured some of the pirates and rescued a Dutch ship they were looting. Wentworth's reaction was to personally knight the gallant captain. It was the act of a king.

The new monarchy

Monarchy had grown more distant from normal mortals. The Tudors had made themselves personally splendorous, and Henry VIII was certainly capable of organising a very glamorous encampment, but Stuart courts were far more ambitious, bound around with complex mannered rituals expressed in magnificent displays of art, furnishing, elaborate decoration and vast fawning theatrical spectacle. The conviction that power, glory and divine blessing flowed outward from the King and Queen, transforming the world around them, was now extraordinarily strong. This was the message of every masque, and the scale of these performances was breath-taking. They employed hundreds of people in astonishingly lavish spectacles which were adorations of the magic and heavenly power of the sovereign.

The most important performance space for masques was Inigo Jones' Banqueting House in the Palace of Whitehall. The burning of the old House in 1619 had, as things turned out, resulted in greater consequences than ending Ogilby's career as a dancer. It also opened a space for the first classically-styled building in the kingdom. Jones visited Italy, brought back a large number of original drawings by the sixteenth-century architect Palladio, and set about literally importing the architecture of the Renaissance. It made a stunning contrast to the existing architecture of Whitehall, a Tudor muddle of black and white and red-painted timber and plaster. This new style would spread imperiously over the whole land, publicly proclaiming wealth and power. We think of it as modern, but in the seventeenth century "modern" meant vernacular (or "gothic") architecture; the new Banqueting House was "antique". The classical world was associated with high status and luxury. The original Banqueting House, which had been built for James in 1606, was of brick and stone with a tiled roof, a rather strange large house surmounted by a belfry-like tower. When Jones was given the task of rebuilding it after the fire, he clearly saw this space of dance and entertainment, the world in which Ogilby had his being, as the central display-space of royal authority. He considered building a sacred-styled space based on a basilica.[11] He may have decided that this would not be ideal for masques, and determined instead to make direct visual reference to Roman imperial splendour. The Earth may no longer have been the centre of the heavens, but in this space the heavens were always centred on the King and Queen.

It was a vision that would reach its apotheosis (quite literally) with the installation of Rubens' Banqueting House ceiling panels. Part of the novelty of the antique style of architecture was that the rafters were hidden by a flat ceiling, offering a new possibility of decoration. The work was commissioned in 1629, and completed in 1634. Rubens was artist and diplomat, working to glorify the Stuart monarchy and negotiate peace between England and Spain.

Peter Paul Rubens was the leading artistic promoter of the counter-reformation. In 1622, to celebrate the canonisation of Loyola, the founder of the Jesuits, he was commissioned to paint an altar-piece for the Jesuit church in Antwerp. The Catholicism which had destroyed the Winter King and Queen in Bohemia had a fierce energy derived not from popular piety but from a sense of authority based on power. It sought to take people's feelings by storm and work in them the inner revolution for which Loyola had campaigned. Rubens' painting, *St Ignatius Casting Out Devils,* is a manifestation of the energy of that inner revolution. Loyola, glowing in red and gold, stands calmly over a writhing, boiling struggle. Twisted wraiths of demons flee, shining cherubim hover over them. It is a picture alive with the screams of the exorcised and the exultation of their release. The picture's turmoil increases towards the bottom, towards the foreground, and the eye-line is down there near the floor, where the bodies writhe. The whole design is intended to sweep the onlooker into the tumult as a participant in that moment of terror and exhilaration, to experience the overwhelming and triumphant power commanded by Loyola.

Rubens was the iconographer of the new Catholic vision. His audience was thrilled with images in which their focal plane was pitched low, as though they were present kneeling, looking up at the drama. It is obviously significant that Rubens was fully accepted as the painter to interpret British royalty in a Protestant land. The Stuarts clearly shared a Roman Catholic vision but without the Pope, and installed it on the ceiling. In the theatre of the masque the viewer is not simply kneeling at the foot of transcendental events but must look up towards heaven to see them.

The painting celebrates the union of the crowns of England and Scotland with, at its centre, the bodily ascension of James I and VI into heaven. Rubens apparently originally intended a painting of Psyche being received into Olympus,[12] but that image of a mythical mortal being accepted among the gods was replaced by a very real human. The picture perfectly marries the King, divinity and alchemy, as Charles' father is transmuted into an eternal and incorruptible form. Can the son of such a figure be thought of as mortal clay, shitting and pissing with the rest of us? Kings now transcended mortality, according to their own propaganda.

It was the message of the masque made permanent, installed on the ceiling of the Palace of Whitehall's performance space. By a wonderful irony, it rendered the theatre useless. Once the canvas was fixed to the ceiling, masques could no longer be performed there because the flaming torches that lit them would blacken the painting. Installation was delayed for two years. Six years later Charles would walk under that ceiling to his execution. By that time Wentworth had been beheaded. But for the time being, monarchy was spectacle, government was spectacle, and Ogilby, that most useful servant, an expert on masques and dance working in an imitation Royal Court, was imbibing and learning to manage spectacle.

He must have had a role in organising state occasions. Wentworth's situation in Ireland was more precarious than

that of a real king, as he was personally unknown with no
connection to the place, and clearly only there on a short lease
at the King's pleasure. He had concluded that the power of
ceremony was more significant and meaningful than brute
force, and the men who arranged those ceremonies could
determine the fate of the colony.

The first great public ceremony mounted after Ogilby's
arrival in Dublin was the opening of the Irish Parliament on
14 July 1634. It began with the Lord Deputy processing to St
Patrick's Cathedral. First came an earl in his robes, carrying
a ceremonial sword and another bearing a ceremonial cap.
Then came the man himself, accompanied by Ogilby and
the rest of his chilling and stately black-armoured guard,
with their black feathers and black horses. Behind trooped
all the bishops and peers. From the Cathedral they moved to
the Castle, where the State Opening of Parliament was, in
Wentworth's opinion, performed "with the greatest civility
and splendour Ireland ever saw".[13]

That procession belonged as much to the world of masque as
to that of public ceremony. Five months earlier the playwright
James Shirley had written a masque, *The Triumph of Peace*,
which began with a fabulous procession from Ely House
down Chancery Lane to Whitehall. It was led by the King's
Marshall and his men followed by a hundred members of the
Inns of Court in gold and silver lace. This was the lawyers'
show of obeisance. It was necessary because the radical
Puritan Gray's Inn lawyer, William Prynne, had produced a
1,000-page condemnation of the poisonous immorality of
dramatic performance in which he insulted the Queen. This
was the volume in which Prynne denounced mixed dancing
as lascivious. Busy people, presented with a huge book which
they are told they need to be aware of, turn first to the index

to get an idea of it. The King looked at one index entry in particular: "Women actors, notorious whores". His Queen had already been prudishly criticised by some for her performance in a masque, and was about to appear in another. Prynne was charged with high treason and brutally punished, and the Bar had to perform an extravagant act of obeisance. Shirley, who was the playwright of the Cockpit and a friend and associate of Ogilby, was chosen to write the masque as he was also a resident of Gray's Inn. The lawyers were followed in procession by the performers: two music chariots; one of lutenists and the other of singers, all elaborately costumed, followed by the actors, with the lead performers in four chariots. It created a stunning impression, carefully reported to Wentworth, who kept a close eye on masque performances in England.[14]

Wentworth wanted the Irish to learn to see the political world as the masque made flesh. On the day after its opening he explained to the Irish parliament how to understand the difficulties King Charles was having with the parliament in England in terms of a malevolent spirit of darkness which could easily be dispersed like the resolution of a masque in a single beam of light and truth.[15]

There seems to have been a real conviction that the fairy-tale world of the masque had some reality and could be inhabited.

Exporting theatre

Ogilby was not in Wentworth's household as just a dancing master and trooper, or even an organiser of official spectacle. Wentworth's understanding of the use of theatricality meant that Ogilby was there as a missionary, to convert the natives.

This was not a religious conversion but a cultural one. He was to assist in transforming Irishmen into Englishmen, and this magic was to be performed in a theatre. He would establish the first theatre in Ireland. The Puritan tide had now closed the few provincial playhouses in England, but Wentworth was no Puritan. He saw theatre as the crystallisation of English civilisation. It was a view expressed in a dialogue between two law students in a play put on near the Inns of Court in 1633:

> Give me Johnson and Shakespeare; there's learning for a gentleman. I tell thee, Sam, were it not for the dancing-school and playhouses, I would not study at the Inns of Court for the hopes of a Chief-Justice-ship.[16]

Ogilby was this world incarnate. Colonisation through the seduction of literature and performance, rather than physical force, is an important weapon in the modern world. It is sometimes referred to as the use of "soft power". We are familiar with the efforts of the Alliance Française, the British Council and the promotion of American movies in Latin America by the US foreign service.[17] In fact we are so familiar with it that we may find it hard to grasp that the conscious use of culture and performance as a tool of imperial government was a complete novelty in the 1630s unless we look back to ancient Rome, which sought to Romanise people through the theatre of gladiatorial shows, performed throughout the empire.

Ogilby was starting a completely novel form of colonisation which, as things turned out, steadily conquered the world. Theatre was the jewel in the crown of Englishness. Shakespeare had been succeeded by an array of popular playwrights. Until the Puritan tide began to run, roughly one Londoner in eight went to the theatre every week; this was an audience comparable to that for cinema in the 1930s. Ogilby seems to have grasped that he could advance the policy of cultural imperialism and make a successful business out of it, and Wentworth backed him. He had never done anything like this before in his life, and he must have been very confident of Wentworth's support to suddenly launch not just into theatre management, but also into a significant building project when theatre was under attack in England. Ogilby built the theatre with his own money (possibly borrowed).[18] The cost was extraordinary, £2,000.[19] It was an investment. Dublin offered nothing like the size of audience available in London, which had about fifteen times as many inhabitants, but it was as large as Norwich, the largest provincial city in England. And although it had no purpose-built theatres, it had a population of theatre-goers. In 1617, Barnaby Rich's *The Irish Hubbub, or The English Hue and Crie* had Dublin characters who would have clearly been a natural part of the Red Bull's audience in London, and who had nothing better to do on a Dublin afternoon than consider whether they should stroll off to watch a play.[20]

Wentworth was himself keen on theatre. A play was staged for him in the castle as part of his first Christmas and New Year festivities; it must have been Ogilby's first experiment in putting together a drama in Ireland. The play was part of an elaborate long day of feasting and gambling. The only record of it is from Wentworth's guest the Earl of Cork. He did not mention the name of the play or its quality, just that it was acted by Wentworth's gentlemen and that in the course of the evening he and the Lord Chancellor lost money to their host at dice.[21] Two years later Wentworth invited them back to see another play. Cork said that after dinner and gambling they were taken to see tragedy performed in the parliament house and then sent home. So far as he was concerned, this "was tragical, for we had no supper".[22] The tragedy was doubtless heightened by the fact that he lost again; he was down "six pieces", which might be £8,000 today. Loftus, the Chancellor, who was also there again, was luckier, and this time Wentworth too was a loser. When a theatre review and a gambling result were competing for diary space it was really no contest, so far as the Earl of Cork was concerned.

Wentworth obviously felt that drama could work its magic, even if the Earl refused to be impressed. A few months later Ogilby's theatre was opened in Werburgh Street.[23] This was not at all comparable to the castle performances staged for Wentworth's private enjoyment.

Werburgh Street was a small street outside the castle, with a church, saddlers, a surgeon and a scribe as well as the house of the Lord Chancellor, Sir Adam Loftus.[24] The theatre was of a very modern kind. Elizabethan theatres, like the Red Bull and the Globe, were open courtyards furnished with a stage, with the audience standing in a "pit" and in galleries, equally visible with the actors. But a new kind of "private" theatre had emerged in recent years, a closed in, covered hall with decent seating and controllable lighting, by oil lamps and candles, giving a new intensity and intimacy to drama. The Cockpit was such a theatre. It was a less democratic space; seats were normally six times more expensive in the private theatres. These politely luxurious rooms provided the stage for a new kind of play, the Jacobean revenge tragedy of intense emotion, violent action and startlingly compelling lighting effects, but all contained within a decorous box that would not spill barbarity onto the street outside. That is, of course, why the Red Bull's audience resented their company moving to the Cockpit and burned it down. Webster had explained their dislike of *The White Devil* by saying that "most of the people who come to that playhouse resemble ignorant asses".[25] The Werburgh Street theatre was intended to "reduce the public presentations of tragedies and comedies to the proper and harmless use whereby those recreations formerly obnoxious were made inoffensive".[26] It seems that the mere fact of its existence was not enough to put other, unwelcome pop-up performances out of business. That would be why Wentworth appointed Ogilby Master of the Revels in Ireland in February 1637 with the power to permit and forbid performances (the authority of the Master of the Revels in England not reaching across the sea).

The theatre "had a gallery and pit [i.e. a balcony and stalls], but no boxes, except one on the stage for the then Lord Deputy of Ireland".[27] The stage was a bare platform with an upper gallery. We know little about the early life of the theatre except that Ogilby was not winning the competition despite his notional licensing powers. He concluded that cultural imperialism of a mulish people needed stick as well as carrot. In 1636 it was felt necessary to pass an Act of Parliament in Ireland banning "common players of interludes … jugglers and minstrels", who were lumped together with beggars, scam-artists, quacks and chancers. The fact that the act specifically outlawed people pretending to be Egyptians, or wandering about "in the habit, form, or attire of counterfeit Egyptians" suggests that Ogilby was up against a really popular entertainment that owed nothing to English court-liness. I think most of us would want to see this show, but the Dark Riders would probably not permit it.

The Egyptian attire of the period would have had nothing to do with the sphinx or Tutankhamen; all that imagery was quite unknown. "Egyptian" identity equated with "Gypsies", and this was probably an attempt to suppress groups claiming to be gypsies. But there is another possibility.

This is the period when the bardic roots of Irish history were putting forth new shoots and redefining Irishness in the context of the new colonialism. The story of Ireland was told in a stunning eleventh-century work, *The Book of Invasions*, which has never lost its power to shape the Irish sense of identity of land and people. It tells of the Irish descent from Goídel Glas, a Scythian who was present at the fall of the Tower of Babel, and Scota, a daughter of a pharaoh of Egypt. Their descendants left Egypt and Scythia at the time of the Exodus of Moses, and came to Ireland via Spain. The invasions that followed, successful and failed, were then all experienced in the context of an ancient pre-classical tradition. For eight years, 1616–24, in the "contention of the bards", poets from northern and southern Ireland contested their versions of history. The debate was being constantly re-fashioned, and defined the Irish (and Old English) notion of their proper relationship to English sovereignty. In 1634 Seathrún Céitinn, known in English as Geoffrey Keating, a Roman Catholic priest, poet and historian, published *Foras Feasa ar Éirinn* ("Foundation of Knowledge on Ireland") in Irish, which traced the Irish story from the creation. It was banned, but was hugely influential over the next century. The legend said not only that that the Irish were descended from an original migrant to Iberia, but that this hero's name had been "Míl Espáine", Soldier of Hispania, and that he had fought for Spain. The story was sufficiently potent in the seventeenth century for Irish refugees in Spain to be given all the rights and privileges of Spanish subjects.

Is it possible that some kind of pageant of Irish history was going on in Dublin, telling the story of this Egyptian ancestry, and it was being swept from the streets? Was Ogilby an officer in a drama war? Of course the question that mattered then was what was he putting on to win the audience and recoup his investment? We have not a jot of evidence of his first plays, and it seems that to fill the house he was relying on bear-baiting and boxing.[28] He needed actors and a playwright. So he went shopping.

Colonising thespians

In June 1636 Wentworth sailed back to England on a heavily armed royal ship, and it seems he took Ogilby with him. There they were able to secure the services of James Shirley and some of the actors of the Red Bull and Cockpit Theatres, all of whom were counted among Ogilby's friends, together with some musicians. Shirley, the creator of the great processional masque *The Triumph of Peace*, was exactly what Wentworth needed. It was a buyer's market; all London theatres were closed at the time because of an outbreak of plague and none of the new signings had any other work. It seems they all travelled to Dublin with Wentworth in the same royal ship in November.[29] They disembarked to discover that the Primate, an energetic Calvinist called Ussher who shared Prynne's view of the immorality of acting, had closed the theatre lest it bring down a divine punishment of plague (which was obviously what had happened in London).[30] Ussher was the man who, in 1650, famously calculated from biblical evidence that the world was created at 6 p.m. on the eve of Sunday, 23 October 4004 BC.[31]

The theatre was re-opened. And hardly anyone came. Shirley wrote a preface to one of Middleton's plays, put on in Dublin 1638, in which he complains that the audience he had been enticed to delight seems to be dead and buried:

When he did live in England, he heard say,
That here were men lov'd wit, and a good play …
This he believ'd, and though they are not found
Above, who knows what may be underground?
But they do not appear.

In fact he wrote prefaces to all the plays that were presented, and they are a litany of complaints about the audience. This is probably not what Ogilby had hoped for. Shirley says they would buy tickets for bear-baiting or cudgelling, but not for plays.[32] In 1639 Ogilby moved on from allowing the audience (mostly the Dublin court, nobility and students) to see the delights of London theatre. He needed to find something that would resonate better with them. It may have been a mistake to expect Shirley, however well intentioned, to have a feel for the task. He titled his first play written for Dublin *St. Patrick, for Ireland*. The comma is important: this title is not a barnstorming slogan but an offering. The prologue says with a kind of desperation that

We should be very happy, if at last,
We could find out the humour of your taste.

The use of "we" (the colonisers) and "you" (the colonised) was not an encouraging opening. This prologue is written by a deeply unhappy man, who actually says that he knows that some of them have come simply to show that they don't like what is on offer.[33] Shirley tried to satisfy them by including slapstick, moving idols, serpents, fire and the performance of magic. The prologue ended with a promise that if the feedback was positive, he would write *St. Patrick Part 2*. He didn't.

The Dublin theatre was now in a cauldron that was being steadily heated. Wentworth's quasi-monarchical rule was seen as arbitrary and contemptuous of the established Irish nobility. He had set out to make Ireland pay its way, so he reviewed everybody's property titles with an eye to increasing royal rents. Of course he quite often found that their paperwork wasn't quite right and repossessed the land. Being a very fair man, he treated everyone's complaints with equal disdain – Catholic, Protestant, Old English, New Irish, all the same to him. And then there was the business of religion.

Wentworth was a close friend of the anti-Puritan Archbishop Laud, who was enraging huge swathes of the population by forcibly suppressing Low Church rites, insisting on the use of a new Anglican prayer-book with its rituals and images. Ireland was rather cowed, but in Scotland this was the trigger for rebellion. Henry VIII had established that the King was head of the Church in England, but that did not make him head of the Church in Scotland. Charles seems not to have understood that. He could appoint bishops, but they had no sway over the "presbyteries", regional assemblies of Calvinist ministers. He outlawed the Presbyterian tradition of extempore prayer, insisting that they stick to their Church's prayer book. When he was told that there was no such book he authorised Laud to prepare one and declared that any minister who did not use it was a "rebel and an outlaw". That was the trigger, in 1637, for an outraged howl of anguish which swept through Scotland. Charles refused to consider any compromise. The Presbyterian church, faced with what it saw as destruction, drew up a National Covenant which required every Scottish householder to swear opposition to every innovation in Church and Government made since 1603. By the end of May 1638 the Covenant had been accepted by the majority of Scots everywhere except for the remote area of the Western Highlands, Aberdeen and Banff.

The New Irish were predominantly Presbyterian Scots who had settled in Ulster, and Wentworth poured oil on the fire by demanding that all adult Presbyterians in Ulster sign the "Black Oath" against the covenant. Those who refused would be heavily fined or imprisoned for an indeterminate time. Many Ulster Presbyterians fled to Scotland.

In April 1639 Charles gathered his forces at York to suppress the Scottish Covenanters by force. He had no professional army: he was summoning a feudal levy from an aristocracy that had very little in the way of men or equipment for war, even if they wanted to supply them. The Ogilvie clan was his most dependable support in Scotland, and he turned Lord Ogilvie, the head of the clan, into the First Earl of Airlie. He also hoped that Wentworth would send forces from Ireland. It was not a clever plan, and the whole operation turned into a chaotic shambles. In September 1639 Wentworth was recalled to England to advise Charles on what to do next. The King wanted an effective army to confront the Covenanters, and needed Wentworth to find ways of paying for it which would bypass the reluctance of Parliament to help. In January 1640 he was made Earl of Strafford. He still ruled Ireland, but his place was really now in the thick of English political strife.

Making an Irish theatre

With his patron away, Ogilby did not commission anything more from Shirley. He evidently decided that the programme of cultural imperialism, and of presenting London theatre to Irishmen, was on rocky ground. Instead of the theatre making Englishmen of the Irish Ogilby began helping the Irish take it over themselves. He turned to Henry Burnell, a wealthy landowner and amateur playwright. Burnell was from an Old

English family, well established for generations in Dublin; his father-in-law was the Earl of Roscommon. Politically Burnell was suspect because of his Catholicism and he was no sympathiser with Wentworth or the theory that Charles ruled by Divine Right. But he might well be just what the theatre needed.

Wentworth arrived back in Dublin in March on a flying visit to hold a Parliament which would provide the money to pay for an Irish army for Charles to use against the Scots. He got it by offering the Irish Catholics – Burnell's section of the population – reforms they had been demanding for years. Ogilby and Burnell seized their moment; the play was rushed into production. The day after the opening of Parliament, Burnell's *Landgartha*, the first published play by a native Irish author, was acted at the theatre. That was on St Patrick's Day, 17 March 1640, during Lent, when theatres were normally shut. The audience must have been filled with the Old English grandees.

To an audience well used to reading allegory, Burnell's play about the struggle of Norway against Swedish colonisation, with Danish help, was more than just a good romp. It had meaning. It was also seen as a direct theatrical response to Shirley's English view of Ireland, and the author said that his audience did not need the visual tricks of *St. Patrick*. The Dublin audience got a magnificent "tragie-comedie" that opened with an Amazon carrying a battle-axe, and verses written by Burnell's daughter Eleanor, the only female Anglo-Irish poet of her time.

The theatre had evidently found its feet at last, and *Landgartha* was published in 1641 "as it was Presented in the New Theatre in Dublin with Good Applause". That may mean that part of the audience was cheering meanings that it was reading into the play – Burnell says in his afterword to the printed edition that "Some (but not of the best judgements) were offended."[34] There was no sequel to *St. Patrick*, but Burnell wrote a follow-up to *Landgartha* and it seems the original was frequently repeated.[35]

On Good Friday, 3 April, Wentworth (now the Earl of Strafford), his work done, hurried back to England. A few days later he was followed by Shirley and the London performers. Their theatres were open again and they wanted to go home. Ogilby was left behind. He was still nominally in Strafford's service, but his pupils (Strafford's family) had gone to London and he was free to quite literally run his own show. His theatre seemed to be making an income, and he was beginning to become confident of his own literary voice. He had been doing some scribal work for Wentworth (he had very fine handwriting) and had been creating his own version of Aesop's fables in verse, probably to entertain the children that he was teaching. Of course he had to work from an existing translation, as he knew no Greek. It is probably at this point that, having lost his playwright and many of his actors, he tried writing a play himself, *The Merchant of London*.[36]

And then it all began to go horribly wrong.

Life 5. The Life Redacted

Rebellion

In November 1640 Charles, having run out of alternatives, finally called a Parliament to ask for the funds for his army against the Scots. This provided the opportunity for them to rein back a king who plainly believed that he should not be fettered, and who was using every manner of device to raise money without their consent and impose his own rules on religion in the face of a popular puritanism. Strafford was their particular enemy, especially as he had suggested that his new-funded Irish Catholic army could be used to crush dissent anywhere in Britain. The creator of the Black Riders and the Black Oath was now called "Black Tom". In March 1641 Strafford was put on trial for treason in Parliament. Ogilby's old employer, Ralph Hopton, was one of Strafford's fiercer attackers. Strafford's defence, that it could not be treason to carry out the King's wishes, was so unanswerable that the trial was abandoned, but Parliament then moved to execute him by an Act, a "Bill of Attainder". Charles had promised to protect Strafford, but in the face of a virtual uprising in London he gave his assent. Ogilby's patron was executed on Tower

Hill on 12 May 1641, before what was said to be a crowd of 300,000. That was surely an exaggeration. 300,000 was pretty much the entire population of London.

There followed a kind of deathly stillness in Ireland. Officially, the Earl of Leicester was Strafford's replacement as Lord Deputy, but he never set foot in the country. Taxes gradually stopped being collected, the new army was slowly disbanded. The administrative powers of the Irish grew and the King's diminished. But the breakdown of power in England meant that the rancorous division between Catholic Old English, Presbyterian new settlers and Dublin administration was inevitably going to erupt. Irish Catholics heard of the victories of the Covenanters against Charles and his surrender to them of swathes of Northern England. They were told that the Scots had petitioned Parliament to kill all the Papists of the three kingdoms. The Catholics could not sit on their hands. There was a vacuum of power, it was time to listen to ancestral voices and take back their destinies. They "nowe expected the fulfilling of Colum Kills Prophecie: which (as they did construe it to be) was That the irish should conquer Ireland againe".[1] On 23 October 1641 the Old English and Gaelic population launched a bloody attack against the English and Scottish settlers and planters, murdering thousands. John Ogilby's theatre was immediately closed by order of the justices, and soon afterwards is reported to have been turned into a "cow-house".[2]

Aubrey recorded that Ogilby "ran through many hazards" in the rebellion.[3] There was no shortage of hazards. The uprising in Ireland was no mirror of the English Civil War; the first Irish rebels were royalist, Ulster Catholic gentry whose main concerns were their own rights and privileges. They made an attempt to attack Dublin Castle, but it was meant to force the administration to support them.[4] With the failure of that attack, the rebellion spread and became chaotic. Its events are recorded (with problematic reliability) in an extraordinary collection of 8,000 witness testimonies which amount to the world's first war crimes depositions. Typical among its pages is an account, dated 12 October 1642, of the fate of a wealthy English family living in Dungannon, in Ulster, at the hands of men from Newry. The householder, James Rowan, was seized and held captive for six months and then killed. His wife set out with their four children and many servants to seek a secure place of safety. The deposition says that they

> were all most cruelly murdered by the rebels in the highway (to wit) the mother was knocked in the head being great with child, and 2 of her children were hanged over their mothers shoulder before they murdered her. And her other 2 Children were knocked in the head and so killed, and at the same time and place 14 of her servants were also murdered by the Rebels.[5]

It is a report of a sadistic massacre committed by a large band well used to killing. They were large enough to overpower at least ten adults. Their weapons were not guns or swords but cudgels and ropes. They are accused of cruelty beyond the dashing out of children's brains. Hanging children in front of their pregnant mother is not an act that can be easily understood. It is also striking, to a modern reader, that while the suffering mother and her four children qualify for a degree of empathy, the killing of fourteen servants is reduced to "also". No note is taken of whether they were men, women or children, or how they died.

This body of material, unparalleled anywhere in early modern Europe, was never intended to bring peace and reconciliation. It is a 31-volume catalogue of reasons to hate. The cruelty and massacres were on both sides, but the emphasis here was on Protestant victim-hood and native Irish savagery. Protestant Ireland has nursed its memory to this day. One of the most ruthless outrages was when a hundred Protestants were thrown from a bridge into the River Bann at Portadown in County Armagh. The Orange Order Lodge at Portadown still carries a banner depicting the massacre when they parade every 12th of July.

By the spring of 1642 England was also being torn apart. The King abandoned London. He was refused access to Hull in April and his army unsuccessfully besieged the city. Civil War had begun. Charles formally "raised his standard", declaring he was at war, at Nottingham in August. By now the whole of Ireland was embattled, and the catastrophe magnified to monstrous proportions. Over the course of the Civil War in England, it is reckoned nearly 200,000 people died from wounds and disease, out of a population of about five million. Multiplied by twelve, to compare with today's 60 million inhabitants, that would give the grotesque figure of two and a half million dead. But Ireland suffered horrors on an unimaginably vaster scale. In 1652 a soldier wrote that he could ride twenty miles and see nothing but hanged men. Then came the inevitable famine. In the thirteen years of war that began in 1641, Sir William Petty estimated that over 600,000 died. That was over 40% of the population. The figures are disputable; perhaps they were only half that, perhaps even a little less. But the scale of death and suffering was to soak the soil in unforgotten blood. The dead would haunt the land through the retelling of their stories with a level of pain that has never healed. Perhaps it never can.

Rathfarnham

It is a mystery why Ogilby was still in Ireland. We do not know where he was, or what kept him. His employment had not necessarily ended with Strafford's execution. As Master of the Revels he had a position and presumably a salary, though it seems unlikely, to put it mildly, that there was much revelling for him to master. The only part of his original duties that still had any meaning was to do with his role as a trooper. With his company all departed, and his work in Dublin made meaningless, he ought surely to have returned to England. But he seems to have felt that with dancing finished there he had nothing to go back to, and preferred life in Dublin. In England he was a servant for hire, a highly specialised tutor with no social position and a rather dubious identity as "a Scot", stereotyped as an uninvited immigrant on the make. In Ireland there were around 100,000 Scots settled by royal request in the colonisation process. This was the land where Ogilby had, for the first time, acquired a socially respectable position in his own right, as Master of the Revels, and was evidently welcome in the homes of the leading citizens as a member of society rather than a servant. That is borne out by the next thing we know, which comes from the horoscope drawn up by Elias Ashmole. At the bottom of the page, as we have seen, is a list of six crucial moments in Ogilby's life. On 14 November 1642, he was in Rathfarnham Castle, within five miles of Dublin. It was his birthday. The castle blew up.

Rathfarnham was the fortified stronghold of the Loftus family, Englishmen who had taken advantage of the Tudor plantation to make themselves into figures of wealth and power on a scale beyond anything they could achieve in England. Ogilby came to know and depend upon these great men, and felt at home among them; they were the power, ruthlessness and sweetness of government in Ireland. The master of Rathfarnham, Sir Adam Loftus, was Vice-Treasurer of Ireland, who had been at the very first play that Ogilby had put on, to entertain Wentworth's guests in January 1634, and he had lost money gambling there. The castle had been built by Sir Adam's grandfather near to an old Norman fort. It is a thick-walled four-square fortified house with a substantial square tower at each corner, sitting in open countryside. It was defended by fortified outbuildings and its own little army.

October 1642 had seen the first pitched battle of the English Civil War, an indecisive struggle at Edgehill. Charles marched on London, and the day before Ogilby's birthday his forces were confronted in a stand-off at Turnham Green. Charles withdrew to Oxford, which became his base for the war. None of that news had yet arrived in Ireland. But war was obviously underway and Ireland was in chaos. What was Ogilby doing at the castle? He may have simply retreated there to shelter behind its walls. Some people did that, but they were people who lived in exposed locations, not on the doorstep of Dublin Castle.

It seems more likely that his presence was social. Sir Adam's son, Dudley, was twenty-four years old and had only recently come back from Oxford. He had studied in Dublin at Trinity College, which had been founded by his great-grandfather. He was fascinated by, and a brilliant student of, ancient middle eastern languages. He was a phenomenon, reputedly able to understand twenty languages and already involved in translating Ethiopian into Latin. Forty years later, his pupil Jonathan Swift said that all the languages he knew were etched in lines on his face, and satirised his big nose, huge legs and substantial sexual appetite: "No Tartar is more fair, no Athenian better hung."

When he graduated in 1638 he had gone on to Oxford. As soon as he completed his MA there, in 1641, he had to return to the family castle to take over its defence while his father was fully occupied in Dublin. Dudley had absolutely no military experience. He was a princeling able to pursue his fascination with ancient languages. The area around the castle was being raided, animals were stolen and killed, people feared for their lives, but Rathfarnham was well protected by its own military force, large enough to ensure the security of its supplies from the land around it.

Dudley Loftus obviously knew Ogilby and must have spent quite a bit of time in the company of this engaging literate trooper and musician. Ogilby's military experience would presumably have been interesting, not so much as a fighting man but as a logistic planner who had seen something of war. In fact Ogilby would inevitably have seen the gruesome similarity between what was happening outside the castle walls and the miserable horrors that he had witnessed, and were still continuing, in what we now call the Thirty Years' War. He was also capable of more direct usefulness, handling secretarial work and writing official documents, as he had done so for Strafford. This would seem to be the significance of Aubrey's note, at this point in the story, that "He writt a fine hand". His quill work was evidently as fine as his mastery of dance, theatre and courtly display.

Although the castle was in a dangerous situation, there is no account of anything so violent as a full-scale attack in 1642. So why did it blow up? The whole place was, of course, literally a powder keg vulnerable to accidents. Multi-layered birthday cake had just been appearing in better-off households, made inside a wooden hoop, though we cannot assume that Ogilby had such a cake with lighted tapers to blow out. But the explosion could have been the by-product of an entertainment. Sometime in 1642, Dudley married. He may well have engaged Ogilby to mount some sort of event for those who were in the castle – even, perhaps, a masque, with candles and torches. That might do the trick. It seems that the Vice-Chancellor, Adam Loftus, who had been Ogilby's neighbour in Werburgh Street, was also there, which suggests a family gathering.

The explosion may have been no accident, however. Dudley's bride was the twenty-year-old Frances Nangle, daughter of one the oldest and most important of the Anglo-Norman families. This was an odd choice as her father Thomas, 19th Baron of Navan, was one of the leaders of the rebellion. In 1642 he, along with Matthew and Jocelyn Nangle, were named in Bills of Attainder, the same form of legislation which had sent Strafford to his death, and which confiscated all their property.[6] What was Dudley doing?

It was such an extraordinary marriage that it seems possible that Dudley had some idea that he was building a bridge between the English plantation and the Anglo-Irish aristocracy. He is described as having a reputation for being extremely foolish and perhaps this is why. He does seem to have been genuinely trying to reconcile enemies, and he played a significant role in the eventual peace agreement between the Royalist government and Parliamentary forces. But in 1642 he must have been going out on a limb. Did his bride's presence open the door to someone who dropped in on Ogilby's birthday with evil intent?

It was a birthday to remember, no doubt about that, and years later Ogilby reported it to Ashmole. He would also tell

Aubrey. He felt he had been lucky to survive. He never again taught dancing. But his blowing up was as metaphorical as physical. In the years that lay immediately ahead, the years of bloody war and of severe puritan morality across Britain, there was no place for revels, masques or the theatre. Trapped by his convalescence in the home of a scholar and antiquarian, he was now in an unfamiliar environment where the highest values were not physical but intellectual. He took to it with enthusiasm and energy. We have his own words for it:

> I being left at leisure from former Imployments belonging to the quiet of Peace wherein I was bred, instead of Arms, to which in parties most began to buckle, I betook myself to something of Literature, in which, till then, altogether a Stranger; And drawing towards the Evening of my Age, I made a little Progress, bending myself to softer Studies, adapted to my Abilities and Inclinations, Poesie:[7]

He began taking Latin lessons from a Gray's Inn friend in Dublin, Mr Chantrel, who was chaplain to Wentworth's right-hand man in the castle, Sir George Radcliffe. In 1640 Radcliffe had been tried for treason by Parliament, which probably left Mr Chantrel with the time to do some extra tutoring.

The door to an entirely new world was opening for Ogilby, the world of classical literature. He seems to have quickly grasped that the values and philosophy he had learned as a dancing master were derived from the great writers of classical antiquity, at whose feet he now began to sit. At a time when Parliamentarian ferment and the great mass of radical political pamphlets stormed around the precepts of the Old Testament, empowering every man to be the judge of his ruler, Ogilby was starting to read his way into the pagan literature resurrected in the Renaissance, and recognising in it the arguments of order and cosmic law that empowered royal authority and the patterns of the dance.

At the same time, the dance itself was forming patterns that would slowly develop and shape the narrative of Ogilby's life.

Hopton

On 6 July 1643, seven months after Ogilby was blown up, Sir Ralph Hopton was blown up too. Hopton was too close to a powder cart after a battle on Lansdown Hill, outside Bath.

Ogilby's old employer and military commander had raised a force to fight for the King in the West Country. His accident was quickly followed by a major victory which gave the Royalists power over the whole region, including Bristol. This opened up a new connection with Ireland. He was appointed lieutenant-governor of Bristol and spent two months convalescing. In September he became Baron Hopton, and was then appointed general. He was desperately short of soldiers, but now that he controlled Bristol that could be changed.

Charles I was very conscious that he needed to bring back the 10,000 or so English troops that had been sent to suppress the Irish insurrection, but that required a deal with the Irish Catholic rebels, a fleet of transports that were not available in Dublin, and a place to land them. Chester had been the port for Ireland earlier in the century, but the Dee was now too silted-up for Chester to be useful. Ships of any size would come to and from Liverpool, but Liverpool was now the base for six Parliamentary men-o'-war. The capture of Bristol changed the situation, offering both a port and ships.

It is probably not a coincidence that, according to a note on his horoscope, Ogilby joined the service of the new Lord Lieutenant of Ireland, James Butler, Marquess of Ormond, in 1644. Ormond, who came from the "Old English" aristocracy of Ireland, had been commander of the King's forces against the Irish Catholic rebels and then, on Charles' orders, negotiated a truce that was supposed to allow him to send troops to England to aid the King. In January 1644 Ormond was made Lord Lieutenant, charged with turning the truce into a permanent peace. That seems to be when Ogilby entered his service, an event he regarded as significant as his worst injuries and illnesses, his marriage, and his original engagement to go to Ireland. His appointment was secret: there is no evidence of it from any other source. In the preface to *Africa*, in 1670, Ogilby provides an autobiographical sketch, in which his story starts around 1643. At last we hear his own voice, but he is using it to conceal his past as much as to tell it. He paints his time in Ireland as the story of a retired gentleman whose only battle was "no less a Conquest, than the Reducing into our Native Language, the Great Master and Grand Improver of that Tongue, Virgil, The Prince of Roman Poets". It seems unlikely that the Royalist warlord in Dublin hired him to translate Latin epics. The Lord Lieutenant never mentioned him in any surviving document. The evidence is clear that after the Restoration, Ormond, the most powerful man after the King, was Ogilby's patron and friend. But what use had he been in Dublin? Ormond was in the middle of a war. He did not need an entertainment supervisor or dance instructor.

Ogilby may have had some role as a scribe, as he had done for Strafford. But it is a bit of a puzzle why Ormond, who had deep roots and extensive connections in Ireland, needed to employ a man like this. The likeliest explanation is that he was expected to play a role in connection with the movement of troops to England. His most obvious value was that he knew and was trusted by Hopton, Charles' General in the south of England. If some kind of a correspondent or go-between were needed between Hopton and Ormond, Ogilby would have been very useful. The possibility that he was acting as an agent, moving between Ireland and England, would certainly explain why his employment was so carefully concealed.

Potentially, there was more. In addition to the English and Welsh troops that could be brought back, Ormond was to negotiate for Irish Catholic soldiers. The dangers of bringing such forces into the Royalist army were obviously very great, as they were regarded with horror by the King's supporters, but Charles was desperate and Ormond dutiful. It was very clear to Ormond and Charles that the addition of thousands of men from Ireland, at a time when the competing forces mustered around 14,000 men each, would decisively settle the outcome of this struggle. Ogilby was a capable organiser and could handle logistics and supplies, whether for actors or soldiers. The friend he tried to defend physically at Gray's Inn was described as a quartermaster; so was his pupil Lacy. The term meant someone who went ahead of the troops to prepare their quarters.[8] Ogilby was clearly a man who could operate on his own initiative, was utterly reliable and, from his experience in the Low Countries, would understand the needs of an army. Perhaps these were rare qualities in the Irish forces that Ormond would, Charles hoped, be sending into Wales and the West Country, and who would have absolutely no notion of where they were landing or how to survive there. But Ogilby never mentioned anything at all that he did in Ormond's service.

His employment was so secret that it still had to be hidden throughout the rest of his life. We would not know that Ormond ever employed him at all were it not for the single line of cypher in Ashmole's horoscope. We have only one piece of evidence of the dangerous undercover work he was doing. It is in *Britannia*.

Transporting troops

Ogilby's great road atlas, published over thirty years after he entered Ormond's service, proclaimed that it was "An Illustration Of The Kingdom Of England And Dominion of Wales: By a Geographical and Historical Description Of The Principal Roads thereof". Right at the start of this tale I said that Ogilby's choice of "principal roads" is very strange. One of the strangest is the shortest road in the book, 17½ miles shoe-horned onto a page near the end tracing a route along the Welsh side of the Dee estuary from Chester to Holywell via Flint. Holywell's only significance was as exactly that – a Holy Well. It was a Catholic shrine to St Winifred, a place of pilgrimage which any Protestant should have seen as a centre of Papist superstition. The path was awkward and most pilgrims preferred to cross the sand from Chester when the tide was out. This little road was not put in the book for illicit pilgrims. It was not in any normal sense a principal road, just an open trackway which was used by a few strangers who needed a finger-post five miles from Chester to point the way, and then stopped for refreshment at an ale house called The Star Chamber to drink the health of Catholic martyrs.

The text that accompanies this road is oddly phrased. Although the journey is supposed to be north from Chester, with the estuary to the right, the list of "backward turnings to be avoided" on the road assumes a journey from Flint to Chester in the opposite direction, with the sand on the traveller's left. It is evidently based on notes which Ogilby made long before *Britannia* was being created, when Ormond was sending soldiers down that road. Ogilby was probably in charge of the logistics, and may even have been accompanying them. Ogilby describes the journey to Chester, not from it. This road had a military function, and is part of the covert meaning of *Britannia*. It is there for reasons that flow from Ogilby's secret life, which began when the final curtain fell on life as performance. In the six months from October 1643, some 3,000 troops from Ireland were landed in the West Country.[9] In addition, Bristol supplied ships that were desperately needed for moving troops from Ireland to the only other landing-place available, in Flintshire, North Wales.

The original idea was to bring them over as a single force, but there were not enough ships and no harbour. In the event one of the first shipments of men was to assist Royalist forces in Cheshire and north Wales in November 1643, when the area was being over-run by Parliament's forces. The discussion of where to land was curiously ill informed. The King recommended Chester, but only small boats could reach there. Ormond suggested the Wirral, the peninsula between the Dee and the Mersey, but access was vulnerable to Liverpool's men-o'-war and there was no way to avoid being trapped there once ashore. The idea of Beaumaris was mooted, as was Holyhead, and the ludicrous consequence which would follow, moving an army over the Menai Strait, was apparently not seen as an insuperable problem. It should have been. The landing was eventually made in the Dee estuary close to Flint Castle. That was the only landing site being discussed which offered the possibility of getting troops safely into the theatre of operations.[10] The road from the landing site is the road from Holy Well to Chester. That is why it is carefully traced and demonstrated in *Britannia*.

This should be the first clue as to the book's real agenda. Another route explores in depth the "road" from North Wales to the suggested landing sites of Beaumaris and Holyhead. Travelling from Chester to Holyhead, once you left Conway you had to walk along the foreshore. If for some reason you decided to make the journey when the tide was in, you had to clamber over the Great Stony Head, Penmaenmawr. That massive cliff has had the stuffing knocked out of it in the last three hundred years, with quarrying and road-cutting softening its angry face. *Britannia* says the path over it is difficult and dangerous, with a sheer drop to the sea on one side and an insuperable overhang on the other. It was better to go six miles on the sand when the tide was out. That is fine for an individual but not for a large body of troops. You needed a day when low water came between 9 a.m. and 3 p.m., so that you could cross in daylight. You started three hours after high water and had at most five hours for the journey. After the six miles along the coast sand, you struck out across the tidal flats towards Anglesey, covering nearly four more miles before the ferry could pick you up and carry you across the narrow channel to Beaumaris. If you were late, you drowned in the rising water.[11] I filmed this crossing under the guidance of Dr Mike Roberts, a marine archaeologist from Bangor who had explored the tidal flats thoroughly. With, as they say, hilarious results. My, how we laughed.

I believe we may have been the first people to do that walk since the bridge opened in 1826. If you lingered (as you do when filming) you found your feet being sucked into the lique-fying sand. The ferry was traditionally summoned by blowing a horn, the ferrymen being based in a tavern in Beaumaris. There were stories that if they felt they needed more money they would sometimes leave the traveller to drown and rob the corpse. Just didn't hear the bugle, you see.

Of course the ferry disappeared long ago, but David Jones, a Beaumaris lifeboat man, generously agreed to pick us up in a suitable rowboat. The idea was for him to make more than one trip, as there was a film crew on the crossing too, but it turned out we were not going to have time for that. So as the water rose around my waist, the Beaumaris lifeboat came out to rescue us. One feature of the journey we did not attempt was to get a horse off the sand and into the boat. Apparently that was done by the passengers lifting its front legs in and then encouraging the rest of the beast to clamber over the gunwale without swamping the boat.

Attempting the route, in either direction, with 1,500 men and supplies would have been suicidal. The only army to have tried it since Roman times was in 1282, when one of Edward I's vassals, having landed an army on Anglesey, tried to get them across to the mainland on a bridge of boats. The tide came in part way through the operation and their armour finished them off.[12]

But sitting planning the crossing from a room in Dublin in 1643, it was hard to check these things out. There was obviously a need for a proper map. In 1644 a version of Saxton's sixteenth-century map of England and Wales was re-published to help in exactly this situation. Known now as "The Quartermaster's Map" it was issued in twenty sturdy sheets to be folded as a pocket-map, "Useful for all Commanders for Quartering of Soldiers".[13] But without showing roads it did not solve the problem.

In June 1645 the King suffered a catastrophic defeat by the Parliamentary army at Naseby and retreated into Wales, awaiting the landing of Irish reinforcements. He was presumably buoyed by the successful landing of a hundred Irish soldiers at Conway Castle in April.[14] If Ogilby was indeed involved in planning military movements across the Irish Channel, he would have spent a considerable time in the close study of the Quartermaster's Map. It seems highly likely that his experience in Ireland, covert and close to the centre of power, involved preparation for invading England and would have a great deal to do with his work for King Charles' son after the Restoration of the monarchy.

The reality was that after the battle of Marston Moor shipments of men from Ireland were few and far between. The last seems to have been 160 men, English and Lorrainers, enrolled as Roger Mostyn's Foot and sent from Dublin to Wales in February 1646.[15] After that, the prospect of sending more Irish soldiers to England collapsed, and Ogilby's position must have become meaningless. In May 1646 the royal forces in England were utterly crushed, and Charles surrendered to the Scots at Newark. He pretended that he was converting to Presbyterianism to gain time, sow division between Parliament and its Scottish allies, and find a way to rescue himself. The Scots decided to keep him in Newcastle. The Prince of Wales fled from Cornwall to the Scilly Isles and on to Jersey.

In Ireland, the situation was as confused and messy – and wretched and murderous – as it is at the time of writing in Syria. The Catholic "Confederates" were in effect an independent state in the south, divided between loyalty to the King and loyalty to the Catholic Church. They had their own General Assembly and Supreme Council in Kilkenny, with their own army and navy. The Protestants were divided between Royalists and Parliamentarians. In reality, savage warfare was being conducted between militias with their own local agendas and large ideologies. Ormond successfully fought off a siege of Dublin by the Irish Confederates by laying waste the country around his capital so the besiegers could not survive in it.

Ormond was still trying to negotiate with the Confederates without giving concessions to Catholicism that the English would never accept – not knowing that Charles' special envoy, the Marquess of Glamorgan, had made a secret treaty giving exactly those concessions. On this basis he had been arranging for a large Catholic force to sail from Waterford without revealing to Ormond that he had agreed, in effect, to restore Catholicism. It all erupted on 26 December 1646, when the newly arrived Secretary of State, George Digby, dramatically accused Glamorgan of high treason. It is hard to imagine a more powerful moment of drama in the Council chamber. Glamorgan said that he was acting on royal instructions and that the Lord Lieutenant had known everything; he had given him a sealed envelope containing his secret instructions. Ormond took a while to remember it, then had it brought. He had been told not to break the seal without fresh instructions from the King. Now the seal was broken, and everyone was agog to see the contents. It was a mass of meaningless shapes. Glamorgan had forgotten that it was in cypher, and did not have the key. That was the end of Glamorgan and of King Charles' Irish Catholic army.[16] The situation was chaotic.

Shipwreck

Both Ormond and the Confederates now desperately needed to send their agents hurriedly and secretly to the King and to the French. Dublin was blockaded, but a small anonymous barque – probably meaning an open two-masted vessel – was found with a willing crew at Drogheda, about thirty miles north. Letters were written, messengers were found, and on New Year's Day they slipped quietly down the Boyne en route to a secret landing near Liverpool. As the defeated Hopton had already fled with Prince Charles to the Scilly Isles, Ormond must have ordered Ogilby to go with them. It was a long way; cold, wet, rough midwinter sailing in a vessel too small even to have a recorded name. The journey ended abruptly and violently on a beach at Holyhead, where they were driven ashore by a storm. Ogilby must have known that Ormond's father had been wrecked and drowned there in 1619, and he would have been pretty sure he was done for. Their helmsman saved their lives, managing to get around the rocks that wait off Holyhead to smash boats that lose control. Oddly, this was not one of the incidents listed on his horoscope. Our information comes from Aubrey: "He was undone at the Irish rebellion. He was wrecked at sea, and came to London very poor."[17]

The small group of passengers managed to get to land and found an inn, where they were quickly picked up for interrogation. Among them were Ormond's agent with a letter for the French ambassador in London, and a lieutenant-colonel of the Irish confederates who was taking a message to the King in Newcastle. The confused story that came to Parliament's ears was that an invasion was being organised from Ireland, that the French King and the Papacy were being kept informed, and that six ships were ready to bring confederate troops from Waterford. There were a few other passengers, and one of them must have been Ogilby. Books and manuscripts were seized, surprising luggage in such a vessel. These were evidently his Virgil in Latin and his manuscript translation. They were examined and deemed of "no publicke concernement". Everyone picked up from the ship was taken to London as a prisoner in chains while Parliament tried to discover what it could about the Irish Royalist plot.[18]

Ogilby would have had some connection with the purpose of the voyage; he obviously knew Digby and Ormond, but in Holyhead he just looked like a middle-aged and insignificant scholar. He was evidently released in London and given back his books.

The apparent revelation that the King was still looking for an Irish Catholic army must have played some part in the Scots deciding that he was insincere in his interest in Presbyterianism. In February they handed him over to the English Parliament. Ogilby never wanted to talk about what had happened.

When Parliament got hold of Charles he was imprisoned at Hampton Court. Ormond, who said that he "preferred English rebels to Irish ones", handed Dublin over to the Parliamentarian army in February. He immediately took his wife and children to London, where he became engaged in secret negotiations between Charles and the Scots, which led to a new Civil War.

As for Ogilby: everything was gone. He had left London some fifteen years earlier, a man on the make with an immensely powerful patron and a remarkable position. He had built an entirely original career as the first theatrical impresario in Ireland and when that was destroyed he became a confidante of the Lord Lieutenant involved in trying to help his embattled King. He had been brought back to London as a penniless prisoner and by the time he was released it must have seemed that he had no future. His original patron, Strafford, had been beheaded, his next, Ormond, was a leading statesman on the side that was being defeated. He had been a Master of Dance in a kingdom which hated dance and regarded it as the work of the Devil luring good people to sin. But he still had his manuscripts and he had not been wasting his time in Dublin. He had been carefully translating the works of Virgil. All of them! It might seem surprising that his hundreds of pages could survive a shipwreck, but the agents' incriminating letters had also survived and Ogilby's military experience would undoubtedly have taught him how to keep his goods dry in a carefully made waterproof oilcloth pack. The translation was virtually complete.

He just needed to start his life again. And he did not waver from his sense of purpose. John Ogilby was not a nostalgic man. When, in his great 1675 atlas, he traced the suggested military routes for Irish troops of the 1640s, it was not because he was remembering some past adventure. His interest was far more forward-looking.

Life 6. The Poet

Translation

Ogilby made his inglorious return to England in January 1647. That was a terrible, bleak time. 1646 had been a year of plague and famine from end to end of the country. In the north-west, recorded deaths were nearly four times as high as usual,[1] while in one typical small Somerset community, Wiveliscombe, 468 people died between October 1645 and August 1646. That was at least a third of the population. At Wells Sessions in 1646–47 the high price of corn was considered as being "to the great detriment of the poor in this time of dearth and scarcity", and people had no choice but to steal.[2] The world in which he had been a master of dance was now a desert. The heat of puritan zeal had burned it dry. His theatre had gone the way of all theatres; they were closed by law and if anyone did put on a play the actors were whipped and the audience fined heavily. Delivered as a freed prisoner to London, Ogilby was a man reduced, in cash terms, to nothing. But he still had in his hands what he believed was the passport to a new future: his translation of the complete works of Virgil.

We have come a long way from the time when every educated man was at home in Latin. Its retreat has accelerated dramatically in the last fifty years. Up to 1960 no one was allowed into Oxbridge without a Latin qualification. Even after other subjects moved on, law schools still insisted on Latin. Today, in a world awash with communications in every language, the public presence of Latin outside the web and church services is restricted to weekly five-minute news bulletins from Finland and from Bremen which knew neither Roman Empire nor Roman Church.

The long withering away of Latin fluency had just begun by 1647, and Ogilby was well aware of the significance of that. He had lived his whole adult life among educated men to whom Virgil was supposed to be as familiar as the Bible, but he was not one of them. He had left school at eleven, and had settled to learn Latin in his forties from a clergyman in Dublin when Ireland was soaked in blood. He said his translation had been made "among people returning to their ancient barbarity".[3] It seems that in Virgil he found a new understanding of the world. He was convinced that there was a new kind of readership, people who had not grown up able to read the language easily but who would connect with the text.

Others had translated parts of Virgil's work into English, but no one had ever seen a reason to publish a translation of the complete works.[4] Ogilby, though, saw this as the key not only to his own future, but to that of Britain. The more terrible the political and social crisis became, the more important he thought it was to see the world through Virgilian spectacles.

The *Aeneid*, the poet's great epic, was created at the Emperor Augustus' request as a literary monument to imperial Rome. Famously supposed to have been laboriously written at the rate of three lines a day, it was part of the bed-rock of

European civilisation. It is the story of the Trojan Aeneas and his legendary wanderings, which ended with the birth of Rome. The moral of the story is that although the ancient heroes suffered bitterly and endured grim experiences, these were necessary steps on a greater journey. Over time Rome was destined to rise and Augustus' benevolent imperial power was fated to emerge from it. Rome's great empire is the proper destiny of the human condition, in which monarchical authority and the wellbeing of society are the two faces of a single golden coin.

It is not easy for us to understand the powerful connection that a certain kind of Englishman was making with Virgil at this time.[5] The modern Penguin translation claims that the poem remains relevant today, but not as a monument to the greatness of empire. The translator's introduction empha- sises Virgil's sense of "the price of empire": "it seems to be a price we keep on paying, in the loss of blood and treasure, time-worn faith and hard-won hope, down to the present day".[6] Virgil is certainly not a simple flag-waver for imperial triumphalism and his story-telling is profoundly troubled, but his narrative is propelled by a destiny that leads through many challenges and tragedies to an impressive future. That is how Virgil was understood in the middle of the seventeenth century. What we have lost, and what was then so powerfully felt, is the sense that Virgil reveals with compelling authority a divine purpose working in time. The great sweep of ancient history, forcefully told and experienced in the poetry, is the evidence of that purpose, a purpose both meaningful and moral. Past and future are connected in a structure played out by human heroes but not designed or controlled by them.

Virgil teaches that civilisation has a history that has retained its overall design and ultimate imperial destiny even through periods of incoherent chaos. This was, of course, just such a period. It was also a time when many gentlemen no longer had much facility with reading Latin.

In London, Ogilby re-connected with James Shirley. Shirley, who had inevitably abandoned theatre, was now making a living teaching. Ogilby wanted someone to check his work, and must have asked Shirley to help. Shirley was educated at Cambridge and it seems probable that he provided introductions to teachers there. So Ogilby walked to Cambridge. Under Parliament's rule, the Earl of Manchester had unceremoniously turfed out about half the college fellows, putting his own preferred Puritans in their place. The ejected fellows were now just sitting at home, trying not to starve, with nothing to do.

Once there, he found the help he wanted. According to Anthony à Wood, who took his information from Aubrey, "his great industry and greater love to learning being discovered, was encouraged by several scholars there, who, in compliance to his zeal, resolved his many doubts put to them".[7]

By the time he had the manuscript ready for the press he can have had no more doubts about his decision. This new world had no room for the old Ogilby. His old calendar of courtly display, based around the masques of Twelfth Night and Shrovetide, was now meaningless. In June 1647 Parliament had passed an Ordinance abolishing the feasts of Christmas, Easter and Whitsun. They were Roman, they were Pagan, they were Superstitious. Many people felt that this Puritan revolution had turned the world upside-down, and this was not what they had expected:

> Listen to me and you shall hear, news hath not been this thousand year:

Since Herod, Caesar, and many more, you never heard the like before.

Holy-dayes are despis'd, new fashions are devis'd.

Old Christmas is kickt out of Town.

Yet let's be content, and the times lament, you see the world turn'd upside down.

...

To conclude, I'le tell you news that's right, Christmas was kil'd at Naseby fight:

Charity was slain at that same time, Jack Tell Troth too, a friend of mine,

Likewise then did die, rost beef and shred pie,[8]

Pig, Goose and Capon no quarter found.

Yet let's be content, and the times lament, you see the world turn'd upside down.[9]

Huge numbers had died, and many felt that the victory had not gone to defenders of constitutional rights but to zealots. Charles had been militarily defeated but remained King, and in 1648 a new eruption began, now against Parliament. It was partly a popular revolt against the imposition of strict Puritan rules. It developed into a second Civil War, which was bloodily suppressed. Power was now divided between Parliament and its army; at the end of 1648 the army finally purged Parliament. The process had begun that would lead to Cromwell's "Protectorate".

Ogilby now had the manuscript ready to print, and he knew the man to help him. John Crook had been the King's Printer in Dublin in the glory days of Ogilby's theatre, 1638–39. He was established in London and would have been the obvious person to receive the manuscript. On 10 October 1648, Crook entered it in the Stationer's Register as a sixpenny volume called *Virgills Workes or Poems Translated into English Verse by Mr John Oglebe gent.*[10]

Lessons of Virgil

This was the first published translation of the totality of Virgil's three great works; ten *Eclogues* ("drafts"), the four books of *Georgics* ("agricultural things") and the twelve books of the *Aeneid*, the epic story of Aeneas and the birth of Rome. He began with the *Eclogues*, the first of which deals directly with civil war – in this case the civil war that followed the death of Caesar. The theme was painfully familiar to the men he moved among, and would become more sharply relevant as the new order tightened its grip. It is about having been dispossessed, and what comes next. Ogilby used Virgil to offer hope and comfort to Royalists who seemed to be losing their entire world. He implied that dispossession would be followed by some kind of restoration.

The theme is established on page 1, in Virgil's dialogue between two herdsmen whose lives were torn apart by the civil war and dispossessions that followed the killing of Julius Caesar.[11] The whole work is presented as a teaching on how a wise and patient man should behave in the face of political whirlwinds, even when he has lost everything. Ogilby found a startlingly contemporary world in the *Georgics*, suggesting that there was covert activity taking place behind the scenes:

Happy is he that hidden causes knows
And bold all shapes of danger dares oppose ...

He did not just translate Virgil into another language but into another context. The original text speaks about the wise countryman who gathers the produce of his land and

... has not viewed
the laws in iron, the Forum's madness, the public records.

In Ogilby's hands, that countryman is catapulted forward
1,500 years:

... nor ever saw
Mad Parlements, Acts of Commons, nor Sword-Law

The *Aeneid* begins with the Trojan Aeneas, having sailed away
from the destruction of Troy, being washed up by a storm on
the coast of Carthage. That must have resonated with Ogilby.
He had sailed away from the destruction of Dublin; he too
had been shipwrecked. Underpinning his translation is the
expectation that the old order will re-assert itself. The war is
lost but that is not the end. Now begins the quiet waiting, and
for the first time we get a sense of what kind of man Ogilby is.
He uses Virgil to state a message of dispassionate confidence
in the inherent order of the world, with astonishing authority.

He had no doubt of the power of divine providence to
restore and enhance the greatness of the country in which he
was formed, and never stopped seeing into a positive future.
His material losses may have been great, but his real treasures
were his contacts, no matter what disasters overtook them. It
seems that he never lost an acquaintance, and was evidently
treasured by some very significant Royalist figures.

Ogilby certainly had friends who came from the world
of Royalist plots and secrets. For example, he presented a
signed copy of the book to Wentworth's friend and secretary,
Sir Philip Mainwaring.[12] In 1634 Wentworth had appointed
Mainwaring as Secretary of State for Ireland, keeper of the
signet and member of the Privy Council, with a salary of
£200 plus £100 for "intelligence",[13] i.e. espionage. There

5. Thomas Wentworth, First Earl of Strafford, and His Secretary Sir Philip Mainwaring, by Van Dyke.

had been a great deal of secret agent work going on among Ogilby's friends in Dublin. Mainwaring was now living in penury in Oxford.

There is a wonderful double portrait of Wentworth and Mainwaring painted by Van Dyke around 1640. They are shown in a very plain room which opens onto a landscape below. They have been interrupted in the middle of the work of government. Black Tom Strafford is dressed like a puritan. He sits heavy and rather sadly stern, part turned to the artist.

He has a letter open in his left hand, resting on his lap. He has been dictating his response. Mainwaring is close behind his right shoulder, seated at a table and writing to his lord's dictation. More flamboyantly dressed in scarlet, with a neat ginger beard and a mass of unkempt curly hair, he leans forward to look anxiously at Strafford's face. It is not a picture of equals; more like a great lord and his hound. The picture radiates a sense of oppression and conspiracy, there is clearly a story going on and we are intrigued by it.

Ogilby's Virgil is not simply a literary work. It spoke to a very specific, wealthy, Royalist audience carefully engaging in secretive politics and waiting patiently for a future he signalled to them. The dancing master had announced that he was still in business, even if his presentation of cosmic order was no longer expressed through dance. Instead of turning men into polished courtiers, he had taken on the task of becoming their host in the world of Augustus to help them prepare for a restoration he never doubted.

Seymour

Ogilby's Virgil was published with a quite remarkable dedication to "William, Marquess and Earl of Hertford, Viscount Beauchamp, and Lord Seymour". That established for all to see that he was under the care and patronage of one of the greatest Royalist magnates remaining in Britain. Seymour was a highly cultivated man, and the dedication was a statement of his endorsement of the work. It was also an enthusiastic abasement at the feet of a noble patron, demonstrating that Ogilby had conversational access to the great man. It is quite possible that he was a guest under Seymour's extensive roof. Certainly Aubrey says that the

Earl "loved him very well". The dispossessed Earl was certain that in time the old order would be restored and that ill-considered conspiracies would only delay that outcome, and that was the core of Ogilby's message. Seymour was the right man for the dedication.

Ogilby's old patrons were gone. After surrendering Dublin to Parliament, Ormond joined the King at Hampton Court in the autumn of 1647. He then went on the run, and in March 1648 travelled to Paris to join the Queen. That month, too, Elizabeth, Sir Ralph Hopton's wife and Ogilby's one-time pupil, died in Jersey, where she had gone with the Prince of Wales' party. Their escape there had been arranged by her husband. His surrender meant that the war was over. When he heard of his wife's death he too left for Jersey, and then followed the Prince to the Hague. That was the home of Prince Charles' aunt, Elizabeth of Bohemia, whom Hopton had so romantically rescued after the Battle of the White Mountain.

But this was not the end of John Ogilby. Strafford was dead but his children had grown up and moved in powerful Royalist circles. Ormond had left the country, but his endorsement of his hidden servant would still open any grand Royalist door. They didn't come much grander than William Seymour.

Before the war began, according to Edward Hyde, "though he was a man of very good parts, and conversant in books both in Latin and Greek languages, and of a clear courage ... he was so wholly given up to a country life, where he lived in splendour, that he had an aversion, even an unaptness, for business".[14] Hyde was Chancellor to both Charles I and II and organised the Sealed Knot conspiracy to restore the Crown. He meant that Seymour had no interest in the pursuit of lucrative offices at Court. He was a thoughtful defender of the law and what he understood to be the constitution, so he found himself aligned with the King's opponents in the years leading up to the outbreak of war. But he stayed away from Strafford's attainder and in 1641 the King, trying to draw him closer, made him governor to the Prince of Wales. As Parliament tried to impose its authority over him he drew away from it. By the time war came he regarded the King's party as the lesser evil. He became lieutenant-general of the south-west and south Wales, raised 2,000 men, and was engaged in the conquest of Somerset. He was Hopton's commander and linked up with him to defeat Sir William Waller's forces at Lansdown (where Hopton was blown up). They went on to capture Bristol. After that Seymour withdrew from a military role, accepted the Chancellorship of Oxford University, and concentrated on trying to bring about some settlement between the two sides.

That, of course, failed. On 30 January 1649, King Charles I was taken out of a window of the Banqueting House onto a balcony where his head was chopped off. He passed under the Rubens ceiling that celebrated the supposed apotheosis of his father. The world that created that ceiling, the world that Ogilby had inhabited, of courtly order, ceremonial performance, the ritual dance of aristocratic and royal authority, had seemingly ended. Later that year, Parliament made dancing at the Inns of Court illegal.[15]

As for teaching dancing as an expression of harmony and love, that was not the Puritan perspective. In 1633 William Prynne, a member of Lincoln's Inn, had denounced "amorous mixed lascivious dancing" and claimed that in classical antiquity dancing was all single-sex and certainly not gymnastic.[16] Prynne was one of those who opposed long hair for men, short hair for women, theatre and the celebration of

Christmas. In the late 1630s a member of the Middle Temple said that in the past "the measures were wont to be truly danced, it being accounted a shame for any inns of court man not to have learned to dance, especially the measures. But now their dancing is turned into bare walking."[17]

From Ogilby's perspective, the law itself was outlawed. His Virgil was issued with an Imprimatur, the sign of royal approval, but was probably printed after the King was dead. Seymour's household would now be regarded by Cromwell's government as a nest of conspirators. The Council of State controlled where the Earl was allowed to live, and wrote to him in March 1651 that "we are informed that many dangerous and disaffected persons resort to your house, and that several of your servants are such".[18] The dangerous and disaffected that resorted to Seymour's house would be Ogilby's audience, his clients and his students.

Seymour was one of the surviving grandees of the old world. In 1618 his wedding had been celebrated with a masque at fantastic cost, to place his union with the Earl of Essex's sister in a framework of heavenly order.[19] He had stayed with Charles throughout his trial, and acted as one of his pall-bearers after the execution. But he did not regard the destruction of the monarchy as final and irrevocable, and nor did Ogilby. Ogilby's Virgil makes it plain that all this is a terrible tempest which will eventually and inevitably blow itself out. Translation of the great work allowed Ogilby to make it accessible to those for whom Latin was a chore or a closed book, and it also allowed him to gloss, interpret and present the masterpiece in terms that conveyed his vision of its political and cultural meaning right here, right now. But this was just the beginning; the book itself was not intended to be left as a mere text. In his address to his patron, he said that "when time shall ripen" he would present it with "more ornament of Sculpture". He intended to turn the book into a hall of entertainment and instruction, where a nobleman or king would inhabit Virgil's world. In 1649, that would have seemed a very bold vision indeed. Most people were more concerned with the future than the past.

The new Europe

The revolutionary tempest that had blown away royalty from Britain had not started on that island and did not end there. The political geography of civilisation had been blown away across most of Europe. That was only possible because its structures, glamorous and pompous though they were, had already been hollowed out.

The foundations of those structures had been built on a universal church, but they were everywhere local and particular. The church or abbey that dominated any fifteenth-century settlement was rooted in the broad sweep of Catholic faith that reached from the Norwegian Sea to the Mediterranean and from the Atlantic to the lands of Turks and Russians, but it identified with that settlement alone, and each settlement was proudly distinct. Most people would describe themselves as belonging to a particular city or community with their personal status defined by their trade or their title. Their rights were a form of community property, different from those of people in other communities, formulated in treasured charters, treaties and declarations. They were called "privileges", private laws (*privates leges*). In the sixteenth century the Netherlands alone had a distinct legal code for each of over seven hundred communities[20] – on average, one set of laws for every three hundred adult men. Three hundred miles away on the Rhine, the citizens of the Free Republic of Strasbourg assembled once a year in front of the Cathedral to renew their proud oath to the city's constitution. They knew that their Cathedral was the tallest building in the world, and that their city had been home to Gutenberg's press.

That press, of course, became the instrument that broke Christendom to pieces. After the Reformation people acquired a new identity through their religious affiliation, and Christendom fractured murderously, but within each realm rulers still recognised that their subjects had their own communal associations with distinct rights. Power was everywhere shared between great lords and local assemblies, called Estates, Cortes, Parliaments or Diets – assemblies of nobles, clergy and burgesses which maintained the privileges of their members and had to be consulted on the grant of taxation to the ruler.

This structure had collapsed violently across the whole continent, as rulers found themselves obliged to raise more money than their subjects would allow. They needed it for a new level of competitive luxurious display, they needed it as feudal service had been replaced by cash payments, but above all they needed it to compete on the battlefield. The new gunpowder warfare with its dance of pike and musket, siege warfare, artillery and heavy cavalry, combined with the ever-growing weight of administrative work, meant that rulers needed much more money than in the past. At a time when agriculture around the world was yielding less, because of cyclical changes in the climate, governments needed a larger share to keep themselves going. The privileges of their subjects would have to go. A new political philosophy was on the march, and private law would have no place in it. The theory was stated very firmly in France in 1576 by Jean Bodin: "We see the principal point of sovereign majesty and absolute power to consist in giving laws to subjects in general, without their consent."[21] This became the firm opinion of the Habsburgs and the Stuarts, as well as of the French Bourbon monarchs.

Bodin's argument was rooted in notions of cosmic harmony, which he dressed up in the costume of mathematical reasoning that neither he nor most of his readers actually understood. He demonstrated the harmonic validity of royal absolutism by an argument that involved saying that 4 is to 6 as 2 is to 4, which it isn't.[22] Kepler pointed out that this was silly, but Bodin's argument was what kings wanted to hear so the appearance of intellectual strength was all that mattered. The Divine Right of Kings would remain balanced on fine-sounding nonsense until it toppled.

The financial demands and attacks on privileges were challenged by outraged and fearful burgesses and nobility. The rebellion of Estates had started in the Low Countries, then erupted at the other end of Europe, in Bohemia, in 1618. It became an unstoppable epidemic, different in each place as local rights, local privileges, local traditions confronted, and were confronted by, baffled, angry and determined rulers. As Harrington put it, power was "blown up" in Spain, France, Germany, Holland, Switzerland and of course in England. Everywhere the language of dispute was the same – it was about traditional rights, liberties and privileges, and the arbitrary power of autocrats.

The Thirty Years' War which had begun at Prague's White Mountain in 1620 had churned up the whole of Europe and hugely increased the numbers of men in unproductive and expensive armies who needed to be paid in coin. It was a war for control of the vast territories of the Holy Roman Empire, from Tuscany to Hamburg, from Brussels to Vienna. No one has any clear picture of the number who died in those lands.

The figure used to be estimated at two in every three, about fourteen million people. It is now reckoned that the population "only" fell by about four million.[23] Or perhaps it was nearer eight million.[24] No one will ever know.

In 1648 the dust was settling. For the previous four years an epic negotiation had been conducted, involving the Holy Roman Emperor, three hundred or so territorial rulers of imperial lands, and the Kings of France and Sweden. At the end of it all, the Peace of Westphalia produced a new map of Europe. It is often said that the Peace gave birth to state sovereignty; from this moment on, Europe was a continent of states with frontiers in place of feudal territories with vague borders and independent cities.

The result was different in different places; in France, the autocratic King became an all-powerful despot; the rights of Parliaments and Estates were made negligible. Twenty-one miles away in England it was the ruler who lost power and Parliament that was triumphant.

Either the sovereign had to go or the privileged communities had to be broken. In the Dutch Republic the Habsburgs were thrown out and towns retained their autonomy, but over on the Rhine, Strasbourg's independence had no future after the Peace of Westphalia, and the oath-day vanished not long after as the city was swallowed up.

England was not included in the Peace but shared in its vision of separate sovereignty which filled the space within the state's borders, where it stopped abruptly. The Great Seal, which had shown King Charles enthroned on one side, and riding in arms on the other, was replaced. It now showed the House of Commons in session on one side, with the Speaker's chair in place of a throne, and a map of England, Wales, Jersey, Guernsey and Ireland on the other. The map was cut off at the Scottish border. The Republic of England was now a fully paid-up member of the new Europe whose map was a net of frontiers. The payment, over the whole continent, had been made in blood.

Ogilby had been trained in a cosmic vision of the dance, embracing the heavens and the Earth, and groups whose separate privileges were underpinned by the Common Law. In the new Europe, each state set out to demonstrate that it was a universe in itself, with its own sovereignty and undifferentiated power over its citizens. That power might seek to be as great in a republic as in a monarchy: Puritan rule in England asserted its authority to overthrow local privilege and tradition in the name of the Commonwealth. York, for example, had proudly asserted its privileges with an annual oath-day like that of Strasbourg. All the citizens gathered in the Guildhall to hear the civic officials swear to do everything in their power to maintain "the Right of this Citie". In 1645, after the city's surrender to Parliamentary forces, it also surrendered its charter. Local privileges would survive, but they would no longer be a defence against the sovereign power.

Ogilby understood that now that the old Europe was gone, its literary and cultural foundations needed to be re-packaged for England. Virgil had to be made available to this new people, as a basis for building a new future. His, and the nation's. This would also be the thinking behind *Britannia*, a work which over-rode the local and particular, and laid out the roads that opened up all communities to the sovereignty of the King's Highway.

The scattered network

Ogilby remained at heart a teacher, who understood and completely believed in the essential meaning of the courtly dance. As a teacher and as a man of masques and theatre he had been displaying mirrors and examples of the underlying order which gives structure, as he saw it, to heaven and earth. He could not believe that his life would never have its order restored, or that society would never settle back into its proper form. We have no letter or memoir from him explaining this, but he made it clear nevertheless. In fact he spoke a great deal on the subject, but in an extended form of literary ventriloquism. He spoke through the mouths of classical poets. That was his answer to the question of what he could do now. He never lost his delight in managing theatre, but the most important performances he would present from now on would be in the pages of books. A number of grand houses now had quiet new spaces, library rooms, dedicated to showing them off, and he decided to claim a place there.

Private libraries were central to the changes taking place in society, politics and intellectual life. The place of the book had changed significantly in less than fifty years. In Merton College Oxford there is a monument to Thomas Bodley, creator of the great Bodleian Library. It shows the scholar as a Renaissance man, surrounded by personifications of Music, Arithmetic, Grammar and Rhetoric. The pediment above his head is supported by stacks of books laid flat, their spines hidden, their page edges and cover clasps showing. This was how books were kept in 1613, when Ogilby was learning the dance. They were closed away for private study.

At that time great houses were designed to accommodate large retinues and were dominated by ceremonial space. A gentleman's books were normally kept in a small private space reserved for meditative study. It was often called a closet, and the commonest book in its small inventory would be the Bible. There were wealthy humanist intellectuals such as Sir Thomas

6. Thomas Bodley memorial, Merton College, Oxford.

Moore with dedicated libraries in imitation of the Romans, but these were more likely to be in special buildings than in a room in the house. Books were frequently stacked flat as on the monument. Their spines did not usually have titling. In some houses large book collections were hidden away in chests.[25]

But the age of great retinues had ended along with the masques and entertainments. Houses had become more private places, and a person's social standing was now enhanced by evidence of reflection, scholarly interest and engagement with political debate. Books quite literally came out of the closet into a social space, the library, where they stood in proud ranks on shelves and turned around, presenting their titles on decorated spines for others to admire. John Ogilby would now take a significant and growing place in this new and very modern territory.

Making a new life

The Virgil was very well received, and Ogilby was evidently well rewarded by Seymour. He also sought the patronage of the Merchant Taylors, and was rewarded with a payment of £10 in exchange for the private circulation of his text.

Having returned to London, he took one more step in the direction of re-making himself. The once pretty boy who had spent his life in the company of dancers and actors decided that having completed a half century in one style of life, he needed a wife for the next. He was now setting up his own household. His choice for mistress of the house, Christian Hunsdon, was a careful one, and the marriage took place on 14 March 1650. She was in her sixties, about seventeen years older than he, the widow of a Merchant Taylor with a house in Blackfriars. Her father had been in the service of the Earl of Pembroke, Hopton's patron, and the dense network of connections that sustained Ogilby may well have played a part in this match; Pembroke's successor would subscribe to Ogilby's publication of Virgil four years later. Christian Hunsdon was wealthy, with one child, a daughter, married to a Monmouth gentleman named Morgan.

The Morgan family was heavily involved in a very novel scientific activity, the new art of clockmaking, and this would introduce Ogilby to people, ideas and ways of thinking which were quite new to him. The Clockmakers Company was the youngest of the City Companies, less than twenty years old. Medieval clocks had been driven by great weights with a swinging bar controlling the weight's descent (the pendulum had not been invented), and were for churches and public buildings. They were made by blacksmiths. A way of using a spring was invented in the mid-fifteenth century, and that opened the way for an entirely new kind of timekeeper to develop, personal and requiring more complex and sophisticated mechanics. By 1630 English clock-making was meticulous, impressive and rapidly developing. The Company was set up to control access to the "Art and Mystery of Clockmaking" for twenty miles around London, and there were Morgans at the heart of it from the time it was set up; Richard Morgan was one of its founders. William Morgan must have been about twelve years old when Ogilby became his step-grandfather, and two months later the boy started on an apprenticeship to a clockmaker.[26] There were around a dozen Morgans who were masters or apprentices in the Company during William's education there.

William Morgan was apprenticed to Simon Bartram, who was one of England's premier clockmakers. Bartram became Master of the Company for 1651 and 1652. There is a splendid example of his work in the Metropolitan Museum of Art, an ornate pocket-watch made around 1630.[27] The market for such objects, which existed in England and France, was a wonderful example of the hunger of early adopters for a technology which had yet to be born. This watch has no minute hand; it had no pretensions to accuracy. It was a beautiful personal ornament, and an expression of faith in the idea of measuring, slicing and dissecting time, but until the invention of the balance-spring a watch would drift away from the true time by several hours every day. Even a fixed clock would be out by fifteen minutes every twenty-four hours. It was only around 1657 that an English instrument-maker,

Robert Hooke, came up with the idea of the balance wheel, and shortly afterwards a Dutch instrument maker, Christiaan Huygens, made a working watch with it. Huygens had also just invented a way to exploit Galileo's observation of the regularity of a pendulum to build the first pendulum clock, which had an astounding accuracy of fifteen seconds a day. 1657 was the year a London clock-maker, Ahasuerus Fromateel, who had started out as a blacksmith making turret clocks, sent his son to the Hague to learn the secret of pendulum clocks.[28] The next year he advertised the first such clocks in England, and William Morgan completed his apprenticeship. Morgan would eventually become Ogilby's partner, and would bring with him a trained understanding of cutting-edge mechanical science that would be essential to the transformation of John Ogilby into the man who mathematicised the land.

But that lay in the future. Ogilby was now, for the first time in his life, master of his own household. Completely re-born, he was now a man of substance with a literary presence. This was just the beginning. The Virgil was respected, even admired, but he was not yet ready to produce the grander version he had promised Seymour. In the meantime, to establish himself on the bookshelves of the gentry and nobility he needed to produce something more enchanting:

> I, greedy of more, having tasted the sweetness of a little Fame, would not thus sit down, but ambitious to try my own Wing, endeavored to Soar a little higher.[29]

Aesop

He set about revisiting the work he had done in Ireland for Wentworth's children, retelling Aesop and adding his own verses. He could barely read a word of Greek, but Aesop had been translated so many times into Latin that he was regarded as a Latin author. There were also many English translations, most recently a 1646 edition for schools. Besides, this text may have been inspired by Aesop but it was actually written by Ogilby – a text that should have been some 80 pages was increased to 236! He obviously delighted in the playfulness of the story-telling.

Ogilby's interpretation of Aesop appeared in 1651, and was very successful. It went through at least five editions in the next fifteen years. He employed multiple voices to give it life and character, a variety of forms and verse and changing line lengths. Aubrey and Pepys admired it. When a less refined translation appeared in 1673, *Aesop Improv'd*, it claimed to be a simplified version of "the famous Oglesby" for a less cultured audience.

"The famous Oglesby" did not lack confidence, and he had an extraordinary plan to make this book unforgettable. This is where the "sculptures" appeared which he expected one day to add to the Virgil. They were full plate engravings, and he commissioned 82 of them from some of the finest engravers around. Now that books were visible as objects of worth and status, he would provide them as luxury status symbols. Besides, since gentlemen might find it necessary but wearisome to actually read through a whole book, illustrations would certainly help.

Ogilby was now placing himself firmly in the new reality. The world of masques and theatre was little more than a memory. It is true that his *Aesop* was excellent masque material. There was no longer any theatre for Shirley to work in, but he wrote plays for the students at his school. *Aesop* had opening verses from him commending it to this very particular audience. Shirley would actually write a masque, *Cupid and Death,* based on Ogilby's text, which was performed for the Portuguese ambassador. But that was not Ogilby's objective. He was creating a book which was a virtual theatre for the luxuriously cultured mind, and where political morals were laid out to help the next step on the way:[30]

> No government can th' unsetled vulgar please,
> Whom change delight's think quiet a disease,
> Now anarchie and Armies they maintain,
> And wearied, are for King and Lords again.

Nothing like this had existed before in Britain. The only comparable English non-fiction book that I can trace with extensive printed illustrations is *The most delectable history of Reynard the Fox,* which was published in various editions from 1620. But that was a considerably less classy act made up from charming, rather crude woodcuts. The *Oxford English Dictionary* credits Ogilby with being the first person to describe book illustrations as "sculptures".[31] The *Reynard* illustrations are two-dimensional and quite medieval; Ogilby's "sculptures" have a trompe-l'oeil or scenic character. Each illustration is a theatrical scene, now to be enjoyed in a world without theatre. No public theatre had used scenery, but the masque theatre of the court and great private houses did, and it is that audience which Ogilby was serving.

The engraver was Francis Clein (or Cleyn), a German living in London. He copied some of his images from a sixteenth-century Dutch illustrated Aesop by Marcus Geeraerts the elder.[32] Geeraerts was a landscape painter known for his habit of including a squatting, urinating woman somewhere in the picture.[33] Clein had to refine the work; Ogilby's audience would not have appreciated Flemish earthiness. But there is also a great difference in the sophistication and elegance of line in Ogilby's edition. The Dutch version has a roughness which is endearing but far from glamorous.

No one would have opened this book without expecting to find hidden or overt subversive material. England was now ruled by a strong man whose claims to popular authority were backed by military repression, and agitation for change was met by a heavy hand. According to one historian, on a conservative estimate a third of the peerage was imprisoned in the Tower of London in the years surrounding the King's execution.[34] The opening praise came from the poet laureate, William Davenant. It was signed off "From the Tower Sep. 30. 1651". Davenant was, as everyone knew, a prisoner awaiting trial for treason.

In these pages, Aesop's fabulous beasts are living in the same country as the reader; they speak of covenants and covenanters,[35] of the "Solemn League and Cov'nant", of civil war, of Cromwell's regiment of Ironsides and sequestration of property, the punishment suffered by so many of his modern readers. Ogilby's Aesop was a monarchist addressing a culti-vated readership who saw rebellion against the Crown as criminal and were determined that the monarchy should be restored. There are four fables about the killing of the royal hart: in one he is dismembered by the lion; in another he is driven into exile by the horse, who forever after must be at the mercy of the soldier who helped him get rid of the hart. It would take a pretty dim reader not to get the point.[36]

It appeared at the same time as Thomas Hobbes' *Leviathan*, which argued that the English had the demonstrable right and duty to dump the King. He said that people are not created as subjects but make a covenant to hand over their personal sovereignty to a ruler with autocratic and unchallengeable power in exchange for his protection. But there was no King in England, so the old contract was extinguished. "The obligation of subjects to the sovereign is understood to last as long, and no longer, than the power lasteth by which he is able to protect them."[37] It was logical that there should now be a new overlord, with a new contract of limitless authority. Cromwell was actively seeking reconciliation with the Royalists, and encouraged them to accept Hobbes' argument. The poet Abraham Cowley seems to have done so, saying that it is time to abandon loyalty to the monarchy once "the event of battle and the unaccountable will of God" have removed it from Britain.[38] Ogilby rejected that argument, and his work was to counter Hobbes not by logic but by the use of fables and their morals. His theme is disturbance of the proper order by war and a military regime, and its inevitable restoration. He translates the great authors of antiquity into another time as well as another language, speaking on their behalf about the ideal society, where people were born into their place, depended on grace and patronage, and where (at least in poetic terms) the noble and chivalric virtue of loyalty was honourable, unbreakable and without a price.

How much of a risk was Ogilby running in standing so boldly in the company of "malignants", as Royalists were now officially described? Certainly falling foul of Parliament was no joke; Davenant was truly in fear for his life.

A well-known poet and playwright, he had established his career as a favourite of Queen Henrietta Maria just before Ogilby had gone to Ireland in Wentworth's service. Shakespeare used to stay in his father's tavern in Oxford and Davenant encouraged the belief that he was the great man's illegitimate son. He started writing masques for the court in 1635 and it had been part of Ogilby's job in

Dublin to study them for Wentworth. In 1638 Charles I, at the Queen's insistence, had made him poet laureate, and the next year he had been given permission to build his own theatre, but these were Puritan times and the project was blocked. Davenant turned to desperate remedies and was involved in a plot to seize London for the King in 1641 (before the Civil War). The principle "The show must go on" can be taken too far. When the plot disintegrated he had carried on, intending to seize the Tower, a theatrical irony that would become evident ten years later, when he became an involuntary resident there. The plot failed and he was declared a traitor by Parliament. Briefly becoming a soldier, he fled to France after the battle of Naseby and was appointed Charles' emissary to Louis XIV. After the King's execution, Henrietta Maria had appointed him Lieutenant-Governor of Maryland, where he was supposed to replace the Parliamentarian appointee, but he was captured at sea by a Commonwealth ship. That is why he was now in the Tower awaiting trial for treason, giving Ogilby a wonderful quote to open the book:

> Yet in thy Verse, methinks, I Aesop see
> Less bound than when his Master set him free:
> So well thou fit'st the measure of his mind.

Davenant was always rather strapped for cash, and it seems very likely that the quid pro quo for this promotional verse was that Ogilby, who had money and connections, should arrange help to make his confinement more comfortable. Ogilby was certainly in the business of bringing together a Royalist readership, and proudly so. As well as using an endorsement from a traitor in the Tower, his *Aesop* was openly dedicated to two Royalist conspirators from Seymour's family, the Earl's son, Lord Beauchamp, and his son-in-law, the Earl of Winchilsea.

Winchilsea had recently married Seymour's daughter Mary. He had been a vigorous military supporter of the Royalist cause, providing auxiliary troops (horse and foot) at his own expense. In 1651 he was a closely watched man. Beauchamp was already imprisoned.

How did Ogilby get away with this? He was obviously running a risk, but it was evidently a calculated one. A writer who wrote an obviously inflammatory tract, aimed at a wide public, was courting punishment, but the ambiguity of metaphors for a small and wealthy audience who were already under suspicion and surveillance was, as it turned out, not worth prosecution.[39] In fact the book was a great success. As Ogilby wrote nearly twenty years later, "so happy prov'd the Version, and so fairly accepted, that of me, till then obscure, *Fame* began to prattle".[40]

He did not become a prisoner in the Tower. But the next chapter of his story was certainly written there, as he came into contact with three inmates in the months before *Aesop* was published. They were Lord Beauchamp, William Davenant, and the brother Ogilby did not know he had, the man who would start a new movement in the dance of his life.

Life 7. The Gentleman

The Tower held an extraordinary small community of like-minded gentlemen and nobles, mostly living in in their own dank apartments, with their own furnishings, servants, books and writing materials and whatever food and drink they cared to order. Of course they paid for all this, but these were not people without resources. In 1630 one prisoner, Sir John Eliot, wrote "I have no news to give you but the happiness of this place, which is so like a paradise that there is none to trouble us but ourselves". It was a touch ironic, but this was not a letter from a man chained in a dungeon. The air was bad, but an indication of conditions comes from Eliot's complaints when he was put under a stricter regime in mid-winter: he was moved to a room "where candle-light may be suffered but scarce fire. None but my servants, hardly my son, may have admittance to me".[1] Most prisoners were not on such a regime and it was not particularly hard for a harmless poet like Ogilby to arrange visits. He went there in 1651 to visit Seymour's son Henry, Lord Beauchamp, to whom his *Aesop* was to be dedicated. It was a Seymour tradition to be imprisoned in the Tower, a penalty of having a slight claim to the throne, and Beauchamp's father wrote "It seems it is a place entailed upon our family, for we have now held it five generations, yet to speak the truth, I like not the place so well but that I could be very well contented the entail should be cut off and settled upon some other family that better deserves it".[2] His imprisonment was due to his involvement in trying to put Charles II on the English throne. It was a story that had begun in Scotland, and it involved the Earl of Airlie, the head of the Clan Ogilvie.

Ogilby meets Ogilvie

Beauchamp was a dashing and personable young man. He had started putting together the Western Association in 1649, after the King's execution, to prepare for a rising against Parliament. In April 1651, before the conspiracy really got under way, he was arrested and put in the Tower, where he was kept until the uprising was crushed in September at the Battle of Worcester. Ogilby must have visited him to get permission for the dedication of *Aesop*. That must be where he met Davenant. Beauchamp certainly knew the Poet Laureate. And the Poet Laureate knew the Earl of Airlie's son James Ogilvie, who also happened to be imprisoned there. James Ogilvie was on a particularly relaxed regime, generally confined but allowed out into the City on various occasions.[3] In 1643 Beauchamp, Davenant and James Ogilvie had been together with Charles I and Henrietta Maria in Oxford.[4] Davenant must have brought together Ogilby and Ogilvie during this shared time in prison, between 1651 and October 1653. That is when the old dancing master discovered for the first time the Ogilby family secret: that he was a member of the family, born not in Edinburgh but in the castle of Airlie by Kirriemuir. He was evidently not the person he thought. He was James Ogilvie's uncle, and brother to the Earl.

He knew the truth by the end of 1653, when he asked Ashmole for a horoscope. Ashmole's note says that he was born at "Killemeure 10 myles north from Dundee". The spelling had changed a little and the town is actually about 20 miles north of Dundee, but this was the secret that Ogilby ended up protecting so firmly. The point was not the place of birth by itself, but the family that lived there.

Airlie Castle was more of a quiet retreat than a massive fortification. Kirriemuir was a prosperous market place for agricultural produce, wool and flax. But Airlie had lost a good deal of his wealth in feuding, and to stand loyally by the King against the overpowering Scottish Covenanters in the 1640s required military strength that his family did not have. It was a principled and heroic position, the stuff of legends and ballads that you don't really want to be part of.

The mysterious arms

We know that Ogilby understood he was the Earl's brother because in 1654 he declared it in a kind of cypher. No one recorded it in writing, but this is the story Ogilby published, in a language few understand, the cypher of heraldry.

Years later, Aubrey had been warned to be suspicious of the old man and smelt danger: "he is a cunning Scott and I must deale warily with him, with the advice of my friends".[5] He noted that Ogilby had a coat of arms, which was odd for a tailor's son. He described it as "a lion passant gardant crowned[6] ..., a mullet for difference ... the crest is a ½ virgin in an earle's coronet holding a castle".[7]

Aubrey was an expert on heraldry, but said nothing more. He could see that these were the arms of the Earl of Airlie, the seventh Lord Ogilvie, with the addition of that mullet, a

five-pointed straight-sided star over the lion's back. He understood the significance of this crest with the Earl's coronet, which
must be why he thought Gadbury was mistaken about him
being born in Edinburgh and made a note to press Morgan on
the subject. But he was evidently unable to do more than hint at
what he understood, and no historian seems to have noticed. A
coat of arms – especially a Scottish coat of arms – is specific to
a particular person, so marks of difference are added to distin-
guish between members of the same family. The "mullet" is
such a mark. Today it would signify that he was a third son, but
according to the Court of the Lord Lyon, which is in charge of
Scottish heraldry, the system was not quite so formalised in the
seventeenth century and it simply indicates a "cadet", a younger
son or brother, or a member of a junior branch of the family.

Ogilby first claimed his true identity at the age of fifty-
three, not by using the crest but just the "charge", the lion.
That was when he began producing a series of fine illustrated
books which open with a full page portrait of the author. It
first appears under the portrait in the middle of his name
in his magnificent translation of Virgil in 1654. His name is
Latinised, "Ogilvius". He did not display his arms on a shield,
but on a cartouche, an oval normally reserved for women, and
he elegantly distorted this cartouche into a vaguely shield-like
form. The Earl has a plate dedicated to himself in this volume
and his own coat of arms appears with his name on a plate
on page 290. His name too is Ogilvius: the plate's dedication
is "Jacobo Ogilvio" (To Jacobus Ogilvius). The escutcheon is
a shield with a crest on top, a motto beneath and two bulls
acting as bearers. His artist has a different, more forthright
style, but the central heraldic image is the same as Ogilby's,
without the mullet. They were evidently declaring themselves
to be brothers.

7 & 8. Ogilby's and Airlie's arms in *Virgil* 1654.

The final plate in the book is dedicated to Edward Bysshe, the Garter King of Arms, so we can be sure that Ogilby was entitled to his coat of arms.[8] In fact by the time Aubrey made his note of the arms, in the 1670s, it would have been a criminal offence to use them improperly. In England, people have sometimes been a little carefree over the use of arms to which they were not entitled. The rules of the College of Heralds are not part of the Common Law, and there is no punishment for simply giving yourself an unauthorised coat of arms. It just makes you look a bit silly. But Scotland is different. There the rules are enforced by the Lord Lyon, and his Court has the sanction of criminal law behind it. It is a real court, and by an Act of 1592 Lord Lyon was authorised to fine offenders a hundred pounds "And failyeing of payment thairof That thay be incarcerat in the narrest prissone Thairin to remane upoun thair awin chargis during the plesur of the said Lyoun".[9] The Court had been extinguished under the Commonwealth, but would be re-established in 1662, after the Restoration, and the Airlie family took such things seriously.[10] Since Ogilby was using Scottish arms we can be absolutely certain that he believed he was entitled to them, and that he was indeed who the coat of arms proclaimed him to be.

The House of Airlie

When Ogilby learned his real identity, the clan was at its lowest ebb. The inevitable consequence of being loyal to the Stuarts was given additional brutal emphasis by the heritage of clan enmities. The Ogilvies had been enemies of the Campbells since the middle of the sixteenth century. Lord Ogilvie was a staunch Royalist. The Covenanters' uprising against the Crown in 1639 had been led by the Earl of Argyll, the head of Clan Campbell. While John Ogilby was putting on plays in his Dublin theatre, his elder brother, the Lord of Airlie, went to York to pledge his arms for the King to attack Argyll, and was immediately promoted to an Earl. The family motto is "A Fin" ("To The End"), and that applied both to enmity to Clan Campbell and to unwavering support to the Stuarts, whatever the cost.

Ogilby knew nothing of his connection to the Earl of Airlie, but his life was bound up with what happened in Scotland. Charles' assault on the Covenanters was a disaster, and he brought Wentworth back to England to find money for another attempt. Parliament would not agree to fund Charles' Scottish war, so he and Wentworth proposed bringing over an Irish Catholic army, removing anti-Catholic laws there in return. The Scottish Covenanters then spoke of invading Ireland to prevent any such thing, and in 1641 the Irish Catholics responded with their own insurrection.

That was the insurrection that closed Ogilby's theatre and ended up drenching Ireland in blood and hatred. And by then the Earl of Argyll had set about demolishing the House of Airlie.

In the summer of 1640 the Earl of Airlie had taken an army into England to support Charles and avoid having to take the covenant. He left his eldest son, the next James Ogilvie, in charge of his estates. This was the James Ogilvie who must have told Ogilby the truth about his birth. In 1640 he had been about twenty-eight years old and held the title of "Lord Ogilvie".

> Argyle has raised a hunder men,
> A hunder men and mairly,
> And he's awa doun by the back o' Dunkeld,
> To plunder the bonnie house o' Airly.

Few people have a passage in their lives shaped into a ballad that is still sung 350 years later. It is not a good thing to happen. Argyll is said to have brought 5,000 men to the assault. The setting of the ballad is unclear: Argyll attacked the Earl's castles of Airlie and Forter. Either could be "the bonnie house of Airly". The expression refers to a family, not a building; "the House of Airly" does not mean Airlie Castle any more than "the House of Windsor" means Windsor Castle.

James Ogilvie refused to surrender, but rather than attempt a hopeless defence he cleared out. According to the ballad-maker, the castle attacked was still occupied by James' mother, the Earl's wife. She was in truth in Forter, a sturdy fortified tower defending the head of Glen Isla.

Argyll burned both the castles of Airlie and Forter, and completely ravaged Airlie's territory: "They have not left him in all his lands a cock to crow day."[11]

The ballad ends with a mystifying cry of defiance and loyalty from the Countess:

"O, I hae seven brave sons," she says;
"The youngest ne'er saw his daddie;
And although I had as mony mae,
I wad gie them a' to Charlie!"[12]

The origin of the ballad is unknown; its oldest surviving record is a hundred years after the event, and there were many subsequent variants, but this line of a youngest son who never saw his father is in all of them. The lady in question had only two sons. But the Earl's father had at least six sons, and one, the Master of the Revels in Ireland, that ne'er saw his daddy. Is this line a misplaced memory from that earlier generation? But how could the ballad-maker know anything about it? It is all a little odd.

Disposing of a baby

John gave his date of birth as 1600. The Earl was born around 1586. How is it possible for the author of *Britannia* to be a brother of the Earl if he is not in the records? The answer is that there are no coherent records; there is no record of any births, and references to siblings appear more or less at random. It is clear that the Earl, whose name was James, did have one younger brother called John, but he was born about 1587 and died in 1625. He dictated his testament on his death-bed, and described himself as the "brother german" of James, Lord Ogilvie of Airlie (James was not yet an Earl).[13] "Brother german" means a real, unquestionable full-blood brother. This was the year when our John Ogilby had himself been near death from malaria, and it looks as if the testament emphasised "brother german" to ensure that there is no confusion with the John Ogilby who was known at court.[14]

The Earl's mother, Jean Ruthven, produced an unknown number of children before her death in 1611. Their births are unrecorded, but seven of them appear in later documents. At this point we run out of evidence and have to look at circumstantial material, because the likeliest explanation sounds more like a fairy-tale than real history. There are plenty of fables in which a grown man discovers that he is really the son of a noble house, raised by a humble retainer who is not his father after all. Usually the retainer is a shepherd. In this case, it was evidently Lord Ogilvie's tailor.

This bizarre tale has its origins in a bitter feud between the murderously aggressive men of two clans, Ogilvie and Lindsay. The clans had strongholds about four miles apart just north of Arbroath, the Ogilvies at Bolshan, the Lindsays at the House of Dun (both were demolished in the eighteenth century).

When John Ogilby was born the head of the Ogilvie clan was James, the 5th Lord Ogilvie, who was about sixty. The man who seems to have been John's father was this man's eldest son, also called James. As the heir, he was called the Master. He was engaged so ferociously in the Lindsay feud that they fought a pitched battle in March 1600, around the time when his wife would have conceived John Ogilby. The Scottish Privy Council demanded huge sums in bail (sureties) from him and placed him under house arrest in his castle at Airlie, at the head of Glen Isla, just east of Kirriemuir. Refusing to submit, he was proclaimed a rebel at Edinburgh Market Cross in June. In January, when the baby was a few weeks old, the King fined him £5,000. That was a fortune in a country which did not have much currency in circulation, and where agricultural rents had fallen nearly 80% in real terms over the previous forty years.[15] Now the Master "brooded with a green and yellow melancholy".[16] A Lindsay stabbed and killed his brother David in Edinburgh. Children were an encumbrance: his fifteen-year-old heir was packed off to the continent, where he stayed until 1605. Eventually, in 1603, the Master illegally walked out of Airlie, joined up with his brothers, and led a full-scale armed raid with guns and primitive artillery against the Lindsays. The King denounced him as "a person perjured and defamed" and he lost the whole of his bail money – £10,000. He was pretty much ruined.

John Ogilby's destiny must have been sorted out by the Master's father, the 5th Lord Ogilvie. In 1606, when the clan chief knew he was dying, he set out the precepts by which the Master's eldest son should live when he became the Lord of the House of Airlie.[17] He was drawing on lessons from his own past which he did not care to set down in a letter: "What in my time, I have done for the welfare of my house my Charter Chest will testify." This was the philosophy of rule, not the details. His guiding star, the basis of all action, was the welfare of the House. This was the essence of Airlie morality, and must explain what they did with baby John. The House was comparable to a Kingdom, and must be kept strong. It is probable that one of the things he did in this cause was to arrange for Jean Ruthven's third son to disappear, perhaps because the child's parentage was doubted. She and her husband may not have seemed to be in a position to make babies when this one was conceived.

The baby was, it seems, given to an altogether peaceable clansman, the tailor John, and his wife. They were probably a childless couple living in Edinburgh. Around the time of the birth, the Master was a wounded animal in a spectacularly

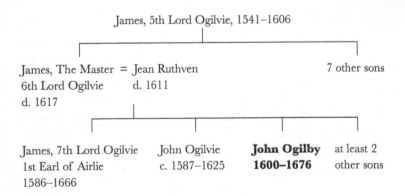

James, 5th Lord Ogilvie, 1541–1606

James, The Master = Jean Ruthven   7 other sons
6th Lord Ogilvie   d. 1611
d. 1617

James, 7th Lord Ogilvie   John Ogilvie   **John Ogilby**   at least 2
1st Earl of Airlie   c. 1587–1625   **1600–1676**   other sons
1586–1666

bad mood. His father had to do all he could to hold the House together. This baby would be better out of the way.

In 1600, John Ogilby the tailor was probably one of Edinburgh's merchant craftsmen of real substance, who worked out of rich apartments in the tall houses lining the wide streets. He may at this stage have been much wealthier than the Master, at least in terms of bags of silver. He may have helped the Master with the bail payment. Whatever the reasons, it seems the tailor and his wife were given the baby to raise as their own. John Ogilby evidently did not learn the story of his origin until he was over fifty.

It may not be a coincidence that the tailor's enrolment as a Merchant Taylor in London took place just when the 5th Lord Ogilvie wrote the letter to his grandson.[18] The old Lord was dying, loose ends were being tied up, and the boy would have a better future closer to the royal court than in what seemed to be a depressed Edinburgh. The Airlie clan may well have played a role, too, in purchasing young John's apprenticeship, a role concealed by the story he later told of a quite unbelievable lottery win. It is quite clear that the Merchant Taylors played a role in deciding the boy's future, and the

House of Airlie may have had a hand in rescuing the tailor and his son. The Master had inherited the Lordship around the time the tailor went to London. His wife, Jean Ruthven, young John's mother, died in 1611. It seems entirely possible that she did what she could to help her transplanted son from her deathbed, supplying the money to release the tailor from prison and secure the apprenticeship. The lottery win was metaphorical.

The undercover aristocrat

It seems clear that when Ogilby first started publishing books, he did not think that he was close kin to an Earl. His first books, his 1649 translation of Virgil and *Aesop's Fables*, in 1651, have frontispiece portraits of him but they carry no coat of arms.

In 1654 he republished Virgil in a large, glamorous and heavily illustrated edition. Here he presented himself as a new man.[19] The careworn, slightly bedraggled translator with tired eyes and a knowing look has become glossy, confident with a fine wig and a noble coat of arms. He gives the impression of a man who has come into his birthright. Johannes Ogilvius, as he styled himself, was a member of a noble family.

The final title-plate appeared in 1658 and was used for almost all of his subsequent publications including some of the copies of his description of Charles II's coronation. Since the Garter King of Arms was required by the King to check that volume for correctness, we can be certain that Johannes Ogilvius was entitled to his lion and mullet. What is more, at the Restoration he added the crest of the Earl of Airlie, which Aubrey says he was still using in the 1670s. Ogilby was declaring a close connection not just to an aristocratic

9, 10, 11, 12. Ogilby's frontispieces: top, as a scholar in 1649 by
William Marshall and 1651 by Richard Gaywood: below, as an
aristocrat in 1654 by William Faithorne and 1658 by Pierre Lombart.

lineage, but also to a political position. The Earl's wealth had been destroyed, but he nevertheless found the money to be a patron of John Ogilby's fine and very expensive edition of his translation of Virgil. This was almost certainly a move in a long-term strategy to bring back Stuart rule and destroy Argyll. To understand how that would work requires a complete re-evaluation of Ogilby's work and position, which has been carefully hidden from history. There were plates dedicated to a hundred English patrons and just one Scot, himself. The illustration on his page is for the start of Book 5 of the *Aeneid*, and shows Aeneas declaring a ritual celebration of his father. The picture looks like a celebration of their shared fatherhood, like some kind of coming-out. Given that no one seems to have noticed John Ogilby's claimed identity down to this day, that comes as a bit of a surprise.

At the time, only a small number of people would have been literate enough in the language of heraldry to read what he was saying. A coat of arms set out, for those in the know, its holder's place in a social network. So in what way was Ogilby hiding his roots? And why was it so important to do so?

It seems likeliest that Ogilby was told to keep the truth about his birth secret to avoid attaching scandal to the House of Airlie. He was permitted, and encouraged, to show that he was acting as a member of that House, but not to say a word about his parentage. Even the use of the coat of arms was circumscribed; he got to choose who would see it. The British Library has a copy of his 1662 volume *The Entertainment of Charles II*, including his frontispiece portrait with his coat of arms. It has other copies where the frontispiece is not there. Similarly, Trinity College Cambridge has a copy of his Homer made for Isaac Barrow, the Lucasian Professor at Cambridge in 1665, which does not have the dramatic new frontispiece with the crest of an Earl. These large illustrated volumes were not bound until they were purchased, and that is when the illustrations were put in place. Ogilby's books were not mass produced. Each purchaser received the version which they desired, at least so far as the leaves of pictures went. And it may be that they also received the version which Ogilby desired. His coat of arms was shown to the people permitted to see it. It seems as though receiving that page was the equivalent of a masonic handshake. It was a sign.

The astrologer's evidence

Of course, we know that there was one person to whom he revealed the truth about his birthplace, when he was fifty-two years old. In 1653 he confided in Elias Ashmole, a professional consultant, on whose discretion he could rely. Ashmole was an antiquarian and lawyer fascinated by science and mathematics, remembered today as the founder of the Ashmolean Museum in Oxford. Ogilby consulted him as an astrologer.

In Ogilby's understanding of the world, astrology was not just a way of seeing into the future. Information about the details of a person's birth allowed the mapping of the whole cosmos at that instant in time, and that map would be a complete description of the person. Possession of someone's horoscope was similar to what we might hope for from having a read-out of their DNA, with their whole identity laid bare. That was not a risk he could take, given the life he had led and was still leading.

We stand at the end of three centuries of confidence in scientific reason. Ogilby was living through what is now described as "the scientific revolution", which we confidently think replaced a mystical and magical understanding of the world, copied from one book to another, with one based on pure reason and experiment. The arcane scholarship that studied hidden links between heaven and earth is now dismissed as unscientific superstition.

But astrology was a hugely successful industry in England in 1653, because people were desperate to know what was going to happen to them. The foundations of their lives had been drowned in the maelstrom of the Civil War. Some quarter of a million Scots and English had died in a conflict which ripped apart the very basis of society. Ogilby and Ashmole had been born into a world in which the hierarchy of authority extended upwards through church and aristocracy to the King and God, but all of that had been wiped away.

The King had been tried and beheaded by his own subjects. All that was left of the old constitution was finished off in April 1653, when Cromwell forcibly abolished Parliament and summoned a new one of his own devising, "The Parliament of Saints". That would last only a few months before Cromwell sent it packing and inaugurated the military dictatorship of Britain: "Oliver Cromwell, Captain Generall of all the forces of this Commonwealth, is declared Lord Protector of the Nations."

In 1653 no one knew what was going to happen to themselves, their families, their estates, their lives. The astrologers really did have a way to turn lead into gold – the lead in question being moveable type. One family in three was buying an annual almanac in which (often under the pseudonyms of long-dead or fictional precursors) astrologers set out the events of the year to come, accompanied by weather forecasts, harvest predictions and other handy information. One of the most successful, *Merlinus Anglicus*, was written by Ashmole's friend William Lilly and was selling some 30,000 copies a year.

Astrologers had never enjoyed such a position before, and never would again. There was even a Society of Astrologers, which held an annual Feast in London. Ashmole regularly attended it, with about forty other members. In 1653 it had been held on 14 August, when the horoscope was spectacularly agreeable. That was important; two years earlier Ashmole had spent several days trying to digest his portion of the feast and had only managed it when a fellow-member gave him a piece of bryony root "to hold in my hand". It worked, despite the fact that Ashmole seems to have quite literally got the wrong end of the stick: the root is a dangerously powerful emetic.[20]

The Astrologers' Feast must, sadly, have been a rather dull affair because it was very important not to attract the hostility of radical Puritans. No one wore a pointy hat; that was way out of date. (The fourteenth-century theologian Duns Scotus had said that pointy hats help channel divine thoughts to the brain, but he was now seen as such an obscurantist that the headgear was known as Duns' Cap, and its wearers as Dunces.) They carefully avoided bad language and any discussion of politics and religion. They were also cautious about alcohol, with no one proposing any toasts. There was a sermon, which took the standard form of demonstrating from a Biblical verse that there was *absolutely* no contradiction between godly Christianity and the business of astrology – which made it quite clear, of course, that this was their biggest problem.

Ashmole had spent the last ten years studying astrology and alchemy. In 1652 he had produced the *Theatrum Chemicum*, a collection of twenty-nine old English alchemical texts in verse, which he felt was their most appropriate form. Poetry, he said with approval, has a secret energy that is designed to conceal as well as to teach.[21] Ogilby may have chosen him because he was a recognised authority on the genealogy of the peerage, so much so that at the Restoration he would become an officer of the College of Arms, the Windsor Herald. This was, then, a way of investigating and authenticating his claim to noble blood. He waited three months before telling him in absolute confidence that he had been born in Kirriemuir.

Ashmole eventually created two surviving horoscopes of him. One, John Ogilby commissioned. The other, which is the vital source of biographical information that we have been using, Ashmole probably drew up around 1680, after its subject was dead.[22] This is the one with a list of significant events in his life. It looks as though all the information for this was collected at his consultations in 1653; the latest life-event listed is in 1650.

The final book in which Ogilby used his coat of arms was an atlas of China, which did not come out until 1669 but which had 1668 on its title page. By then the Airlie connection had lost its significance. But when he had first discovered it, he had used this hidden connection as effectively as possible, as we shall see. The themes of Ogilby's life are secrets, hidden signs and conspiracy. They are the themes of *Britannia*.

The Virgil patrons

When he met Ashmole, Ogilby was devising the great edition of his Virgil translation that he had promised Seymour he would make in 1649. In 1670 he described the transformation of the book like a butterfly emerging from a chrysalis: "From a Mean Octavo, a Royal Folio Flourish'd. Adorn'd with Sculpture, and Illustrated with Annotations ... being Publish'd with that Magnificence and Splendor, appear'd anew, and taking Beauty, the fairest that till then the English Press ever boasted." He also described the other truly remarkable feature of this book, its sponsorship by an astonishing array of the super-rich, its pages "Triumphing with the affixt Emblazons, Names and Titles of a hundred Patrons, all bold Assertors in Vindication of the Work".[23] What this meant was that each of the full-page illustrations was identified with a patron, whose name and coat of arms were displayed at the bottom of the page. They were all stakeholders in the publication. Twenty of them had no personal title of nobility but they belonged to noble families and each of their plates was dedicated "Armigero", to the bearer of a coat of arms. Ogilby too was an armiger, presenting himself in the frontispiece with his own arms. He was no longer a commoner but now revealed as "a gentleman borne".

No book had ever been published in this way before. It has been described as the first example of "subscription publishing",[24] but it is a mistake to see this as a crowd-funded commercial venture. Ogilby calls the stakeholders "patrons", not subscribers, and there is no evidence that the book was for sale. Now that we know the history of the years that followed, we can see the preponderance of men (and some women) here who were engaged in plots to overthrow the Commonwealth and restore the monarchy. The hundred patrons included a marquess, a marchioness, six earls, three countesses, six barons, four viscounts, seven baronets and a number of the wives, sons and daughters of these august persons. Strafford's children, William, Ann and Arabella, for whom Ogilby had originally translated Aesop, are there. The first six plates are dedicated to the Seymour family, which was rightly regarded with suspicion and fear by the government, and six more follow further into the book. The picture dedicated to Henry Seymour, Lord Beauchamp, is especially poignant as he had just died, aged twenty-eight, following his incarceration in the Tower. It illustrates Eclogue 5, in which two shepherds mourn and poetically celebrate their dead companion, Daphnis, the mythic inventor of poetry. The picture shows the shepherds below, and in the sky Daphnis ascending into the realm of the gods. He is not portrayed as a shepherd, but as a young warrior with a crown.

He was in the company of warriors biding their time. Two other plates are dedicated to men who had died for the cause. More than two-thirds of the living patrons are readily identifiable as people engaged in or close to conspiracies to bring back the monarchy. They include John Ballasys, one of the six members of the Sealed Knot. The Sealed Knot's secret strategy, in the dedicated service of the exiled King, was organised by Edward Hyde, Earl of Clarendon. Hyde later explained that

> they would not engage in any absurd and desperate attempt, but use all their credit and authority to prevent and discountenance the same, so they would take the first rational opportunity, which they expected from the divisions and animosities which daily grew and appeared in the army, to draw their friends and old soldiers who were ready to receive their commands together, and try the utmost that could be done with[out] the loss or hazard of their lives.[25]

Here are Philip Egerton, who would raise a troop of horse for a rising five years later, and Philip Warwick, who had fought at Edgehill and would help to arrange the restoration – as would Anthony Ashley-Cooper and Nicholas Wilde, more subscribers to fine plates.

Here too are John Penruddock, Thomas Peyton, Richard Thornhill and John Grenville, who formed a significant part of the high command of the Action Party, which took over from the Sealed Knot just around the time of the book's publication.[26] There were at least four participants in the Battle of Worcester, others who would be involved in Penruddock's forthcoming rebellion of 1655 and five of the conspirators in Booth's rising of 1659.

A good number of the patrons were great ladies – thirteen of them – who were as committed to the cause as any men. A significant number of husbands and wives, brothers and sisters, had separate dedications. They were not subscribing in order to have a copy each. Their inclusion was a commitment to what the book represented. Some, such as Nicholas Steward, appear to have acted as a patron without having any money: Steward was fined £1,500 for supporting the King but that was cut to £100 because he was broke.

The volume was a testament to the patrons' taste, learning, patronage and modernity. But there was more to it than that. These people were co-owners of the project, sharing in his reading of Virgil for Britain, ready to act when called. The book's overt message was that they needed patience. Its covert message was their roll-call.

So what of the dozen or so patrons who have still not been exposed as members of one conspiracy or another? It seems unlikely that they were simple innocents who persuaded Ogilby to let them put a picture in his book. These must be people who, like Ogilby, have managed to stay under the historians' radar. They include two poets, and two of the men to whom Shirley dedicated his work. Some we can be sure were hidden undercover. One of the plates, for example, is dedicated to Viscount Chichester. He had been a member of Ormond's Privy Council in Ireland, when Ogilby was working there, and had been a key negotiator with the Confederate Catholics to bring soldiers from Ireland to the royal army in the west of England. When Ormond surrendered Dublin to Parliament he handed over Chichester as a hostage. In 1651 Chichester married a woman who became a patron of Protestant dissent (in London as well as Ireland), actively encouraging just the kind of division the Sealed Knot was waiting for. The plate with his name is a picture of the Trojan Horse, but its significance would have been missed at the time. Then there was Nicholas Lechmere, a thirty-three-year-old Puritan Parliamentary lawyer. He was an overt Parliamentarian, and had been present at the Battle of Worcester. Prince Charles had stayed in his house there, but not at his invitation. He was on the other side, and his diary records his part in Cromwell's day-long battle for the city. It does not record Charles Stuart's remarkable escape, in which he somehow got out through the only unguarded gate, the first in a series of seemingly miraculous evasions (including hiding in an oak tree) which eventually got him to safety. It is possible that Lechmere's diary for the day did cast some light on this, but the last three lines of the entry have been erased.[27] In 1654 he was known as a pretty hard-line Puritan, but might that deletion conceal a treasonable blind eye to Charles Stuart's escape? This diary, having contained no opinions on the wider world at all through the Interregnum, would flower with Royalist enthusiasm as the Restoration of "the most excellent Prince Charles the Second King of England" approached. Who knew in 1654 that Lechmere was a closet Royalist? It looks as though Ogilby knew and was known to every one of his patrons – at least those that were still alive. And although the Merchant Taylors Company were not enrolled as patrons, he presented them with a copy, along with a copy of his *Aesop*, for which they stumped up £13 6s. 8d.[28] What was their connection with this club of patrons? Actually, it was remarkably strong. The headmaster, William Dugard, had set up four printing presses in the school in the 1640s, and in 1650 printed *Defensio regia,* a French condemnation of Charles' trial. He was arrested and sent to Newgate, his presses seized and his family evicted. Milton intervened with Cromwell to get him released and reinstated at the school, and he was then given the job of printer to the Council of State.[29] The story illustrates the risks of publishing "seditious" material. He is today considered to have been a turncoat.[30] Ogilby's sending his books to the Merchant Taylors suggests that the headmaster had not, after all, changed sides.

The book was not a commercial production, but a commissioned one. It appears to be the membership card of an elite and dangerous club, and each member received the membership list in its pages. They were by no means the only Royalist conspirators, but they were an inner core of trusted nobles and their friends.

Ogilby's re-adoption

Of course, Ogilby was not the creator of this project. He had simply wanted to produce his magnificent illustrated book. But he now found that he was being given "the Encouragement of Noble and Generous Personages, mentioned in their several Pieces", his new and startling group of patrons. At their head was Seymour, to whom the book was dedicated "For discharge of my Obligation", but the frontispiece showed that it owed a great deal to Airlie too. The House of Airlie's actions had two consistent themes: unwavering loyalty to the Stuarts, and the defence of the House itself. Ogilby must have been patronised by Airlie, and given the story of his identity, because Airlie believed it would serve these ends. From Airlie's perspective, these goals were identical. The restoration of Charles II would mean the overthrow of Argyll, and the restoration of clan Ogilvie. The House of Airlie would regain its place, its wealth and its security. But in 1651, when the Battle of Worcester was lost, Charles had made a desperate escape abroad and the Royalist network had been smashed. To re-build it required the most secret and careful co-ordination across Britain between those who would work for the day when he could be brought back. This was a time of spies and secret agents. It was hard to know who to trust, and it was even harder to circulate such a list in a safe form. *Virgil* was a useful part of that list. It was an extraordinary book, regal in its appearance and pretensions, monarchist in its argument and philosophy, and listing in its magnificent plates what we can now see, but the authorities at the time could not, a community that could be relied on when the day came.

It was a truly noble book that would have a dignified place in noble Royalist circles that shared an undimmed vision of the proper order of the kingdom. This translation of Virgil was now the most glamorous printed book ever seen in England. When Ogilby was a child he had seen the way great men and women made their display through the creation of lavishly decorated fabrics. He was now offering that service through a lavishly decorated text. His original translation had been a low-budget operation. It had been published by an old friend, John Crook, and sold for sixpence. Crook had also published *Aesop* with its "sculptures" but for this Ogilby needed complete control over the whole process, from acquiring the paper to printing, binding and distribution. He did all the work in his own house, in King's Head Court in Shoe Lane. His patrons required the very best, so he commissioned the illustrations from the best print artists in the country. Many were by Hollar; many others were by Cleyn, the chief designer of the Mortlake Tapestry Factory under Charles I and the Commonwealth.[31] The plates alone must have cost over £1,000.[32]

This new *Virgil* was a luxury production with extensive marginal notes (largely drawn from existing foreign editors) that were interesting and learned. But it was the look of the thing that was astonishing, taking the printed book to a new level of physical refinement. According to Anthony à Wood, it was "reserved for libraries and the Nobility".[33] And its larger format meant that it would stand more proudly on the shelf.

The political content had been clear from the start of the original edition. Ogilby begins with the first *Eclogue*, set in the terrible aftermath of Rome's civil war between Julius Caesar's assassins and his avenger, Octavian. This epic bloody struggle culminated with the destruction of Brutus at Philippi in north-east Greece. Some 50,000 victorious returning troops were rewarded with land in Italy, which meant that tens of thousands of people had their estates confiscated. The resonances were obvious to readers whose own estates were being "sequestrated" by Parliament. The poem opens with two shepherds who have lost their land. The new edition, directly commented on the use of "sequestrations", pointing out that although it is not what the original says, the modern parallel justified it: "the Version may very well by rational consequence be admitted".[34] Virgil's story develops into the rise and greatness of Octavian, who becomes Augustus, and the text was now glossed in a way that told the knowing subscribers to anticipate the return of Charles II from his exile in France to deal at last with his father's executioners. The patrons were being advised by the old dancing master, in the name of Airlie and Seymour, to put aside passion in favour of patient cunning. They should appear to make an accommodation to the new power, and secretly prepare for the inevitable moment when it would begin to fracture. That would be the time to act, so that natural order could re-assert itself and justice be done. His new notes deliberately focus the reader on the crime of Caesar's assassination.[35]

Ogilby was a very discreet man, completely trusted by, and now owned by, people who intended to replace Parliament and restore the Stuart regime.

Learning Greek

The wisdom of his advice to be patient, which coincided completely with the views of Seymour, was wretchedly demonstrated the very next year. At least six of his patrons were active in the uprising that has taken its name from one of them, Penruddock, who was executed. The book was dedicated to another of them, Heneage Finch, Earl of Winchilsea. The rising was botched, it had lost all surprise by the time it happened, but the main lesson of this disaster was that there was no appetite for a return to armed struggle. Ogilby's patrons must wait, and in the meantime Ogilby must make a living. That was why he became a client of Elias Ashmole, one of the patrons of the *Virgil*.

Ogilby had met him in 1653 and asked for a horoscope. Someone had arranged for Ashmole to be included as a patron, and directed Ogilby to him. That is when he decided to seek guidance on the next stage of his career. He had decided to produce a new translation of Homer. This was a very odd thing to do, since he did not know the language and would have to learn it from scratch. He was asking Ashmole for advice on when to start!

This was an extraordinary effort for a man in his fifties, especially if he needed to earn a living, and a huge reputational risk. His own explanation was that he had been persuaded that he could produce a great epic himself, but had to prepare himself properly to try: "My next Expedition with Sails a Trip, and swoln with the Breath of a general Applause, was to discover Greece ... in which I had a double Design, not only to bring over so Ancient and Famous an Author, but to enable myself to better carry on an Epic Poem of my own Composure."[36]

There was a common belief among Royalist writers that there was a need for someone to create a major contemporary epic poem to rank alongside the classical models. The object was to establish a moral and cultural bedrock for the re-building of monarchy in a way that would help educate and inspire a Prince and deprive the Puritans of narrative authority over the minds of Englishmen. There had been a number of abortive attempts over the previous decade to produce such a work.[37] Now Ogilby had become convinced that he was the man to do it.

To do so, he decided, he had to immerse himself in Homer as he had already immersed himself in Virgil. Shirley had already found him a tutor, a Scottish teacher in his school called David Whitford.[38] The current English translation had been published in 1611 by George Chapman, the secret author of the masque which had lamed Ogilby thirty-four years before. In "bringing over" Homer, Ogilby intended to supplant his nemesis, the writer who created the character Prognostication. Up to his death in 1634, Chapman had been one of London's most successful playwrights, and was a friend of Shirley.[39] Chapman's version was well regarded by the majority of readers, who could not read the original. Three years after Ogilby consulted Ashmole, Samuel Sheppard wrote of "Mr Chapmans Incomparable Translation of Homer's Works" that

the learned may well question it,
Whether in Greek or English Homer writ.[40]

Sheppard himself had had an abortive crack at creating an epic poem of the Civil War,[41] but without feeling any need to improve on Chapman's version of Homer, which represented thirty years of intermittent labour.[42] It read well out loud, but Ogilby would know that Chapman had worked largely from a Latin translation and had often freely interpreted rather than translated; he added over 4,500 lines to the *Odyssey*. Perhaps more importantly, it was clear to Ogilby that Chapman's translation concealed Homer's firm commitment to, and preaching of, absolute monarchy. When Ulysses went around Agamemnon's ships to argue them out of deserting the battle of Troy, he reproved subversive grumblers among the seamen by telling them there could only be one commander. In Ogilby's version, Homer would say, as Chapman's did not:

No good did many Rulers ever bring;
Let one be Lord; in Jove's name one be King.

He intended to produce a translation which would clarify Homer's commitment to "the Divine Right of Princes and Monarchical Government".[43] It could not be challenged for accuracy, and, with Shirley's help, would be equipped with a formidable battery of scholarly annotations. This was an extremely demanding investment of time and energy, and he needed to know that it would pay off. A modern Ogilby would doubtless go to a business consultant: in the seventeenth century that role, along with market and currency predictions, was the work of astrologers.

Ashmole noted his first encounter with John Ogilby as occurring at 7 p.m. on 1 October 1653.[44] This is very precise, but Ashmole was, after all, an astrologer. And it was an important moment, because, as things turned out, it would complete Ogilby's transformation. He waited several months before getting to the nitty-gritty. At 11 p.m. on 20 December the astrologer set about using his arcane knowledge to pick the most propitious date for Ogilby to begin his language studies.

The technique used, called the "election" of a time, involved casting two horoscopes, one a natal chart, and another for the moment when a new enterprise should begin. This meant that the reading could be very full, providing far more information than had actually been requested. In this case, Ashmole's charts seem to have persuaded Ogilby to do more than learn Greek. Immediately after they were drawn up, he launched himself on a bold new career as a self-publisher. This would position him for his greatest achievement and lead eventually to *Britannia*. It had evidently been a spectacular horoscope.

Whether or not the stars and planets had any influence over Ogilby's affairs, we can be reasonably confident that his astrologer did.

The basis of a horoscope was the division of the sky into twelve "Houses", divisions of the sky which ruled different areas of life. The astrologer used his tables to draw a chart showing the place of the planets and signs of the zodiac in relation to each other and to these Houses at a particular moment in time. We know roughly what conclusions Ashmole would have drawn because his close friend Lilly had published a massive work called *Christian Astrology* in 1647, the first book in English intended to allow anyone with patience and a capacity for arithmetic to try their hand at it.

Lilly's text provides some guidelines on how Ashmole would have interpreted the chart. The most relevant feature of Ogilby's natal chart, apart from the generally cheery observation that every single planet is ascending, is that Mercury is in the Second House, the House of Fortune and, as luck would have it, the "cosignificator" of the House:

> Mercury well placed represents a man of subtle and politic brain, intellect, and cognition; an excellent disputant or Logician, arguing with learning and discretion, and using much eloquence in his speech, a searcher into all kinds of Mysteries and Learning, sharp and witty, learning almost anything without a Teacher.[45]

What is more, Mercury is also very well placed in the chart drawn for the moment of the question. In fact Ashmole has made a note that it is strengthened by Venus. We can only speculate about that – it seems unlikely that it is a reference to his seventy-year-old wife.

The message was that there is no time like the present. He could get on with learning Greek as soon as he liked, and he would be good at it. His teacher would be one of the masters at Shirley's school, David Whitford.

But Lilly has more to say about a man who has Mercury well-placed in the Second House: "if he turn Merchant, no man exceeds him in way of Trade or invention of new ways whereby to obtain wealth". In the chart drawn for the moment of asking, Ashmole noted that Mercury, which was already well placed in the natal chart, was now augmented by the power of the moon. In Lilly's words, where there is a Mercury–Moon alignment, "The man learns many

Occupations, and frequently will be tampering with many
ways to trade in."[46] Ashmole made a note that, according
to this chart, "1654 & 1655 may probably prove miraculous
years."[47]

1654 was the year Ogilby published his illustrated Virgil
translation, which was a major event for him but not really
miraculous. Miraculous, to Ogilby and Ashmole, meant the
restoration of the monarchy. The *Virgil* seems to have been
part of that effort, but it did not lead on to much of a result
in 1655. Just the wretched failure of Penruddock's uprising.

Discovering subscription publishing

One feature of the horoscope was Mercury appearing in the
same house as the Sun, which could, to the optimistic mind,
suggest that any "new ways whereby to obtain wealth" would
be well rewarded. This he desperately needed, as once his
illustrated translation was published he had to finance himself
while learning Greek. So he set to work on a new way to
obtain wealth, one to which he had already been introduced
by the *Virgil* itself. His exclusive invitation-only group of
patrons could act as a basis for producing a new book that
would be simply a luxury piece of furniture, an ornament in
any ambitious or pretentious library, without any input from
Ogilby beyond the design of the book. He would invite the
Royalist nobility to subscribe, paying for their own plates.

It was a very new idea, but not entirely original. In fact
there was now emerging something that looks from a distance
like a Royalist Book Club. The antiquary William Dugdale
had successfully solicited his own circle of Royalist friends
to pay for plates in his history of the monasteries, *Monasticon
Anglicanum*, which appeared in 1655, and was preparing a

History of St Paul's Cathedral financed the same way for publication in 1658.[48] Dugdale's subscribers did not have much overlap with Ogilby's, however; his focus was essentially nostalgic. He described monasteries that were now extinguished, a cathedral that was now crumbling.

Ogilby's patrons were now asked to become subscribers. They were being invited to share not in a British past, like Dugdale's subscribers, but in the Roman imperial experience, and he set about the production of a Latin text of Virgil using the same glorious "sculptures" as the English version, with their dedications, printed on heavy paper with an appropriately imposing binding and gilt edging. It was published in 1658. There was no scholarly apparatus or explanation of Virgil's morality, just the wide-spaced text. The dedication was to William Wentworth, the son of the Earl of Strafford, his mighty, executed and attaindered patron. William Wentworth had been allowed to return from exile in 1652, taking an obligatory oath not to practise as a Catholic, and was apparently leading a quiet un-political life. This dedication was of a piece with the bland commercial purpose of the volume. Ogilby had no qualms about proudly reminding his readers (in Latin) of his service to the Earl. Here the subscription list was rather different from the club of patrons to the translation. Twenty-six of them did not appear in this volume; some simply could not afford it, some were not interested, a few were dead.

Ogilby retained control of the project and kept his secrets well. He managed not to appear in a single letter, diary or official document during the entire interregnum. There was certainly a need for concealment in 1658. Ormond made a secret visit to England (which had to be hurriedly terminated when it was betrayed) to see what prospect there was of a successful rising in conjunction with Spanish ships and troops gathered in Flanders. The conspiracy was discovered, guards were doubled, Dunkirk was besieged. The ships were destroyed by Cromwell's navy, and Dunkirk actually became a British possession in June.[49] In August, Ashmole's home was raided and his study ransacked by soldiers who claimed they were looking for the King.[50] Ashmole, like all Ogilby's trusted contacts, kept nothing incriminating. His "diary" was written up retrospectively, and contains just two mentions of Ogilby: the day they met and the day he died, with not a word about their relationship. The note of his death is quite striking, as one of only three deaths in the diary which omit any relationship to the deceased, such as "my old friend" or "my cousin". One of them was his closest friend, the astrologer Lilly. The other was Mrs Ogilby, the year after her husband. Ogilby was evidently close to Ashmole, but Ashmole kept anything which might give away Ogilby's connections to Airlie, and to royalist subterfuge, well hidden.

By inviting his patrons to re-subscribe for a patently non-political Virgil, removing or losing dedications to some of the most notorious plotters such as Courtenay, Grenville and Thornhill and then replacing their names on the plates with some very unexceptional wealthy people, Ogilby may have been providing some cover of innocence to them all. But the need for conspiracy would soon evaporate. It was not a viable long-term business plan.

The invention of crowd-funding

Ogilby's efforts were obviously pretty fully bent on completing and publishing his translation of the *Iliad*. As he moved on from mastering the language to completing the translation, he was faced with the problem of funding what he knew had to be a luxury volume produced to the same very high standard as his *Virgil*. The difficulty was the cost, which he reckoned at an astonishing £5,000.[51] He did not have that kind of money, and there was no reason why most of the core funders of the Virgils would want to cough up for this.

The Lord Protector, Oliver Cromwell, died on 3 September 1658. His son Richard succeeded him, but it was clear that this pseudo-monarchy was dissolving. A new Parliament was elected to resolve the government's crippling debt problems, and it was a much less hard-line Puritan body than the last. It included moderate Presbyterians and a number of crypto-Royalists. It also had a restored House of Lords, though as no one could agree on its name it was now called "the Other House". Richard Cromwell was no military man and the army, convinced that this new Parliament would abandon them, first threw out the Parliament and then threw out the new Lord Protector. "Tumbledown Dick" went home, and then wandered off to France incognito.

It was time for the principle of subscription to be opened to a wider public, people who would support a book for its own sake rather than as a covert commitment to a cause. This was how a great Polyglot Bible had been published in three volumes, from 1652 to 1657, and that had worked. So Ogilby went public, putting out an appeal for people to subscribe to have their names on plates in the book. He explained that each "sculpture" would cost him at least £10, and for £12 paid in instalments a subscriber could take an interest and be named on plates in two proposed books, the *Iliads* and the *Odysses*. If they preferred to spend less and forego the plate, they could subscribe £6 as Acquaintances.[52]

The result was not as successful as he needed. It is obvious that the Virgil finance was not given to him for purely bibliophile reasons. In 1651, when he gathered his original hundred patrons together, he had no track-record as a luxury publisher – just the *Aesop*, which was not of the highest quality as a physical production. Yet now that he was at the top of his game as a publisher, and his work was known to be unrivalled, only forty-seven people paid for plates in the *Iliads*. This book of around 600 pages is less illustrated than he must have hoped, and the payments for plates barely covered their costs, leaving a great deal to be covered by conventional sales.

Just nine of the subscribers were from his original exclusive list of Virgil supporters; they included Strafford's son and daughters. There was also James Compton, who had not only been one of the Sealed Knot but was also a great bibliophile and patron of actors and playwrights, the poet Thomas Stanley and Edward Bysshe, the Garter King of Arms. The Seymours were not backing it, and without them the only really major supporter who remained with him was Anthony Ashley-Cooper. Ashley-Cooper was one of the key players in bringing about the return of Charles, and would become one of the small group who would run the country for him. This was a very important connection for Ogilby.

Ten of the people who had been brought in to replace missing subscribers to the Latin Virgil of 1658 also bought into Homer; and then there were twenty-eight new people taking an "Interest". The most significant by far was Ormond, one of Charles' small group of advisers in his negotiations for the throne. With Ormond and Ashley-Cooper as his enduring patrons, Ogilby was very well placed to know in what direction the political winds were blowing. His dedication to the new king makes it clear that he was bringing the *Iliads* out ahead of Charles' return, which happened in May 1660. It was probably published in March, when the Long Parliament was dissolved. That was when even the old hard-line Puritan William Prynne, who had condemned dancing, royal actresses and Christmas, and had his ears cropped, called for a restoration of the monarchy. Ogilby refers to the caretaker figure of General Monck, who now controlled the sequence of events, as "the Harbinger of You", saying "we are cheered into a Belief, that we shall again see a glorious Day of peacefull Serenity". Ogilby had gone into Ireland when Charles was three years old, and had never been in his presence. He seems to have intended the publication as a letter of introduction and recommendation to the returning sovereign.

Some of the people buying space in the book were evidently riding piggy-back on this opportunity. The dedication plate of John Denham, for instance, gives his title not as a Count or Baron but as "Regiori Operum Praefecto & Curatori Generali", a strange construction which probably means Surveyor-General of the King's Works. This book was published before the King had been allowed to land, and when the Surveyor of Works was a Parliament appointee, John Embree. Denham maintained that he had been appointed to the role by Charles in 1649, when he was with the exiled court at St Germain; there was now a competition for the job involving heavy-duty lobbying. The function of this plate, in a volume which was clearly intended to be presented to the restored King on his arrival, was to stake his claim. It evidently worked. Denham, who had no particular competence in building work, was appointed in June 1660.

John Ogilby was sufficiently well placed to know what would happen next, and so discreet about his sources, that he seemed to be driven by "a prophetic spirit". That was John Aubrey's sly interpretation of his decision early in 1660, "foreseeing the restauration of king Charles II, and also the want there might be of Church Bibles" to produce the largest and most beautiful edition of the King James Bible yet seen. This had already been published in 1659 by Frank Field, printer to the University of Cambridge, sponsored by the Vice-Chancellor, the Master of Jesus College. It had not sold. Ogilby, who may have known Field from his stay in Cambridge, simply bought it up and hurriedly added some plates from Hollar and some bought in from an Amsterdam publisher. He must have got it for a song. The printer had already been paid by his sponsor and seems to have become aware at a surprisingly early date that his Puritan copyright would soon become worthless and that the book's sponsor was about to be sacked from his Mastership. Only a very suspicious person would think that Ogilby was advising him. Ogilby later explained that this acquisition was not opportunism or insider dealing, but a pious sacrifice: as he was "dressing" his own books with

> all the Splendor and Ostentation that could be, I thought it also Religious, and the part of a good Christian, to do something for God's sake, to adorn in like manner, with Ornamental Accomplishments, the Holy Bible, which by my own sole Conduct, proper Cost and Charges, at last appear'd the largest and fairest Edition that was ever yet set forth in any Vulgar Tongue.[53]

He had it ready for presentation to Charles on his arrival.

Charles landed on 25 May, and arrived in London on the 29th. He immediately began distributing goodies to his supporters, though usually goodies that did not cost him much directly. Ogilby's good friend Ashmole, for instance, whose diary is normally so very reticent, suddenly bubbles and fizzes with the excitement of rewards. He was introduced to Charles on 6 June, and twelve days later saw him again and was made

Windsor Herald. Four days after that he was installed in Henry VIII's closet in Whitehall. In September he was given the Comptroller's Office in the Excise, overseeing customs duties, which were a significant part of Charles' income. He may have been chosen as being less likely to plunder the office than most other people, though he was aggressive in pursuit of his own interests. The Ashmolean Museum is based on his collection (for which he demanded a grand building), which was itself partly wrested from the collection of John Tradescant. He fought and defeated Tradescant's widow for it at Chancery, leaving her ruined; she committed suicide.[54] Of course he did not have any understanding of accounting, and the Comptroller's office was simply a sinecure. An even less appropriate sinecure was handed to him the following February: "Secretary of Surinam in the West Indies". His diary note suggests that he had not known where Surinam was. He certainly never went there, but there was a small British colony there and therefore some income. He was also made one of the commissioners for recovering the King's goods, which was the one position handed to him which made some sense. As an antiquarian, he did actually know about the plundered royal treasures, their history and value. He may have been placed there to temper the aggressive counter-plundering undertaken by the existing Commissioners, who were tearing apart the houses of the Interregnum establishment searching for anything of value: they were entitled to 20% of whatever they "recovered", and it was becoming a problem.[55]

Ogilby might have hoped for some crumbs of his own from the royal table. He was making striking gifts. Both the *Iliads* and the Bible were big, heavy tomes. The Bible, in two massive volumes, was as difficult to shift in space as it was commercially. Seven years later Pepys refused to buy an as yet unbound copy from his bookseller on the grounds that it was simply too big to bother with.[56] It was also fantastically expensive, perhaps £25 before binding. In 1661 Ogilby presented a copy to the House of Commons which voted to pay him £50 but the Lord Treasurer refused to pay, insisting the money would have to come from the Privy Seal. He was not just missing out, he was being swindled! He appealed to the King, who immediately issued a warrant for the money.[57] Naturally other publishers were soon playing catch-up, and in 1661 Ogilby petitioned for all other illustrated bibles to be banned for ten years. That was never likely to be granted.

The *Iliads* is so forbidding that the British Library presented me with a trolley rather than leave me to stagger off with it. The translation is uninspired, more concerned with accuracy than memorable expression, and each page has its wide margins stocked with small print of scholarly exposition, like a copy of the Talmud. The whole book gives off a sense of quasi-religious awe, and it does feel as though he was placing it alongside the great King James Bible that he was producing simultaneously as another sacred pillar of British civilisation.

Master of the Royal Imprimerie

In his dedication to the King, Ogilby stressed that Homer had important lessons. First, this was a book to inspire conquering Emperors, and Alexander the Great had been illuminated by it, "by whose light he trac'd the way to universal Empire". He also pointed out that Homer is "a most constant Assertor of the Divine right of Princes and Monarchical Government". Ogilby was constantly working for the most absolutist form of monarchy, in the belief that this was the most natural and proper form of government.

The obvious model for this form of government was France, and King Charles II was more familiar with France than with England. From Ogilby's perspective, one striking feature of this centralised state was its control of the physical appearance of the printed page. In 1640, when the imagery of print on the page was being dominated by the Dutch Protestant presses and their elegant typefaces, Richelieu set up the Imprimerie Royale. The finest books, published with royal approval, carried the subliminal message of French royal supremacy in their very typeface, a new design used by a printer named Jannon. Jannon was a Protestant, like the Dutch printers, but he happened to be French. That, in Richelieu's eyes, made him the King's obedient subject and his font part of the national patrimony. He seized both. The printer ended up working in the Louvre and his punches and matrices are still in the care of the Imprimerie Nationale. The signature Dutch typeface was Garamond, which has a cool elegance that conveys clarity and reason. Jannon is very similar but less symmetrical, with more contrast in the letter strokes. It has a baroque authority that makes it most suitable for printing pages designed to impress. Of course it suited Ogilby perfectly, and he petitioned for the right to use the font. On 21 January 1661 his petition was granted. He clearly wanted Charles to establish an equivalent of the French Imprimerie, and his plan was evidently meant to be supported by his presentation of fine books to the newly arrived King. In fact he was given the title of Master of the Royal Imprimerie. It was a step on the road towards the absolutist, centralised British Imperium he expected, but it was a very tiny step. There was no actual Royal Press. There was no salary either. There was never much possibility of Ogilby's house becoming the home of government printing. He had, however, been able to connect himself to Charles' desire to be seen as having come into his own as a real monarch, a fellow to the ruler of France. If having a Royal Imprimerie was part of the role, Ogilby would represent it for him, and proudly used the title on his front pages.

The next question was what Ogilby could do in his project of promoting the natural and ancient order of society while making a decent living. A new subject matter beckoned. He had petitioned the King for and was granted the right for thirty-one years to print a series of mathematical works in Greek and Latin, including works by Euclid, Archimedes and Ptolemy.[58]

This did not mean that he was chasing a new kind of customer. It can be hard to appreciate that the division between arts and sciences that seems so totally natural today was completely absent in the seventeenth century. Science and mathematics were wonderfully exciting studies for anyone who wanted to understand the world better. The ancient world's understanding of cosmology was seen as worthless, and knowledge had to be built on new discoveries, but the question of whether the same applied to other branches of science was being urgently discussed, and the question was especially alive in the case of mathematics. There was no such person as "a mathematician"; everyone who was interested in rational argument had an equal right to be heard. One debate was whether mathematics was a science at all. Aristotle had said that scientific knowledge is based on understanding causality, but a mathematical proof is not a demonstration of cause and effect; a logical analysis can show that the angles in every triangle add up to 180 degrees, but that analysis is not the cause of the fact. So if mathematics is not a science, what is it?

Mathematics was being transformed by a combination of discovery and invention: Napier had discovered logarithms, and now complicated sums were calculated using "Napier's Bones", an early version of the slide-rule. That was how you could do arithmetic without knowing your tables. In fact the very concept of numbers was changing. Napier had developed and refined the use of the decimal point to represent fractions, and numbers were released from the straight-jacket of representing physical objects. Two-fifths was no longer written as two-of-five things (2/5) but as a number in its own right, 0.4. A new world was opening up every bit as exciting as one discovered across the oceans. Infinity had now been given its own mathematical symbol. Just as the telescope and microscope revealed a hidden cosmos of the infinitely great and the infinitesimally tiny, so new ways of writing down and thinking about numbers opened up an unexplored realm that stretched from concepts of infinity to calculations of the immeasurably small.

The inexpressible number "pi" was being calculated to a degree of refinement impossible with old-fashioned fractions. Newton would compute it to fifteen decimal places in 1666. Measurement using these new decimal-point numbers was creating abstract metaphors of the physical world in a purely theoretical space that could now be investigated. This was a far greater new world than America. Eventually we would all migrate there, leaving the old world of solid numbers and roman numerals in a dimly-remembered past. But in the mid-seventeenth century, it was a new, strange and exciting territory. Many people engaged in these challenging mental voyages were concerned that those who wanted to travel with them should have a good grounding in classical mathematics, because this was a study which really did build on the past in order to strike out to new horizons. The difficulty was that the original sources had undergone a transmission from antiquity that left them confused and corrupted. Modern translations aimed to improve them by re-writing what they said. A French Jesuit explained that "most of those who learn Euclid's Elements are frequently very dismayed because they don't understand the usefulness of the difficult propositions, ...: so I have thought it appropriate ... to make them as easy as I can. This has obliged me to change some demonstrations ...."[59]

In England, this work was being undertaken by Isaac Barrow, who Ogilby must have known and who was, in 1660, preparing an English translation of Euclid that people would be able to understand. Barrow had been a poor but brilliant young scholar studying classical and modern languages at Cambridge when Ogilby arrived there looking for help with his translation of Virgil. He was known as the leader of a group of Royalists there. He survived as a Cambridge fellow by pretending (not always successfully) that he was a Commonwealth supporter, but to become a fellow he had to take an oath to study divinity. To evade the obvious trap he turned that into a study of church history, leading to astronomy and on, naturally enough, to geometry. He was extraordinarily gifted in the new mathematics, inventing new techniques for computing infinitesimal fragments of shapes and laying the foundations for what would become Calculus. He was Newton's tutor, and when Newton eventually spoke about standing on the shoulders of giants, Barrow's powerful deltoids would have been in his mind. In 1655 he produced a simplified English primer on Euclid. It was printed by Frank Field, who Ogilby would be dealing with in 1660 as he acquired the great Bible which Field printed. He was well-placed to know that Barrow was planning a full-scale Euclid translation that year.

He may also have known of Barrow's plans from Heneage Finch, the 3rd Earl of Winchilsea, who was one of Ogilby's most committed supporters. Monck had installed Finch in Dover to welcome Charles to his kingdom, and then in October 1660 the Earl took his family off to the Ottoman Empire. He was a Cambridge man, with a strong interest in Classical literature, a courtier and then a Royalist plotter in the Interregnum. It would be surprising if, before his departure for Istanbul, he did not meet Isaac Barrow, who had been forced abroad in 1655 when he found that his political and religious views were too well understood for him to be allowed the Chair of Greek. Barrow had travelled across France and Italy to Constantinople, returning to England in 1659 after many genuinely exciting adventures. He was an obvious person for Finch to get to know to learn about Constantinople.

The English Euclid would have probably been a particularly attractive project for William Morgan to be involved with. Ogilby's step-grandson had finished his apprenticeship and had decided to stay in London rather than return to his mother's home in Wales. He had learned the mathematics, the mystery and the craft of clock-making, but his knowledge might well be better used helping Ogilby than devoted to clock-making. However, the mathematical texts project died when Ogilby was given a commission on the scale of a blockbuster movie. He was to write, produce and direct a coronation.

Life 8. The Pageant Master

Charles would need a coronation.

This was not the normal transfer of sovereign authority to a new ruler. The air that people breathed needed to be changed. The dry oxygen of Puritan utility had to be perfumed with the intoxicating magic of royalty, banished by the Commonwealth. This coronation had to conjure the convincing vision of monarchical authority restored. Authority is mysterious stuff. Its power does not flow from force or argument, though of course it uses both. It is built on the process of internalising the values of the ruler by the ruled. A king's subjects must believe in his right to be their ruler and in their own proper place as loyal and subordinate.

The great question which King Charles' standard-bearers had to face was how to make people know that his enthronement was not just one more revolution. There had been so many constitutional revolutions in a short while. In 1668 Thomas Hobbes wrote an incisive account of them called *Behemoth, or the Epitome of the Civil Wars of England*. Charles II forbade its publication. It takes the form of a dialogue between a student, who knows nothing, and an instructor who surveyed the whole panorama "as from the Devil's Mountain". To ensure that his pupil has taken in all he has explained, the instructor eventually sets his pupil a test:

> Seeing there had been so many shiftings of the supreme authority, I pray you, for memory's sake, repeat them briefly in times and order.

The student's response is impeccable, brisk and dizzying. He begins with the eight years, from 1640 to 1648, when sovereignty was "disputed between King Charles I and the Presbyterian Parliament", after which the King was executed, the House of Lords was shut and power was held by the Commons, in the Long Parliament, which ended in the hands of a faction called the Rump. The third holder of sovereignty, from 20 April to 4 July 1653, was a council of state set up by Cromwell. That was junked and replaced by Cromwell's parliament, "which was called, in contempt of one of the members, Barebone's Parliament". On 12 December supreme power was seized for the fifth time, when Cromwell became Protector. After his death the student enumerates how sovereignty was batted around six more times in two years:

> Sixthly, from September the 3rd 1658 to April the 25th 1659, Richard Cromwell had it as successor to his father.
> Seventhly, from April the 25th 1659 to May the 7th of the same year, it was nowhere.
> Eighthly, from May the 7th 1659, the Rump, which was turned out of doors in 1653, recovered it again;
> and shall lose it again to a committee of safety,
> and again recover it,
> and again lose it to the right owner.

The "Restoration" certainly looked like one more revolution of a gambling wheel, and there were many people who did not think the game had necessarily ended. In May 1660, one of the regicides, Edward Ludlow, said he found "the wheel to goe round soe fast" that he could not tell "where it might rest". It was Ogilby's job to change that. Another public figure wrote privately about a compass-needle spinning round and repeating its directions, "and who knowes not wither this dance may not like others end in the same measure they began".[1] It was time for the old dancing master to step forward.

Charles and his brother James had seen this problem addressed and brilliantly managed when Louis XIV reclaimed his rule in Paris. The monarch had not been decapitated but as a young boy he had been forced to flee with his mother, the regent, while France disintegrated. When Charles and James were refugees in Paris, Louis was unable to enter the city. In 1653 he reached fourteen years old, attaining his majority; his commander won a victory under the city walls, and he rode in to claim his throne there. He was met by popular celebrations, and then something had to be done to create the magic of monarchy around him, to spin France into its place in a cosmos where royal power was absolute. What was done there, amazingly, was a dance.

This was not just any dance, but a dance never seen before, a work of genius performed by the French and English courts in harmony. *Le Ballet Royale de la Nuit* was a show performed in the Louvre on 23 February 1653, beginning at dusk and lasting the whole night, thirteen hours. It was not a masque and had no story, but it did carry the narrative of a masque. It displayed, in forty-five scenes with astonishing costumes, the entire range of French society in the metaphysical structure of a night, the long descent into darkness, chaos and malignancy that would in England be presented as an ante-masque, and then the inevitable victory of the shining light of day. The glorious final triumph, personified by Apollo, the Sun, was Louis dancing in a golden head-dress. James, Duke of York, danced the spirit of Honour. As day broke, at the end of this magnificent quasi-religious performance, the new cosmography of France was born, in harmony with the whole cosmos, under the absolute and benevolent authority of its dancing boy-king, Le Roi Soleil. It was repeated five times in the next ten days, in a phenomenal test of stamina.

Louis had needed to throw fairy-dust into the eyes of the court and the nobility, because that was where royal authority had broken down. His target was not the population at large, who generally retained their attachment to the mystery of monarchy while blaming all evils on the monarch's advisers and their local seigneurs. He did not trouble with an expensive coronation, and settled for a very unobtrusive religious ceremony. His concern was to make the nobility worship him, and he went on to corral them in a new pen which he called the palace of Versailles.

Charles did not have to spin a web around the nobility of England; they were his loyal cavaliers. He needed to dazzle London. James I had never doubted that the city was crucial to his rule; that was why he had come to the Merchant Taylors when Ogilby was a schoolboy there. But Charles I had watched London turn against him and become a Puritan stronghold. What was needed now was not a dance but a coronation that would literally take over the city and inspire it with the vision of monarchy. It would do the job of the *Ballet de la Nuit*, but for a far greater public, on a much larger scale. London under the Commonwealth had come to dominate the nation, and once London was seduced, England would be secure.

Ogilby was given the job by a special committee of the Common Council of London set up to run this operation.[2] His

task was to turn Charles' progress from the Tower of London to
Whitehall leading up to the ceremony on St George's Day into
a memorably potent national experience that would snuff out
any idea that there could be any more alterations to sovereignty.
Of course Charles himself took a very close interest in how this
would happen. Everything Ogilby would do had to be approved
by the King, who had to have complete confidence in him. The
smallest miscalculation could pull the rug from under the "restoration". On the surface, England was awash with enthusiasm for
its King, but there were many people at every level of society
who profoundly regretted the collapse of the nation's great
experiment with moral democracy. That obviously included
many thousands of officers and soldiers of the New Model
Army, which had been the idealistic driving force behind Puritan
government. In December, they had been banished twenty miles
from London unless they had legitimate business there, and the
banishment was re-stated for the coronation.[3] So Ogilby dared
not get this wrong. He also dared not play it safe.

He was now well known as an authority on classical epics,
but that does not explain why he was thought to be the
right man for this job. It must have helped that he had been
responsible for ceremonials at Wentworth's court in Dublin
and had created and run his own theatre there, writing some
of the material himself. But it was his work and contacts after
Wentworth's fall that must have been the convincing factor.
Charles' closest advisers included Ormond, who knew Ogilby
very well, and John Grenville, who played a central role in
negotiating the restoration and was a patron of Ogilby's *Virgil*.
He was trusted by some of the most powerful men around the
King, and was in their confidence. Ogilby was known to them
as the man who combined theatrical and poetic expertise
with a very specific vision of the ideal monarchy, and who

obviously had the skills to present and propagandise that in a way that would connect with a large audience. So he was brought to Charles' notice and put to work.

The procession

The cavalcade which Charles required was meant to be mind-blowing. Wenceslaus Hollar's depiction of it as a strip drawing covers five double pages, four strips to a page.[4] It begins with two hundred horse guards, riding five abreast, followed by eight hundred mounted courtiers, judges and aristocrats, and another thousand lesser nobility, attendants, footmen and guards who were walking. Hollar seems to have lost the will to draw after the twelfth strip, in which he tried to depict fifty-one barons. By the time he got to "Earls in number 31" he just stuck in two riders in a bunch of less impressive pedestrians. Charles appears in the twentieth and final strip, the only rider in a forest of halberds (axe-headed pikes) carried by Gentleman Pensioners and Equerries and the Yeomen of the Guard. The endless black-and-white miniature figures indicate the fantastic scale of the cavalcade but of course completely fail to convey its noise (trumpeters and drummers, horses and crowds) and the dazzling display of golden and bejewelled costumes and harness. The entire route right through London was freshly gravelled and decorated with tapestries and banners. Conduits and fountains ran with wine. Flamboyance, extravagance, the celebration of apparently limitless luxury and power, made a deliberate contrast with the age of Puritan democratic restraint that was now so clearly ended. One Duke's horse harness was set with an estimated £8,000 worth of pearls and diamonds, and the Duke of Buckingham's costume was said to cost £30,000. How you spend the equivalent of tens of millions of pounds on a suit of clothes is hard to grasp. All that glittered may not have been gold, but that was because it was silver, diamonds and precious stones. Pepys said that the procession was so dazzling that it was sometimes impossible to watch.[5]

But a procession, no matter how spectacular, was not sufficient to install a new and permanent constitution in the national psyche. The challenge was how to transform the procession into something with a compelling transcendental resonance, with very little time to invent and prepare what would be done. The King announced his processional route on 9 February 1661. He would be crowned on St George's Day, 23 April, and the procession would be the day before. Ogilby had ten weeks to invent, script, design, build, cast and rehearse a theatrical spectacular unlike any other. It was a triumph of logistics, man-management, artistic invention and the super-lative self-confidence of a sixty-year-old in full song. Pepys said he was "sure never to see the like again in this world",[6] and Clarendon that "the whole Show was the most glorious in the Order and Expense, that had ever been seen in England".[7] Like any good showman, the organiser devised a souvenir programme which could be bought on the day, and which included a list of credits for the heads of the technical depart-ments including carpentry, joinery and the music. They were said, in a spirit of confident prophecy, to have "performed all to Admiration, and, considering the Shortness of the Warning, much beyond what could have been imagined".[8]

Arches

The dynastic Catholic rulers of Renaissance Europe had occasionally been installed in some major city by a *joyeuse entrée*, a procession which imitated a Roman triumph and which was intended to overwhelm the population by the splendour of its pageantry, moving though hastily-erected grand-looking wood and plaster arches decorated with symbolic figures and surrounded by poetical performances. It was a grand flowering of the Renaissance pomp of Catholic dynastic ambition. This device had appeared in London for James I's coronation in 1604,[9] when seven prettily and elaborately decorated arches were erected on the coronation route where music and entertainments were performed without any particular common theme beyond the celebration of the event. The arches, fifty feet high, were flamboyant and delightful, quintessentially Elizabethan. One had on its top a model of the city. James hated the whole day. Charles I had declined any such event in London, but he did have to attend one in Edinburgh, when he went to be crowned King of Scotland in June 1633. A poet was engaged to help design this and write speeches to be performed. Seven rather sober arches and staging-posts were erected, less ambitious than London's in 1604, and a series of performers, some playing symbolic characters such as Caledonia and Planets, kings and worthies, performed set-pieces which were intended to flatter and honour the King while setting out a narrative to educate him.[10] He was told to make passion yield to reason's doom, not to raise up any "paranymph" who might attract him by a "frizl'd leape, quaint pace or painted face", and was generally welcomed into the grave delights of a Calvinist utopia. It was as much about Edinburgh as about the King. This audience was unlikely to be awestruck by the power of majesty, and if they had been, the organisers might have felt that things had not gone quite right.

But the power of majesty and the majesty of power was now going to blow everyone away. Ogilby decided at once that his show would be based around four arches which would be consciously classical in design, and whose decorations would be allegorical arguments so dense that the general audience would know that beneath the breathtaking, dazzling surface were profundities understood only by their rulers. The central idea was to connect the King's procession with what he saw as the original source of celebratory arches, the triumph of a victorious Roman Emperor. That, he explained at the very start of his two books about the event, was the starting-point and meaning of what was being done. This was not to be understood as an event which was local in space or time. It was proclaimed as a re-appearance of the imperial power of antiquity, resonating forward to a respectful posterity. The obvious difference between London's arches and Rome's, as he saw it, was that these were only temporary and "by reason of the shortness of Time" were wood and plaster instead of marble, but these arches "far exceed theirs" in number and "stupendious Proportions". In fact they were so "stupendious" that each was a great monument and a theatrical space in its own right, a hundred feet high and with room for up to forty performers and musicians.

The architecture which "far exceeded" Rome's was credited to the city surveyor and "another Person, who desires to have his Name conceal'd". This mysterious character was Sir Balthazar Gerbier, a Dutch art agent, miniature painter, secret agent, double agent and jobbing architect who would not have been anyone's natural choice as a creative artist. He had briefly been Charles I's Master of Ceremonies in 1641, but was so obviously duplicitous that he ended up fleeing to France after two years and staying there until the Commonwealth. He then set up a school of espionage in London in 1649 ("horsemanship, foreign languages, cosmography, and the construction of military fortifications") which collapsed in a year. Pepys said one of his books was "not worth a turd".[11] Sir Balthazar had been an anti-monarchist who preferred to keep his head below the parapet even after the parapet had collapsed. He wrote *The None-Such Charles his Character* (1651), an attack on the King and his purchase of "old rotten pictures", but kept his name secret. He then took advantage of the looting of the "rotten pictures" to pick up Van Dyck's "Equestrian Portrait of Charles I" and Titian's "Charles V with a Hound" and turn a quick profit. He had been a hopeless Commonwealth spy and in 1659 went on a gold-hunting expedition to Guinea. His daughter was murdered in a mutiny in May 1660 and he came back to Europe complaining that he was the victim of a conspiracy. So what did Sir Balthazar Gerbier have to offer? The answer was a wonderful illustrated volume showing a pageant designed by his close friend Peter Paul Rubens. Gerbier had hosted Rubens for nine months in London, and had access to the artist's designs for the arches, facades and gateways which he had created for Archduke Ferdinand's entry into Antwerp in 1635. Gerbier could not be seen to work on the coronation without proclaiming himself a hypocrite, but he was desperate for money and Ogilby needed access to Rubens' designs.[12]

The Rubens pageant had been a rather grim, if extremely expensive, mask over a very tough reality. Ferdinand, who was essentially a prince of the Church rather than a war-lord, had been driven by the force of circumstances into leading his own army through the middle of the Thirty Years' War in 1633, and by dint of his sheer obstinacy and faith had won astonishing victories, effectively annihilating the Protestant army of Sweden and taking a number of important cities including Antwerp. The city into which he made his *Joyeuse*

Entrée had once been the greatest centre of wealth in northern Europe. Now it was a desolate ruin, its river, the Scheldt, was blockaded, grass grew in once busy streets. Rubens certainly portrayed a vision of dynastic power linked into a cosmic destiny, but his arches also presented unhappy images that spoke of a depressed present and a frightening future. In an act of desperate lobbying by the city fathers, near the end of the procession Ferdinand was shown the female image of the city begging for help as she was abandoned by the god of commerce.[13] But for Ogilby the point was not the allegory used on Rubens' arches, but their structure. Those arches were built not just for passing through, but as gigantic performance spaces.[14] That was what he needed for London.

The procession was just part of the event. It was "the Entertainment" of the King, and this Entertainment was conceived in a different way from that presented for earlier Stuarts. This was a single coherent narrative performed as a five-act drama, a platform performance with the audience (the King) moving from one arch-shaped theatrical space to the next and ending the next day with the coronation itself. Ogilby was re-creating the Continental pageant on a new footing. Charles did not appear as a great prince bringing his glory into a city that he now owned – the Entry into Antwerp was just that – but as a king taking his place on a waiting and proffered throne. This was a neat sleight of hand. Londoners would see the story being performed not as the projection of dynastic power over a city, but of the city's authority over a kingdom in the royal name. Charles was assuming his seat at the centre of a national empire reaching over all Britain and the surrounding ocean. The subject of this play was the story of a new Augustus come into his proper and divinely ordained imperial inheritance, centred on the prosperity of London and the loyalty of his subjects. Every aspect of the pageant was part of a flamboyant visual demonstration of the spiritual order being put back into balance, so that political action would have meaning and authority. This was the mother of all masques, in which human affairs were once more harmonised with natural law through the transcendent power of majesty. The thunderstorm which happened to erupt at the close was proclaimed as heavenly applause, the eruption of approbation from a cosmos as engaged by this ceremony as the meanest member of the audience.[15]

The first four acts of this pageant-drama were on arch-stages spaced out over a mile, right through the City, and cost £10,000. The ordinary public, like Samuel Pepys, could watch and be astounded by the lavish brilliance that passed before them, and be impressed (or depressed) by it. For them it would have to be enough to sense that something amazing was happening around them, and that they were part of it. The Restoration that Ogilby was demonstrating, and that the population had to enthusiastically embrace, was not a restoration of Charles. What was restored, according to this show, was a golden age of royal rule and British identity. Proper rule was back, and with it came the old festive calendar. Tomorrow was St George's Day, and the King was St George. Mayday and Christmas would follow. The world that had been turned upside down had been righted. But the full experience that Ogilby had constructed was invisible to those watching from a single vantage point. It was, as with a masque, designed to be seen by the King. The only way the rest of the population would learn the narrative of the Entertainment was by buying the programme.

As in a masque, the audience were by their very presence also participants. As in a masque, the most noble attendees had the most glamorous roles and the speaking parts were taken by professionals. A masque normally began with an "anti-masque", the presentation of a world ruled by chaos and disorder. That was how the procession's story unfolded. After the cavalcade passed one group of singers on a stage and another on a specially constructed balcony they arrived at the first gigantic arch, where a woman portraying Rebellion, in a torn crimson robe covered with snakes and serpents, was mounted on a many-headed hydra. She had a crown of fire, a bloody sword and a magic wand, and was accompanied by Confusion, a twisted and deformed hag in tatters, crowned with ruined castles. Eighteen drummers and thirty trumpeters proclaimed the start of the play – so startlingly that the Duke of York's horse threw him twice and Charles had to invoke Health and Safety and have the volume turned down. A wind ensemble and ten actresses took over, two of whom, Rebellion and Monarchy, had speaking parts. The movement of the King around the Arch brought a transformation from Rebellion and Confusion by way of the Royal Oak in which Charles had been secreted after the Battle of Worcester, through the appearance of Loyalty to his landing and acclamation, labelled (in Latin) *The Arrival of Augustus*. Rebellion and Confusion were routed, and the King was able to pass through the arch and begin his Coronation progress. Rebellion was banished to the stygian depths:

> Must He enter, and a King be Crown'd?
> Then, as He riseth, sink we under Ground.

The arch was decorated with a trophy of decapitated heads, including a representation of Cromwell. Surviving regicides had been executed in October, and Cromwell had been dug up and his head put on display. It is a very recent sensibility that finds such displays barbarous; his head was kept as a memento for centuries.

The whole show was heavily buttered with quotations from and references to Virgil and his narrative of inevitable imperial authority. Rebellion is Satanic, Charles is Aeneas founding Rome, and his entrance is also presented as the modern equivalent of Augustus' return to the city after the defeat of his father's (Julius Caesar's) murderers.[16] The combination of messianic and golden-age images with the conflation of Charles as Saint George destroying the dragon that was the Rump Parliament added up to a powerful rhetorical message that did not need to be much explained to work on the public. They were jammed into place on the processional route, so they had no vision of how the images worked together, but they were then free to examine these huge structures for a year afterwards.

Above that first arch, standing on sky-high pedestals, were statues of James I and Charles I labelled not "King James" and "King Charles" but as divine beings – "DIVO JACOBO" and "DIVO CAROLO". This was, Ogilby explained, in imitation of the Roman tradition of recognising dead emperors as gods. He quotes Seneca on Augustus, "Made by his son's great Piety a God".[17] In the middle, highest of all, was Charles II, with a list of attributes in Latin (Emperor of Britain, Greatest of the Best, Destroyer of Tyranny and so on), ending SPQL. Roman state inscriptions and the standards of the legions carried the legend SPQR, meaning Senatus Populusque Romanus, The Senate and People of Rome. Under Augustus and his successors, this was of course a cypher for the absolute power of the Emperor. SPQL meant that London was the new Rome.

The procession moved on, past the white-clad nymphs and seven trumpets of Cornhill, and various other performances including a boy dressed as an Indian on a camel, "led out by two Black-Moors, and other attendants" who scattered jewels, silks and spices among the spectators and recited a loyal offering of the East India Company.

That naturally led to the next set, the arch of Naval power. On one side stood Father Thames, on the other the deck of a ship with sailors, and the story here was of Charles as the British Neptune, Emperor of the Seas. Pepys, Treasurer of the Navy, sat overlooking it. As with the first arch, Ogilby's text is a dense mass of classical references which embed Charles in the authority of antiquity. The imagery of this arch is the richest of the four, and it takes far more space in his description than the others. It is an attempt to create a visual, speaking and singing encyclopaedia a hundred feet high that combines the projection of global power, commerce and the arts and sciences in a single bewildering performance. The performers and pictures were teachings on different systems of representing numbers, the attributes of the world's conti-nents and London's trade as well as geometry, cosmology and music, all dominated by the assertion of King Charles' natural right to command the seas. Perhaps the only part that was immediately comprehensible for less cultured citizens was the blood-curdling song of the "sailors" on one side of the arch, who lustily celebrated unspecified triumphs over Turks and Belgians "Till their scuppers ran with Gore". The funda-mental message was of enthusiasm for "trade" enjoyed as a delight in plunder on the King's behalf:

King Charles. King Charles, Great Neptune of the Main!
The Royal Navy rig,

And We'll care not a Fig
For France, for France, the Netherlands, nor Spain.
The Turk, who looks so big,
We'll whip him like a Gig
About the Mediterrane;
His Gallies all junk, or ta'ne.
We'll seize on their Goods, and their Monies ...

By now it was clear that the Puritan notion of political order
as a Commonwealth answerable to Biblical authority and the
individual conscience had been replaced by royal absolutism,
the celebration of loot and the glorification of power. This
modern celebration of Charles' progress to the sacrament of
his coronation was untroubled by any reference to religion.
Virgil, not the Bible, was the sacred text of this drama, and
significance was expressed in luxurious display, not humility
or moral worth.

It is true that the third arch represented a religious structure,
but the religion was not Christianity. This was the Temple of
the Roman goddess of Concord. The arch was dominated by
a three-headed giant combining symbols of England, Scotland
and Ireland. Inside the arch were a dozen performers and two
dozen violins, and there was still room for the whole procession
to pass through, enjoying a musical and poetic celebration of,
and thanksgiving for, the suppression of war in the three
kingdoms. The very existence of these entertainments was
an important part of the theme of Restoration. Theatre
and music had been outcast and suppressed by Puritan
government, and performances had only been possible in
discreet private homes.[18] Now pretty well every professional
musician in London was needed for this very public show, as
were a significant number of theatrical performers. It seemed

that they could only be seen and flourish when there was a king, and the closest thing to a Christian message in the whole entertainment was the celebration of Charles as a royal messiah:

> Comes not here the King of Peace,
> Who, the Stars so long fore-told,
> From all Woes should us release,
> Converting Iron-times to Gold?

On went the procession, past probably its least impressive show, the figure of Temperance, "mixing Water and Wine". Untypically, Ogilby seems unable to explain what it is doing there. Intemperate extravagance was restored with the presentation of a thousand pounds of gold to the King, and the procession moved happily on through lines of musical performance to the final arch, the "Garden of Plenty". This was dominated by images of Bacchus, the god of wine, and Ceres, the goddess of harvest abundance. Here the King took possession of a land of fertility as the spring arrived after a grim winter, again with musical performances. The "paranymphs" that had been denounced to his father's face in the Edinburgh coronation had been practising their frizl'd leapes and quaint paces, and were smiling seductively with their painted faces. Presbyterian rule was over. As the procession moved on through Temple Bar, leaving the City on its way towards Whitehall, it passed a display of wild and domestic animals with living statues and more music. The whole journey, just over four miles long, took an exhausting five hours.

The final act of this drama was the next day, the Coronation itself, and the man who would manage the staging of that was one of Ogilby's Homer subscribers, John Denham. It was Denham's job to arrange the throne-building and other construction work, such as paving Westminster Hall, that was needed for the formal religious and feasting ritual of Coronation.[19] For his essentially practical and relatively small-scale work, this high-rolling syphilitic jolly court playboy was made a Knight of the Bath, just one order of chivalry below a Knight of the Garter. The Bath was the only order whose members marched by right in the Coronation procession, ranking just below the Knights-Marshal. Ogilby, on the other hand, received no honour at all, not even a simple knighthood. Yet he had a far more significant, far more creative and indeed astonishing role. He had just one day to make the Coronation into unforgettable magic. He was in charge of "the poetical part" of the event, and had the whole of London as his theatre. Ogilby would never be a courtier, or even much of a gentleman. He was entitled to the Ogilvie arms, but he was in trade, a book publisher with a shop in his home. That was not the kind of man who could ever be received at court except as a petitioner. His talents and value were understood well enough, but his reward would have to come in other ways.

The Common Council of London had the Chamberlain pay "Mr. John Olgleby the poet" a hundred pounds for composing the speeches, songs and inscriptions, along with a payment of nearly £10 to his step-grandson, William Morgan, for acting as his assistant. But the most significant reward would come from his souvenir programme, and then from the large well illustrated commemorative version which he brought out the following year. This was closely modelled on the volume produced for the Antwerp entry, the *Pompa Introitus Ferdinand*, which he had probably got from Gerbier. It was a dramatic expansion from the 32 pages of his original text to a large volume with 165 pages on the procession, plus a substantial description of the actual coronation provided by Ashmole, now the Windsor Herald. This led to a degree of conflict with the new Garter King at Arms, Edward Walker, and Ogilby was ordered by the King to let Walker oversee and correct that part of the text. The book itself was more a lavish compendium than an account; the original 1661 book was subsumed into it, and people were evidently able to have whatever relevant illustrations and inscriptions they wanted bound into it. But the main point was that Ogilby was given royal protection of his copyright in it.

From the perspective of the Ogilvie clan, the (re)-adoption of John Ogilby had served its purpose. The Marquess of Argyll, their hated enemy, was put on trial for high treason in 1661, and just when it seemed he was about to be acquitted for lack of evidence, a bundle of letters suddenly appeared which removed his defence and his head.

The old order had been restored, and the clan no longer needed John. But, in any case, he had his sights set elsewhere. Master of the Revels in Ireland.

Master of the Revels

In May 2012, the first purpose-built Restoration theatre in Britain re-opened to the public after being dark for 225 years. This was where plays of Goldsmith and Sheridan first appeared, where Garrick played Hamlet, where the first production was seen of a British play written by a woman. It was the second theatre built by John Ogilby, whose contribution has only recently begun to be properly recognised. For a while utterly forgotten except by a few antiquarians and theatre historians, Smock Alley theatre has now been brought back to life. Like Ogilby's first theatre, it was built in

Dublin. If the city is today associated with a great theatrical tradition, that has something to do with this surprising man whom Charles II re-appointed in 1661 to the position of Master of the Revels in Ireland. He was not supposed to have the job. Charles had already given it to William Davenant in November 1660.

Davenant had led a surprising life since he had penned the encomium for Ogilby's *Aesop* in the Tower. Instead of being tried for treason, John Milton negotiated his release, and he was pardoned in 1654. Poets in the Civil War have an admirable record of saving each other from execution irrespective of their allegiances.

Remarkably, Davenant then set up a private theatre in a room of his house in London, producing new plays by Royalist writers including himself. He put together a company there which put on the first opera in England, *The Siege of Rhodes*. This theatre was run as a business; he managed to get permission for the show from Cromwell's Puritan government by saying it was an evening of "recitative music", and probably used some of the very expensive ticket money to grease some palms. It was an extraordinarily innovative production with five composers working on Davenant's text and with a performance by a respectable married lady with a good singing voice, Mrs Coleman. Enthusiastic theatre historians now describe her as England's first professional actress, though this seems to have been her only performance. The French actresses who had made an appearance in the days of Charles I had been booed off stage.

The show's originality was not limited to the presence of Mrs Coleman. Davenant was a key figure in theatre's shift from Shakespeare's world of medieval all-male performance on bare boards with very basic costumes, a few props and no scenery, into a space inspired by the vision of the masque with elaborate costume design and mechanically operated changeable sets. Davenant had written masques himself and the scenery for *The Siege* was designed by one of Inigo Jones' pupils. The play's entry in the Stationers' Register calls it "a mask".[20] This was a place where female performers were very properly present. There was painted, moveable scenery, with five separate sets including the fleet of Suleiman the Magnificent, with painted side flats creating perspective and hanging borders above the stage. The show was entirely contained within a proscenium arch. Up to now a theatre had been a galleried public open space, the "wooden O" which could as easily be a cockpit or a bear-baiting display, or else a simple indoor platform facing benches and galleries, with some of the audience on stools on the stage. This was now replaced by Davenant's closed-off and expensive pictorial show which kept the audience and players in different worlds. Here a glamorised and heightened vision of events in a distant place and time was brought alive before the audience's very eyes, with the emphasis on vision. This was a new entertainment that combined the narrative energy of theatre with the staging techniques that had been used in masques, all for a wealthy paying audience. After the restoration Davenant was ready to go public with it and make some serious money.

In August 1660, he was granted a renewal of his unworkable patent to set up a theatre, but under very different, post-Puritan circumstances. Before the Commonwealth, playhouses, plays and performers had been licensed by the Master of the Revels, and the old Master, Sir Henry Herbert, was quickly re-appointed in June 1660. But then Charles decided to exert a far more direct control over theatre. He was familiar with the French system, in which there was a court theatre under the direct control of the King. That would not be realistic in England, but he could and did control who would run theatres. He limited the number of patents to just two: one for Thomas Killigrew, who was effectively his court jester, and the other for Davenant. Both were authorised to use scenery. The Royal Warrant was issued in August, and immediately created an obvious conflict of powers with the Master of the Revels. It is probably for that reason that Davenant applied for, and was granted, the position of Master of the Revels in Ireland, where Sir Henry's writ did not extend. It was perhaps just a precautionary measure by a shrewd businessman/courtier. He was now fully occupied, as was Killigrew, in building and establishing their new scenic theatres in London. There is no sign that Davenant ever intended to build a theatre in Ireland, a country he had never visited.

Ogilby had originally been given the title of Master of the Revels in Ireland by Strafford, of course, but that was not a royal patent, just the Lord Lieutenant acting as a viceroy. That grant had become meaningless with the destruction of the Werburgh Street theatre. Ogilby was now busy with his plans for expanding his publishing operation. Why would he want to engage with Ireland again? It would require a substantial investment of money that he did not have, and Dublin was a very insecure place with a host of bad memories. Cromwell had, of course, turned Ireland into a republic. It had been effectively controlled by one of his sons, Henry, and after Oliver's death Henry became governor-general under his brother Richard. He quit after Richard's fall and there was a confused struggle for control of Dublin Castle which ended with it being taken by Royalists. Charles was not declared King of Ireland until May 1661, six months after Davenant's appointment. Monck had been made Lord Lieutenant, but did nothing to take up the post. There was still a question in English minds about whether Ireland was at peace, and there were constant stories flying around of plots and rebellions, fuelled by enthusiastic forgers.

But Ogilby had stayed in Ireland for as long as he could possibly cling on there, and he clearly decided that he wanted to return. Back in 1641, when his theatre had been destroyed, he preferred the sadness and danger of Dublin to the life of an unwanted dancing master in England. Now he at least had some kind of celebrity in London, but he might have felt less enthusiastic to leave if that had been reflected in the grant of a title. He felt the pull of Dublin, a city where he evidently believed he could live a larger life, and so Davenant needed to be dispossessed of "his" title. He addressed himself to the King in tones of genuine hurt:

> Your petitioner had a graunt from the Right Honourable Thomas Earle of Strafford then Lieutenant of Ireland for the enjoying and executing the place and office of the Master of the Revells of that kingdom which after his great preparations and disbursements in building a new Theatre, stocking and bringing over a Company of Actors and Musitians and settling them in Dublin fell to utter rueine by the Calamities of those times to the utter undoieng (by the Damage of Two Thousand Pounds att lest) of your petitioner.[21]

He firmly requested that Davenant's "pretences" should be put aside and the Irish title and patent be granted to him.

Charles, of course, received a great many plaintive requests from gentlemen who had lost fortunes through their attachment to the Stuart cause, and even when the petitioner had remained with him in exile, he was not noted for spontaneous acts of generosity when it came to restoring other people's losses. So it is rather surprising that Charles simply reversed the grant he had made to Davenant and gave Ogilby the "new erected" post of "Master of all and every our Playes Revells masques and enterludes within our said Kingdome of Ireland" on a permanent basis, with the monopoly right to build theatres and put on plays.

The whole story is very odd. Ogilby seems to have pressed his suit at the very time that he was frenetically busy putting together the Coronation procession; the first surviving indication that he was given the job came in March 1661. Why would the King act so strangely and humiliate Davenant for the sake of a mere useful tradesman whom he had first encountered a few months earlier? Why was Ogilby interested in the wasteland that was Dublin early in 1661? And how did he persuade a wealthy patron, Thomas Stanley, to finance his building an entirely new theatre there? Stanley was a poet and Ogilby used his translations from Greek; he was an ardent Royalist who wore a black armband in memory of the executed King, and founded the Order of the Black Riband. He was a friend of Ogilby, was one of the patrons of his 1654 *Virgil* and subscribed to his Homer. But what had Ogilby said to explain what he was up to and persuade Stanley that this was worth putting money into? In September 1661, when Ireland was still in a state of decay and confusion, Ogilby had his patent re-written to include Stanley's eleven-year-old son. The boy's father was obviously making an investment, but it was an odd one. You would have to have what Aubrey called a "prophetic spirit", and others might call inside information, to know that Dublin was about to change dramatically.

The explanation for all these mysteries must be traced back to Ormond, Charles' most powerful adviser. In a few astonishing months since the landing at Dover, he had accumulated a stack of offices including Commissioner for the Treasury & Navy and Lord High Steward of England. He had also been made a Duke. Monck was in charge of Ireland but had told the King that he did not think he could bring any harmony to the colony, was unwilling to go there, and recommended that Ormond take over. The result was that in the summer of 1661 Ormond began preparing, negotiating and choosing staff for the role he would be given. Ogilby had been at Ormond's right hand, silently and evidently usefully, during the bad times in Ireland, and Ormond had subscribed to his Homer. The Duke would have had no hesitation in preferring Ogilby to Davenant. The potential of a theatre in Dublin to be a force for good or harm in the new Ireland was obviously very great. For Ormond, Davenant was an unknown quantity who might simply deliver nothing. Ogilby was known and trustworthy. No contest. Ogilby demanded and was given the job of Master of the Revels in Ireland two months before Ormond was appointed. If it had been done later it would probably have been harder to move Davenant aside.

Ormond set out for Dublin in July 1662. Ogilby was probably travelling in his train, with his step-grandson William Morgan, while it seems Mrs Ogilby stayed behind to manage the publishing business. Ormond was displaying as much pomp as he possibly could, plainly intending to carry the overwhelming magnificence of the Coronation into Ireland to establish the new order there. The weather, though, was unhelpful. They found it impossible to sail out of Chester, and so walked across the Welsh sands to be ferried to Anglesey and overland to Holyhead. The crossing from there to Dublin, which must have been full of unhappy memories for both Ormond and Ogilby, was so rough that the ship was feared lost.[22] Once the new Lord Lieutenant landed, the public celebrations were described as "a kind of epitome of what had been lately seen at London upon his Majesty's happy Restoration". A Protestant from a great Irish Catholic family, he set about turning Dublin Castle into a palace, from which he would rule untroubled by the limitations on power which would frustrate Charles in London. The Irish Parliament was nothing like as challenging as the English, and the constitutional settlement which Ormond achieved in Ireland left him a great deal of freedom. He was a kind of Prince Palatine, Ireland's senior nobleman ruling in the name of the King of England and seen by some Irishmen as belonging in their own royal tradition. An anonymous poet compared him, in Irish, to the eleventh-century High King Brian Boru.[23] He was a subject, not a king, and he held his post at the pleasure of the Crown, but in practical terms he had more power than his master.

Ormond had been in Paris with Charles in 1648, staying out of reach of the English Parliament, when civil war had erupted in France. The Fronde began as an uprising of Parlements, French regional tribunals, defending their traditional liberties against royal power and royal taxes. Paris became too dangerous for French royalty, but this was not a re-run of British events. The French rebels had no Protestant ideological energy to temper and radicalise their self-interest. The Crown was able eventually to crush both the Parlements and the subsequent aristocratic uprising. Four years after Charles I was executed, the French monarchy ended up in a position of absolute power. It was also wealthy and cultivated. Not surprisingly, this was the obvious model for British Royalists to envy and aspire to.

Dublin was never going to be more than a very miniaturised and provincial pseudo-Paris; its population was well below

50,000, and was dominated by the Castle, Trinity College and the Cathedral. Its intense and ambitious social life revolved around this limited axis. The potential theatre audience came from the church, the nobility and placeholders of the court, the garrison, the lawyers of Trinity College, and the traders who serviced the city. Ogilby had returned to a city in a far worse state than it had been even in the insurrection. A third of its remaining population had died in a plague in 1652.[24] About two-thirds of the Dubliners of 1662 were English. Streets were unpaved, rubbish was everywhere. But Ormond intended Dublin to grow, and it would double in size by 1670. Ogilby's theatre opened in October 1662. This was the first Restoration theatre built in Britain. It was built on vacant land at the back of a couple of houses on Blind Quay,[25] reclaimed (and it would eventually be revealed, unstable) land on the riverside. Ogilby occupied a house on the quay, presumably living at the back of his theatre. This was the largest public theatre in Britain, significantly larger than its only rival, Davenant's converted tennis court in Lincoln's Inn. According to Katherine Philips, Dublin's most important female dramatist and literary star, Ogilby's theatre was far superior.[26]

It was a rectangular space with a platform for actors which occupied as much floor space as the audience. This stage was divided half-way back by a proscenium arch, a structure suddenly making its British debut in a purpose-built theatre. It was like the Palais Royale theatre of the French court, designed for a deep perspective of changeable wings ("shutters") and backdrop scenery creating depth and spectacle, with overhead scenic panels for the sky and with stage machinery. Inigo Jones had first introduced sliding and flying scenery changes in masques at Whitehall, and somehow Ogilby was able to import the architectural know-how to make at least some of this happen, though there is no surviving evidence of how it all worked.[27] Musicians sat over the proscenium. The audience was on rows of upholstered benches facing the stage, with a central box at the back for the Lord Lieutenant and other boxes for the nobility to see and be seen. There were three galleries, whose occupants' status declined as they went up. The stage was lit with oil lamps along the front and with candles. Ormond's attendance there bestowed as much kudos on the viceroy as he did on the theatre.

Without the help of a useful London plague, Ogilby had some trouble assembling a company of actors. He could only attract professionals by outbidding London, which resulted in the King issuing an order that he return one of his players to Davenant. Others were part-time actors with trades or from the garrison. The world to which Ogilby was inviting his audience was certainly not Irish, but nor was it English. He opened, before the theatre was fully fitted out, with what were evidently meant to be crowd-pleasers – a Fletcher comedy which had played at Werburgh Street and was seen as an attraction, and then Shakespeare's *Othello*, which was a kind of banner for post-Puritan entertainment. It was very theatrical, exotic, melodramatic, with a relatively small core cast, no staging challenges and the novelty of a sensual relationship with an actual woman. Women were at last to be seen on stage, though we know nothing of any woman who was in this production. Thomas Killigrew had used it as an opener for his theatre in London, with Prince Rupert's mistress playing Desdemona. Pepys enjoyed the show. The strange London theatre tradition of dressing the Doge and Senators of Venice with feathers in their hair was scrupulously followed. This certainly created an effect, though more modern spirits in the audience thought it was not the desired one.

What followed in Dublin was very different, and established the remarkable nature of this theatre. The stage was ready, the scenery was finished, £100 – a small fortune – had been spent on costumes (by the Earl of Orrery), all society was gathered. The Lord Lieutenant, Ireland's leading nobles, everyone who could afford a seat and wanted to be seen to be associated with the new, modern high society of Dublin settled down to watch a play that was nothing to do with London's theatrical tradition, or Ireland's either. The play was about Caesar and the death of Pompey. People with an interest in theatre would have known of the play on that subject written by George Chapman about fifty years earlier, but Ogilby had no interest at all in promoting Chapman's work. That would now be replaced in the theatrical lexicon by the spectacular presentation of Corneille's *Pompey*, translated from the French by Britain's first female playwright, Katherine Philips,[28] better known as "The Matchless Orinda". The future had arrived, and landed in Smock Alley.

Orinda was a social phenomenon, an extremely capable cultural hostess who created an association devoted to female friendship. Its members took on avatar names, and Orinda was hers. She arrived in Dublin at the same time as Ogilby and Ormond, ostensibly to pursue a property claim connected with her Welsh husband, and was immediately lionised. The combination of a highly original mind, literary skill, constant social brilliance and deference in a beautiful and apparently modest young woman – no wonder the Earl of Orrery immediately became her patron, sponsored her writing and paid for the costumes.

Corneille was a product of Cardinal Richelieu's determination to create a new kind of drama that would act as moral and aesthetic propaganda for the heroic and virtuous nobility the Cardinal wanted people to associate with the French court. The *Mort de Pompée* had been written in 1642 at the height of the playwright's success. Caesar had been played by Molière. The plot revolves around two powerful women, Pompey's wife Cornelia and Cleopatra.

This was the play that Orinda chose to bring into English. It was not just an artistic whim, but part of a coherent cultural programme on the French model. It was utterly new to Britain in many ways, and symbolically echoed the theatrical form of French tragedy by being written entirely in rhyming couplets. This show launched a British theatrical genre of French plays in translation. It was a perfect choice for the new theatre from a technical viewpoint. Corneille had carefully constructed it according to Aristotle's (and the Academie's) insistence on unity of time and place, with all the action off-stage, so the whole play consists of dialogues on a single day in a single set. One problem with this culturally advanced idea was that British theatres needed to entertain their audience for the three hours between lunch and dinner. Corneille's text would barely fill two hours, and in a closed, badly ventilated room with oil lamps would eventually be drowned out by very cultured post-prandial snores.

Orinda and Ogilby transformed Corneille's static presentation into a far more theatrical entertainment, a vision of a new operatic theatre, grown out of the music and glamour of the masque and its dances. They created newly composed songs and dances, extending the show by linking the five acts and involving characters who Corneille had never thought of, including Pompey's ghost.[29]

The play is about the aftermath of a Roman civil war, but modern commentators have found it difficult to read any obvious political message in Orinda's translation. The central narrative concerns Ptolemy's catastrophic belief that he would please Caesar by killing his enemy Pompey. Caesar was angered because he wanted to stage a public reconciliation with his enemy and so resolve the legacy of war. There was an unstated but obvious parallel on offer with Charles' commitment to forgive all his father's enemies except the actual regicides, but Charles could not accept any identification with Caesar and the play went into oblivion. The real message, which did leave a legacy, was the fact of the performance, creating a courtly story-space which is meant to be apolitical in its acceptance of, and delight in, the status quo.

Ogilby was now connected to Orinda's social world, which extended far beyond Dublin and was based not on patronage but female friendship. It included the Duchess of Ormond and the King's sister-in-law, the Duchess of York. Orinda made sure that the Duchess of York had an early copy of the play.[30] Two weeks after *Pompey*, Ogilby mounted *The Generall*, an entirely original work by Orinda's passionately enthusiastic sponsor, Roger Boyle, Earl of Orrery. The son of the Earl of Cork, he was one of the leading figures in Ireland. He had played an important role (on both sides) in the war and in the Commonwealth. He was also enthusiastic about theatre, as a writer as well as a member of the audience, and a friend of Davenant. He had written to Ormond in January 1661 (so before Ormond was named as Lord Lieutenant) that "When I had the honour and happiness the last time to kiss his majesty's hand, he commanded me to write a play for him … Some months after, I presumed to lay at his majesty's feet a tragi-comedy, all in ten feet verse and rhyme … because I found his majesty relished the French fashion of plays, (rather) than English."[31] He had already written *The Generall* in 1660, a drama about the conflict between a Sicilian king and a usurper which was a theatrical presentation of his own moral conflicts, a demonstration of his submission and of the need for a settlement which ignored any thought of revenge by the new regime on the old. That also happened to be the official policy, so all was obviously well. At the heart of the drama were all the issues of love and honour that were so much part of Orinda's discourse, and Boyle had been engaged with the subject before she ever arrived in Dublin. On the night that the Smock Alley Theatre first opened, the actors had been taken from their own show to Boyle's house, where they had performed a private version of *The Generall* for a very special invited audience.

The theatre was a huge hit, culturally and financially. As early as January 1663 it was reported to Whitehall that "Mr. Ogilby gets money apace".[32] *Pompey* and *The Generall* were both presented in London after their Dublin premieres, which placed Ogilby and Dublin at the very centre of the new theatrical culture that so dominates our picture of Restoration life. He did not have Nell Gwynn but he did have an orange-seller, offering symbols of ultra-fashionable aristocratic luxury from an orangery modelled on those at Versailles. Pepys saw his first orange tree in Richmond Park in 1664. Ogilby was putting on the latest successes from the London stage – *The Adventures of Five Hours* and *The Cutter of Coleman Street*. Orinda had been trying to read *The Adventures of Five Hours* when it was snatched away and hurried across to Ogilby.

But things were not going quite so well among the thespians, who seem to have been involved in ever-growing disputes. That report to Whitehall about Ogilby's financial success said that he made money "and his actors reputation". Actors like good reviews, but the implication was that they were not being paid what they expected. The preparations for *Pompey* were marred by arguments over the music and dances. Within a few months of its appearance Orinda was writing that there were arguments over the play's publication and, as the theatre closed for the summer, she predicted that the performers would be seen again being played by comedians themselves, in "a Farce or a Puppet Show at London called *Ireland in Ridicule*".[33] Meanwhile a cathedral chorister who had been one of the singers was severely censured by the Church for having anything to do with a theatre. In June 1664 Orinda wrote: "There is a Plot discover'd here, but what to make of it I know not; and indeed 'tis so unlucky an Age for Plots that even those on the Stage cannot thrive: for the Players disband apace ...."[34] Whatever was going on, Ogilby was withdrawing or being pushed aside. Blind Quay was being re-developed (the name was moved to a different street) and he had to move house. He seems to have abandoned the management work, or had it removed from him. Ormond appointed one of his own household, a soldier with theatrical ability named Ashbury, as deputy Master of the Revels and theatre manager.[35] The issues may well have been financial; the theatre was a luxury product, and Dublin was in financial ruin, without money to clean its streets of ordure or pay for the piped water. And actors do so like to be paid.

As a poet in London Ogilby had been lionised, and (with less false modesty than Orinda, who claimed to be embarrassed by fame) he revelled in it. The time had come to go back to London and presumably re-join his wife. His return probably coincided with *Pompey*'s production at Court on 14 July.[36] William Morgan stayed on to help run Smock Alley and be Master of the fractious Revels of Ireland. Ogilby had a publishing empire to protect, new projects to launch and a new administration that he needed to butter up. It was time to get back to making books.

In the autobiographical sketch he wrote a few years later to introduce his volume on *Africa*, he did not even mention the building and running of Smock Alley. This was a self-promotional text and there was something about the Smock Alley story that he wanted forgotten. He succeeded in hiding the story; we do not know what had happened that would harm his reputation. In his own account he jumped directly from what he had done before his return to Dublin (the Coronation and his huge Bible) to his re-entry into publishing. "Next, in order to the compleating of *Homer*, I fell upon his *Odisses*, which I Dedicated to His Grace the Duke of *Ormond*." Nothing to see here, move right along. He was prepared to say that he was fed up and in need of some more diverting work, but made no mention of theatre. He was simply "weary of tedious Versions, and such long Journeys in Translating Greek and Latin Poets, Works asking no less than a Mans whole life to accomplish".

Return to London

If Ogilby had really made a lot of money from his theatre in Dublin, he must have squandered it pretty quickly, because he was certainly strapped for cash by the time he arrived back. He was a printer and publisher but was not a member of the Stationers' Company, and needed protection from its closed shop rules. In May 1665 he petitioned the King for a fifteen-year copyright on all his publications to date. He mentioned that this was "according to the use and custom of foreigne Princes for the encouragement of Authors". He immediately received a warrant granting it from Baron Arlington, Charles' Secretary of State. It warned the Stationers not to interfere with him.[37] That was an exercise of the royal prerogative setting aside a statute, the Licensing Act of 1662. Ogilby was being sheltered by a power which made many men very suspicious of the King's idea of his own authority.

It is not at all clear what made the Secretary so responsive to John Ogilby's request. Baron Arlington was developing into the *eminence grise* of the English court. It was a position for which he had apparently been designed by Central Casting, wearing a sinister black patch across his nose which advertised a wound he had received in the Civil War, when he was a young servant to Charles I's Secretary of State, Lord Digby. He had become secretary to the Duke of York, then Charles II's agent in Madrid before the Restoration. Two of his relatives were inscribed in the 1654 *Virgil*, that roll-call of grand Royalist conspirators. He came back in 1661 to be given a parliamentary seat at Charles' insistence, and was quickly promoted. A tall, extravagantly dressed and stately figure, he was very well read in classical literature, and a trusted associate of Ormond, so he would certainly have known Ogilby's character and qualities. Ormond may have put in a good word. Arlington probably also knew of Ogilby through the theatre, because his aunt was married to Killigrew. In 1638 he had written a poem as a preface to two of Killigrew's plays, which expressed his lifelong belief that human virtue reached its highest perfection, in life as in masques, in the royal presence.[38] He was a man who operated quietly behind the scenes, and who was concerned to ensure a well-ordered and well-financed administration by manipulation and knowing exactly who was doing what. He was very close to Charles, who liked and trusted him. In fact there was a private staircase from Arlington's office in Whitehall to the royal apartments.[39] This was, of course, a status that created powerful enemies, such as the Duke of Buckingham, who wrote his own assessment of the man in the form of "Advice to a Painter To Draw my L. A-----ton, Grand Minister of State":

> First draw an arrant fop, from top to toe
> Whose very looks at first dash shew him so: ...
> Two goggle-eyes, so clear, tho' very dead,
> That one may see, thro' them, quite thro' his Head.
> Let every nod of his, and subtle wink
> Declare the fool would talk, but cannot think.
> Let him all other fools so far surpasse
> That fools themselves point at him for an ass.[40]

For Ogilby he would become a figure of power who could be relied on. And when the time came, it seems Arlington would put him to use.

Plague

The immediate need for cash could be solved using an insight Ogilby had received in his childhood; he needed to hold a lottery. He had great stacks of unsold and unbound books; they were luxury works, and he decided to charge the remarkable sum of £2 a ticket. At that price, people needed to feel reasonably confident of winning. It was in fact a theatrical exercise in remaindering; Pepys bought two tickets and won two books, *Aesop* and *The Coronacion*. The draw began on 10 May, but as this was a "standing lottery" it carried on for as long as people bought tickets.

The problem with this brilliant plan was that his market was drying up as the plague began to crawl though London. London was a stinking city of open drains and raw sewage, where almost a half a million people lived in wildly varying conditions and where many of the grand houses of old

Royalists had been abandoned during the Commonwealth and were now rat-infested tenements. Rat infestation was, of course, the problem. By the time Ogilby's lottery opened, the plague had taken hold around the docks. On 30 April Pepys was writing of "great fears of the sickness here in the City". By July, with the death rate ten times normal and the city petrified with fear, a large number of the lottery-ticket buying public were well away from London.

In terms of simple statistics, London's Great Plague of 1665 was less severe than either the plague of 1603, which kept James away from his capital city when he should have been crowned there, or the plague of 1625 when Hopton and his fellow soldiers returned from the Netherlands. In 1603 the mortality was over 22% of the population; in 1625 it was over 20%. In 1665 it was a "mere" 17.6%.[41] But it is that epidemic which has registered in popular memory as a death-mountain like that of the Black Death, which may have killed 40% of the population. One reason may be that this was the final great outbreak, but no one could have known that. Another of course is that London now had a vastly greater population, more than double that of 1625. There were more deaths in London in 1665 than there had been people alive in the city a hundred years earlier. The sheer scale of deaths – over 80,000 highly infectious bodies had to be disposed of in five months – was beyond anyone's experience. The Bills of Mortality greatly under-reported what was taking place. According to the Duke of Albemarle in one week when 7,000 deaths were reported, a further 7,000 were unreported because of home burials in people's gardens.[42] Burials were supposed to be by night, but as numbers grew and nights shortened that became impossible. Imagine a city churchyard where diggers are at work every day on thirty graves. That was St Brides, and it was by no means the busiest. St Dunstan-in-the-West ran out of land and started tipping bodies into a common grave: St Brides soon began doing the same. Far more burials were needed at Aldgate, where a huge pit was opened. Coffins were remembered as niceties of another age; these were times for shrouds and speed. In some places common graves held up to forty corpses.[43] The noisy shouting and swearing of the corpse-carters and the perpetual tolling of bells drove people to abject terror or to a determined affirmation of their own lives. Pepys said he never had such a jolly time.

It has been said that more than eighty London printers died during the epidemic. Ogilby did not intend to be one of them. At the end of May the court evacuated up-river to Hampton, and Ogilby abandoned his lottery to move nearby.

By death and flight, the population of London was halved and the bookselling business was a memory. By July all parks and gardens were shut, all entertainments barred, the churches deserted, the streets empty except for single hurrying figures or the delirious dying. It was clear that the epidemic was not just of bubonic plague, with its distinctive black swellings, but of disease itself in every manifestation. Death from "spotted fever" increased twenty-fold, consumption eight-fold; dropsy, convulsions and "rising of the lights" (now said to be croup) were killing people on an unprecedented scale. Old age and childbirth, rickets, over-eating and bad teeth were all striking people dead with an unfamiliar swiftness. No one understands to this day what was happening. The folk-memory, which has something to commend it, is that London had grown into a monstrous pustule which would consume its inhabitants relentlessly until it was purged by incineration.

Ogilby had left London for Kingston upon Thames. It was not an entirely safe retreat: 122 of its 2,800 or so inhabitants perished,[44] but that was a quarter of the death rate in London. He had retreated to Hircomb's Place, a medieval house that was the family home of a minor courtier and Middle Temple lawyer named Robert le Wright.[45] Le Wright was in his mid-fifties and was living as a bachelor, his "perfidious" wife Gratiana having deserted him "basely and utterly" two years earlier.[46] He had no children. The French ambassador was also there. He was the unmarried illegitimate son of Henri IV, about the same age as Ogilby.

Ogilby probably came to be there because of the network of admirers of Elizabeth of Bohemia that had shaped so much of his life. Le Wright, like Hopton, had abandoned his studies and gone to fight for her and Frederick; he had been recruited by his old schoolmaster and Cambridge tutor, who became Chaplain to one of the English generals at Arnhem in 1628. There he would have met William Craven, an immensely wealthy Londoner, orphaned son of a Lord Mayor, who joined the fight three years earlier when he was seventeen. Craven had fled abroad after a disastrous affair with the wife of a minor Yorkshire dignitary in her early forties which unexpectedly produced a daughter. When he arrived he fell for another older married woman; this one was King Charles' sister, Queen Elizabeth of Bohemia. There was an entire community of unmarried dashing English gentlemen who adored her, and he was the most devoted.

Craven evidently remained on good terms with le Wright and about thirty years later arranged the ill-fated marriage of his daughter to his friend. After the Restoration, Craven came back to London where he stayed through the plague, helping to maintain order and donating property for burial grounds. A man of determined conscience who spent £3,000 buying people out of London's debtors' prisons, Craven gave

Elizabeth Stuart shelter when she eventually returned a widow to England and she died in his house.

The story-teller

Living in Kingston deprived of theatre and publishing, Ogilby was back in the situation he had known in Rathfarnham, behind castle walls with a grim world outside. There he had studied Virgil; now he returned to Aesop, becoming, to his own delight, a story-teller. He became "Designer of my own Fables, and at last screwed myself up to a greater height, finishing two Heroick Poems, viz. The Ephesian Matron, and The Roman Slave".[47]

The two "epics" were poem-stories rather than full-scale Virgilian or Homeric narratives. He published them with his newly invented fables in a single illustrated volume, *Aesopics*. The fables were rather delicious, and his animal-character parodies of a pompous judiciary and greedy lawyers suggest that his host, who played no role in the life of his Inn, was no great fan of its members. It looks as though he might even have been influenced by le Wright's take on the inevitability of proper order being restored. Ogilby had taught that the universe is driven by a master-plan that requires endurance to pass through the bad times until it inevitably rights itself. Being legally trained, le Wright saw this in terms of inexorable and ruthless justice – reflecting "So sure, how slow soever, is God's vengeance" – rather than the operation of natural law, and that seems to have shaped Ogilby's narratives.[48] For example, there was a well-known fable of the crow that perched on a sheep to save the trouble of flying. When the sheep said he wouldn't get away with that on the back of a dog, the crow replied, "I despise the weak and yield to the strong. I know whom I may bully and whom I must flatter; and I thus prolong my life to a good old age." In Ogilby's hands the crow also happens to be a lawyer, envious when he sees an eagle fly off with a sheep to eat, who tries to do the same. The greedy crow-lawyer soon realises he has over-reached himself, but when he tries to drop the sheep finds that his talons are caught fast in the wool and that's the end of him. Instead of the triumph of ruthless pride, we have the just punishment of a greedy barrister.

The poems were his first attempt to make his voice heard in its own right, rather than speaking through characters in plays or pointed translation. The whole volume had a moral and political purpose, which was to be conveyed through story-telling rather than argument.

The Androcles story has a natural place in the volume, being associated with Aesop, but Ogilby has turned it into a much larger and more political fable than the original. It sets out a political vision which, we will see, will inform his work on *Britannia* a few years later.

The source tale was a supposedly true story of a Roman runaway slave who sheltered in a cave where he was confronted by a lion. The animal was in pain because of a thorn in its paw, and Androcles removed it. The lion then looked after him as if it were a faithful dog, until Androcles could no longer stand the isolation and returned to Rome. Condemned to be thrown to the beasts as a runaway, he was confronted in the circus by the very same lion, which treated him with affection. He was released, the lion was awarded to him, and Androcles was said to have been seen afterwards walking round with the lion on a leash.

Ogilby's readers knew the story, and would not have expected the lion to be a human king, magically transformed into a beast retaining the power of speech. But that is how

Ogilby tells the tale. The beast introduces himself as a very recognisable ruler faced with very recognisable rebellion – but in this case the cause is his own weakness, brought about by stepping on the thorn:

> Soon as they felt me weak, and thus disarm'd,
> Each-where tumultuous Commotions swarmed,
> Much 'gainst my Evil Counsel they alledge,
> Prerogative trampling down by Privilege ...

Androcleus removes the thorn and lances the infection, and the lion offers him shelter, food, clothing and beautiful women – "Pure Virgins, not Decays, piec'd up and vamp'd" who he can enjoy with "varying Joys, and fear no After-claps". This unusual Lion, far more humanoid than the anthropomorphised beasts of the Fables, leads him to refreshing water and a comfy bed. Fully recovered, King Lion then confronts his rebellious subjects advancing in arms, and makes promises to them which seem remarkably similar to the promises Charles II made as the basis for his restoration.

This, it turns out, is just a feint. Once secure, he suddenly reveals his full power and falls upon them in bloody slaughter. Soon the court is fully restored. There is no criticism of this duplicity. In fact it is clear that this ruthless and violent approach to re-establishing fully authoritarian royal power is one that Ogilby endorses.

It was a nasty world out there, and Ogilby was quite comfortable with brutal ruthlessness. That is evident in the other poem, *The Ephesain Matron, or the Widow's Tears*. The story comes from the *Satyricon*, written at the time of Nero, which is a satire on the behaviour and pretensions of ordinary Romans. A widow extravagantly mourning her dead husband by staying fasting in his tomb for days is seduced by a soldier who drops in when he is supposed to be guarding a set of crucifixions nearby. While the two of them are hard at it, relatives of one of the crucified criminals make off with the body to bury it. The guard is now liable to be executed for dereliction of duty, so the widow, who had been a very model of pious loyalty to her spouse, helps the soldier nail up his body on the cross to hide what has happened. Her tears were evidently insincere.

In Ogilby's hands the story takes an extravagantly gruesome twist. That may have been encouraged by le Wright, whose wife had deserted him "basely and utterly" two years earlier.[49] The widow has only been in the tomb for one day when the soldier arrives; she eats with him in an upper chamber and leads him on. She then retreats to the tomb warning the soldier that she will knife him if he follows – but he, of course, pursues her.

Venus, overseeing all this, decides to leave him to it while she goes off to resolve an issue with a man who spent a while without a woman, "forc'd to forage, lately got a Clap; / and well recover'd, vows no more to roam". The association of women with venereal disease, which also happens in Androcleus, gives us our only glimpse into Ogilby's sexuality, and perhaps that of some of the fellow-guests in Kingston to whom he must have read his new work. It is rather a sad one. In this story, female sexuality appears to disgust him, and it is the widow's lust that drives the horror. She accepts the soldier's advances with alacrity and they turn the tomb into their love nest. When he discovers the theft of the body he is guarding, though, a simple substitution will not do. The stolen body was very distinctively mutilated. The widow sees no problem here and tells the soldier that as a practised killer he should chop away at her husband's corpse: "What Maims you please, and Mutilations make." He lacks the stomach for it, so the lady strips off and does the job herself:

> And first his Hand, which she so oft had kis'd,
> Without compunction, sever'd from the Wrist;
> His Ears crop'd off, his right Eye out she tears,
> Where once small Cupids danc'd in Crystal Sphears;
> His Nostrils slits, His Lips, whereof she sipt,
> Balm mixt with dew of Roses, off she whipt;
> When thus she said, If this Sir, will not serve,
> Say where you please, and I will further Carve

This grotesque and gruesome comedy is then suddenly ended by the re-appearance of Venus in a blaze of light and music, and very cheery about the mutilation: "With a dead Husband to make bold, what harm?" In the blink of an eye she puts the corpse back in the tomb, the stolen body back on the gibbet, and everyone lives happily ever after.

This Heroic Poem appals with its sheer outrageousness, and reading it even now, that shock can make you laugh out loud. It belongs less to the world of Virgil than to that of the blood-soaked tragedies of the theatre. In fact its setting in a closed sepulchre made it an ideal candidate for candlelit staging. This, of course, was Ogilby's milieu, and Jacobean tragedies were crowd-pleasers which the King evidently relished. *The White Devil* was revived at Drury Lane in 1665, and *The Changeling* and *The Spanish Tragedy* were played at court in 1668.[50] Gore and sex were entertainment. This poem may well be an adaptation of a play which he wrote but which was never put on. Its unity of time and place conforms very well with French theatrical rules, as represented in *Pompey*, but now dressed in the gory aesthetic of English theatre. Ogilby's vision of the universe was not a nice one, and the spectacles through which he viewed the world, at least in those terrible times, were not rose-tinted, but blood-splattered. There was no bubble of sanctuary where anyone could pretend the world was comfortable, not even Kingston upon Thames.[51]

The new epic poet

His great poetic work was still to come. This was the venture on which he had started out with his consultation on learning Greek, back in 1653. The creation of an epic for these epic times was the great Royalist poetic goal, attempted by Abraham Cowley in 1643 and 1656, Samuel Sheppard in 1648 and Davenant in 1651. These were all unfinished, their authors overwhelmed by the struggle. Ogilby alone had the determination and endurance actually to complete a full-scale Royalist epic poem. He was determined that it was not enough to give the British their English Virgil and Homer. They needed their own twelve-book epic in which their own semi-legendary hero struggles against adversity and creates a new future for the world. In the mould of the Christian saviour, the Briton would not triumph until after being martyred. The future Britain would be seen to rise from his death as the phoenix rises from its own ashes. He thought it was just what was needed. The hero was, of course, "our Miracle of Hero's, Charles the First, being the best Pattern of true Prudence, Valor, and Christian Piety".

At least that is what Ogilby said in the preface to *Africa*. What *Carolies* actually contained we do not know because none of it survives. We can take it that the story would be based on the structure of the *Iliad*, with Charles I a modern Hector, whose noble leadership demands the loyalty of his followers, whose morality deserves emulation and whose death is noble self-sacrifice for his people in defence of a great cause. All we have left of Ogilby's epic is eight lines, and on this evidence no one since the author himself has regarded its loss as a tragedy:

> Mirror of Princes! Charles the Royal Martyr,
> Who for Religion, and his Subjects Charter,
> Spent the best Blood Injustice Sword e're dy'd,
> Since the rude Souldier Pierc'd our Saviours side,
> Whose Sufferance, Patience, reach'd to such a height,
> For Angels onely with Sun-beams to write:
> No mortal Hand, less my unworthy Pen,
> Fit to Display the best of Kings and Men.

Of course epic poetry is not to be read as if it were lyric. Its power and effect builds over long passages, its sweep draws in the reader and creates a world through sheer scale. But still, what survives is not very encouraging.

For the last two hundred years Ogilby has been regarded as a bad poet. "His pretensions to praise of any kind can scarcely be supported: he has neither animation of thought, accuracy of taste, sensibility of feeling, nor ornament of diction."[52] But that was not how he seemed at the time. Edward Phillips, Milton's nephew, who was educated by the great man, acted as his occasional helper and eventually inherited his papers, described Ogilby as "one of the prodigies of our age"; "in verse, his Translations of Homer and Virgil; and which is the chief of all, as composed propria Minerva, his Paraphrase upon Aesop's Fables; which for ingenuity and fancy, besides the invention of new Fables, is generally confessed to have exceeded whatever hath been done before in that kind."[53]

If the *Carolies* had been published, perhaps that judgement would have been confirmed. Then he would probably never have created *Britannia*.

Life 9. The Atlas Maker

Apocalypse

> Here is wisdom. Let him that hath understanding count the
> number of the beast: for it is the number of a man; and
> his number is Six hundred threescore and six. (Revelation
> 13:16–18)

The Bible ends with a prophecy. When the moment came,
in 1666, no one should have known more about the coming
apocalypse than a publisher. There was a profitable industry
selling prophetic works based around the Book of Revelation.

In autumn 1665 the plague deaths diminished, and Ogilby
returned home to the King's Head Court in Shoe Lane. London
filled up with people once more over the winter. Shoe Lane was
a mass of workshops, taverns, brothels and heaving tenements
running between Holborn and Fleet Street just west of the city
wall. Pepys visited a tavern there which was so squalid that he
felt uncomfortable going in. He records that he had his first sight
of cock-fighting in Shoe Lane. He was jammed into a heaving
mass of apprentices, bakers, brewers, butchers, draymen, "and
what not", an utterly unfamiliar world of shouting, swearing
and outcry betting, Astonished, he watched these apparently

penniless men not only bet three or four pounds at a time, but keep going until they were £10 or £20 down.[1]

This was an area outside the walls and outside the law. £20 might not have been so hard to come by as Pepys supposed.

There were at least a dozen closed courts off Shoe Lane. According to the Hearth Tax records, King's Head Court alone had 29 households and 85 chimneys, implying a population in that one little alley of over 400 souls. Some of the houses were surprisingly large, and there were huge differences in wealth in this Court, but no other home there came close to Ogilby's. In fact he had two buildings there, one with three hearths, and the other with twelve, enough to be a substantial inn.[2] He was a most respectable and highly respected man, even though he was a tradesman and poet with no status. So far.

His masterwork was ready. The manuscript was complete, the printing done, the pages stacked, it was almost ready for binding. After seventeen years of interpreting the greatest literature of Greece and Rome, it was time for him to produce his personal masterpiece. This was the imposing epic poem that would establish his reputation as a master to be spoken of in the same breath as the ancients. The subject may have been the making of a royal martyr, but the object was the making of John Ogilby. It was time. It was done.

If Revelation wasn't warning enough, Ogilby had Evans, a leading astrologer, as a neighbour. But the prophets were all taken by surprise. The fire started on Sunday, 2 September, in Pudding Lane, a mile to the east of King's Head Court. A woman could piss it out, declared the Lord Mayor, and stomped away. Even if he was wrong – and no woman tried – there was the Fleet River, the City wall and then an entire city between Ogilby and the fire. It would take a truly pessimistic mind to think he was in any danger.

And I heard a great voice out of the temple saying to the seven angels, Go your ways, and pour out the vials of the wrath of God upon the earth. (Revelation 16:1)

And the fourth angel poured out his vial upon the sun; and power was given unto him to scorch men with fire. (Revelation 16:8)

That was the morning of Day 1. The houses in London's alleys, passages and courts were made of wood, covered in pitch, filled with fuel for the fire. By the morning of Day 2 printers and booksellers within the city walls knew they needed to be scared. As the roaring inferno sucked in what oxygen it could the narrow pedestrian alleys became chimneys, funnelling the roaring flames up into the sky, devouring everything. The temperature reached over 1,700 degrees. Human bones turn to ash at 750 degrees. At Newgate, the great iron chains of the prison melted. London had become an incinerator.

The city's booksellers had the use of a strange little church, St Faith's, which was actually in St Paul's crypt. They decided to move as much as they could into St Faith's, whose stout stone walls were protected by the larger frame of the Cathedral. Surrounded by a large open space, it would keep everything safe. They labelled each pile of books and carefully blocked every gap in the church through which a spark might enter. Just in time.

St Paul's was vulnerable because it had wooden scaffolding for repair work, but St Faith's stood firm while St Paul's burned above it. When the upper part of the great cathedral was on fire, its stones cracking in the inferno, some brave soul went down into St Faith's and opened the stout door a crack to check that all was well with the books.[3] The fire up above was starved of oxygen, and as air rose in the searing heat, pressure dropped. St Faith's was full of oxygen, and relatively cool, so air pressure was much higher. St Faith's poured out oxygen as though it were petrol. The fire looked down and exploded into the bookstore. The cathedral was now incandescent, its eight acres of lead roof were liquefied and pouring down onto whatever remained below. Most of the stock of London's book trade was sealed in and turned to ash. At 9 o'clock that night a fourteen-year-old schoolboy, William Taswell, was reading a small book at Westminster by the light of the St Paul's inferno a mile away. It is the only medieval cathedral to have vanished from England.

Some of Ogilby's stock had been with London printers and was now atomised. But most of it was in his home outside the wall and across the Fleet. He saw no reason to start moving it. There was no angel of wrath pouring fire out there. At this stage it does seem that the fire got a bit personal. A gigantic tongue of flame contemptuously leapt over the city wall and the Fleet River, and pounced on the crammed alleyways of Shoe Lane. There was no time to save anything. King's Head Court quite simply disappeared from the face of the Earth. With no lead roof to seal it, Ogilby's stock turned into fiery leaves, swirling up into the hot dark sky.

Carolies was gone. The Great Fire took every copy and the original manuscript of Ogilby's masterwork. He was sixty-five years old, and heartbroken among the smoking ruins. "This long intended Edifice, my own great Fabrick", "the pride, divertisement, business and sole comfort of my age".[4]

There had been thousands of almanacs of astrological predictions, and ready buyers for the mysterious Mother Shipton and Nostradamus. Their forebodings were riddling and unclear, but everyone knew that 666 was the number of the beast of the Book of Revelations, and 1666 was named as the year of the Last Trump, or something equally fearsome. Perhaps they were living through it. Nostradamus' incomprehensible verses on the burning of the city had been published in Booker's Almanac for 1666. Pepys heard that Prince James said "that now Shipton's prophecy was out".

Seventeen miles to the west, Lady Elizabeth Carteret was at her home at Cranbourne Lodge, on the edge of Windsor Great Park. She had noticed that after the long dry summer the Thames was exceptionally low. A strange hot wind had been blowing for days, and late on the night of 3 September fragments of ash and burned pages began floating down from the dark sky. Lady Elizabeth saw that one of the scraps was still partly legible. It said, she remembered, "Time is, it is done."

Samuel Pepys was particularly attracted to Lady Elizabeth, and at the peak of the plague the previous year he had dreamed of a night with her. Now, months after the fire, he was at a dinner party where she spoke of these drifting embers as her own personal prophetic revelation.[5] They were discussing prophecies of the apocalypse, and the words must have put them all in mind of the Book of Revelation: "It is done. I am the Alpha and the Omega." Among Ogilby's stock were the unbound leaves of his huge and lavish Bible, awaiting buyers who were prepared to pay £25 for a book the size of a piece of furniture. These words were at the top of the last folio in the bundle, and became part of the swirling ash.

The devastation was indeed apocalyptic. Smaller fires continued to burn until it finally rained on 9 September, and then the man who had hosted Ogilby at Kingston, Robert le Wright, set out to explore what had happened. He must have gone by boat to the Tower, and then picked his way through the ash. He does not say whether he walked along Thames Street, or took a route further north to Lombard Street and

Cheapside. It would have made no difference: the streets had vanished, there was not a single building to interrupt his view across the wasteland apart from the stone stumps of a few burned-out churches. St Paul's was a broken wreck. He continued along Ludgate Hill, past the unrecognisable ruins that had once been Shoe Lane and Ogilby's print works, down to Fleet Street. He was walking a mile and a half through what had been, a few days ago, by far the greatest city in the land, dense with people, memories and the weight of antiquity. There remained, so far as he could see, absolutely nothing. This inconceivable catastrophe was made even more vivid by seeing, in Whitefriars, that there was a habitation still standing; just one tenement, a monument to a vanished city. In it, one man, a butler of the Inner Temple, still somehow clung to the belief that he was in London.[6]

Of all the trades in the city, none was as hard hit as the booksellers.[7] One estimate was that £150,000 worth of books were carbonised – about £150 million in modern money. Ogilby reckoned his own loss of home and stock at £3,000 and was left with just £5. At sixty-five years old, he was simply wiped out: "Fall'n into a low condition, groaning under a double burthen of Sickness and Poverty, and almost quite despairing, the Work that might have Boy'd me up once more, thus irrecoverably lost...."[8]

Some people were destroyed by the annihilation of their world. James Shirley and his wife, who lost their home to the flames, died just a few days later. They did not have the strength to carry on. Ogilby was made of tougher stuff. His response to the destruction of his life astonished Anthony à Wood:

He had such an excellent invention and prudential wit, and was master of so good addresses, that when he had nothing to live on, he could not only shift handsomely but would make such rational proposals, which were embraced by rich and great men, that in a short time he would obtain an estate again. He never failed in what he undertook, but by his great industry and prudence went through it with profit and honour to himself.[9]

Ogilby had taught his great Royalist audience, through his reading of Virgil, that suffering bitterly and enduring grim experiences were necessary steps on a greater journey. He believed that, and never wavered; it was his strength. Looking over the ashes of his unsold books, he simply realised that he had been freed from them. He had been sharing an overcrowded house with a vast quantity of unsaleable volumes, as the market had changed and his customers, those once dispossessed and powerless Royalists, had moved on:

... since his Majesties Restauration, the minds of those restored to former Fortunes, or rais'd to several Advancements, were more abroad, and not at leisure to look on such private Divertisements at home; so that those later Volumns, which in course were Printed to perfect the former, remain'd a Drug, until the insatiate Flames, at once, and in one bad Market, clear'd me of my Store, and House also.[10]

He set about the business of creating a new home where he could create quite different books for the new reader. Perhaps influenced by le Wright's discovery of the sole surviving house in the ruins, he set out to build in the same street, Whitefriars.[11] Of course he was penniless, so he turned to his old supporters for help, and they delivered it: "... many of my Friends, the Worthy Patrons were more favorable to my Endeavors, when under a Cloud, than after Shining in full Lustre" and in particular it seems that his Merchant Taylor connections must have helped him secure some work.

It was work in a completely new field, where he had no experience whatever. Anywhere in Europe, official positions were given to people with the right connections: outside of medicine and the law there was no such thing as a professional qualification. Ogilby got himself and Morgan appointed "sworn viewers" by the Corporation of the City. The job was a traditional one for resolving property disputes between neighbours, usually nuisance issues or disputes over boundaries. The posts had been held by men like Edward Jerman, whose family had been carpenter-builders in the City for generations. The fire was the best thing that ever happened to Jerman, who now had undreamed-of opportunities to rebuild London from the ground up. He was enrolled in a group of men charged with surveying the ruins, determining where boundaries had been and supervising rebuilding. They were led by Robert Hooke, now the Professor of Geometry at Gresham College. Their old jobs as city viewers were suddenly vacant, and Ogilby and Morgan were employed. After the fire the expertise required for this work was presumably more diplomatic than technical as people came back to the embers.[12] The posts seem to have been sinecures as the surveyors for rebuilding were soon dealing with the work the sworn viewers had done before the fire, and in July 1668 the first clerk of the Mayor's Court was instructed to attend Jerman and the other surveyors when they viewed and resolved disputes "as hee useth to doe of the views of the common viewers of this Citty".[13]

The work that Ogilby and Morgan were left with evidently introduced them to a whole new world, the world of people Jerman was engaged with. They knew nothing of surveying, but somehow they gained this experience and within six years

Ogilby was putting together "the most accurate Survey of the City of London and Libertyes thereof that has ever been done", and the Court of Aldermen backed him wholeheartedly.[14]

The world of the coffee house

The fire had wiped out the whole of Ogilby's London universe, which revolved around Shoe Lane and St Paul's. Robert Hooke was an habitué of the coffee houses, and as soon as they got back on their feet, Ogilby settled himself in one. It was called Garraways, and it was the centre of the life of the new London. The city was getting back on its feet with incredible speed because it was a tremendous hub of global commerce. Further up river, at the palace of Whitehall, Ogilby's books supported royal pretensions to an Augustan Imperium. Whitehall was the centre of *The Empire of Great Britaine*, depicted in Speed's 1612 map. But the City of London had no royal palace, and was the place not of Imperium but, as Ogilby would put it in the dedication to *Britannia*, "The Great Emporium and prime Centre of the Kingdom". At the centre of the world was London, which grasped the globe with tentacles of seaborne trade extended by the goldsmiths of the Exchange.

The reconstruction of the Exchange was an absolute priority, and that commission was given to Jerman, who soon found he had no time to continue as one of the City's new surveyors because he was too busy rebuilding the place. Ogilby was given a space in the new Exchange. At the centre of everything, the real hub of business, dealing, news and global commerce was the small cluster of coffee shops around the Exchange. Their gravitational pull held everything together; this was where science, trade, books and speculation exercised their irresistible pull, ingesting as they worked libations carried almost daily from the farthest corners of the planet.

Thomas Garaway was a member of a great merchant family which traded with most of the known world; a Garaway was Lord Mayor of London before the Civil War. Thomas had survived a shipwreck in West Africa and made a fortune in gold and ivory before setting up a house to supply coffee and tea. It was called The Sultaness Head, and he had declared it open in 1658 with an advertisement in the copy of the Gazette that announced the death of Oliver Cromwell. Its initial attraction was the novelty of an exotic infusion from China, the first public sale of drinks of tea. It was the most up-to-date and fashionable gathering place for gentlemen whose interest reached around the world. They were already used to coffee from Turkey; their eyes were not fixed on the French or Spanish, but the Dutch, who were their competitors in the most lucrative markets of Africa and the Far East. There were a number of coffee houses fighting for trade in the alleys around the Exchange before the fire. The most successful was The Great Coffee House, just across Cornhill in Exchange Alley. This was a spillover from the Royal Exchange, a place to relax, gossip, make deals and enjoy a rather expensive beverage (a penny a cup). After the fire, the plans were for more substantial buildings in broader streets around the Exchange, and the owner of the Great Coffee House could not afford the terms he was offered. Garaway leapt into the breach, and Garraways Coffee House, as it is now spelt by historians, re-appeared in Exchange Street. It was the new centre of gossip, of deals, of plots, of fashionable whispers. It was also a vital place of unobtrusive government eavesdropping, and it would be very surprising if Ogilby was not being used as an occasional informant of what was in the pungent air.

Robert Hooke was thirty-two when the new Garraways opened. He had been a student at Oxford, an ardent Royalist during the Protectorate, and became an assistant to Robert Boyle, the chemist. Boyle was the nephew of the Earl of Orrery, and Hooke was much lower in the social pecking order, but in the pursuit of scientific understanding, master and servant worked as equal partners. When the Royal Society was founded in 1660, to encourage the advancement of natural philosophy through experiment and observation, Hooke was appointed Curator, responsible for providing the experiments. He became Gresham Professor of Geometry in 1664. He was an astonishingly energetic enthusiast in almost every field of science and mathematics, and worked especially at studying microscopy, producing the stunningly beautiful volume *Micrographia* in 1665. His precise drawings of louse and flea, with details invisible to the unaided eye, stunned with their terrifying beauty. The louse unfolded to four times the size of the book, its flawless detail a triumph of observation, measurement, new science and artistic skill.

The presence of the sworn viewer Ogilby promoting his fine books in the same rooms would have created a degree of awareness of each other, but Hooke may well have been more interested, at first, by Ogilby's step-grandson, William Morgan, the sometime clock-maker.

Hooke was intrigued by clock mechanisms, and had begun work on the problem of using a pendulum in 1655. The clock was one of the most obvious markers of a shift from a pre-modern relationship between humans and the cosmos. Our idea of a clock is intimately connected with numbers, but the word itself derives from "cloche", a bell, and medieval clocks existed to ring out public declarations of the time for prayer. When the clock was given a "face", it was a visible model of the universe, in which a hand or sometimes an image of the sun travelled around the central Earth, pointing to the hours as a mechanical sundial, with noon being the highest point on the dial. The original triumphant offering that a clock gave to mankind was that it operated in the dark of night as well as in the bright light of day, and that it made all hours of day and night the same length, irrespective of the season. Clocks had poor accuracy, and the invention of "clock-work", the spring-driven mechanism, did not do much to help because a spring unwinds more slowly at the end than the beginning. A device had been devised to try to counter this (a cord was wound around a conical drum, so that as the spring slowed the mechanism speeded up), but it was a very approximate correction. A minute hand would expose the clock's inaccuracy cruelly, but it also would make no sense; if a clock face shows the sun going round the Earth, what does the minute hand show? It could only have a place on the dial once the sun had stopped going round the Earth, as it did after Galileo.

Hooke's interest in microscopy was a natural development from the telescope. Since it was now clear that the true nature of things is hidden from human sight, there was a huge task confronting the natural philosopher, unexplored continents both vaster and more accessible than those across the sea, and whose potential riches were so great as to be incomprehensible. To explore this world required a new intellectual discipline which recognised that it is a place where cause follows effect not according to chance or divine intervention, but according to rules. This was most clearly evident in the movements of heavenly bodies revealed through telescopes, and in the late 1660s the Royal Society's journal carried papers which spoke of the "laws of motion". These were laws of a completely new kind, which have no moral authority and no sanction. There is no punishment for breaking a law of nature because it cannot be broken. Its operation is inexorable in a universe that works entirely mechanically. The world was to be understood not as a place of sin and salvation, but as a great clock whose mechanism had merely to be examined and described. The experts on its laws would not be priests (or dance masters) but clockmakers.

Accurate time-keeping was particularly important for scientific observation: the essence of an experiment is that it is repeatable, but if the measurement of time is somewhat random, that makes a lot of experiments rather meaningless. Time is also fundamental to geography. How far one place lies east or west of another is measured in the minutes that separate noon at one from noon at the other. The problem of making that measurement would remain intractable for about another century. Timekeeping is also essential for timetables, which were starting to appear in the mid-seven-teenth century as commercial carriers ran systematised routes around the country. The rhythm of life was changing, thanks to the clockmakers. Hooke made watches (which never worked) and seems to have conceived the watch balance spring around the same time as the pendulum appeared, in the late 1650s. It was an interest which he never lost, and he had a close relationship with Tompion, the master clock-maker. Hooke's so-called diaries only run for a few years from 1672, but in those years at least it is clear that he knew Morgan very well. This has been obscured by the index of the published version of the diaries, which ascribes every mention of Mr Morgan to Francis Morgan, an architect who appears far less often. The indexer had no reason to suppose that there was more than one Morgan in Hooke's life, though it is perfectly clear from some entries that references to Morgan without a first name are to Ogilby's grandson.[15] In fact William Morgan appears in Hooke's diaries considerably more often than Ogilby.

However it came about, it is clear that immediately after the fire, John Ogilby realised what it meant to be a modern man. He was not particularly enthusiastic about it, especially as being modern meant learning contempt for the great classical authors whose work he had been so assiduously translating.

Augustan poetry had, he complained, now been dumbed-down in favour of "Rough Satyr, Rude Travestie, and Rhime Doggerel" and a newly arrogant clique of "Moderns [who] confidently avouch, that we in this more Refin'd Age, speak better things ex tempore, than what hath been Recorded by the whole Rabble of Antiquity". In fact his great masters were now seen as simply tedious (a charge that would ultimately transfer to him personally), and that "our Brisker Youth, and more Sublime Wits, should be ashamed to peruse, much more to follow". But complaining was pointless. Having seen how the market had shifted, Ogilby set off in pursuit of his departing customers: "A new Gaggle drowning the old Quire of Melodious Swans, I resolv'd to desist; and shutting up the Fountain of the Muses, left Clambering steep Pernassus."[16]

Mount Parnassus was the home of the muses and Apollo, and he had spent his whole life on its slopes. But now there was a new kind of book to be made. When he was learning to dance and teach the Old Measures in Gray's Inn, and laying down the intellectual foundations that had carried him this far through life, he would have read Thomas Elyot's 1531 *Boke named The Governour*, which set out the cosmic pedagogy of dance and showed how it teaches deep understanding of the world. Elyot also described another important key to understanding, which was the combination of maps with history. They offered education through pleasure:

> For what pleasure is it, in one hour to behold those realms, cities, seas, rivers, and mountains, that scarcely in an old man's life cannot be journeyed and pursued: what incredible delight is taken in beholding the diversities of people, beasts, fowls, fishes, trees, fruits, and herbs? To know the sundry manners & conditions of people, and the variety of their natures, and that in a warm study or parlour, without peril of the sea, or danger of long and painful journeys? I cannot tell, what more pleasure should happen to a gentle wit, than to behold in his own house everything that within all the world is contained.[17]

Ogilby was a businessman and a teacher, with things to reveal and money to make. He dashed off a petition to the King explaining that, being ruined by the Fire after twenty years of work and with the profits that had finally arrived being burned away, he now really needed a licence to import 10,000 reams of the best paper from France to put him back on his feet.[18] Not a single page was to be occupied by the old choir of melodious Greek and Roman swans. He would lay out the world for education and pleasure. He decided that his first new pages were to be colonised by the Chinese.

He was in his new house in Whitefriars by 1668, and the first work of his new incarnation appeared the next year. It was *An Embassy from the East-India Company of the United Provinces, to the Grand Tartar Cham Emperour of China*. China was the largest economy in the world, and there was nothing to be learned about it in English except for a translation of a Jesuit description of the country under the previous dynasty.[19] There was business to be done there, the Dutch had got their foot in the door. In 1654 the Dutch East India Company sent ambassadors to China in the hope of acquiring trading rights on the south coast. The text Ogilby published was an account of the trip written by the steward to the embassy, a seasoned explorer called Johan Nieuhof. He described a journey of 1,500 miles through China, which took two years. When his account was published in Amsterdam in 1665, modern China became an open book, at least to the Dutch. It immediately appeared in French, and the following year in German. But the English had to wait for Ogilby, and what he had to show them was not just a place to do business.

In the terrible years up to 1648, when Europe was being "blown up", China too was in violent upheaval. It had been sucked into the European trade orbit by large-scale imports of silver from the Spanish mines at Potosi. Until recently, historians believed that the great silver mountain of Potosi was excavated to provide silver for Europe, but metallurgists have now shown that Europe's silver came from Mexico, and the Potosi silver went west, to the Philippines and China,[20] in exchange for porcelain and silk. For the first time China began using silver as currency. Europe had suffered massive inflation from the huge Spanish acquisition of American gold and silver, the inevitable effect of an increase in the money supply without any increase in production. When the impact of huge price rises was made more emphatic by a run of bad harvests, as happened in the first half of the seventeenth century, the result was a rash of wars and uprisings and the emergence of a new political order. The revolutions in Britain were simply one part of a general change, and China was just as seriously affected.

Historians disagree vigorously and fundamentally about just how the supply of silver affected China's economy. The story played out very differently, of course, from in Europe. Chinese cities, far larger than Europe's, were dominated by officials, not by merchants. There was no new mercantile ideology, no struggle over liberties and privileges that would transform the culture. But everyone agrees that things went horribly wrong in China in the second quarter of the century.[21] It was devastated by famine and torn apart by war. Nearly 12 million people, over 11% of the population, perished in the twenty years to 1646, a human disaster similar to the Thirty Years' War but over a far larger area, overwhelming the largest and most successful economy on Earth. (European states were self-important minnows by comparison. In 1650 the largest economy after China was India, whose gross domestic product was ten times Britain's.)[22] The ruling Ming dynasty was decisively defeated in the early 1640s by Manchu from the north, who called their state the "Great Qing". The Manchus captured Beijing and gained complete dominance in 1644.

Qing rule was ruthless. Men who maintained the old Ming tradition of wearing their hair long in a top-knot, and refused to show their submission by shaving the front of their scalps and wearing a pig-tail, were executed. In one city, Jiading, almost the entire population was slaughtered. What emerged was a centralised absolutist state in which all commercial and administrative power was held in the hands of the Emperor. The purpose of the Dutch East India mission that *The Embassy* described was to establish trade relations with the new Qing Empire.

Nieuhof's account of the embassy included material from recent Jesuit descriptions that were already available in Holland. The publication had been a triumph of Dutch book production, with 150 engravings largely taken from Nieuhof's interpretation of Chinese materials. Ogilby stated perfectly clearly that he had "English'd" Nieuhof's text himself, a claim which has been comprehensively dismissed. In fact he probably read Dutch quite well, having spent almost a year as a hostage in 1626–27 after being captured in the Dutch-speaking territory of Dunkirk (the district of Dunkirk remained predominately Flemish-speaking into the nineteenth century, and the local Flemish dialect is still used daily there by about 20,000 people).

Ogilby added material from two more Jesuits, one of whom was the head of the Beijing observatory. He had the illustrations faithfully copied, and printed the book at his new-built home in Whitefriars. But this was not the same kind of vanity publishing as his earlier illustrated works: there was no dedication to a patron, and only one picture named a sponsor, one Sir Archibald Erskine, who had his coat of arms on the opening map of China. He was no great nobleman, and is not an easy man to identify. He seems to be the Rev. Sir Archibald Erskine of Augher in Ulster.[23] This book had to justify itself on the open market, without the cushion of noble well-connected subscriptions. There was a tremendous hunger for knowledge of the world as it existed right then, rather than 1,500 or more years before. This hunger for knowledge was the drive behind the creation of the Royal Society in 1660. Its members were gentlemen with an active interest in the world, and the Royal Society was as much a part of the new commercial city's life as were the coffee houses and the Exchange.

Rather than let the commercial success of his new book compete with his surviving pre-fire stock, Ogilby decided to make it available in a lottery with the remnants. As new houses were built for gentlemen who had lost their homes, they obviously needed fine and fashionable books for their new-made bookshelves. But faced with dramatic losses and expenses, many who hungered for it might baulk at paying £4 for a volume. So they could take a punt. A five shilling ticket was a genuine lottery ticket, but for anyone spending five times that there was a guarantee of winning more than 25 shillings worth of books. The value of prize volumes varied from £2 for the *Entertainment* to £25 for the great Bible; the other prizes included *Virgil*, the *Iliads*, the *Odysses*, *Aesop* and, of course, *China*.

Ogilby also had a message for his readers, and it was the same message he had been teaching through his literary translations. The story of the Dutch Embassy was the story of a failure, and at the heart of that failure was the disconnect between Dutch and Qing understanding of political authority. After the account of the mission comes a description of the Chinese Empire. It begins:

> Now the Kingdom or Empire of China hath been Govern'd from Age to Age, in a series or long prescription of Time out of mind, by a Single Person, the Supreme Authority being always Monarchical; for both the Power of the Nobles and that of the Populacy are so altogether unknown to the Chinese, that we had a difficult Task when we were at Peking, to make them understand what our Government of the United Provinces was, and what were our High and Mighty Lords, the States General.

Political society was, the Chinese believed, authorised by natural law, and that natural law was profoundly absolutist. The Dutch were not like the Chinese; the Statholder of their Republic was not like the Great Qing. But the British monarch might obviously be compared directly with the Qing Emperor. It is true that Nieuhof spoke of the ruthlessness of the Tartar conquest, reporting that over 8,000 people were killed in 80 days in Canton in cold blood, and over 100,000 altogether, but this was in the context of a civil war and Ogilby's readers would understand that. This account painted an optimistic picture of an empire of immense power and wealth, managed by a thorough-going bureaucracy, which had successfully recovered from that terrible civil war through the effectiveness of Absolute Monarchy, the system ordained, in Chinese tradition, by Heaven:

> The Emperor of China Commands over the Lives and Estates of all his Subjects, he alone being the Supreme Head and Governor; so that the Chinese Government is absolutely Monarchical, the Crown descending from Father to Son.

The Atlas project

It took a while to sell the tickets, but *China* evidently carried the lottery through to a position where Ogilby's fortune was restored. "An Embassy from New Bacavia, to the Emperor of China', ... publish'd in my last Lottery, prov'd so acceptable, that I resolv'd to carry on in the same way hereafter, the whole Business of my Pen."[24] That comes from the next volume he produced, *Africa*. Evidently inspired by the conceit of becoming some kind of literary Genghis Khan, he announced in May 1669 that

> girding himself couragiously for no less than the Conquest of the whole World, making the Terrestrial Globe his Quarry, by a new and Accurate Description of its four Quarters, viz. EVROPE, ASIA, AFRICK, and AMERICA, and teaching them English, bring home in triumph illustrated with large Maps, and embellished with various Sculptures ... and New Remarks, the product of our later Discoveries.

This was not exactly an original idea. He knew that engravings were already being prepared for a world atlas by Richard Blome. That book, which appeared in 1670, was *A Geographical*

Description of the Four Parts of the World. But it was a single small volume with just 24 maps copied from a French world atlas of 1658 by the French geographer and mapmaker, Nicolas Sanson. Ogilby's plans were no less derivative, but far more grandiose. But he needed the copyright protection that Blome had from the Stationers' Company, and he was not a member.

So he was given it by the Crown. He secured copyright protection for a description of the whole world in a series of volumes to be printed under the general title of *An English Atlas.*[25] On 10 May 1669, he issued proposals for five volumes: Africa, America, Asia, Europe, and Great Britain.[26] The last of these would eventually acquire a life of its own and become his lasting monument, *Britannia.*

The first volumes appeared with breathtaking speed. The first quarter of the world to be overwhelmed and subjected to Ogilby's imperious folios was Africa, and the great volume he produced in 1670 opened with a re-iteration of his fifteen-year copyright protection, this time signed not by Arlington but by the King himself. It was followed immediately by the *Atlas Japannensis* (1670), then *America* (1671), *Atlas Chinensis* (1671), and *Asia* (1673). The speed and energy of his work did not mean that it appeared skimped or hurried on his large, thick pages. The Japan volume opens with a description of the Earth's place in the cosmos and a recitation of the book of Genesis down to descendants of Noah's son Shem, from whom he argues the Japanese are descended (and thus are children of Adam like the rest of humanity). He then launches on a history of navigation and discovery since the introduction of the compass, with long and dramatic accounts of voyages and conquests, before eventually admitting his reader to the company of the Japanese, "strangely different in their nature from all other people". He then traces the history of the

Dutch and Portuguese in China, and does not return to Japan until he is over sixty pages into his text.

Having copyright protection of his own did not mean he had any qualms about plagiarising others. The creation of an empire invariably involves plunder, and it was entirely in keeping with the times that Ogilby took his plunder from the Dutch. *Japan* is translated from a book by Arnold Montanus, so is *America*, and the rest from works by Olfert Dapper. The originals were splendidly illustrated and produced by the same printer who had produced the Dutch edition of *China*. Ogilby plainly had a deal with him.[27]

In his introduction to *Africa*, Ogilby cheerily explained that he had started work on the book by doing some research, but happily soon found that was not necessary:

> a Volumn lately published beyond Sea in Low-Dutch, came to my hands, full of new Discoveries, being my chief and only Business to enquire after, set forth by Dr. O. Dapper, a Discrete and Painful Author, whose large Addition, added to my own Endeavors, hath much Accelerated the Work.

King Charles granted him the right to import the paper for it tax-free, and away he went. His dedication to the King explained that this was the first part of

> a New Model of the Universe, an English Atlas, or the setting forth, in our Native Dress, and Modern Language, an Accurate Description of all the Kingdoms and Dominions in the Four Regions thereof.

London was rising from its ashes, and so was he:

> I also, Dread Soveraign, feeling a Spring of Youthful Vigour, warming my Veins with fresh Hopes of better Times.

And as for his king: Charles had a project of his own which precisely matched Ogilby's view of how a sovereign ought to rule. The King wanted information about his kingdom that would open new possibilities of power over it. That was the reason why in 1671 John Ogilby would find himself appointed Royal Cosmographer with the job of inventing a new way of knowing the kingdom and a completely new way of presenting the result. He would need the spring of youthful vigour. He did not know it, but he was about to start the greatest work of his life, the magnificent and completely original creation called *Britannia Vol. 1*. He was seventy.

PART 2

The Journey to *Britannia*

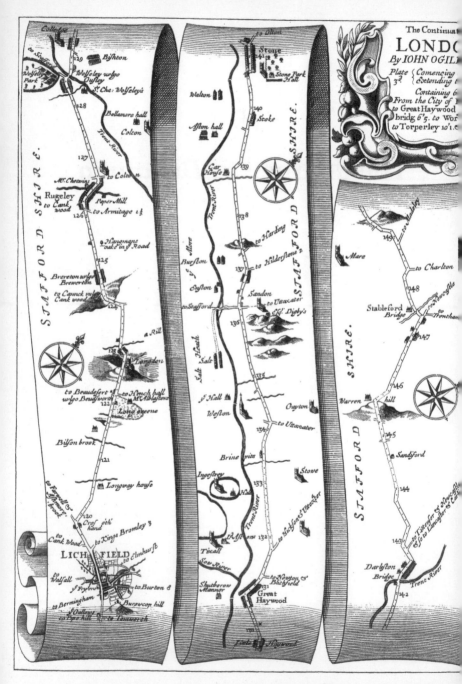

The Continua
LONDO
By IOHN OGIL
Plate { Comencing t
3ᵈ { Extending t
Containing 6
From the City of
to Great Haywood
bridg 6'5. to Wor
to Torperley 10'1.8

13. *Britannia*: The Road from London to Holyhead, Lichfield to Chester.

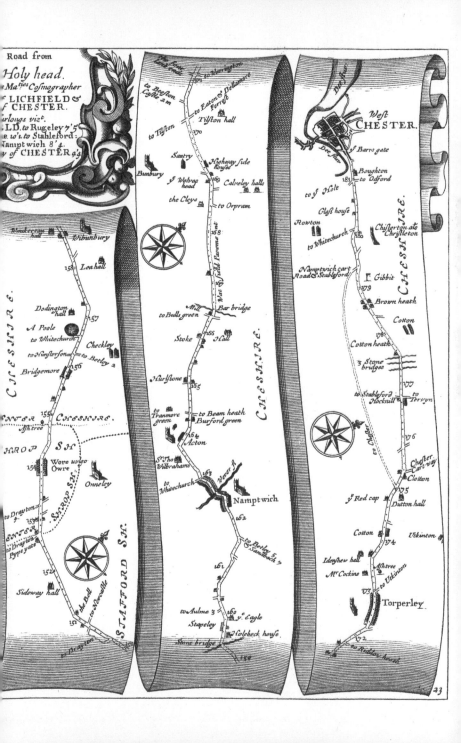

The Use of Maps

The mysterious book

The dedication to *Britannia* addresses Charles II in a rotund and flamboyant flourish:

> I have attempted to improve our Commerce and Correspondency at Home, by Registering and Illustrating Your Majesty's High Ways, Directly and Transversely, as from Shore to Shore, to the Prescrib'd Limits of the Circumambient Ocean, from the Great Emporium and prime Centre of the Kingdom, Your Royal Metropolis.

But that does not mean that it was an atlas of commercially useful roads of the day. The first of "the Principal Roads of England and Wales" to be displayed in *Britannia* goes from London to Aberystwyth, in Cardigan Bay.

It is very hard to imagine anyone in late seventeenth-century London wanting to get to Aberystwyth. By the time you reach the third plate, and Aberystwyth is revealed, the road being shown did not actually exist. The text says the town consisted of less than a hundred houses and a completely ruined castle.

There is no evidence that anyone wanted guidance to it. People found their way around the country by following printed itineraries, with lists of the towns to pass through on any particular journey. These were very widely available and indicate the roads that existed at the time. The itineraries of the day did not mention Aberystwyth at all.[1] Ogilby's road can be traced to Presteigne in Wales, but from there on much of it was simply not there. The route he shows is an imprecise drovers' track to the coast. In the text this is described as "altogether open, as well as Mountainous and Boggy even to Aberistwith", a route which "lies through a kind of morass". It was completely impassable to wheeled transport. He does not mention the fact, but heavy loads had to be moved overland to Aberystwyth on sledges.

What was in Ogilby's mind, to present this as the very first of the principal roads? It was not just because Aberystwyth starts with an "A". The itineraries of the period do have a town on Cardigan Bay that starts with an "A", but it is not Aberystwyth. They show how to get to Aberdovey. Unlike Aberystwyth, Aberdovey was at the end of a real road. It went through Wolverhampton, Shrewsbury, Welshpool and Machynlleth. It was the site of the customs-house for this section of coast,[2] and unlike the "road" to Aberystwyth, this was an official post-road. Post-roads were supposed to be maintained by the local authorities. Every parishioner was liable to perform six days' road maintenance work a year if called on by the parish's Surveyor of Highways, who also had the power to commandeer materials. There was a well-developed postal system, with changes of horses kept at staging-posts (post offices). In 1681 postage was two pence per sheet for the first 80 miles and another penny for any extra distance. Post was meant to travel from London at the rate of

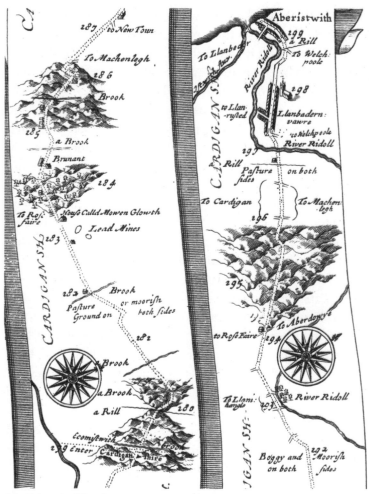

14. *Britannia*: The 'boggy' road to Aberystwyth.

120 miles in 24 hours, so it was said that a post from London to Newcastle on Monday could expect a reply on Friday.

Ogilby starts his book with a list of the post-roads, mentioning the Aberdovey road, but does not show it in the main part of the book. So there is a puzzle with understanding how Ogilby has chosen these roads. There is also a puzzle with understanding why he has left others out, including some far more important than the road to Aberdovey. For example, what has happened to the road to Liverpool?

It simply isn't there. *Britannia* opens with a map of England and Wales showing "all the principal roads actually measured and delineated". "Leverpole" is shown as a named spot, but there is no road connecting it to anywhere else. It does not appear in the gazetteer.

Liverpool was a real place, and people did make journeys to it. The way to get there is set out in an itinerary published in 1666,[3] and the town was certainly included in other guide books as a commercial port which provided an outlet for the industries of Manchester.[4] Between 1626 and 1652, Lancashire quarter sessions (which handled matters concerning Manchester) had to concern themselves with the state of highways between Liverpool and Warrington at least seventeen times.[5] That makes no sense if there had been no road. If Ogilby's work was designed to help the flow of commerce, the road to Liverpool should have been included and the port described. So why is it left out?

Ogilby does say that he had to drop many of his measured roads because there was no room in the volume, but a later opportunity to remedy this omission was not taken. In 1679 his partner and executor, William Morgan, produced a handy little pocket book listing all the roads in *Britannia* and adding many that had been measured but not included.[6] There was still no road to Liverpool. It had evidently been deliberately ignored.

The pocket book had none of *Britannia*'s strip-maps. There was just a sketch map of the roads, "that if you do not find in the book the road you would go by, by finding in the map the place where you are, and wither you would go, you may easily see what road will bring you thither". Unless, that is, you wanted to get to Liverpool, which was not shown at all. It was mentioned in a list of towns at the start of the little volume, but with no indication of where this mysterious place might be found.

This makes it hard to believe that Ogilby was mainly interested in improving commerce, because Liverpool was the main port for Dublin. He had served in Ireland in the household of its Lord Lieutenant, Wentworth, and must have known that Wentworth's luggage had been sent by road to Liverpool for shipping. That was back in 1633. The earliest picture of the town, made five years after *Britannia* was published, shows a substantial stone seaport with some two dozen ships bustling about. A young tourist, Celia Fiennes, who visited shortly after that, wrote in her diary that she had seen "a very rich trading town, the houses are of brick and stone, built high and even so that a street looks very handsome. The streets are well paved. There is an abundance of persons who are well dressed and fashionable. The streets are fair and long. It is London in miniature as much as I ever saw anything." The road was a pack-horse track which came across the Pennines from York and Hull, and it is shown on a map of 1668.[7] It was only notionally a highway, but that was true of several of the routes shown in *Britannia* and was not grounds for exclusion. Commercial carriers had regular runs arriving in London from Liverpool every Thursday, returning next day.[8] Just a few years later London traders were bringing their American trade to Liverpool and sending goods on to London by road, rather than take the risk of having their ships captured by the French.[9]

Britannia's main purpose was not promoting commerce, and Ogilby was not telling the truth about it. There had to be a much more compelling reason for this prodigious expenditure of time, effort and vast sums of money.

The way-wiser

In the early 1670s, John Ogilby's wheel travelled more of the land of England and Wales than any wheel had ever done. He called it a "way-wiser" – a road-knower. It carried no baggage, no passenger. It was followed by its caretakers, guardians of this scientific instrument that was measuring its own journey as it rolled through towns and villages, over hills and bridges, crossing bogs and moors, year after year restlessly onwards with no final destination. Its circumference was 16½ feet, one fortieth of a furlong, with a wooden handle to be pushed along and a clock-face that recorded the distance. One of its servants kept the rim clean, and another used a compass to note its direction. In 1675 a new way of knowing the world was born from these revolutions. For the first time, a European country had a map of its roads.[10] *Britannia* laid out 73 roads in strip drawings from town to town.

This lavish volume bound its shifting, archaic and mysterious land in elegantly-wrought fetters of scientific delineation. It created a new image of reality for which 26,000 miles of road had been physically measured inch by inch. It contains a hundred beautiful engraved plans of roads of England and Wales as winding ribbons chopped into sections. It is not a map, that bird's eye view of countryside filled with rivers, hills, forests and habitations. Places not on the selected roads simply do not exist in this *Britannia*. But those roads are generally depicted with extraordinary care and accurately portrayed. Rivers, hills, forests and communities are there not by right, but only as aids to understand and follow the roads. That is

15. The way-wiser, from the frontispiece to *Britannia*.

why great houses, streams and bridges, notable features and the nature of the land are spelt out along the way. It is the record at one inch to the mile of thousands of actual journeys. The most significant fact about each place was how it could be approached and left behind by Ogilby and other strangers. *Britannia* was a new way of understanding the kingdom.

There is an accompanying text giving descriptions of towns and villages on the roads, and details of markets, resources, antiquities, local histories and the names of inns. Portraying each road in its own space, rather than in a landscape, Ogilby's strip-maps were the ancestors of route planners created by motoring organisations which eventually evolved into the navigation system of our vehicles. But why did he do it? We see the world as John Ogilby presented it, as a place for journeys. We never realised what else he was showing us, or why. Today Ogilby's luxury book is regarded as a beautiful and innocent creation, its sinuous elegant strip-maps seductive and charming. It was apparently not necessary for this pretty thing to trouble itself with issues like politics. But this is a façade. This book had a secret and well-constructed purpose.

The mind of a mapmaker

To begin to understand *Britannia* we need to realise that no European had ever thought they wanted anything like it. It seems so obvious to us that people need maps showing roads that we can't easily grasp that people understood the world in a way that did not require them. We are so sure that people must have wanted road maps that we imagine their existence even when there was no such thing. The Peutinger Table, often called the first road map, is a schematic diagram of the road network of the Roman Empire from Ireland to India. It shows distances between towns and was probably originally carved on marble in the heart of Rome. Today what survives is a thirteenth-century parchment copy, a third of a metre wide and nearly 7 metres long. Ogilby pays homage to it as the ancestor of his own work, but it is not a road atlas. It is a display of the length of Rome's arms, in all meanings of the word.[11]

We may similarly misread medieval maps. There is a fourteenth-century map of Britain, the Gough Map, which has east at the top and marks London and York in gold. It shows routes between towns as red lines whose lengths are marked in leagues – one league being the distance to be covered in an hour (on a good day).

It looks to us like a road-map, but that is because of our way of seeing things. In fact the few roads that existed – London

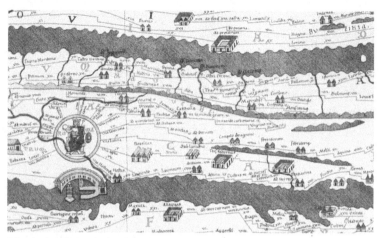

16. A section of the Peutinger Table: Italy with Rome centre left, Croatia above; Africa below.

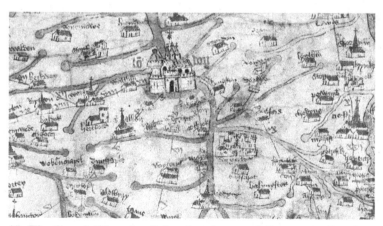

17. The Gough Map: detail showing rivers and distances to London.

to Dover, for example – are not shown. The red lines seem to represent off-road journeys, presumably for royal officials. It is a statement of the King's power, an English equivalent of the Peutinger Table, a vision of Edward III's reach across his island empire with helpful notes on it about the mythical history of the kingdom.

Nobody needed a map of roads. Scholars and apprentices moved around guided by their own networks of colleagues. Most merchant expeditions were by ship. Inland trade was generally moving goods and animals to and from markets, and those involved already knew where they were going. The word "travel" did not even exist until the fifteenth century. Before then, people said "fare", as in "farewell". The hint of finality was clear. It comes from Norse and Frisian, connected with distance and voyages. In Norse, a "Farman" was a seafarer. But then *The Voiage and Travaile of Sir John Maundeville, knight* appeared, a pilgrim guide built around the story of what we now know is a fictitious character. His "travail" meant hard labour, hardship, suffering, and the word seemed so appropriate for the experience of moving any distance over land that we have used "travel" ever since.

Not even pilgrims needed route-maps. There is a very celebrated visual itinerary of the pilgrimage to Rome drawn by Matthew Paris, a monk at St Albans in the thirteenth century. It shows the route on illustrated strips, with each resting place one day's travel from the one before. The pilgrim's daily walk, his Journee, gave birth to our word "journey". It does seem to have been an inspiration for Ogilby's strip-maps.[12] But this itinerary gave no information about way-points, cross-roads or even directions, and was not meant for use in the real world. Monks could study it at leisure, making the pilgrimage in their minds.

Once engraving appeared the situation could have changed. At the end of the fifteenth century an A3-sized sheet called the Rom.Weg, the path for Rome, was printed in Nuremberg for its tourist market, "since man has the inclination to experience foreign countries and strange things". It was in German, not Latin, and the market must have been travellers to the Holy Year celebrations of 1500. It mapped routes to Rome from Poland, north Germany and the Netherlands.[13] The distance between towns was shown by dots: counting them gave accurate road distances. Who were these secular unguided wanderers? Perhaps the likeliest customer was a pick-pocket. There are hardly any surviving copies.

The Rom.Weg ignored other important trade routes. In 1501 it was re-drawn with a different market in mind.[14] Nuremberg was promoting itself as the new imperial capital. The Peutinger Table had showed that all roads led to Rome, but only one road was shown there now, the road from Nuremburg. To show Nuremburg as the imperial hub, a lot of important routes that had been on the Rom.Weg had to be rubbed out. In their place, new roads were drawn by arbitrarily marking direct routes from town to town, with the distance dots evenly spaced, taking no account of the actual course and length of the roads.

This cunning device to misdirect travellers did not encourage any great desire to see roads on maps. It was reproduced in ever more inaccurate versions over the years until being abandoned in favour of text itineraries.[15] Engraving allowed maps to become more common, but their purchasers did not expect to see the layout of the roads.

In the early seventeenth century John Speed's beautiful county maps showed unconnected settlements in the landscape. Counties were countries in miniature, with their own proud histories which Speed represented in the crests of their ancestral lords. This was "chorography", the visual representation of the story of the land. The King's Highway was not seen as the skeleton on which it hung. The wealthy

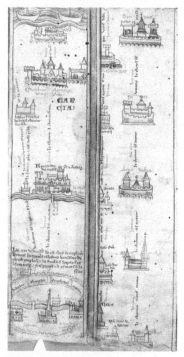

18. A page from Matthew Paris' itinerary.

landowners who bought expensive copies of county chorographies were subscribing to a picture of Englishness that was not rooted in their sovereign but in the estates of their peers. England belonged to its major landlords.[16]

The need for a guide

By the 1670s road travel had become commonplace but it was still normal to make a will before going any distance. Problems of travel in the period tend to be exaggerated in modern eyes, but the roads were bad and people were sometimes reported to drown in pot-holes. One diary records a journey to London in May 1695 when the road at Ware was so deeply flooded that coach passengers had to swim and a pedlar drowned. But that was exceptional.[17]

So long as you made your journey between April and September, stuck to a popular route and had plenty of money a cross-country journey could usually be done safely enough. But there was still a problem in finding the right road, and it is easy to see why later generations have supposed that *Britannia* was designed to help. Travelling alone across territory that you had never seen before was very difficult. A traveller could choose to ride with the post-boys for three pence a mile for horses plus four pence per stage for the post boy, so the journey from London to Newcastle would cost about £4. That is equivalent to the price of a taxi today. Stage coaches, also called flying coaches, were cheaper and more comfortable on the routes where they existed, but slower than post-horses. They cost about a pound for a hundred miles and covered 40–50 miles a day. You could hope to travel from London to Oxford or Cambridge in a day, and Bristol in two.[18] The very wealthy even travelled in their own coaches and paid road-menders to patch up impassable stretches.

That was what Samuel Pepys did when he tried to take a holiday shortly before work began on the road atlas. In June 1668 he was thirty-five years old, a civil servant making more than £500 a year. He had just bought his first coach, comfortable, light and modern with leather suspension and glass windows. This was a very new kind of vehicle, designed for showing off. The idea was to trot prettily around London wearing obviously expensive clothes, visible but protected from the weather. Samuel was enthusiastic to be bolder. He set off with his wife, her maid Willett and his cousin's daughter

Betty for a short tourist trip around southern England. The idea was to cover 300 miles in nine days, rising early so as to see as many sights as possible. He immediately discovered that the roads were a problem, and had to pay road-menders to get him out of London to Barnet. That was just the first such occasion and the coach suffered a "mischance" near Newport Pagnell. He decided that to get to Stonehenge and to cover the ground from Bath to Bristol, he dared not use his precious vehicle.

He also needed expert guidance. The moment he left London he was, literally, in uncharted territory. He knew the places he wanted to visit, but had very little idea of how to find them. The land was the private intellectual property of its residents. Unfamiliar travellers did not belong and could not cross it without their help. They were foreigners. Pepys used the word to describe people who lived outside London, and once he left the city, he became one himself.[19] He needed to hire local guides. In some cases inn-keepers rode out to help their guests. Others were highly-paid professionals acting as personal travel agents and bodyguards, like the guide who took the party all the way from Huntingdon to Oxford for £1 2s. 6d. On a couple of occasions when they travelled unaccompanied Pepys had been quite worried, especially when they crossed Salisbury Plain at night. The area was notorious for armed highwaymen. After that, they found a guide to escort them over the Plain from Salisbury to Bath, but he led them onto an unusable path.

They abandoned this path and "with great difficulty" found a road to a town, where there was a small inn. They arrived about ten at night. The only room there already had a pedlar in it. They "made him rise", and Pepys and his wife installed themselves. A folding bed was put up for Betty and Willett.

"It seems, had we gone on as we intended, we could not have passed with our coach, and must have lain on the Plain all night."

The following morning they found the beds were full of lice, "which made us merry". Pepys paid off the guide (only two shillings for this one) and they were led to the next town by the landlord. But Pepys did not bother to hire a guide to lead his coach home from Bristol to London, presumably thinking that it would be perfectly safe and obvious where to go. They got lost on the seventeen-mile journey from Newbury to Reading. It was humiliating, and he got into a bit of a strop.

The published help available to Pepys was of little use. One cartographer, John Norden, set out at the end of the sixteenth century to show the roads of Britain but he only completed a small part of his project. He also produced a table of distances between towns, but these are given as if the land was a flat Euclidean plane. He dismissed real-world distances as misleading "by reason of the curving crookedness, and other difficulties of the ways". The only printed guides available to a traveller were lists of towns on the route from A to B, but without any directions. Many of these itineraries were printed in annual almanacs that were published for general household use and usually hung on a nail over the fireplace. The core of every almanac was the list of astrological predictions for the year, but they also included all sorts of reference material: medical advice, information on the care of animals, tide tables, times of sunrise and sunset and, of course, road itineraries. And in a land with few signposts every branch track and crossroad offered the chance, as Pepys discovered, for an unintended visit to the wrong destination.

The itineraries included distances, which were usually wrong and made more confusing by the fact that there was no standard length to a mile. For example, a typical itinerary for Pepys' journey from Bristol to London ran:

> Bristol to Marshfield 10, Chippenham 8, Marlborough 15, Hungerford 7, Newbury 9, Reading 15, Maidenhead 10, Colnbrook 7, London 15

There was no reliable way for a traveller to measure how far they had gone, so perhaps it did not matter that this itinerary is nineteen miles less than the actual journey. But of course that depends on what you mean by a mile.

The expression "a country mile", which translates as "much too far", is a reminder of the days when miles were as long as anyone felt they should be. The account of James I's progress into England in 1603 was annotated by its London publisher, who pointed out that to understand the energy of this king who could ride nearly thirty-seven miles in under four hours, you had to know that these were not the tiddly little miles used in southern England but "the miles, according to the Northern phrase, are a wey-bit longer than they be here in the South".[20] The variations were extraordinary and highly localised, from the 3,208 yard mile of Northamptonshire to the 1,689 yard mile used in Lancashire. Bizarrely, that measure was being used on the road into Warrington from the north, but as you continued south towards Chester the mile grew by 75% to 2,970 yards.[21] London and Westminster had a mile of eight furlongs of 660 feet. That was set in legislative stone in 1593, when the plague was sweeping through London and the theatres were shut. A brief Act of Parliament tried to limit overcrowding by summarily forbidding building new houses or subdividing old ones within three miles of the two cities, and defined what it meant by a mile.[22] This "statute mile" was to be used in legal documents[23] and by the Post Office,[24] but it was by no means universal.

Communities were separated from each other by ancestral territorial boundaries, and units of weight and measure were matters of local tradition, not national standards.

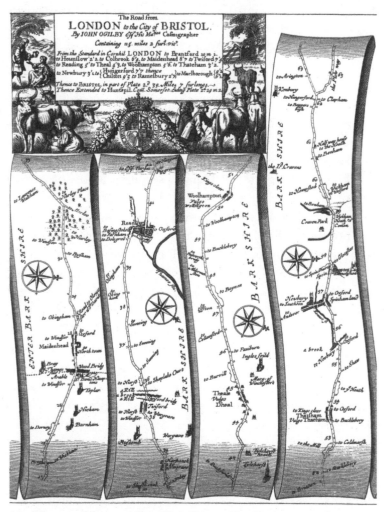

19. *Britannia*: The road from Reading to Newbury.

Britannia certainly changed England and Wales into lands that could be travelled without local knowledge or help. Ogilby's beautiful strip-map of the road from London to Bristol did not just show every physical feature on the way but also gave local names. Between Newbury and Reading, Pepys would have learned that places he was trying to find – Theale, Woolhampton and Thatsham – were locally known as "Dheal", "Wollington" and "Thacham". The secrets of the landscape, which gave a living and power to guides, had been uncovered and made public. The private intellectual property of each locality was now in the hands of anyone with access to the book.

Following Ogilby's roads would certainly be a more precisely described journey than one from an almanac. But the book would not replace a local guide or serve as an almanac-substitute. It was not a cheap and cheerful object hanging on a nail but a fantastically expensive luxury possession.

Travellers still did not think they needed a road map. One was published around the time of Pepys' carriage trip, but it was never more than a curiosity. Tucked away in the British Library is a pristine sheet, a Royal folio (20 x 25 inches) dated 1668, showing a map of England and Wales.[25] It says that it was "Printed, colloured and sould by Rob Walton at the Dyall in Little Brittaine with all Other mapps". It never was coloured; that and its wonderful fresh condition indicate that it was never sold at all until it passed into the hands of a dealer in antique maps, on to a collector and so, in 1910, to the British Museum.

It appears to be a proof copy of an advertising promotion to help Rob Walton draw business to his new address. It is bordered with decorative vignettes of towns, with two larger images of London – one showing the city as it had been, with old St Paul's prominent. He used to sell his maps from

St Paul's churchyard. The other picture of London was even larger, showing the fire at full throttle. That was the disaster that had destroyed his shop. He had now relocated and needed to get the new shop up and running by showing off something special. The map is astonishingly finely detailed yet highly legible and it carries an advertisement for more and fuller maps "sold at the same place as this is".

County boundaries are indicated, hundreds of towns are named and shown. But something more was offered, and this was unique: "The Roads or highways are playnly layd forth by two small lines from towne to towne by which any one may playnly see the way from One place to an other. By TP 1668." TP was Thomas Porter, who wrote various travellers' guides which Walton had published. They were a well-established map team, and this was a brilliantly novel idea. But it was not meant to be of any practical use. It was not sold on a stout folded sheet or bound in a cover. The seas include some interesting monsters and two ships in combat. It was an exercise in dexterity and a demonstration of expert knowledge. They had taken the standard reduced version of Saxton's 1583 wall map which, like all maps of Britain, showed no roads, and shown that they could add "Roads or highways".

"Road" was a very modern word, which first appeared in the 1590s (the traditional term was "way", and "road" had simply meant a ridden journey). It is clearly used here as a synonym for "highway". "Highways" were roads capable of carrying waggons, and as Ogilby says, these were largely arteries for London. The city was served by around 200 waggons and at least 150 gangs of packhorses every week, carrying far more goods on the roads by value than travelled by water.[26] But these highways faded away as London became more distant. The map shows only one highway west of

Bristol, running to Plymouth; the only ones in Wales were to Denbigh, Cardigan and St David's.

This map was a one off which no one seemed to feel needed repeating. Wenceslaus Hollar, the celebrated engraver who worked for many years with Ogilby and would make a major contribution to the look and quality of *Britannia*, had begun work on a similar project the year before, but no one was enthusiastic enough to see it through. An opportunistic publisher of legal textbooks in Gray's Inn now got hold of the plates and printed Hollar's map with the claim that it showed "the Highwayes and principall Roads, thorough the Kingdome, never before expresd in any such mapp".[27] Well, it showed a few of them. The only known example of it is in the Royal Collection at Windsor.[28] The "catalogue *raisonée*" of Hollar's engravings, by Richard Pennington, simply describes it as a map of England and Wales and does not mention that it displays roads.[29] These maps were soon forgotten.

In 1665 Porter and Walton had produced probably the most useful of the itinerary books that were actually used as travel guides. That included a conventional two-sheet map without roads, accompanied by a printed list of "High wayes" and the itineraries to be followed in going from one town to another. The novelty maps of roads were of no practical value.

But they are immensely valuable to anyone trying to assess the roads in *Britannia*. Hollar actually completed a much better version of his road-map while Ogilby's atlas was being put together, or very soon afterwards. He shows all the post-roads, even if they did not qualify as highways.[30] These maps by Hollar and Porter confirm for us what roads were actually in use, the post-roads and routes used by carters and stage-coaches when Ogilby started his survey. They make it clear that in many cases, Ogilby goes off in a very different direction.

He must have been familiar with these single-sheet maps. Ogilby's book has an introductory double-page map showing the roads in his atlas just as Porter showed them, imitating the convention of double lines for a road, which avoids confusing them with rivers. He too uses dotted lines for county boundaries. Porter has a plaque off the Welsh coast showing "The Scale of English Miles". Ogilby's map is to the same scale as Porter's, but he moves the plaque down to the entrance to the Bristol Channel, so that he can show three scales: "Vulgar computed miles" (as used by Porter), the smaller "Direct Horizontal Miles" and his even shorter "Dimensurated road miles".

Ogilby puts a royal coat of arms in the same position as on Porter's map, off the Northumberland coast, and re-edits the cartouche to read "A New Map of the Kingdom of England and Wales Whereon are Projected all the Principal Roads Actually Measured and Delineated by John Ogilby Esq. his Ma'ties Cosmographer".

It all looks very similar. But the roads are not the same at all. They confirm beyond all doubt that Ogilby was not mapping "the Highwayes and Principall Roads, thorough the Kingdome", surveying instead some most peculiar "roads" and ignoring very important ones. Hollar's finished map shows the road to Aberdovey and omits Ogilby's strange road to Aberystwyth. Both Hollar and Porter show roads from York to Liverpool and Hull, which Ogilby leaves out. As we have seen, according to Ogilby there was no road to Liverpool. So what is his book about?

Maps revealed the information needed for the exercise of power, and Ogilby's work, too, served that purpose. But he was representing the land in a new way, to serve the needs of a very small market. Its production cost was quite phenomenal; the budget could be calculated to be hundreds of millions of pounds in modern money. It required the exploration and accurate measurement of tens of thousands of miles of tracks, paths and causeways, the work of the finest engravers, the collection of detailed information about every town and village on the roads and the invention of new ways of drawing landscape. It weighs nearly 8 kg, and is solid with grandeur and self-importance, too huge and too precious to carry on a journey. And some of its routes are, to put it gently, unexpected.

The use of the atlas

At first glance, the frontispiece to *Britannia* looks like an advertiser's vision of the way this product will improve your life. It shows travellers venturing boldly and happily towards the sunny uplands, map in hand. But they are using an individual sheet, not the whole book. One historian suggests that purchasers would tear out pages as they needed them,[31] but it would be astonishing if anyone really did that.

At the time of writing (2016), *Britannia*'s published price of £5 translates to nearly £750,[32] which is ludicrously expensive for a book. It compares with a modern built-in car navigation system, but of course it was not built in to a vehicle, and weighs nearly as much as a one-year-old child![33] There is no evidence that anyone used it to make a journey, or that it was designed for a commercial market.

The test of the commercial attractiveness of a seventeenth-century publication, like a modern movie, was not what was said about it, but how quickly it was pirated. That did not happen to *Britannia*. A few months after it appeared, the strip-maps were printed without the text as *Itinerarium Angliae,* a less expensive visual itinerary, and a few months after that individual sheets were being sold, presumably for people like Pepys. But the atlas was not a commercial hit, and pirated adaptations did not begin to appear until 1719, over fifty years later. Then Thomas Gardiner produced a cheap and portable version of the strip-maps as *A Pocket-Guide to the English Traveller*, saying that the original book was just "an Entertainment for the Traveller within Doors". By then that was true, as it is now, and this is the accepted view of the book today.[34] But all that money and effort was not spent just to enable road-surfing for couch potatoes. *Britannia* was not a tool for virtual journeys undertaken as meditative exercises. So what was it?

Ogilby said in his dedication that its usefulness was perfectly obvious. He reminds the reader that ancient Persian monarchs, Alexander the Great and Julius Caesar all ordered lists of roads and distances. But as he goes on to say, his measured distances and pages of description represent something quite new – as do the beautifully detailed strip-maps. So what did he mean by saying that this massive tome, which could only be consulted in the library of a wealthy man or in a university, would help to "improve our Commerce and Correspondency at Home"? "Correspondency" meant communication, but it also meant things agreeing with each other. Somehow this book is supposed to increase commerce and harmony. That sounds like some vague pious hope, but the money involved was far too great to be spent on nothing more than whimsy.

Ogilby certainly knew of other uses for accurate road measurement besides helping individual travellers. Although he listed a few ancient empires that had tabulated their roads, he did not mention the most modern, the Chinese. But he knew about it. In his second book on China, the *Atlas Chinensis* (1671), he included a Chinese table of "The

Roads, and Distances of the great Cities of China one from another". The text stressed their "exceeding curious" practice of measuring distances between provincial capitals using "a Scale of Furlongs written by the Chineses themselves". There was an ·obvious connection between the roads, the accurate measurement of their distances, and the Qing postal system, which, he said, meant that news spread through the whole empire in a few days.[35]

The lesson of China was that measuring roads and the associated control of communications was at the heart of the centralisation of power. Was this what this book was really for? There is good reason to think so, and that takes us into the territory of plots and conspiracies that had actually played such a large part in Ogilby's carefully hidden life.

In 1670, the King had decided in the most absolute secrecy that he needed to throw off the shackles that he had accepted as the price of his restored monarchy. He should become, like the ruler of France and the Emperor of China, the absolute master of his land. To achieve this, he would need money, armed strength, ministers who would carry through the plan, and detailed knowledge of the kingdom. There was a conspiracy afoot. And *Britannia* was part of it.

The Secret Treaty of Dover

A Tale of Two Kings

The origins of *Britannia* can be traced to a decision taken between the King and his sister Henrietta in December 1668. While Ogilby was hard at work with what he called "the conquest of the whole world" between the covers of his great atlases, Charles was secretly contemplating the conquest of his own kingdom. The two projects would eventually coincide.

Henrietta, known in France as Minette, was married to Louis XIV's brother. The positions of the kings of France and England were very different, and the three Stuart siblings felt that this needed correcting. When Charles had fled to France in 1651, after the collapse of his forces at Worcester, he was twenty-one years old. He arrived in a kingdom that was in the throes of its own terrible Civil War in which regional Parlements and disaffected nobles violently challenged royal authority. That struggle had begun with an insurrection in Paris in August 1648, just as Parliament was wrapping up its military victory in Britain. It was called the Fronde, the word for the slingshot which Parisians used to shatter the windows of the mighty, and which David used to kill Goliath. It grew into a monstrous catastrophe which may have cost around a million lives over five years, more than the total death toll in the English Civil Wars.[1]

In 1649, when Charles I was executed, ten-year-old Louis and his mother had to flee Paris. When Charles II arrived there the French king had escaped to the provinces with his mother and her chief minister, Mazarin. Charles moved into the Louvre, and was the only king in Paris until 1652. Monarchs were an endangered species in Western Europe. Only four still held their thrones, two on the Iberian peninsula and two in Scandinavia. None of these ruled unfettered. Philip IV of Spain was in desperate trouble, faced with a revolt of Catalonia and the complete loss of Portugal, where a new-made king ruled by the grace of his nobles and was never permitted to be crowned. Frederick III of Denmark was only elected king by the nobility once he swore never to involve the kingdom in a war. That just left Queen Christina of Sweden, who was not exactly a model of successful monarchy. A highly intelligent woman, she made a public show of ruling by Divine Right while being quietly cynical about the idea, and would convert to Catholicism in 1654 not because it justified absolutism but because it gave her the excuse to abdicate, change her name and go to live in Rome. The Pope then described her as "a queen without a realm, a Christian without faith and a woman without shame". So in 1652, a betting man might wager that the Age of Kings was being rapidly ended. But then Louis became legally old enough to rule, and his forces, commanded by Marshal Turenne, returned to the walls of Paris to win a decisive victory in the Faubourg St Antoine. He was then taken in a coach into Paris by Turenne and his mother, gambling that he would not be attacked by the populace. He was delighted and relieved to be cheered and welcomed by a city that was utterly weary of war and where some 20% of the population were literally starving. France had a king again. This quite extraordinary young man would rapidly change everything.

The Stuarts, having experienced bitter defeat in England, were now participants in the beginning of the Royalist triumph in France. Turenne's right-hand man on the battlefield was Charles' nineteen-year-old brother, the dashing James Stuart, whose contribution was generally regarded with admiration. Turenne had poor eyesight and had used James as his spotter. Now the Stuart brothers watched the remarkable spectacle in the Louvre which established Louis as the Sun King. A national theocracy was born and nothing was ever the same in France again. In the words of Bishop Bossuet, whom Louis would appoint to tutor his son, "The royal throne is not the throne of a man, but the throne of God Himself".

While the English Parliament ruled supreme, the Parisian and other regional Parlements of France were reduced to cyphers. Louis developed a powerful and wealthy centralised sovereignty in which popular opinion was only permitted to express submission. Charles' mother and sister moved into the Palais Royale with Louis and his brother Philippe. Theirs was the world that John Ogilby believed would inevitably come into being in England. But when Charles' restoration came, it did not give him that sort of power.

His sister stayed in France and married Philippe a month before Charles' coronation in London. Her brother-in-law Louis' revenues were 23 million livres, around £2 million. Brother Charles, by contrast, had been handed a throne whose feudal rights had been abolished, whose estates had been dramatically reduced, and whose income came from grants of taxation. By 1670 Louis' income had trebled, largely thanks to Jean-Baptist Colbert's management of finances and the economy.[2] This was a trick that Charles could not achieve while Parliament controlled the purse-strings. It paid lip-service to the notion that the King ruled by Divine Right, but did not give him the power to make law or impose taxes. He had to understand that the royal prerogative, the sovereign power of the King, was limited by Parliament's prerogative, and the King would receive what Parliament chose to give him. It was definitely not as much as Charles wanted or needed. His power to rule as he saw fit was sharply circumscribed. The Earl of Rochester, poet, courtier and debauchee, is credited with the memorable lines:

> Here lies our sovereign lord the king,
> Whose word no man relies on;
> He never says a foolish thing,
> Nor ever does a wise one.

Written on Charles' bedchamber door, this connects with Rochester's belief that the King's political acts were shaped by his mistresses rather than his own ideas, which the Earl foolishly stated too clearly:

> His scepter and his prick are of a length;
> And she may sway the one who plays with th' other

Rochester was banned from Court for that. But Charles supposedly accepted the criticism on his door as having a different significance, and replied "That's true, for my words are my own, but my actions are those of my ministers." He felt he was a prisoner of a system that he should command.[3]

His inability to restore royal power to what it had been in 1640 was painfully obvious to him. In other kingdoms, kings were now becoming more powerful and their lands were prospering. It began with Frederick III of Denmark, who had originally ruled under the strict control of his nobles. In 1660 he had been able to institute absolute rule by decree. That had been made possible by a military victory over Sweden, which made him the most popular man in the kingdom. Portugal was moving in the same direction, under a Prince-Regent, John, who would take the throne as an absolute ruler. Charles married John's sister. Kings were no longer on the road to extinction, but it seemed clear that for monarchical government to work, shackles on royal power needed to be broken. Charles felt that his position as a hamstrung, hobbled monarch was intolerable. Something must change, and that needed to be something that made England look more like France.

His brother and sister believed strongly that this involved converting to Catholicism, which was seen as a religion that endorsed the King as an instrument of divine power. This vision was spelt out by Jacques-Bénigne Bossuet, who provided the philosophical underpinnings of Louis XIV's rule:

> Firstly, royal authority is sacred; secondly, it is paternal; thirdly, it is absolute; fourthly, it is subject to reason. God establishes kings as his ministers, and reigns through them over the peoples....So princes act as ministers of God and his lieutenants on earth. It is through them that He rules His empire.[4]

This was not a proposition likely to be endorsed by English Protestants and he was in no position to challenge their view that the King was a partner in government, not the master. The constitutional arrangement of the Restoration in England was that there would be no reprisals against those involved in the rebellion apart from the regicides and a couple of determined Republicans, and there would be religious toleration. Parliament soon interpreted toleration as only extending to Anglicans; Catholics and non-conformists were treated as equally undesirable. Unlike the French Parlements, which had only ever been local forums, the House of Commons was a national body representing over five million people. It had the largest franchise in the world, which had greatly grown as inflation shrank the size of the property that entitled a man to vote. A few years later, Daniel Defoe addressed the Speaker as one "Commanded by two hundred thousand English-men", which was believed to be the approximate size of the electorate and was probably a pretty low estimate.[5] If they had been as apathetic as a modern electorate they might not have minded being side-lined. But they were not at all apathetic, especially when it came to France and Catholicism.

It would be hard to over-state the strength of popular anti-Catholic feeling in England. As Bossuet's writings indicate, religion was not just a matter of faith. It was political theory expressed in an aesthetic and a performance. Catholicism, with its ritual "bells and smells", celebrated hereditary and institutional authority; puritanical Protestant simplicity and sobriety challenged this with personal conscience and individual judgement. Puritans and Catholics knew which side they were on less through theological dispute over sacraments and grace, and more by their gut feelings of comfort or unease in each other's surroundings. The aesthetic of English nobility and court was Catholic, that of the House of Commons and the City was Puritan. Catholicism was equated with the supremacy of the King over the law and Parliament, and with the influence of France over England. The difference between Charles and a large number of his subjects was that they thought this would be a catastrophe. Anti-Catholic suspicion had reached fever pitch with the Great Fire. There was an unshakeable public belief that the fire was brought about by an international Catholic conspiracy. The government tried to stop people blaming the fire on Catholics and ordered a trouble-making pamphlet to be confiscated and burned by the hangman, but "No Popery" was a rabid cry which was easily taken up.

Catholics in England were barred from public office and religious assembly, and Catholic priests were legally subject to expulsion or death, but these laws were not enforced with any vigour. It is likely that up to 10% of the gentry and aristocracy were Catholic, though their numbers were declining.[6] Charles certainly liked to surround himself with Catholics, and not just for political reasons. His Queen, Catherine of Braganza, had a Catholic household with twenty-eight priests. She was not the only Catholic to share his bed. Nell Gwynn distinguished herself from Charles' other mistresses by calling herself "the Protestant whore".

The discussion of his conversion came when things had gone very badly with Parliament. The King was responsible for paying the cost of running the kingdom, including the civil service, the army and the navy, as well as his personal and family expenses, and the cost was supposed to come from Crown lands, customs and excise duties. That income was about £300,000 a year too low in peacetime. The shortfall, and any extra required for war, had to come from grants made by Parliament. He had been forced to make a humiliating peace with Denmark, France and the United Netherlands in 1667 because he was simply not allowed to spend the amount they could commit to war. The Duke of Buckingham (the son of the great dancer) was supposed to be managing Parliament for him, but in May 1668 it rose for the summer having refused to give Charles the money he needed or to accept religious toleration. They saw him as spectacularly profligate, dissolute and immoral. He restored his relations with Parliament by ceasing to ask for money.

From Charles' perspective this was not working, and so far as he and his closest advisers could see the only way this kingdom could be governed was by decree, without Parliament, and with French financial support. But Britain was allied with other Protestant powers, Sweden and the States-General of the Netherlands, against Catholic France. To get French cash meant switching Britain out of the Protestant world and into the Catholic one.

Charles agreed with his brother and sister that he would consider converting, but he would act only when public opinion should allow it. That would mean that he must have a wave of popular support following a great military victory. That was how Frederick III of Denmark became an absolute monarch. Even then he would need the French king to supply him with money, and the means to put down rebellion. He did not propose having, as he put it, to resume his travels.[7]

This would mean assisting Louis in his policy to take over the Netherlands. Charles would have to become an ally of France, with the reins of power in his own grasp to be used for Louis' advantage, at least in the short term. It should also give him the opportunity to share in the defeat of the Netherlands, with all the political and commercial benefits that should boost his popularity.

On 25 January 1669, according to his brother James' memoirs, Charles spoke to a very select gathering in total secrecy in James' chambers at Whitehall. He had already mentioned his interest in conversion to them: now he spoke of the need to make concrete plans for what could be a very unpopular event. The country was run by a small group of ministers known, from their initials, as the Cabal – Clifford, Arlington, Buckingham, Ashley-Cooper and Lauderdale – but only the first two were brought into this secret. James himself was there: he was much more interested in personal religion than Charles and was in the process of a secret conversion. He had no doubts about the need for Charles to join him. Baron Arlington (Henry Bennet) ran the government with apparently unquestioning loyalty to the King's wishes. Thomas Clifford was on his way to becoming a Catholic. John Evelyn, a well-known intellectual-about-town, described him as "Bennet's creature". Lord Arundell of Wardour, one of the most prominent Catholics in England, was also present as one of the conspirators. The King may not have been keen to impose an absolutist Catholic monarchy on an unwilling Parliament, but some around him, especially Clifford, certainly did like the idea, and Charles was sure that some kind of drastic action was necessary.

A decision was made. The French Ambassador was asked to tell Louis that Charles wanted his help to carry through his conversion, and Arundell was sent to Versailles to negotiate a treaty. It was the most explosive treaty ever signed by a British ruler, and the few people involved knew that. Has any other treaty begun with words like Article 1 of this one?

> Articles so secret and advantageous to both monarchs have been agreed upon that a treaty of similar importance can hardly be found in any period of history.[8]

It went on in the most amazing way:

> The King of England, being convinced of the truth of the Roman Catholic religion is resolved to declare it, and to

reconcile himself with the Church of Rome as soon as the state of his country's affairs permit.

Louis would pay Charles two million "livres tournois" (about £165,000) for his conversion and three million livres a year (about £250,000) as a military subsidy, which Charles would use to overthrow his international obligations and join with France in an assault on the Dutch United Provinces at a time of his own choosing. They would dismember their conquest and share the spoils. Charles' income before this was around £900,000, but it was impossible to reduce his expenditure below £1,200,000.[9] Now he would be able to rule unshackled, without needing Parliament. The Restoration settlement would be set aside, the clock would be put back to before the Civil War.

That was shocking enough. But there was more:

... the King of France undertakes to provide, at his own expense, 6,000 troops for the execution of this design, if they should be required.

In other words, this time the King would not have to rely on his own forces to crush rebellion. The French would invade to help him.

Once this chilling document had been drawn up, the Earl of Sandwich provided a grand escort for King Louis' sister-in-law to visit her brother Charles in May 1670. There were nearly 240 people in her suite.[10] Her husband, frightened of losing her, had forbidden her to go to London, so Charles met her at Dover. Quietly hidden away for a few hours during the ceremonial there, unknown to almost everyone, the secret treaty was signed on 1 June by the French ambassador, Colbert de Croissy, Arlington, Clifford, Arundel and Sir Richard

Bellings, who had worked on it as Arundel's translator. The two sovereigns ratified it, separately and in profound secrecy, three days later.

Its existence was supposed never to be revealed. A dummy treaty (also secret!) was soon afterwards signed between France and England, negotiated by the unsuspecting Duke of Buckingham, which did not mention religion or French troops. This was a smokescreen to hide the real document. When suspicion did arise that something like this had been done, Charles faced down Parliament with a lie:

> I assure you, there is no other Treaty with France, either before or since, not already printed, which shall not be made known.[11]

The plot

The treaty remained a well-kept secret for nearly a hundred years. It required Charles to declare war on the Dutch, the Third Dutch War, but that was also called for by the dummy treaty. The secret clauses were the ones concerning Charles' conversion and its backing with a French invasion, and they were never invoked because the war went seriously wrong. Inevitably, although no evidence appeared of the secret treaty, rumours swirled around that the King and his ministers intended to reduce Parliament to a cypher, institute rule by the royal prerogative and introduce Roman Catholicism at the heart of power.[12] Later historians ridiculed this conspiracy theory. In 1757 David Hume explained that it would have been "absurd and incongruous" for Charles to oppose popular feeling to such an extent. The Crown would never have made itself so completely dependent on Louis. But in 1763, Hume made the only documentary discovery in the whole of his career as an historian, and it was a corker. He was shown James II's memoirs in Paris, and they included the text of the treaty.

Who was the bigger fool – Hume or Charles? Hume's discovery was buried in a later footnote: "One cannot sufficiently admire the absolute want of common sense which appears throughout the whole of this criminal transaction." His only explanation was that Charles was "chiefly fitted for smaller matters, and the ordinary occurrences of life; nor had he application enough to carry his view to distant consequences, or to digest and adjust any plan of political operations".[13] Hume clearly had in mind the Greek word for a man whose mind is confined to domestic affairs and cannot handle political thought. That word is "idiot".

As we have seen throughout this book, people were very good at operating in total secrecy. They often avoided putting things on paper and many routinely burned correspondence after reading. In recent years many historians have said that they do not believe that Charles meant to convert, though that has more to do with the lack of evidence that such plans were really in hand than anything else. We do not know much about the preparations for the execution of the plot, and many historians take the view that it was not serious, just a device to try to get some money out of Louis.[14]

Even after the Treaty had been found there was still no known evidence that preparations were put in hand for the conversion and invasion. That changed in 1937, when it was found in Clifford's papers. It turned out that Clifford had kept both the text of the treaty, and his military plans to deal with the anticipated uprising.[15] We will see those reflected in *Britannia*, which was begun as part of the preparations.

To keep Louis informed about the progress of the plot, Louis and Arlington installed an agent in Charles' life. Minette brought in her retinue a glamorous maid of honour, Louise de Kérouaille. Soon after returning to France, Charles' sister died, suddenly and unexpectedly, which left Louise without any position. Charles, devastated by his sister's death, was persuaded to write to the French king asking for her to return to England as a maid of honour to the Queen. Ambassador Colbert, together with Arlington and his wife, made sure that Charles then had every opportunity to get to know the lady. She was soon in the Queen of England's household and, once she was sure of his affection and had been firmly told what Louis expected of her, in the King of England's bed. Her position was tied to Colbert's support, and that was dependent on her acting as a French agent.[16] The English thought it was perfectly obvious what she was doing, as an anonymous ballad entitled "The Whore of Babylon" makes clear:

> You treach'rous Whore of France, may Rabble's rage
> Seize thee, & not till thou'rt destroy'd assuage.
> The People's Cross, misfortune, constant Pest,
> The Millstone whelm'd upon this Nation's breast;
> Britain's impairer of her honour & Fame,
> The Festering Sore of Majesty, the Shame
> Of English Councils; the Crowns costly load,
> And Prince's thriving Infamy abroad;
> The Commons hater, & false France's friend.
> Lord, from this Basilisk Loyalty defend!
> Permit a change, our ruins to confront,
> Let us be govern'd by an English Cunt.[17]

The widespread suspicion that something underhand was being cooked up with the French was more justified than the most hardened conspiracy theorist might imagine. For the treaty to produce results, three kinds of action were required

– military, diplomatic and administrative. They were all in hand.

The military preparation required was significant. Charles had only a small army, no bigger than the 6,000 men Louis was now going to provide. There was profound suspicion of a standing army. Charles was now preparing to provoke and face down a major uprising, so he would need to have a substantial force, in addition to the proposed French troops, and he would need effective regional strongholds. That meant recreating major fortifications that had been demolished under the Commonwealth. Clifford set about drawing up a briefing and plan of action for the King in an astounding document which he headed "The Scheme", written in the summer or early autumn of 1670.[18] The days of compromise and consensus were over. Clifford was designing the iron fist of real power that Charles now wanted. In June the previous year, the King had written to Minette saying that he was fortifying the main ports and placing them in secure hands. The Scheme begins with the need to give his forces useable fortifications throughout the kingdom. They included many coastal locations, but also inland strongholds, "And magazins armes and amunition are to be forthwith sent to most of these places".

Reading *Britannia* in the light of this, we can see that it evaluates the state of fortifications in each town very soon after The Scheme was drawn up, and shows that a substantial amount of the work Clifford wanted had already been done. The coastal defence works would have happened without any preparations to handle insurrection. They were needed because of the Dutch naval strength. But there were other strongholds which Clifford thought needed to be "repaired or finished" as part of The Scheme and which were more to do with internal control. So it is rather striking that very soon after The Scheme, Ogilby reports that York, Carlisle and Chepstow all had their fortifications renewed and in good order, as Clifford had required.

All manner of devices were found to conceal spending on improving military readiness in 1670. For example, The Scheme required Pendennis Castle to be put back in working order so the Governor was given £3,000 as an unexplained bounty,[19] and the Lieutenant of the Ordinance was granted £12,500 "on the Wine Act",[20] so using royal revenues from import duties. That was enough to buy 700 tons of iron or over 80 tons of bronze.[21] The Scheme went on with recommendations to reform the army, especially the guards (the core of the small standing army), and to appoint discreet loyalists as Colonel of the King's own regiment and as Constable of the Tower. Clifford thought he could increase the size of the guards regiments and the garrisons, bring home the Regiment at Barbados, and equip inexperienced light infantry with small artillery pieces, making them "as usefull at first to quell insurrections as the well form'd troopes". He advised Charles to replace the Lord Lieutenants of the Counties and their deputies with men who would support an absolute monarch against sedition. Charles was also building up his military strength another way. He had command of the militia, a trained citizen force. Militia men were believed to have minds of their own, and the theory was that the King could be allowed command of them because they could not be used to enforce tyranny. That created a loophole.

In 1668, when Scotland was in upheaval against Charles' insistence on imposing bishops and dismantling the Covenanter religious structures, he drew on an act of five years earlier that gave him power to raise a militia of 20,000 foot and 2,000 horse "for suppressing any forraigne invasion, intestine trouble or insurrection".[22] He told the Scottish Privy Council to raise that force, and do it from areas in the country where Royalist magnates held sway.[23] The Scottish Parliament confirmed his absolute power over religious affairs and its Militia Act of 1669, to great alarm in England, restated his freedom to use this militia to deal with insurrection anywhere in Britain. Lauderdale told Charles happily that "In a word this Church, nor no meeting nor Ecclesiastick Person in it, can ever trouble you more unless you please; and the other act settles you 20 thousand men to make good that power."[24] He was very pleased with their military effectiveness: the Act that raised them allowed them to be used wherever Charles wanted, and Lauderdale was impressed by their evident readiness for action: "Those six regiments yow may depend on to be ready to march when & whither you please."[25] They added up to more than three times the size of the army. Of course it was important to ensure that no one else was entitled to be armed, especially the merchants, guildsmen, apprentices and craftsmen who were potentially more deeply attached to Protestantism and liberty than to the Stuart cause. The solution to that was found by the novel device of making it illegal for anyone with less than £100 a year in income from land to have a gun. This was a Game Act, under the pretext of restricting guns to men entitled to hunt. If strictly enforced, this would have disarmed everyone worth less than £100 a year who was not in the militia and whose income was not from land.[26]

The second leg of the project was diplomatic. That involved connecting with the Pope, and around the end of 1670 instructions were prepared for a top secret envoy from Whitehall to Rome. The following April, Arlington presented Charles with the envoy's instructions for approval, but the time was not yet ripe. That would come with the surge of enthusiasm to be created by victory over the Dutch, and they were still Britain's allies. That created an even more challenging diplomatic task. The treaty required a joint Anglo-French war with the Dutch. Clause 5 was quite clear about that:

Both sovereigns will jointly declare war on the States General

This was the French pay-back for the money they were giving Charles. There were, of course, plenty of people in England who could also see the advantage of demolishing their main rival for global commerce. It was also Louis' quite rational conviction that the British would only tolerate Charles' conversion and assumption of absolute power if he could produce a great military victory and be seen as a hero.

The Secret Treaty left the timing of the war to Charles, and there was a long period of uncertainty over whether it would actually happen. It would be, to put it mildly, a controversial and unpopular project. But in July 1671 the pretext for a war against Britain's ally was being actively sought. Temple, the British Ambassador at The Hague, was replaced and his wife and daughter were brought home on the royal yacht *Merlin*, which had orders to fire if the whole Dutch fleet did not strike their flags to her. Fortunately for everyone on board, the Dutch did strike their flags. Arlington then pretended anger that they did not salute firing white smoke as they would have done to a British warship. He explained to the Foreign Affairs Committee, "Our business is to break with them, yet to lay the breach at their door."[27] The pretext for war had been found.

The *Merlin* incident took place on 26 August 1671. By now Charles was reckoned to be more than £3 million in debt.[28] The third leg of the project, the administrative preparation, had also been put in hand. That was *Britannia,* but it was not being produced by Ogilby.

The government survey

The model of an absolute monarchy was France, and Louis XIV's control extended over the whole kingdom. In 1661 Louis had given his chief minister, Jean-Baptist Colbert, enormous power over running France. To get a grip on the country, Colbert had ordered an inventory of France's resources.[29] Something similar was now going to be needed in Britain. There was no power to order the work to be done, so a commercial publisher had to be encouraged, and offered the assistance of the Royal Society. In 1670 a broadsheet advertisement appeared for a book called *Britannia,* which would contain such a survey "in obedience to His Majesties Royal Commands". This did not come from Ogilby but from Richard Blome. He wrote that the King had written "to all Justices of the peace, Sheriffs, Mayors, High-constables, Ministers, and Churchwardens" requiring them to provide information for it.[30]

Blome asked for details of communities, navigation, markets, local government, ports, fairs, the scale of local business and farming, antiquities, important citizens, and whether towns were on highways. His effort to collect information was made with the blessing of the Royal Society; several of its members subscribed to his *Geographical Description of the Four Parts of the World* and the Society considered that the collection of "chorographic" information was part of the creation of a scientific description of the world.[31] William Petty, who had carried out an effective survey of Ireland in the 1650s, was a founder member.

Petty's survey had been done with a thousand soldiers measuring the colonised land for distribution to settlers being installed by Cromwell. The connection between a country-wide survey and the imposition of new rule was obvious, and harked back to Domesday. But Charles had not seized the kingdom – yet – and this survey was launched in the gentle spirit of scientific enquiry and commercial profit. Blome did not have any powers and was not even offering a free copy of the book in return for help.

His Majesty evidently wanted this information, but this was not the way to get it. Blome promised to publish by Trinity Term, which meant by 1 May 1671.[32] On 18 July the Lords of the Treasury approved his petition to be allowed to import the paper his publication needed free of duty.[33] But whatever material Blome had collected was useless and never saw the light of day.

Arlington evidently had a problem. He looked forward to Britain becoming much more like France, with himself in a position much more like that of Colbert. But he needed the tools, and Blome could not complete the work. Never mind; Ogilby, with his customary foresight, had put himself into a position to step into Blome's shoes. In June 1670, when Blome had published his broadsheet for *Britannia*, Ogilby suddenly declared that he was rushing ahead with the British volume of his English Atlas, producing it as the third volume in his series (following Africa and Japan), not the fifth as originally planned.[34] He advertised it as *The Description of the British Monarchy*. It was much more lavish and expensive than Blome's effort, but was also to have descriptions of counties and their great houses.

John Ogilby received his summons to pick up the baton at the end of the summer of 1671, when it was clear that Blome had fallen down on the job. He received a letter in the King's name on 24 August addressing him by the novel title of Royal Cosmographer and saying that his British volume "seems to be of greatest Concern both to Us and Our Loving Subjects".[35] It would eventually be offered to the King as an open book with a coded text, containing "Pregnant Hints of Security" with "fainter indigested representations ... deducible in order to the Security against Civil Dissension".

Ogilby's new job

There are three kinds of evidence that Ogilby's work on *Britannia* was part of the planning for the execution of the Secret Treaty plot:

1 The fact that he abandoned his nearly-finished book when he was given a new brief.
2 The nature of that brief and the royal appointment that went with it.
3 The King's use of the Privy Council to finance the work.

The evidence that he was obliged to change his book is very clear. The letter requiring him to carry out the survey Blome had said he was making came two days before the *Merlin* incident, and went further than Blome's commission. This time information would not be collected on a voluntary basis but by compulsion: the letter required local officials to give him whatever assistance he wanted in conducting a survey. He would also have to trace how to move around the country by actually doing it, and setting up road markers throughout England and Wales.

At the end of November, Ogilby's book was advertised under Blome's title, *Britannia*. It was said to be ready for the press, but the advertisement was confused "... in regard, by his Majesties special Authority, he is to make a particular Survey of every County, as to the compleating of the Maps in a larger Volume then hath hitherto been published".[36] He had already sent out sections of the nearly-finished book to potential customers. One was the Earl of Denbigh,[37] who was unhappy that his family was not being given enough prominence.[38] Denbigh's petulant and apparently insignificant letter of complaint proves that Ogilby was telling the truth about the book being ready for the press, but that it was withdrawn as he set to work on this newly commissioned operation. By the time that war was declared on the States-General in March 1672 it was no longer enough to create new county descriptions and put up signposts. *Britannia* had been transformed into something completely novel, a new kind of map of the kingdom.

If the royal government was going to take control, it needed to know what was where, and that information was unreliable. Colbert had been conscious of exactly the same issue, and in 1668 he had asked the Academy to recommend ways of making more accurate maps of France.[39] He knew that the existing maps were misleading, but it still came as a terrible shock to eventually discover that France's main port, Brest, was being shown nearly 90 miles west of its actual position. The need was every bit as great in Britain, and after the Secret Treaty even greater. If an army was coming from France, it was necessary to know where places actually were.

There simply was no accurate map of Britain, and the Royal Society was not going to play the role of the Academy in solving that problem. The standard map of Britain was produced by Saxton in 1579. It was the first atlas of any country, and it gives England a stolid, rather dumpy form in which the east–west distance from the mouth of the Mersey to Grimsby is the same as the north–south distance from Grimsby to London. That is simply wrong: England is slimmer and more delicate than that. Saxton's errors were far smaller than those on French maps,[40] but the curvaceous east coast has been reduced so that Lowestoft does not thrust out quite so boldly and is shown directly north of Ramsgate. The shapely leg of the West Country, which on a modern map gingerly dips a ladylike toe into the eastern Atlantic, on Saxton's map appears more masculine and robust, delivering a hearty kick towards Ireland that swings it up so that Land's End is shown north of Plymouth. This was the map that Speed used a generation later. Ogilby would not draw a new map of Britain, in fact he uses Saxton's map at the front of *Britannia*, with the roads drawn onto it, knowing very well that measuring the length of a road involves hills and mountains, bends and twists, and a flat map does not reveal much about its length in the real world. He had to show real distances as well as enumerating resources. These are the questions that *Britannia* had to be created to answer.

The French were attacking the problem from a sophisti-cated theoretical standpoint, setting out invisible triangles whose corners were visible landmarks. It took a century to complete the 400 triangles needed to map the whole country. This was not only an impossibly slow process but it provided no information about hills or roads, so the distances that needed to be travelled between places were still unknown. In place of French intellectual theory, Ogilby would map the country with pragmatic empiricism.

This was actually more radical than the French project because it involved the invention of a new kind of geographic image, but he would not say anything like that. It was so different from any existing publication that he did not even have a word for it. It was simply "an illustration of the Kingdom of England and Dominion of Wales". Described as a "General survey of England and Wales",[41] his work was to be presented in two volumes and include an entirely novel form of information, over 200 engravings of the roads of Britain. He called the presentation "ichnographical", a word that literally means "like track-drawing" but which up to this date referred to a ground plan.[42] Ogilby was applying the precision of surveying a building to the whole length of a road, treating it as a one-dimensional structure.

Instead of a map setting out the locations of every significant feature on the fabric of the land ("mappa" was a cloth), it would dissect the country and plot places on disembodied roads, measured "Directly and Transversly, as from Shore to Shore, so to the Prescrib'd Limits of the Circumambient Ocean" by rolling a wheel down every single one of them! It would cost over £14,000 to carry through.[43] He would get wheels rolling as fast as possible and have the engravers at work at once.

The survey was so remarkable and so commercially absurd that it is clear evidence that Ogilby was working to orders. This was an unprecedented operation which went far beyond any commercial publisher's ambition. He was to ascertain distances with the public declaration that it was for postal use. This meant the first standardised calculation of distances on the post roads, an exercise of central power diminishing local autonomy and identity.[44] There was also the bonus of a direct connection to taxation, in the form of postal charges, since these were based on mileages between staging posts and miles were almost all much longer that they should be. There were too few miles and the Postmaster General was losing money. Using statute miles for postal charges, devaluing distance, might be as profitable to the crown as devaluing the currency. *Britannia* constantly compared "vulgar" distances with "dimensurated" ones and so justified higher postage. The post office was farmed out in 1667 for £21,500, and ten years later, after Ogilby had done his stuff, letter postage was costing £50,000.[45]

There had never been a Royal Cosmographer in Britain before. The title existed only in the great world-empire of Spain. A century earlier, Ortelius, whose *Theatre of the World* was the ancestor from which Ogilby's world atlas was descended, had been Royal Cosmographer to Philip II,[46] and at the time of Ogilby's appointment a Dutch astronomer, cartographer and military engineer, Langren, was Cosmographer to the King of Spain on a salary of 1,200 ecus a year.[47] Ogilby's job paid about a twentieth of that – £13 6s. 8d., less than half the pay of the royal locksmith, but the old dancing master, who understood the whole cosmos as an ordered system of patterns and law in which humans had their own proper place, was now part of the Royal Household, employed to map out a universe centred on King Charles. A cosmographer had a grander canvas than a geographer,[48] and looked to the sky. Every single road map in *Britannia* is headed "By John Ogilby Esq., His Ma.[ties] Cosmographer". Charles' government would not have granted any stipend without expecting value for money. This was a post that ought to bring some distinction to the Court, showing that it was as intellectually advanced as those of France or Spain, but if Langren's example was anything to go by, it also carried military implications.

Langren has a crater on the moon named after him. But Ogilby was engaged on earthly matters. Astronomers had devised new instruments to measure what was in the skies over men's heads, while no one knew how to measure the lands under their feet. Robert Hooke's *Micrographia* of 1665 did not just reveal the magnified louse and flea; it ended with a detailed image of Mount Olympus on the moon, revealing it to be a ring of hills pitted with craters. Since Hooke had a good idea of the diameter of the moon, these features could now be measured with more precision than the road from London to Hooke's family home on the Isle of Wight. Almanacs gave the distance from London to the ferry at Southampton as anything from 60 to 64 miles, none of which was remotely accurate. England's first Royal Cosmographer had the task of bringing accurate measurement down onto the earth. That was going to be the striking feature of *Britannia*. Ogilby would reveal the true length of Hooke's journey to Southampton as 78 miles 9 furlongs. His new title was not just an honorific. He would give the administration as much information about how to move over the land as Robert Hooke had provided about the body of a louse. It required that information for military efficiency and the effective control of the nation's resources.

This was not the atlas volume Ogilby had originally intended, but it served a purpose for which his whole life had been preparing him, and to which he was utterly committed. Monarchy would seize the reins of power. The detailed questionnaire which his surveyors were supposed to inflict on every community they passed through, was drawn up in 1672 in consultation with Hooke, Aubrey, Wren and other members of the Society.[49]

By now, Ormond had been admitted to the secret and was part of the conspiracy.[50] There is every reason to suppose that Ogilby, who Ormond trusted completely, would now know what this was about. He had to. The book had been transformed by "Special Encouragement from the King's Most Excellent Majesty", and from "several of the Nobility". By

1674 there was a further element to his title – "Geographic Printer". He was no longer entirely his own man.[51]

Which brings us to the business of financing the work. These road maps, which were to be the greatest work of his life, extended the cost and scale of the operation to something far beyond Ogilby's own resources. His English Atlas project had been bowling along merrily – Africa, Japan, America and China were all produced in 1670–71. They had a straightforward structure, of a largely pirated text and a few maps and illustrations, all beautifully produced, and the British volume was well in hand when it suddenly changed into something new, astonishing and completely original. The budget for it was £20,000.

There are different ways of understanding historic prices. If you just use a standard measure of inflation, this is approaching £3 million in today's money, which would be a startling price but is probably far too low. As a share of the gross domestic product, an equivalent size project today would cost getting on for half a billion pounds.[52] That seems impossibly expensive for a publication, though not for an innovative mapping project: it is probably the amount Google spends each year on Google Maps.[53] But the market for online mapping seems huge and obvious, the market for a luxury book limited and obscure. It is hard to see how it could be funded by normal commercial means. To make matters worse, within a few weeks finance completely dried up in Britain.

The financial crisis was created by Clifford's management of the King's desperate need for money. With a royal coup to finance he evidently thought it time for the Crown to stop paying its debts. This would be a short-term solution, as once Charles declared himself a Catholic, France would underwrite him – though that was of course a secret. On 2 January

1672 the government declared a "stop on the Exchequer". Capital and interest payments due on a large part of the royal debt were simply halted. This threw the banking system into chaos. Charles' principal creditors faced ruin and thousands of depositors with the London goldsmiths lost access to their funds. The notes issued by these bankers, which had been used as money, became instantly worthless. Although the "stop" was announced as lasting for just one year, there was no reason to believe that. In fact the debts involved were not resolved for thirty-four years.[54]

Ogilby tried to drum up private finance, but this was little more than a gesture. His forthcoming projects had been advertised in the quarterly catalogues put out to the book trade since 1668. In the 1672 February catalogue, he advertised that "for the better ease and convenience of those of the Gentry that live far remote, he hath appointed several noted Book-sellers in many of the chief Towns of England; to whom they may repair for further satisfaction, and see a Specimen of each Volume which is already finished" (he had now added China and Africa to America and Japan). He was also evidently exploiting his other Crown office, Master of the Revels in Ireland, to raise a bit of cash. On 7 February an advertisement appeared in Dublin saying that he had granted a licence for a Wheel of Fortune to be set up.[55]

He needed funds on an altogether greater scale than a fairground booth and a few provincial booksellers could drum up, and Charles tried to provide it. He had no cash, but on 6 February 1672 he told a committee of Privy Councillors to quickly find some way of raising the money that would not involve government funds.

The Privy Council must have been told that this had a high priority but of course could not be told why, or how urgently the results would be required. The Council had plenty on its plate and must have been rather baffled by the demand that they work out the financing of Ogilby's book. They were more concerned with organising Charles' unpopular and expensive war against the Dutch at a time of financial crisis. On 15 March the Declaration of Indulgence, which offered religious toleration to Protestant non-conformists, was extended by royal decree to include Roman Catholics. This was seen by many in Parliament as a fundamental move towards absolutism, not just because of the suspicion of Catholics but because the King was claiming to exercise a prerogative legislative power to strike down penal laws. The Lord Keeper of the Privy Seal, Orlando Bridgeman, refused to affix the seal to the document to make it law, and ended up being turfed out of his job. Two days after the Declaration was made, war was declared with the States-General, following an unprovoked English attack on Dutch ships in the Channel.

At this moment, Clifford was saying privately that Charles "might settle what religion he pleased, and carry the government to what height he would" so long as the courts continued to function and people did not fear for their property, "and if, on the other hand, the Fort of Tilbury was finished to bridle the City, the fort of Plymouth to secure the West, and arms for 20,000 men in each of these, and in Hull for the Northern parts, with some addition which might be easily and undiscernibly made to the forces now on foot, there were none that would have either Will, Opportunity, or Power to resist".[56]

The urgent need for an accurate road atlas as a military tool to deal with possible insurrection seems to explain why, during these difficult days, the Councillors, including Sandwich, who would shortly be leading a war-fleet, were obliged to find time to discuss the financing of Ogilby's project at a number of meetings, and to produce their report on 9 April.

The report approved his plan to produce a two-volume work, one of county maps and one of roads. To help finance it, subscribers should be sought and have their "Achievements, Residences and Titles of Honor" inscribed. For £10 they would receive a copy on fine Imperial Paper, or for £5 on inferior Royal Paper. The committee recognised that subscribers alone would not make the project self-financing, but though they approved the publication (as the King evidently wanted), they could not recommend a solution. The best they could do was to ask him to appoint someone to oversee the financing and report on it.[57]

Eleven days later Sandwich, on board his flagship, raised his colours as Admiral of the Blue to battle the Dutch.[58] Frederick III, King of Denmark, had been able to transform himself from a hobbled ruler under the thumb of a council of noblemen into Europe's first absolute monarch on the wave of popularity that followed his defeat of Sweden. Charles was now relying on performing a similar trick. It did not go quite so well.

Only one full Admiral of the Royal Navy has ever died in battle.[59] Sandwich's flagship, the *Royal James,* was a brand-new vessel, the largest in the Navy. Sandwich warned that its anchorage was vulnerable, but the overall commander, James, did not believe him, and the fleet was taken by surprise. Sandwich's body was washed up two weeks later, bloated and putrefying, recognised only from his Order of the Garter.

The hero's body was brought up the Thames in a magnificent pageant, with a grand procession to his burial in Westminster Abbey. If national sentiment could be whipped up over the tragic death of their Admiral, he would not have died in vain. Well, it was worth a try. The States-General seemed to be in desperate trouble as Louis' large army made a successful invasion, reaching Utrecht. The Dutch, panicking, said their condition was "redeloos, radeloos en reddeloos", irrational, desperate and beyond rescue. The Secret Treaty was still on course.

On 11 July the King issued a proclamation saying that he was personally subscribing £500 to *Britannia* and urging "Our Nobility and Gentry, and all others Our Ministers and Officers Ecclesiastical, Civil and Military" and anyone else with money to follow his example. He added that he had appointed three of the Privy Council committee, Bridgewater, Anglesey and Holles, to keep an eye on the subscriptions and report to him on who was contributing.[60] That was a surprising degree of royal involvement, and a further indication that this was not just a private commercial undertaking. Although the naval war was going very badly for England, Charles still had reason to be optimistic. In August 1672 he appointed Clifford, the most pressing advocate of his Catholic policy, as his Lord High Treasurer.[61] Although (according to the French ambassador) Clifford and Charles' Catholic brother James were arguing that the time was already right for his conversion, Charles and Arlington wanted to wait a bit longer, until they could celebrate victory over the Dutch.[62] But the planning for the coup still needed to go forward.

Ogilby's work would obviously be needed much sooner than the two years anticipated by the Privy Council committee, and he was proceeding with the road measuring with astonishing speed. Aubrey wrote in August 1672 that "Mr. Ogilby is writing the history of all England: the map is mending already". Since Aubrey believed that he was working on a history book, which must have been the general survey volume, "the map" must refer to the road-map volume in some form. If it was being amended it was virtually in proof stage.[63] The road map was obviously the most immediately valuable tool for any military planning that would be required, and this means that the main work of road measurement had already been completed.

What's in the Book

The meaning of *Britannia*

This book's main agenda is hinted at in the presentation of the preface. It appears below an illustration of a bookshelf of Ogilby's own publications, with his two-volume Bible at one end and *Britannia* at the other. They are the bookends to a contiguous body of work, in which are the lessons of antiquity and the descriptions of the continents.

In the centre of the bookcase is a shield with his coat of arms transformed. The Airlie crowned lion passant guardant, with its mullet, which his ageing circle of Royalists would

20. Preface heading from *Britannia*.

recognise, has put its foot down and now stands foursquare. It is drawn to fill the space, so that perhaps there was simply no room for it to have one leg raised. But it now looks exactly like the lion that crests the King's own coat of arms, and notionally stands on the royal helmet. It signifies the King's approach. Ogilby used images with precision, and loaded them with meaning.

His life's work as a maker of books is being presented as a structure devised to support the King. This title of this tool of power did not indicate a physical space called Britain, but a political project. This *Britannia* excludes Scotland and Ireland. Other books called *Britannia* were about the three kingdoms. William Camden's *Britannia* of 1577 was a description of the land and history of the islands of Britain and Ireland, including some 50 pages on Scotland. Written in Latin, it was translated into English in 1610 and dedicated to King James, who styled himself "King of Great Britain and Ireland". Speed's *Theatre of the Empire of Great Britaine* (1612) included Scotland and Ireland.[1] Ogilby's *Britannia* was never meant to include Scotland. His announcement of the project, in 1671, gives its title for the first time and says that it is "now ready for the Press" but that to complete it "by his Majesties special Authority, he is to make a particular Survey of every County".[2] That means England and Wales. There is no mention of the Shires of Scotland. Even his most ambitious plan for the work, "Mr. Ogilby's Design For Carrying on His Britannia", which proposed six volumes accompanied by "Four large Maps of the Kingdom of England", gave no thought to Scotland. So what did he mean by Britannia?

Half of the book is composed of text describing the roads and the communities on them. When he published *Britannia*, Ogilby also stripped out this text and published the maps on their own, and this was no longer *Britannia*. It was *Itinerarium Angliae*. *Britannia* did not mean that the maps displayed the territory called Britain.

"Britannia" had taken on a new significance by 1672. That was when Charles II issued the first English coins with an image of Britannia personified. Inevitably, being Charles II, he had the Duchess of Richmond, who he lusted after for years, model for the role.[4] He had packed her husband off to Denmark, where he died that winter. But Ogilby's *Britannia* was not given its title in honour of Charles II's sexual appetite. "Britannia" was the project that lay behind the creation of a new coinage and a new iconography.

The figure of Britannia was the personification of a Roman province which did not include Scotland or Ireland. The model for Charles' coin was a Roman sestertius thought to have been minted in 143 AD to celebrate the crushing of rebellion in the province.[5] Ogilby's book traced the roads in the area of the Roman province and like the coin, this Britannia was about crushing rebellion. The word was not there to represent a geographical territory. On the side of the coin where she appears BRITANNIA is the only word, just as on the Roman original. The other side of the coin looks like none other ever minted. A powerful Roman bust of the King with the laurel wreath of a victor bears not his title but a slogan, CAROLUS A CAROLO. Not so much Charles II as "Charles: The Sequel". Britannia is the personification of Charles' royal project.

This slogan had actually been presented to Charles II by Ogilby when he came to claim his throne in 1660, in a dedication:

May you…see that Prophecie fulfill'd in your Name and Person, Carolus à Carolo Magno Major,[6] which shall ever be

21. Britannia on a Roman coin.

22. Britannia on a Charles II coin.

remembred in the constant Devotions of Your sacred Majesties most humble, obedient and loyal Subject, John Ogilby.[7]

The "prophecie" was an inventive interpretation of a Nostradamus-type text by a German mystic, Paul Grebner, supposedly presented to Queen Elizabeth. It passed through a few other hands before Ogilby gave it this pithy shape, and Charles used it as the flip-side to his vision of Britannia.

Charles issued this slogan-coin to coincide with his attack on the Dutch and in expectation of his seizure of power. The words CAROLUS A CAROLO, given him by Ogilby, indicate that he is harking back to his father's seizure of power and personal rule in 1629. The sequel is proclaimed. The account of towns within the text of the book takes care to mention particular examples of loyalty and disloyalty shown to Charles I.[8]

Reading the secret

Ogilby's dedication states clearly that *Britannia* has a military purpose. He tells the King that he is presenting "the Scale of Peace and War". The Preface that follows goes on to speak darkly of "fainter indigested representations ... deducible in order to the Security against Civil Dissension and foreign Invasion". The message is reinforced in the book's puzzling frontispiece, drawn by the painter and illustrator Francis Barlow and engraved by Wenceslaus Hollar. Barlow was England's first wildlife painter, and he had been using the genre to convey coded messages.[9]

The picture is full of interest, though at first glance quite unsurprising. A high gateway, flying what looks like the royal standard and bearing the arms of the city of London, adorned with sculpture, opens onto a bucolic landscape. The gate's portcullis is fixed open; this was true of all the city's gates, symbolising the age of peace that had dawned with the restoration of the monarchy. The centre of the picture is a fine highway winding up a distant mountain; the land is full of sheep and cattle, there are hunters and fishermen at work. In the foreground the map is being made. Road measurers are using Ogilby's "dimensurator", surveyors sit at a table of

23. *Britannia* frontispiece.

instruments, a group of gentlemen discuss one of the strip-maps. Riders are setting out on the road holding one. There is also a three-man team shown using Ogilby's measuring wheel to measure a road. One person is pushing it along, one is cleaning the mud off the wheel and one is on horseback making notes and checking the direction of travel on a compass. But they are not on the great highway. Instead, they are measuring an obscure and almost invisible track. It seems to suggest that inside this atlas, some important highways might be missing, and some very obscure tracks might be carefully detailed.

That is the first and most obvious visual clue to what this book as about. It is the most obvious because it does not need any background knowledge to interpret it. The rest do, beginning with that great gate.

By the time this book appeared Ogilby was a very well established publisher of geographical works with an expert knowledge of the field. This image is a direct reference to the frontispiece of the best-known atlas of Britain at the time, a collection of maps of the English counties, Scotland and the provinces of Ireland published by John Speed in 1612 as *The Theatre of the Empire of Great Britaine*.

Both show a wall of niches with sculpted figures. It has been said that by displaying Britain's ancient worthies (a Roman, a Britain, a Saxon, a Dane and a Norman) as a unified symbol of the nation, Speed was suggesting a relationship between the atlas and political power.[10] Ogilby is deliberately setting out a much blunter relationship between his atlas and political power. Unlike Speed's frontispiece, the architecture in *Britannia* is positively threatening. Speed shows representative historical types labelled and apparently stuffed on display on a monument. Ogilby shows a fantasy gatehouse that dominates

24. John Speed, *Theatrum Imperii Magnae Britanniae*, frontispiece.

and commands the country beyond its walls, with two rows of serious-looking cannon pointing out from its buttressed sides. It is clearly not one of London's ten gates and is far more confrontational than any of them. Two figures are walking out of it, one carrying a pike.

Ogilby had erected a series of great arches in London for Charles II's coronation procession in 1660, and the top section of the gatehouse is reminiscent of them. It seems to summon the idea that this is an arch through which the monarch takes possession of his city, and now returns to take possession of his land.[11]

25. Coronation arch, London 1661, from J. Ogilby, *The Entertainment of His Most Excellent Majestie Charles II*, 1662.

In fact the King is up there on the arch doing exactly that. The sculpted figures in Ogilby's niches are not like Speed's; they are not ancient worthies posed in eternal stasis. They are wearing modern armour and in conversation. One sports a goatee beard, suggestive of the executed Charles I. His pose is clearly a reference to Van Dyke's 1636 portrait of Charles I in his robes of state, and has the same eye line (level with his waist). His younger neighbour, almost stepping out of his niche, is presenting the land below to the older man. This is an equally clear reference to Philippe de Champagne's 1653 portrait of Charles II, which shows him gesturing towards a sea far below (in that case the Channel) with waiting ships in an identical perspective. It is a copy of the Charles II picture with its body reversed; it is a mirror image. Reversal is a deliberate theme in the whole picture, as we shall see.

In the 1653 painting, shown here reversed to match the engraving, Charles II is signalling his intention to return to his throne. His image on the tower is gesturing towards a fortified harbour town below. Why? Can we identify it? There are clues to the geography carefully planted in the picture.

The road running up the picture goes north from London. That is spelled out by the two travellers just setting out for it. One is carrying a strip-map with a compass drawn on. Any doubts on this matter are settled by one of the three maps carried by the cherubs in the sky. The left-hand banner shows the beginning of a strip from the atlas titled "The road from London to Barwick" (Berwick). This is one of the principal roads of the kingdom, and it is busy. A rider is crossing over the bridge, another is over half-way up the mountain, and between them is a coach with a couple of footmen on the outside "boot" and an outrider. The northern mountain it climbs carries a windmill (prosperity) and a gibbet (law).

26, 27, 28. *Britannia* frontispiece, sculptures on gate. Charles I, by Van Dyke (1636). Charles II, by Philippe de Champagne (1653), body reversed.

So we might expect the fortified harbour to be on the west coast. But look again.

In the bottom right corner, three men are at a table littered with geometric and surveying instruments. They are in some consternation, drawing attention to a large globe of the world in the middle of the table, on which east and west are reversed.

This is not an engraver's mistake: the words "Europe" and "Africa" appear clearly on it, the right way round. Once more we have the theme of mirror-imaging, which seems to be a deliberate clue for how to read the geography of this landscape. East and West have been intentionally reversed. So although the road runs north, the fortified harbour town in the picture which apparently lies to the west is actually on the east coast. This is the town to which Charles II is pointing, showing it off to his father.

The third banner, directly above the globe, shows part of the map of England that opens the volume, depicting the coast and roads of the north-east including Hull. The fortified harbour is Hull. The towers of Holy Trinity Church,

29. Globe on the frontispiece of *Britannia*.

30 & 31. City on the frontispiece (above) compared with a reversed
sixteenth-century drawing of Hull (below).

the largest parish church in England, and of St Mary's,
rise behind the distinctive fortifications. In keeping with the
general theme of mirror reversal (which suggests a playful
reference to the printing process as well as an encoding of the
book's message), the city has been reversed east–west. Hull
had been the first town to resist Charles I, in April 1642, and
that resistance began the war that led to his execution. It was
also the last town to accept the restoration of the monarchy,

in May 1660. The political reversal of Hull had been the final act of the kingdom's submission to Charles II.

The central banner in the sky is a map of London taken from one of the strip-maps, but altered to ensure that the word "Westminster" appears – the word has been put over Holborn. From the bastion that is London/Westminster, the martyred King is being shown that his rebellious kingdom has been tamed.

In that strange frontispiece, on the grass at the foot of the picture, in the shadow of the guns, a group is studying a sample strip from the atlas, headed "The Continuation of the Road".

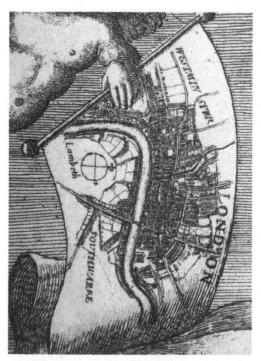

32. Banner from *Britannia* showing London.

The key to the puzzle

The message of this complex image, for those who want to puzzle it out, has more to do with the royal mastery of the kingdom and the subjection of its most rebellious city than simply the making of a road atlas. Ogilby has, by accident, provided us with a key to where to look for coded references in it. It is lodged in the Queen's library at Windsor. The drawing of the frontispiece can be dated to 1672–73 (see below, p. 369). All publications at this time had to be submitted to Roger L'Estrange, Surveyor of the Imprimerie. His job was to monitor seditious publications and limit dissent. He was notorious for his nose for anything suspicious – in fact he was called the "Bloodhound of the Press", and he famously complained that *Paradise Lost* was seditious for suggesting that sunlight after an eclipse "with fear of change perplexes monarchs". He worked thoroughly and ruthlessly; his midnight raids could bring a printer to the scaffold.[12] Ogilby seems to have expected L'Estrange to read the hidden message and either censor it or reveal it, so in the version of the frontispiece which he submitted, every clue to its geography and meaning are removed. To see which parts of the picture are coded, you just have to look for everything that has been erased. To help, I have added question marks where the image has been redacted.

The banners showing the road to Berwick and the map of Yorkshire are blank, the strip-map held by the horseman has nothing on it, the globe with East and West reversed is empty, the sheet saying "The Continuation of the Road" now says nothing at all. It is not that all text is missing – the central banner still shows the map of London/Westminster. But everything that might identify the geography and the true message of the book has been erased. Including, bizarrely, its title.[13] The flag over the gate has been blanked out. It took me a while to realise why, but it would have been the most startling part of the picture for L'Estrange, and a very clear political statement. In place of the lion rampant stood up on its hind legs that represents the King of Scotland, and which should occupy the top quarter next to the flag pole, Ogilby has put a lion passant guardant, with three feet on the ground. That lion represents the King of England. It does look as though in the world of the *Britannia* project, there is no place for a separate Scottish kingdom.

Charles had strong feelings about Scotland. After his father's execution, the Scottish Presbyterians accepted him as their king but there was no question of him ruling by Divine Right. In fact he did not rule at all; they had him in their power. He was a virtual prisoner of the Covenanters, whose support was oppressive and intolerable to him. He did make an escape to the home of his loyal friend Airlie, but was quickly recaptured. He would never forget his humiliation, and one of his objectives as King was to make Scotland as submissive to his authority as he possibly could.

The restoration of Charles' power in Scotland had been far more thorough than in England. He came back with a vengeance. In 1661 he had Argyll executed. Ogilby's brother, the Earl of Airlie, was vindicated at last. Agreement with the Covenant was outlawed and bishops were installed to run the Church in Scotland according to the King's wishes. From 1663 the minister handling Scotland was Lauderdale, a big, rough, boisterous, passionate man who sprayed spittle as he spoke. He would do whatever it took to ensure that Charles' wishes were effective and his power supreme. In November 1669 he reported to Charles that "never was King so absolute as you are in poor old Scotland".[14] This version of the Royal

33. *Britannia*: frontispiece as used.

34. *Britannia*: frontispiece as sent to the censor. The question marks indicate where material has been omitted.

35. Flag over gate in the frontispiece.

Standard made it clear that every vestige of Scottish sovereignty was to be considered ended.

Also missing from L'Estrange's copy is the coach and its outrider on the great highway, which automatically means that it is worth looking at with care. The coach is very small and sketchy, but its form is very distinct – that of a famous and unique vehicle, a gift from a French aristocrat, the Count de Gramont, to the King around 1664. Gramont had known Charles and James in Paris and had danced alongside James in Louis XIV's inaugural ballet in 1653, where they both appeared as "Lovers", along with the 2nd Duke of Buckingham.[15]

Its special status is shown by the footmen and the outrider, who must be a herald. Even without them it would have been instantly recognisable from its shape and the side window. It was the first coach made with windows (so it was the model

36 & 37. Coach on road in the frontispiece and coach given to Charles II by the Count de Gramont.

on which Pepys' coach was based), the idea being that the King's ladies could ride in it around Hyde Park and still make themselves visible as they used to do on horseback, rather than being shut up in a closed box. Gramont had it designed and made in Paris with the help of the Duke of Guise, who spent two thousand louis on it. It had caused a famous spat between two of the King's mistresses over which would ride in it first. The winner was Frances Stuart, Duchess of Richmond. The model for Britannia.

So the coach carried a double message: the royal wheels on these highways were a French gift, and they carried Britannia. Not for L'Estrange's eyes, obviously.

It is clear that the book presents itself in different ways to different readers. To those who are simply looking for an illustration of roads, that is how it appears. That is, of course, how it has been described and used from its original publication until now. But for those in on the secret, it does something else.

The Royal Society

The relationship between information and the King's power was at the heart of *Britannia*. This led to key members of the Royal Society, a predominantly Royalist community,[16] becoming increasingly involved. This does not seem to have been Ogilby's plan. Blome had approached the Society for their advice and approval for his own *Britannia*, but Ogilby had not followed that course. Nevertheless, during 1672 several Fellows of the Royal Society, including Wren and Hooke, became actively engaged with him. They were not men with time on their hands. Wren, the Surveyor General of the King's Works, was already so over-worked that in 1673 he resigned his chair at Oxford. Hooke, quite apart from being the Curator of Experiments to the Royal Society, was fully engaged on a huge number of projects. The Society was Royal precisely because the government needed to know as much as possible about the world, and the development of "physico-mathematical experimental learning", the original purpose of what became the Society, was just what Charles wanted. If the King wanted them to engage with Ogilby, they would, however overworked they might be.

The traditional account of the origins of the Society emphasises that its founders were men interested in experimental and mathematical enquiry for its own sake. Its motto, *Nullius in Verba* ("Take no one's word for it") is as important for examining history as nature, and should certainly be applied to the history of this institution. It was actually brought into being by the hidden hand of the King, who had come back to England with a plan to harness the "new philosophy" in his own administrative, and above all military, service. There has always been a bit of puzzlement over the apparent risk taken by the first members of the society, who would surely have looked highly suspicious. They were a gathering of both Royalists and Parliamentarians involved in arcane investigations in the dangerous early months of the Restoration, when who knows what plots were being brewed. It was surely a surprising relief when at their second meeting they were told that the King approved of their activities and would support them. That must have been because of his enquiring mind and fascination with chemistry? Well, not entirely.

The man who transmitted that message from the King, one of the Society's founders, was Sir Robert Moray. Moray was a Scottish courtier who had once been a Covenanter and a secret agent in Richelieu's service. He was not the most obvious candidate to preside over the Society's first meeting, but he did. He had been part of Charles' court in exile, and by the time of the Restoration they were very close buddies. A volume of his correspondence was published in 2000, showing that Moray was very concerned to match the French system for centralising and exploiting new knowledge in the service of the King, and seems to have developed a plan with Charles for doing this before they ever set foot again in England. The plan was to create a formal structure based on Gresham College, which is what happened within months of the Restoration.

Moray's greatest concern was Britain's military weakness at sea compared to the Dutch, and Charles well understood the issue. Britain's land-based forces were essentially for civil war. Its frontiers were the seas. That is why Ogilby's arch of naval power in the Coronation was given so much more prominence than any other. Ships had changed from being battle platforms for fighting men into floating artillery batteries, and this really did require a new military science. Of course, Charles was genuinely fascinated by scientific enquiry, especially by clocks and alchemy, but what he was after was something that would be of direct use, as quickly as possible. Another courtier, Lord Brouncker, a commissioner of the Navy, became the Society's first President. He was a serious mathematician whose great work was to calculate the ratio of the area of a circle to that of a square drawn over it. Squaring the circle is surely one of the best known arts of government. The other members of the Society well understood what was needed to hold onto their precious royal patronage, so they immediately concentrated on ship design, improving navigation and other scientific and mathematical developments that had an obvious military and commercial significance.[17] The first issue of their journal contained seven papers concerned with ships and the sea. Brouncker had used Gresham College for experiments on gun recoil.

One of the first members of the Society was the King's cousin Prince Rupert, once a dashing Cavalier, now a serious naval expert particularly interested in weapons metallurgy and artillery. He showed them how to make extra powerful gunpowder, and the best way to make shot. He showed them a repeating revolver two hundred years before Colt, as well as mines and torpedoes.[18] The second issue of the Society's journal specified a series of experiments to improve the Art of Gunnery, and it is likely that he drafted that. Perhaps not surprisingly, the progress of these experiments was unreported. Rupert was developing this new science in his armoury in Windsor Castle. With the help of collaborators from the Royal Society he designed a new kind of naval gun, the Rupertino. At the same time the Navy's master shipwright, Sir Anthony Deane, was working with Society Fellows (and he became one) applying new scientific principles to the building of naval vessels. One was the *Royal James,* a brand new 100-gun first-rate ship of the line equipped with Rupertino guns. It was brought into commission in January 1672, just in time for the war with the Dutch. The Royal Society was its midwife. Charles and James intended this devastating scientific weapon system to be one of the principal instruments of that decisive victory over the Dutch that should trigger the Secret Treaty's overthrow of church and state. It was the ship on which Sandwich perished.

Another of the Society's ways of helping the government was its interest in collecting data about the world, and above all about the kingdom, through surveys and quantitative studies. Ogilby's work fitted right in, and it was important for the Society to help him deliver. Hooke already knew Ogilby but Wren did not, and seems to have first become involved with him in 1672, when he put Aubrey to work on *Britannia*.

The measurement of roads

John Ogilby would never become a member of the Royal Society himself. Its Fellows were far too determined to maintain its social exclusivity to admit an artisan entrepreneur. Nevertheless, he was now His Majesty's Cosmographer and actively engaged with the leading figures of the new science. "Science" had once simply meant knowledge, but in these years it acquired a new meaning which became the basis of our civilisation. Scientific authority was now created by accurate measurement. In 1929 the facade of the University of Chicago Social Science Research Building was inscribed with words ascribed to a physicist, Lord Kelvin: "If you cannot measure, your knowledge is meagre and unsatisfactory." The cynic might observe that there is no evidence that Kelvin ever said this and that it suggests anxiety about the credentials of social science. But the point is clear, and it is one that Ogilby understood very well. The act of measurement replaces traditional error with modern truth. The search for precision is an end in itself, and Ogilby rejected Hooke's proposals to attach the way-wiser to a carriage, or to give it a saddle and a second wheel for scooting along, because these speedy creations would not be so accurate.[19] His road atlas introduced his new instrument to measure journeys, displaying it in the frontispiece, at the top of the dedication, in the cartouche on top of the first and last pages of roads, and a couple of others in between. These pages established the 8-furlong mile as the national unit of distance, and the one-inch-to-a-mile mapping standard, which was used by the British Ordnance Survey until the 1970s. His preface begins by proclaiming that the reader will here see Geography transform into a science. That capital G is illuminated with an engraving of the western hemisphere of the globe, with lines of latitude and longitude. From the ancients right up to modern times, he says, maps have been nothing but "guess-plots" and itineraries copied new mistakes onto old guesses:

> No Actual Dimensuration was ever perform'd but a Computation of Distances, by a Cursory Perambulation, made up the Original Work, from Whence, whatever Mr Cambden, Speed, or of late one Blome have since done, are but only Copy'd, with this ill Fate, That as the Original Errors were not onely transferr'd to, but augmented by the additional ones of the later Mapps.[20]

He slightingly (though correctly) describes the single-sheet maps with roads marked on them, by Porter and Hollar, as depicting "Notionary Roads upon imperfect Charts at Minute Scales".[21] The act of measurement changes everything.

Clearly Ogilby regarded his Wheel Dimensurator as comparable, in its capacity to display what had previously been hidden, to the telescope and microscope. And the instrument itself was – well, revolutionary. There was an existing method of measuring land, a chain of 100 links "invented" in 1620 by a clergyman called Gunter. Petty used it to survey Ireland. There were 10 chains to the furlong (furrow-length) and surveyors into the twentieth century had one shoulder permanently depressed from a lifetime of carrying chains. Each hand-made link was required to have an inside measurement of precisely 7.92 inches, which, of course, it did not. Its accuracy depended entirely on the skill of the surveyor, and as it could not be used single-handed "it exposes the Account to Dangers of Mistakes".[22]

The "way-wiser", which Ogilby said was invented by Ashmole's astrology teacher, Backhouse, was the vehicle that would carry guess-plotting geographers into the realm of science. The rim would wear down and dirt would build up, but with regular cleaning and checking it could be more accurate than anything else. His measured distance from Cornhill in London to Aberystwyth is 199¼ miles. He compares this triumphantly with the "reputed" distance, which he claims was 44 miles too short. He seems to have been remarkably accurate. On today's roads the journey is 209 miles. Most of the difference, which is below 5%, is the result of modern roads having to make a few diversions along the way.

Transferring the notes made from the measuring-wheel and a bearing-compass to paper meant marking on miles and furlongs, side-turnings, bridges and rivers, together with compass roses and representations of hills. Buildings, woods and orchards were shown along the road, and dotted lines marked the road edge where it was open, rather than enclosed by walls or hedges. The strips are restarted with a thick line and a new compass rose when they change direction. Road widths are not shown; they are all drawn as double dotted lines one sixteenth of an inch wide, or double solid lines for a road with defined sides in an "enclosed" landscape.

These one-dimensional roads are measured in three-dimensional space. Seen from above on Google Earth in two dimensions, Ogilby's route across Wales from Fishguard to Holywell is about 120 miles. His dimensurator wheel, rolling up and down mountains and around winding paths, covered 150 miles on that journey.

But what was it doing there anyway? We only have one record of a journey made along this road in Ogilby's lifetime, and it was made by a cripple in a handcart looking for a cure at the miraculous Catholic shrine.

The proposals

Britannia was re-conceived in early 1672 as a detailed guide to the country with supplementary plans of its roads, each carefully surveyed. Ogilby engaged, among others, John Aubrey and Gregory King, to work with him on what would have been a remarkable tool for the administration, enabling it to take a much more interventionist role in the life of the country than ever before. A wonderfully intrusive question-naire was drawn up by Aubrey and King working with leading members of the Royal Society including Hooke, Wren and Sir John Hoskyns, who would become its President. The way-wiser surveyors carried authorisation requiring, in the King's name, that justices, local officials and churchmen provide answers. A copy of the questionnaire was preserved by Aubrey.[23] This document made it clear that *Britannia* would be a large volume of text containing the answers collected, supplemented by another volume with plans of the roads of England – no mention of Wales. There had been attempts at surveys before, but nothing quite like this, with a sheet of twenty-two questions being given out by men who held a royal warrant. Some questions were of course directed to investigating landing sites, "Ports, Harbors, Havens, Creeks, Peels, Peers, Watch Towers, Land-marks, Light-houses, Sands, Sholes, Islands, Eits, &c", and any surprises that might be sprung by unusual tides. Other questions, concerning markets, fairs, buildings and information about eminent local people and antiquities had been asked before and were the stuff of previous English atlases. But Ogilby also wanted details of landscape and agricultural use, watercourses, springs, mines and minerals. There were some questions that were designed to catalogue each community's wealth in quite alarming detail, demanding information about "Works and Mines of Gold, Silver, Copper, Lead, Black-lead, Tin, Iron, Salt, Salt-petre, Allom, Coperas, Gems, Precious Stones, Glass, Crystal, Marble, Alabaster, Plaister, Fullers-Earth, Ochre, Tobacco-pipe Clay, Potters Clay, Lime, Chalk, Marl, Freestone, Milstone, Grindstone, Whetstone." The answers were requested to be sent direct to Ogilby, and the respondent was to be rewarded with cash or (of course) books, but alongside that carrot was the stick of the royal warrant.[24]

King specifically says that his work was measuring roads. He spent some weeks "in the middle of winter 1672 in very severe cold weather" surveying roads in Ipswich and Maldon. *Britannia*'s intended purpose as a scientific survey for the post-coup government explains Ogilby's apparently senseless decision, in the late summer of 1672, to add four extra volumes containing new surveys of every county. Of course this put the cost up even further:

> Whereas the Lords Referees computed the charge of Britannia and Book of Roads (to be compris'd in two single volumes onely) to fourteen Thousand Pounds ... upon the present

Design of Six Volumes, and six large Maps, the whole Charge
will amount to twenty Thousand Pound.[25]

Since those Lords Referees had already said that private
finance through subscriptions could not in itself cover the
original cost, Ogilby would hardly have made the project
even more expensive without some firm belief that the money
would be made available. He had been ruined twice, by the
Irish Rebellion and the Great Fire, and his skill in re-building
his fortunes is testament to his good business sense. He was
not looking for another destruction. But he was, clearly, antici-
pating a significant role in what was now, he expected, going
to happen.

By the time of publication the number of volumes had
settled at three. The book which is always referred to as
Britannia was actually *Britannia Vol. 1*, which now combined
text and road plans. It said it described "all the Principal
Road-Ways in England and Wales", and that it would be
followed by Volume 2 with descriptions and plans of twenty-
five cities, especially London, and Volume 3 which would have
"a description of the whole kingdom". Although Volumes 2
and 3 never appeared, the plan of London certainly did. It
became a phenomenal undertaking in its own right, with the
support of the Court of Aldermen.

Strange roads

The choice of roads was fundamental to the royal mastery
of the kingdom. Ogilby was supposed to set out the distances
"from Stage to Stage" on the post-roads, but he has not done
that. Early in the book he presents a detailed list of these
post-roads; there are eight principal roads from London,

with thirty-five routes branching off from them. For example, one route branches off the Chester road at Towcester to go north to Derby and Sheffield. Another branches off closer to Wales, at Stone, going north to Manchester and then west to Liverpool. He has measured the eight big ones, but ignored all but ten of the branch roads, so neither the road to Sheffield nor the one from Manchester to Liverpool are included. In fact Bradford, Sheffield, Wolverhampton and Liverpool are simply not in the atlas. *Britannia* contains around 7,500 miles of roads, but less than 1,600 of those miles were on post-roads. To understand what the book is for we have to look at which roads he is actually showing.

In some cases he has provided alternatives to the post-roads because they were in such a bad state that people had begun to avoid them. For example, there was a post-road to Cambridge, Newmarket and Norwich, which branched off the great north road 33 miles from London, at Royston, where James I had built a splendid house to use while he hunted and raced on the heath. This was a road of great importance. Cambridge was an intellectual hub and Norwich was a manufacturing centre, the second largest city of the kingdom. Imported goods from Kings Lynn and grain from East Anglia were carted to this way towards London. The carts were emptied onto barges on the River Lea at Ware (Ogilby has no interest in that sort of information), but on the way there they reduced the road to sludge or worse. This was unsuitable for the huge number of nobility that needed to travel the route. Between Cambridge and Norwich was Newmarket, a great social centre during the season, where King Charles was a highly competitive racing jockey. The road through Newmarket continued to Euston Hall, the home of Arlington. In 1671 Arlington hosted a two-week-long house party that included pretty much the whole court, and Euston Hall was the scene of a very ribald mock wedding that installed Louise de Kéroualle in Charles' bed (producing Charles, Duke of Richmond, nine months later). The road to Euston Hall, at least if you tried to go via Royston, was unbearably mucky. Pepys travelled it to get to Cambridge in February 1660 and found it "very foul": he turned off before Royston at Puckeridge.[26] An act of 1663 in effect established a precursor of the turnpike here, collecting tolls for the maintenance of the road.[27] Ogilby refers to this as having lasted for three years, so by 1675 the Royston turning was mucky again. The roads he traces to Cambridge and Norwich, to Newmarket and Euston Hall, turn off instead at Puckeridge. James I's house at Royston, which sat on the old post-road, was an abandoned ruin.

But there are much more significant novelties in Ogilby's pattern of roads compared to the post-roads. He adds six new routes to the main roads from London, which he calls "Direct Independants". Together with the eight major post-roads, these form the main arteries of the kingdom. Clearly the first purpose of this work is to promote a vision of England and Wales as being completely oriented around London, and he is very clear about that. It looks as though that is the reason why his road network stops at the Scottish border. He never mentions this oddity. He only recognises Scotland when the road from Carlisle to Berwick wanders briefly across the border, though acknowledging that the post-road to Berwick does continue to Edinburgh. Edinburgh is presumably the problem: five roads went north from the border, and every one of them went to Edinburgh. That meant that the island of Britain had two centres, and that was not the message of this book. It is the atlas of London's supremacy, and the presentation of the roads was obviously shaped by that. In fact before

Ogilby even begins to trace the roads, he devotes 10,000 words over fourteen pages to describing the City of London.

But there is more to his choice of roads than their connection to London.

Roads for landings

Only one of the fourteen principal roads from the Great Emporium does not lead to a harbour. The south-east coast is very carefully explored, with roads to Deal, Dover, Hythe and Rye. The Hythe road was not a post-road, nor was it of any commercial interest as the port was silted up, but it is listed as a principal road. Perhaps it is relevant that the shore was certainly in use by smugglers and it posed enough invasion risk for a defensive canal to be eventually built behind it. The road from London to Newhaven (with its safe harbour) has an unadvertised extension to the fishing village and harbour of Brighthelmston (Brighton) and on to Shoreham, where the harbour was not much used.

There was a post-road from London to Chichester, but Ogilby ignores that in favour of one to Arundel, "where Ships of 100 Tun may ride". This "Road from London to Arundel" turns out to continue along the coast to the harbour town of Chichester. The post-road to Portsmouth, which was a branch off the road to the West Country, was uncontentiously promoted into a principal road from London, but many of these new principal roads lead to places which were of no commercial interest whatever: Aberystwyth, St David's, Holywell, Bridgenorth. That road to Bridgenorth, the only one of the fourteen not to connect to a harbour, is actually listed as going to Buckingham, and the extension to Bridgenorth is a sort of afterthought. Bridgenorth is between

Shrewsbury and Birmingham, and this road connects to Chester and Holyhead.

The next swathe of roads, seventeen of them, are called "Direct Dependants", and are offshoots of London's arteries. They are all identified as "From London to …", though none actually starts from London but from the branching-off point. They include such unusual roads as one to Weymouth which avoids the normal route along the Land's End road and instead follows a path which was genuinely hard to find (even his surveyor got lost). An expert study has failed to find any evidence that this "London to Weymouth" road was ever followed along its length, and it was nowhere near as suitable for travellers as *Britannia* said,[28] but it clearly provided a rather discreet route to London from Weymouth's modern harbour. (He also shows a road linking Weymouth, a Channel port, to Bristol on the Atlantic, which seems to serve no particular purpose unless you have a suspicious mind.) He then lists thirty-one "Cross Independants", which link towns on different London roads. The choices here seem rather strange: Bristol to Exeter was a well-used road, St Davids to Holywell certainly was not. Finally come ten "Accidentals", "such Roads as are not in a Direct Line, but Comprise Two or Three Horizontal Bearings",[29] such as the road from Exeter to Dartmouth, though oddly this section includes one road "From London", which for some reason has not been included in the Direct Dependants. It goes to Poole, the largest harbour in the country, taking in Lymington and Southampton.

The relative economic importance of communities may be roughly inferred from the number of roads leading to them. (The four roads leading to Stilton are an exception: today known for its pungent blue cheese, the only known food that is both slimy and crumbly, it used to be a major crossroads on the great north road, a stopping point on the ancient drove road from east to west.) Seven roads are shown to Bristol, five each to Chester, Oxford and York, and four to Carlisle. You would not guess from *Britannia* that the biggest provincial city was Norwich, which is given little more than 200 words (York, the second city of the kingdom, gets 500; Oxford, Bristol and Chester get around 250). Its economy was based on weaving. It had a huge market, which was such a draw for travelling showmen that employers complained their workforce was being distracted and legal restraints were created to limit the number of shows. Apart from the road through Puckeridge, its only highways were to Kings Lynn (but the road with that title was really a road to the port of Yarmouth, which he noted did a great trade with Holland), and from Ipswich (but the road with that title was really a road to the fishing port of Cromer). He was not interested in Norwich but was very interested in exploring viable seaports and harbours, without drawing too much attention to what he was doing.

There are plenty of other examples of this game being played, such as the road from Oxford to Salisbury, which turns out to be a road to Poole harbour. The road from London to Barnstaple in Devon actually extends to the sea-port of Truro via Padstow, "a Port-Town Trading chiefly to Ireland". But perhaps the oddest is his unobtrusive 94-mile road from London to Oakham, the county town of Rutland, to which is appended as an apparent afterthought 168 miles of road to Richmond in Yorkshire, linking London by secondary roads to the ports of Newcastle on the east coast and Carlisle on the west. The road from Richmond to Carlisle was traced with much more care than the road to Carlisle from the south. That climbs over spectacular mountain scenery; Shap summit is at 320 metres, but you would have no inkling of that from Ogilby, who seems unaware that it is a summit at all.

Right at the start of Part II, I asked why the book begins with the road from London to Aberystwyth. The road makes perfectly good sense until it gets into Wales, and more specifically to Presteigne. The published itineraries would only lead you there if you were on your way to Carmarthen; none of them go due west from Presteigne. But Ogilby does. The standard route to Cardigan Bay, like the post, went further north, from Shrewsbury. But Ogilby sends his reader on an entirely amazing and extremely taxing journey to nowhere.

Once he got past Presteigne, Ogilby began using a graphic technique to suggest going up and down steep hills – the road running over wedge-shaped blocks of hills pointing at each other. This may have been Hooke's idea.[30] But if all you had was the strip-map, without the text, the journey would look fine. Leaving Rhayader the map says the road has "on each side pasture ground". The text, though, reveals the reality. "The Road continues altogether open as well as Mountainous and boggy to Aberistwyth". Twenty-six miles of bog which, Ogilby warned, is "a kind of Morass". Today this remote way is surfaced road, and reckoned to be one of the most beautiful in Britain when passable, but in 1675 it was unused and unusable by any wheeled vehicle. In fact it was not a road, just a set of tracks followed by Welsh drovers taking their clients' cattle to fatten in England. There was no possibility of these gentlemen feeling the need for a massive volume to guide them; any drover who thought he was lost could follow his dog. They knew the way all right. Drovers have told me that it was quite common for their predecessors to sell their Pembrokeshire corgis in London and let them make their own way home. Then they could be sold again next time they went to London. Corgis, with their short legs, were the preferred cattle-herders as they could nip at cows' heels and dodge their kicks.

The explanation for tracing this extraordinary road must be that it connects some lead mines, marked on the road and mentioned in the text, to Aberystwyth. These mines were waterlogged, but in the days of Charles I an entrepreneur found a way to pump them out and to begin producing not just lead, but silver as well. Charles I was now able to make coinage without being dependent on London. The ore went by sledge over the morass to a mint in Aberystwyth castle, then from the end of 1642 to a new mint at his Civil War headquarters in Oxford. This supplied Charles with coins to pay his soldiers in the Civil War, while the mines produced lead for their bullets.[31] The castle mint was brought back into use in spring 1646, until Charles' last army surrendered in March. Aberystwyth may have been a useless ruin in 1675, but it had a significant past, which indicated a possible significant future. When the day came. If the day came.

The cataloguing of resources and manufactures was obviously part of the function of the text, whether it was knitted waistcoats or cherries, millstones or limestone. Those examples were all to be found on a road which would be expected in the book, the road from London to Berwick, the main road to the north. Going off-piste to mark the place of something really valuable indicates one purpose of the atlas. But there are other roads which were as baffling as that to Aberystwyth, and where there is no sign of a useful hill of silver. The road from London to St David's, for example, follows a perfectly normal route to Monmouth, and then strikes out in a most surprising way. Porter's road map of 1668 and Hollar's map of the early 1670s both show the road going west via Brecon, on high, dry land. But Ogilby sends his reader on a journey through Cardiff and along the coast where there really was no road.

Two miles after Kidwelly, the road simply runs into a deep, wide waterway, the River Towy. Far from being a highway for trade, Ogilby's wheel had been bowling down an old pilgrim way. The Towy is wide and, when the tide is running, dangerous. Our oarsmen demonstrated how it was done in their youth and got into difficulties on a fine day. The name of the crossing point, Ferryside, is not mentioned in *Britannia*, and it seems that the surveyor had a tricky time. This probably explains why the very obvious castle ruin there is not marked on the map (though it is in the text), the equally obvious church is not mentioned in the text (though it is shown on the map), and the Lloyd family's sixteenth-century mansion, Llansteffan Plas, is studiously ignored in both. The significance of the place was not as a stop on a highway but as the access point to Carmarthen from the sea. Carmarthen was no longer defended by a wall and castle, and was a key commercial and administrative centre. At some point Ogilby now had to go north to pick up the road to Haverfordwest, he could have done that by going to Carmarthen, but he was evidently more interested in reporting on the sheltered river harbour by the sea.

A brook must then be crossed into Pembrokeshire where another river called Dungledy must be crossed to get to Haverford West. By now the surveyor seems to have been struggling in a strange land with a strange language and may have wondered why he was not allowed to use the proper road. The first part of his journey in Wales would have been very pleasant; the area south of Monmouth was thoroughly Anglicised, and although the poor Welsh lived in hovels (he passes "Houses so call'd" on the way through), he seems to have felt no need to report on inns. There are fine houses along the way belonging to very wealthy families who would have provided civilised hospitality to these well-connected surveyors with their royal warrant. The Morgan family had a very grand house near Carleon. Sir John Aubrey, bart., a relation of the Aubrey who was working for Ogilby, had a substantial pile nearby. But once these luxuries had been left behind, the surveyors were exploring a land that was profoundly alien to them. You would not know it from *Britannia*, but the crossing point on the Towy/Taf is Pilgrim's Rest, a burial place of medieval pilgrims who had run out of money or luck. No ferry is shown on the map. The surveyor did at least survive, and must have somehow got his wheel ashore by Laugharne, the spot now famous as Dylan Thomas' boathouse. You then have to get across a brook which has neither bridge nor ferry to enter Pembrokeshire. The Rivers Clethy and Dungledy must be crossed (in waders?) to get to Haverfordwest, from which you are allowed to proceed to the ruins of St David's Cathedral on dry land. If the end of the journey was a cheery pleasure, that is not hinted at. The text suggests the miserable conclusion of a depressing endurance test: "The Cathedral and Free-School are the only fair Buildings, the Bishop's Palace and Prebends Houses being much ruin'd: the Walls are decay'd, the Inhabitants few, and tho' it still continues an Episcopal See, yet it has not the benefit of a market." Or, apparently, of an inn. What was the point?

The point becomes a little clearer as the surveyor's wheel rolls on from St David's, tracing a road to Holywell, the site also visited by that very short road from Chester. It is a "Cross Independant", which implies that it serves travellers who wished to make this cross-country route, but it is hard to believe that there were any. It is a tough road to follow even today, climbing steep exposed mountains. So why was this road of interest to the author of *Britannia*?

The holy well is supposed to come from a magical spring that appeared when a young virgin named Winifred was decapitated by her spurned lover. Where her head had stopped rolling the water gushed forth. This was not an obvious destination for a commercial traveller's guide to Britain in the 1670s. It was significant to Catholics, because the pool constructed there was the only British pilgrimage site which remained in business throughout the sixteenth and seventeenth centuries. There was a constant flow of pilgrims from England, across the sands of the Dee from Chester. In 1629, when Catholic practice was officially criminal, there were apparently 1,500 pilgrims there including 140 priests. The Jesuits even maintained their own inn there and seem not to have worried about calling the establishment The Crossed Keys, a phrase which some might think had a relationship to the Pope's insignia. Mass was obviously impossible, but taking the waters seems to have been regarded as a good substitute. There were even Catholic conversions here. One person who was using this road around the time the book was published was a young cripple called Cornelius Nichol, who was reported to have been placed by the roadside at Cardigan in a handcart and was pushed by a relay of well-wishers around a hundred miles to the shrine, where of course he was cured. He arrived on 11 June 1674, so the publication of the road in *Britannia* tied in nicely with the promotion of the site.[32] In fact things went rather differently from the way the Jesuits there hoped. According to the Religious Census of 1676, there was not a single Papist left in Cardiganshire by then, which implies that Cornelius did not long survive the miracle, or had regretted his fame and become invisible. Three years later the so-called "Popish Plot" created a national panic and the priest in charge at Holywell, John Plessington, was hanged, drawn and quartered.

This road helps to make one part of the book's covert agenda clear, as a handbook to be used in an anticipated new kingdom under a Catholic king. It is part of a re-shaped kingdom of the Royalist imagination, in a book which can actually be used to create the country it envisions. In fact the Catholic King James II did go on pilgrimage to Holywell twelve years after publication, hoping for a cure for his apparent infertility. The Queen became pregnant thirteen months later, in what was evidently a rather slow-motion miracle, but one which soon convinced the English to get rid of the Stuarts rather than face the prospect of a Catholic heir to the throne. Once again, this was not the hoped-for outcome. If Holywell did deliver miracles, its clients and management needed to be more careful about what they wished for.

This road was not only important as a pilgrim road. It also showed the route from the silver mines that had provided Charles I with his currency to the mill that worked the metal. This "highway" to Holywell was only passable in dry weather. The place-names of the area, such as Ynys-Hir, Ynys Edwyn, Ynys Ediol, Ynys Gragog, indicate that the road linked island ridges through marshland ("ynys" being Welsh for island).[33] The road was not being traced for travelling, but to find out how to exploit what was there.

Most important of all was the fact that tracing the roads to and from St David's allowed the author to present a detailed exploration of all the harbours along the south and south-west coast of Wales, which could have been to assess potential landing places for a helpful army coming via Ireland. The best potential was evidently found at Fishguard which "hath a good Harbor for ships". Many of these small harbours were bases for fishing fleets, and provided decent shelter for fishing smacks and some notorious individual pirates, but that was not enough for the promised French force of six thousand. The expression "Harbor for ships" indicates that Fishguard could accommodate a fighting fleet. In 1797 the French did indeed land an invasion force near Fishguard, putting ashore seventeen boatloads of troops.

The importance of understanding where troops could and could not be landed plainly explains a number of *Britannia*'s roads, including an otherwise baffling road to Flamborough Head. No one could possibly have wanted to go from London to that desolate Yorkshire headland. The text says there was a lighthouse there, but that was not yet true. Charles had authorised the building of a lighthouse, but it was not completed. It was supposedly meant to help avoid shipwrecks, of which there were plenty. But it would have been a guide as much as a warning. This was a significant landing-place for war materials from the continent, as Queen Henrietta Maria demonstrated in February 1643. When the English Civil War began in August 1642, the Queen was at The Hague, partly for her own safety, but she quickly began raising money and arms to help her husband. In February 1643 she landed, not at Newcastle as intended, but just below Flamborough Head, at Bridlington, driven by storms. It turned out to be a good place for such an action.

Her account of the adventure, in a letter to Charles, is magnificent. She evidently relished her refuge on the shore being bombarded by Parliamentary warships. She was driven to shelter in a ditch and seems thrilled to have been spattered with dirt and having a servant killed within seventy feet. The attack was driven off by the threat of action from her Dutch convoy. She was then met by two Scottish military leaders, the Earl of Montrose and "Lord Ogilby". "Lord Ogilby" was the Earl of Airlie's eldest son and heir, now called James, Lord Ogilvie. He was a fearless Stuart supporter. She carted her treasure and armour to York,[34] and James Ogilvie followed, ending up with the transplanted royal court in Oxford. Here Henrietta Maria constructed a replica of her old court before the war, with "her" poet laureate, William Davenant, very much in residence. The road to Flamborough Head had brought that court back to life, and might do something similar again.

Other landing places to explore were the end of the short road in Flintshire which had actually served to bring troops from Ireland in the Civil War, and the road from Holyhead, which he showed to be impossible for an army to traverse. This agenda explains why Ogilby chose to include roads to Aberystwyth, Flamborough, Holywell and Buckingham, while not finding space for Sheffield, Bradford, Wolverhampton and Liverpool.

Off the map

The omission of Sheffield is probably the most significant for understanding Ogilby's sense of priorities. It was the main centre of cutlery-making in Britain, and a Company of Cutlers had been formed in 1624. The tradition of Sheffield blade-making went back centuries. The bullying miller in Chaucer's Reeve's Tale carries an armoury of blades – sword, cutlass and dagger – and tucked into his sock a Sheffield pen-knife.[35] It was not an heroic weapon of war, but it was the product of an important industry, smelting and forging local ore for a national market. The iron workers were individual artisans, who were said in 1723 to be sending 1,500 tons of small blades a year "along roads almost impassable" to Doncaster, where they were shipped by water to Hull.[36] The road was a track for pack-horses, and the hilly, stone-built streets of Sheffield did not see many strangers. Several iron works and mines in other parts of the country were noted, such as those in the Forest of Dean, but their iron was useful for military purposes. Commercially Sheffield was significant, militarily it was not, and cutlery simply did not matter enough on any of Ogilby's scales of importance to have its road included. The same applied to the nearby small town of Bradford. Interestingly, this was not a judgement on the social importance of the town: Wolverhampton, in the heart of the West Midlands, was described by Blome in 1673 as "much frequented by gentry", and indeed Charles I had been there four times, but its road simply did not need to be included as a possible route to or from a harbour or a critical mineral resource, despite its coal and wool. It is significant that none of these towns had any corporate structure or political status.

Liverpool was a very different matter, and was not simply ignored. It was removed. This raises an entirely new set of issues. If one purpose of the book was to enumerate military landing places, why did it not include Liverpool, the port that linked directly to Dublin? If another purpose was to evaluate the resources and economic potential of the kingdom, why did it not include Liverpool, the port that linked directly to the trade of the New World and the export point for Lancashire manufactures? And if it was supposed to be a measured, scientific study of the roads, why did it show one which in reality went to Liverpool, but here stopped at Warrington, deliberately altering the map of that town to make the continuation of the road invisible?

The town of Warrington, on the Mersey, is drawn on two plates of *Britannia*, but the layout of the town is not the same in both places. On the London to Carlisle road, it sits on a crossroads, which goes on the right to Manchester and on the left to Liverpool ("Leverpool"). But shown on the London to Chester road there is no crossroads at Warrington. The difference becomes obvious when both maps are oriented with west at the top.

They are drawn by different hands, and the town is spelt differently. The surveyors for the left-hand map, tracing the road north to Carlisle, recorded that they entered Lancashire from the south and crossed a remarkable stone bridge over the Mersey (where they made an incorrect guess as to the river's course). This bridge was of great commercial and strategic significance, the only one over the river and the key point for communication between Lancashire and the south. It had been fought over in the 1640s. For some reason they identified this spot as "Prescot". They then came into Warrington, where they recorded a crossroads. One road went east to Manchester, and another, Sankey Street, went west to "Leverpoole". But that is not what is shown on the right-hand map, which places Warrington on the road west from York. They entered the town on from the east, but apparently Sankey Street, the road that continued to Liverpool, had vanished. They evidently found they were facing an unbroken line of houses which formed an impenetrable wall on the west side of the road. The surveyors are not unobservant: they do a much better job of understanding the course of the Mersey. But they do not see any trace of the road to Liverpool. The

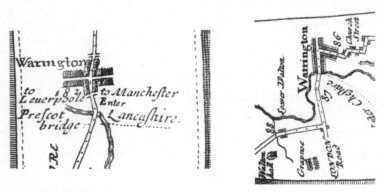

38 & 39. *Britannia*: Warrington on the roads to Carlisle (left) and Chester (right).

map had been blinded and the road to Liverpool cancelled. This would not have been a decision taken on Ogilby's own initiative. The book was not his to change in this way.

The King's *Britannia*

Knowledge, power and privilege

The physical object titled *Britannia Vol. 1* was quite obviously produced for a small and highly privileged audience. Owning a copy made a statement. Its grandeur, weight and superb quality placed it in the same social context as his *Aeneid*, and like that book it had a hundred plates. Ogilby must have supposed that it would have that number of subscribers, and the copper plates were only good for a hundred high-quality impressions.

This was more than a luxury indulgence. It was a weighty and authoritative body of new knowledge, and that knowledge was power. *Britannia* was an anatomy of England and Wales as the hinterland that sustained London, "this Great Emporium and Prime Center of the Kingdom, Your Royal Metropolis", surveying England and Wales with particular emphasis on economic activity, natural resources and communication with possible surprise landing places. The infrastructure of the future Stuart kingdom is made clear by the road network described, in which, as in ancient Rome, the farthest limits are directly connected to the imperial capital. In fact Ogilby makes direct reference to the Roman Peutinger Table in his preface, and understood it very well. The road from London to Aberystwyth, however insignificant, fits this model and starts the book. And it passes by the silver mines that produced Charles I's war chest.

The language of the text attached to the visual itineraries went far beyond a catalogue of resources and markets, creating something like a pilotage book for land voyages. The reader does not simply learn about these roads but travels them. Setting out for Berwick, the reader accompanies Ogilby on a walk through the city that made him:

> From the Standard in Cornhil, (entring Bishopsgate-street) at 20 Poles you pass by St. Martins Outwich Church on the Left ... & 5 Poles farther, Thread-needle-street falls in on the same Hand, wherein stands Merchant-Taylors Hall, a stately new Erected Building ... at 37 Poles you are opposite to Gresham College on the Left, extending backward to Broad-street, Founded (together with the Royal Exchange) by that Worthy Citizen Sr. Thomas Gresham, who Planted therein 7 Lectures, of Divinity, Astronomy, Musick, and Geometry, Civil Law, Physick and Rhetorick; and is now the Place of Congress for the Virtuosi of the Royal Society of London, for improving Practical and Experimental Philosophy.

And so the miles fall away: "At 1 Furlong or 40 Poles, you have ... at 1 Furlong 18 Poles you pass by ... At 135 you come to ...." But though it looks like a book for travellers, it was not. Ogilby does not seem to have put any working guides out of business.

Britannia is a depiction of royal power from the centre to the periphery, and an account book of the business and antiquities of the kingdom's communities. Apart from investigating coastal defences and possible landing-points, he reshapes the map in a way appropriate to a Catholic reader (the emphasis on pilgrim sites) and lays the foundations for more efficient exploitation of its resources in a way that would echo Colbert's use of national resources in France. London depended, for example, on the flow of coal to feed its fires and thus its citizens. The text mentions more than a dozen sources of the fuel, some of which (Neath, Llanelli, Wigan, Sunderland) would not be identified from the strip-maps.

Ogilby was embroiled in something which he would carry through with brilliance, dedication and originality, but which was almost unmanageable. "And we should be in much greater forwardness, if such Persons as seem willing to be Concern'd, would, ... not distract and discourage us ... Some crying, with an unreasonable Impatience, When will it be done?"[1] He would not have got into this without knowing what he was supposed to achieve and what purpose it was to serve. His whole life had been a preparation for it. That plaintive cry, which is on an undated advertisement for a new map of Middlesex, must have been made in February 1673, when Hooke bought a copy of the advertised map.

The "unreasonable Impatience" was being expressed at the start of 1673 because there was a real urgency to the potential need for this book. Ogilby had always brought out his books with amazing swiftness, and the frontispiece shows that publication had been intended for no later than 1673. The drawing is undated, but Ogilby was raised by a tailor; the clothes are precisely dated.

The sovereign set the style for gentlemen, and in 1666 Charles had made a very clear statement of what they should wear. As far back as 1662 he had told Parliament that "the whole nation seems a little corrupted in their excess of living

… in their clothes, in their diet, in all their expenses … I do believe I have been faulty that way myself: I promise you I will reform".[2] His reform, announced on 7 October 1666, was the adoption of the "vest", which Evelyn claimed to have recommended to him, calling it oriental or Persian. It was a long woollen garment worn instead of a doublet and stiff collar, with a topcoat over it instead of a cloak. It was a conscious move away from French style, and Pepys reported that "I know not well how; but it is to teach the nobility thrift, and will do good." Charles wore it in public on 15 October 1666, an event for the world to note. By 1669 this was described as how the English dress. It was the officially approved costume, meant to be as widely adopted as the Mao jacket in China after the Cultural Revolution. All Ogilby's men in the frontispiece are wearing their vests, some with a topcoat. But although Pepys added "it is a fashion the King says he will never change", he did. French fashions came back. In 1674 Chamberlayne's *Anglia Notitia* said that "the French mode again was taken up", and the playwright Elkanah Settle told the King that "vests, your seven years love, grew out of fashion".[3]

Ogilby would not have had his men dressed out of fashion – that would undermine the whole sense of modernity the book was meant to convey. The publication date was clearly intended to be 1673, when Clifford was ascendant, the victory over the Dutch should have been achieved, and Charles should have made himself into a proper Catholic sovereign. But that is when everything went wrong.

The Plot is Dead. Long Live the Plot

By 1673 it was clear that the Dutch War would not after all be any kind of success. The French attack had become

a mess, and with the Dutch fleet still intact the English had
no remaining plan of attack. Charles had put off recalling
Parliament to ask for money. To manage that he had kept the
fleet at sea all winter, notionally blockading the Dutch coast
but really preventing his own ships from coming into harbour
and needing to be paid off. By the end of January his game
was up. Parliament was recalled in February 1673, and once
the House of Commons was in session it offered Charles
£1.26 million on condition that he withdrew the Declaration
of Indulgence and abandoned his claim to suspend the penal
laws. He said that he would take that into consideration, but
doing so raised the dreadful prospect of Parliament refusing
to deliver the funds it had offered. Louis advised him to yield.
In fact the message to Charles was that the French king would
be generous if that happened, and would stop all money if
it did not.[4] Louis had no enthusiasm for England becoming
both anti-Stuart and anti-French, and even less enthusiasm for
Parliament cutting off Charles' income and so forcing him to
make peace with the Dutch. Charles himself petulantly ripped
the Royal Seal off the Declaration of Indulgence and broke it.
In a few months the whole Catholic project collapsed.

In place of the absolutist Catholic coup envisioned in the
Secret Treaty, there was now a Parliamentary anti-Catholic
counter-coup. Parliament passed the Test Act, banning
Catholics from coming within five miles of Westminster, and
Clifford, who had railed against it in a spectacularly ill-judged
speech, was forced to resign. After James refused to take the
Anglican sacrament at Easter his conversion became public
knowledge, and it was confirmed when he had to resign his
command of the navy. In June Charles notified the French
that his own professsion of Catholicism was now not merely
postponed but abandoned altogether.[5] But James and Clifford

managed to arrange for a man of their choosing, Thomas Osborn, Earl of Danby, to take over Clifford's post as Treasurer. And although Charles insisted that James' children were to be brought up as Protestants, he now allowed the heir to the throne, whose wife had died in 1671, to marry a fifteen-year-old Italian Catholic. So Charles set up the probability of a Catholic dynasty, and Louis encouraged the match. Dutch propaganda appearing in England was extremely effective, in particular a pamphlet which presented French policy as an international conspiracy against Protestantism in which British ministers were implicated.[6] Demands were made for Charles to divorce his Queen and marry a Protestant.

The Secret Treaty was now dead in the water. In October 1673 Clifford, its most committed enthusiast, died. According to John Evelyn, he hanged himself with his cravat.[7] But that did not mean that *Britannia* was abandoned, or that the Stuart project to restore royal power was dead. The Secret Treaty had kick-started the creation of the road-atlas, and its driving force was still in place after the Test Act. A shift had evidently taken place in the King's mind from potentially taking the initiative against Parliament, to being prepared to fight against a Parliamentary move to reduce his power. Charles now needed to be in a position to handle a potential insurrection even if he did not become a Catholic. The book still served the same purpose of preparing the ground for the struggle to come. It was a vast work, still evidently incomplete, and Charles wanted it done. In particular he seems to have wanted the inventory of the kingdom to be published along with the road-maps, and that was a kind of bottomless pit.

This was now Ogilby's main work, and he tried to shift more of his back stock to help with the costs. In February 1673 he had set up a standing lottery, with the prizes being unbound copies of his previous publications. It started at Garraway's Coffee House in Exchange Alley on 7 April, and transferred in mid-May to Cliffords Inn Lane, near St Dunstan's Church, Fleet Street.[8] In the summer of 1673, the Queen added her own subscription of £500 to the work. Just as the Commissioners of the Privy Council managed to find time for Ogilby when they were hugely busy, so now Wren and Hooke found considerable time to devote to his project.[9] Robert Hooke, a fellow habitué of Garraway's, was also the City's surveyor and encouraged him by purchasing his China volume in March. On the same day, the King granted Ogilby the licence to import paper for *Britannia*'s publication, indicating that he still needed it. The possibility of further acts against the King's prerogative powers was very real, and Charles believed that he still needed to plan for military action and to bring troops into the country.

In the two years before the eventual publication of *Britannia*, Hooke's diary records over sixty meetings with Ogilby.[10] The King's vision of the future still moved towards France, away from the restoration settlement, and required secrecy and conspiracy. When Parliament met again in October 1673, Charles delivered to it the barefaced lie that there was no other treaty with France than the one already published. Parliamentarians were not at all convinced, and there was a growing drift towards confrontation. In January 1674 an address was presented to Charles requesting that he permanently remove two members of the broken Cabal, Lauderdale and Buckingham, from his presence and councils, and an attempt was made to impeach Arlington. Arlington survived, in relatively minor posts, and continued as post-master general. It was easy to believe that England was moving back towards civil war. The issues that had torn the country apart in the

1640s, the struggle of Parliament against royal prerogative power and its defence of liberty of the subject, were live and kicking.[11] Everyone now understood where these rows might lead and was preparing for the worst.

At this point, in February 1674 Charles enlarged Ogilby's title to that of "His Majesty's Cosmographer and Geographic Printer" and said he had "especiall Trust and confidence in the fidelity, circumspection and ability of my well-beloved Subject and deponent".[12] Calling him the King's deponent signalled that *Britannia* was being compiled to provide information that Charles had demanded and was anxious to have in his hands.

His need for a military and administrative survey had not gone away. Parliament had carried through an anti-Catholic coup. The secret premise on which the atlas had been predicated, as a guide to assist a French military occupation, had now lost its meaning, but whatever followed was likely to involve facing down rebellion, and *Britannia* would still be needed. In his will, written in 1674, Ogilby charged his stepgrandson to complete "the King's Britannia". This is the King's book, displaying the King's geography of his realm, supplied by the King's Cosmographer. *Britannia* now had to adjust itself to a changed purpose. If that were not so, it might have been published much sooner, and included Liverpool. As it was, it remained a work in progress until the King must have suddenly decided that the crisis was upon him.

When Ogilby wrote his will in 1674 Britain's involvement in the Dutch war had finally ended, and Parliament had set about cutting the King down to size. It launched ten bills to reduce royal power over the judiciary, Parliament, taxation, and religion.[13] The restoration settlement was evidently not working and Charles was not prepared to be governed by men whose instincts were clearly not just Puritan but almost republican. Consulting no one, he walked into Parliament at the end of February and bluntly announced that its presence was no longer needed. Convinced that they were about to be arrested, leading members of the opposition burned their papers, cancelled a "party" dinner and bolted.[14] He also shut down the Scottish Parliament, where similar "mad" motions were being debated. Now that the Dutch War was being wound down, 25 companies from English regiments that might have been disbanded, around 4,000 men, were shipped instead to Ireland. This was a way for Charles to keep a standing army at his disposal without creating too much immediate alarm.[15] It might be necessary to use it if the adventure of ruling without Parliament provoked anything looking like insurrection.

In the meantime, Ogilby was trying to keep *Britannia* on the road, and moved on to another major part of his plan for it, the survey and description of London.

Mapping London

This mapping of London was being treated as a venture in its own right, and had been approved by London's Court of Aldermen a year earlier. Aldermen represented the livery companies, and Ogilby, a Freeman of the Merchant Taylors, had used his access to their Court to woo them to help his finances. They paid him £20 for each of the Atlases he produced, which came to £80 by 1672, and then he offered to create a detailed large-scale survey of the rebuilt city for them, which was meant to form the major part of the succeeding volume. The Court gave him the go-ahead and in 1673 agreed to pay £100 towards it. They insisted that the work was supervised by a committee of Aldermen and their own surveyor, Robert Hooke, who was advising him on *Britannia*.

The City was being re-created literally from the ground up, and it may be that its administration needed an up-to-the-minute survey. But the real purpose of creating a map of the new London was to present the city to itself and to the world. All the other great cities of Europe were familiar to generations of inhabitants and visitors. But London had gone, its landmarks and familiar haunts erased, the heart of the city burned away. As Thomas Vincent wrote after the fire, "The Glory of London is now fled away like a Bird, the trade of London is broken and shattered to pieces". Just four years later, Ogilby was able to write of "that Stupendous Miracle! The Raising from a Confused Heap of Ruines (sooner than some believed they could remove the Rubbish) Your Imperial City, ... hereafter to be the Business of Foreign Nations to See and Wonder at". It was time to reveal what had been done, to make it both graspable and astonishing.

By 1672 London was the most modern city in the world, the only one that smelt of paint and sawn timber. Its rivals, Rome, Paris and Amsterdam had all been re-fashioned, but in very different ways from London. They had been re-formed on their medieval foundations according to new imposed visions. Rome, London's religious challenger, had been turned by its recent Popes into a baroque church city with processional avenues meant to represent rays of a star. Paris, London's cultural challenger, was now dominated by new and transformed palaces, the Louvre, the Tuileries, the Luxembourg and the Palais-Royal; it had even acquired a stone royal bridge, the Pont Royal. Amsterdam, London's commercial challenger, had been re-shaped by its burgomasters, governing merchant oligarchs who re-built it on a coherent plan of new concentric canals and exercised more effective city planning powers than the Pope, the Sun King and London's Aldermen added together. Medieval London had not been transformed by a visionary planner but by a careless baker. Although there were soon grand plans to design and build a model city on the cinders, there was no legal authority that could resist London's need for swift remedies that would put its traders back in business. The best that could be achieved were new building regulations.

Londoners simply had no enthusiasm for shaping their city around cosmological certainties. Even at the height of the Commonwealth, when radical visionaries were in total control, they did not create any new statements in stone and simply vandalised old ones. Ogilby became the Royal Cosmographer without ever looking through a telescope, his gaze being firmly fixed on *terra firma*. That would not have been conceivable in Spain or France.

No one actually knew quite what London had become. The Aldermen were the government of the City, but they had no masterplan. The old roots, fertilised by cash, had sprouted vigorously on their own. Although it generally retained its old plan, many of the warrens were gone and the density dramatically reduced. New regulations defined the sizes of streets and houses of different classes, and imposed flat brick fronts. Around 13,200 houses had been burned, but the new streets only had about half that number. In the end about 9,000 houses were built, and a third of those stood empty, while thousands who had lost everything remained in squalid camps of tents. The city needed a precise survey of what had been done, especially as most of the existing maps had also been burned.

To make it financially viable for Ogilby the Court forbade anyone else to undertake such a survey. By now, as Aubrey had seen the previous autumn, the main highway measurements for the kingdom appear to have been completed, and so Ogilby evidently decided to invest some of his remarkable energy in other elements of the great work. In June, he hired Aubrey to carry out a survey of Surrey for one of the planned county maps, but it was the City survey that would be his greatest challenge. Maps of cities up to now had usually been artistic bird's eye views taken from an imaginary position above and off to one side. The streets were depicted in three dimensions, with house frontages and roofs. This was a totally different proposition, a land survey like that of a manorial estate or an architectural ground plan. The surveyor he put in charge, at Hollar's suggestion, was William Leybourn, twenty-five years his junior and a very successful authority on the theory and practice of this rapidly developing science.

Traditionally, the steward of a manorial estate was its surveyor, recording the rights and duties of the tenants and reporting on the yield of a manor for its lord. He would attend the measuring and marking of boundaries, but in the company of an assistant called "the land-meter" and the village elders who knew where the marks should be.

In the spirit of the new learning, the land-meter had now become a geometer, and the new geometrical mathematics were transforming the relationship between humans and the land they occupied. That is why Gunter's hundred-link surveying chain had appeared in 1620. Queen Elizabeth's surveyor, John Norden, published *The Surveyor's Dialogue* in 1607, which discussed the ways to measure land and so better assess its value but still worked with a framework of custom and traditional values. A few years later he wrote that "It is an offence to breake reasonable and lawfull customs, to the prejudice of poore tenaunts."[16] Norden's morality of surveying rather lost its meaning as the colonisation of

America proceeded to draw lines on what was seen as a blank canvas. At the same time, the development of new mathematical surveying techniques allowed governments to gain a much firmer grasp of the economic and military potential of their land, as had begun in France four years earlier. Since Louis XIV's income came largely from a tax on the size of landholdings, this was information of fundamental importance. The huge difference between the tax expected and the tax received had been explained through inefficiency, theft, corruption, local obduracy, and all of that was undoubtedly true. But the size of France and the landholdings within it were known only by tradition and custom, for which Ogilby used the attractive word "guessplots". When the French survey was eventually published in 1682 it revealed that France was almost 20% smaller than shown on previous maps. Louis is said to have complained that his surveyors had lost him more land than any invading army.

Ogilby had been the Sworn Viewer of the City's boundary disputes, so he well understood the significance of a yard on the ground, but that did not mean that he had the geometric and practical knowledge to undertake the first large-scale survey of an entire city. That was no problem. He had not known much about sailing when he captained a ship. In this case he was acting as the equivalent of a theatrical producer, setting out the vision, bringing together the people and resources, raising the finance, resolving problems, overseeing the work and performing the core activity of any producer, ensuring that everyone who was connected with or even heard about the project would be filled with enthusiasm for it.

In 1653 Leybourn had published a best-seller, *The Compleat Surveyor*, the first book on the subject that did not need to persuade the reader that surveying has a value. It remained the standard textbook for the next sixty years. Leybourn had carried out the relatively small-scale survey that was needed immediately after the fire, but this was something completely new, and would re-define urban street-plans. They decided that the measuring should be done with a fifty-foot chain and the plan should be drawn at the scale of fifty feet to an inch. Another recruit to the project changed that. The twenty-three-year-old Gregory King was a surveyor's son who had impressed Hollar and was recommended as a helper to Ogilby just as the survey of London was being planned. He eventually became Britain's first economic statistician, and some forty years after starting work on *Britannia* wrote a memoir of his time with Ogilby.

> He found Mr. Leybourne just newly engaged in making a map of London, and viewing the first essay of that survey he found it was projected at a scale of 50 feet to an inch.[17]

That would have made the finished plan about 17 x 9 feet, too big to be consulted. It is true that this was going to be a flamboyant statement that London was back in business, but as there was no detail in it, just the street plan and the shapes of buildings, King successfully urged that the scale be doubled. That still meant that the fine engraved lines depicting house walls would represent a thickness of just under ten inches, which would be acceptable. Party walls had to be at least 1½ bricks thick under building regulations introduced after the fire. The map could be reasonably accurate to that extent.

The survey, which was published the year after *Britannia Vol. 1,* was more ambitious than the techniques of the time could cope with. It looks marvellous, and its "scientific" credentials are enhanced by the fact that the names of property owners are not displayed (though the homes of

Aldermen are referenced in the index, and it can be used to explore their urban estates). But Ogilby did not realise that Leybourn's surveying was not up to the job. There was no overall framework of reference within which relative positions could be fixed, a problem which was not solved for large urban spaces until the nineteenth century. It did not help that not enough attention was paid to the directions of small lanes and alleys, so many buildings are out of position.[18]

These faults are a result of working at the limit of the surveyor's art at the time. But there is another problem with the map, of a quite different kind. Ogilby had abandoned the old three-dimensional view of buildings on a map, but had introduced a fourth dimension, time. The city was in the process of being built, and his survey, like his road atlas, sometimes carefully, systematically and scientifically measured things that were not there at all, but he thought should have been. Some were expected to appear in the future, some already belonged in the past and had been swept away. There was, of course, no indication of whether any feature shown belonged to past, present or future.

One building that was mapped but no longer existed was Essex House, on the Strand. The Strand is not actually in the City of London, but the map extends far beyond the city walls. It was engraved on twenty sheets, and the city represents less than half of it. It covers Ogilby's London, extending north to Shoreditch and from the Tower to Gray's Inn. Essex House was a run-down palace with forty-two bedrooms, originally built for one of Elizabeth I's favourites, Robert Dudley. It is shown as a grand set of structures entered opposite St Clement's Church, with secluded formal gardens at its back stretching down to the river. But it had fallen on hard times. Pepys was impressed with its ugliness, and like other aristocratic palaces along the Strand it was now in the hands of a speculative property developer. Nicholas Barbon bought it in 1674 and set about demolishing all the houses on this large site and laying out new streets down to a new quay on the river.[19] A plaque there now records the laying out of Essex Street through the middle of the site in 1675. That street is not in Ogilby's map.

So the past was being represented as being there in the present, perhaps because the King himself tried to block Barbon's project and it was still incomplete when the map was finally published in 1676. The future of London was also represented as the present. A recently discovered letter shows that the map was sent to the King in July 1675, about 8 feet 8 inches long and almost completed except for the border design.[20] St Paul's Cathedral was in reality still empty ground. The first stone had been laid three or four weeks before, and it would take thirty-five years to complete. But a cathedral is shown there on the map. It has no great dome. This building had never existed and would never exist. It was the planned cathedral which the King had just approved. The first stone brought when Wren asked a workman for a marker was a fragment of a tombstone which happened to say "Resurgam" ("I will rise"). It seemed a poetic riposte carved in stone to the paper that had fluttered into Lady Elizabeth Carteret's garden during the fire, with its intimation of apocalypse, "Time is, it is done". London was risen, and the plot Wren marked out was imbued with the notion of resurrection, carefully aligned with the Easter sunrise for 1675. That stone was placed over the door. The cathedral on the map is an inspirational anticipation, but Wren eventually built something else.

It is obvious that Ogilby did not think of his maps as slavish representations of geographic truth. They represented some other kind of truth. *Britannia*, with its falsification of the road to Liverpool, was published in September 1675. This map of London raises the same question as the atlas: whose truth was being mapped? Why was Ogilby creating painstakingly measured, wonderfully crafted, scientifically authentic false images of the land?

Britannia was for the King, and the London map was for the Court – not the Royal Court, but the Court of Aldermen. These were the twin bodies dominating Ogilby's world. Charles was the sun, the source of warmth, light and glory, and the Court of Aldermen the moon, pulling on the tides of fortune that brought wealth from around the world. Ogilby's work was to magnify them and help them prosper. Of course they knew that St Paul's did not exist, and that there was an important port named Liverpool, reached by a road from Warrington. The King knew very well, because he knew everything about Liverpool and had only just given his warrant for the building of St Paul's. Several Aldermen also knew Liverpool very well, because they had a close involvement with it.

Take, for instance, Sir Robert Vyner. He was one of the committee of Aldermen charged with overseeing the work on the plan of London. And like Ogilby, he was profoundly loyal to the King, and a master of secret dealing in plain sight.

Vyner

Ogilby had known Vyner for a long time, because Vyner had created the coronation regalia for the great event in 1661. He was the scion of a family of goldsmiths, almost the same age as the restored King. The old regalia had been destroyed by the Commonwealth, and he was hurriedly put forward as Charles' goldsmith. Vyner became one of the King's very best friends and his personal banker.

Bankers matter to kings. Charles II never lost control of Vyner, one of the fattest of all the City's fat cats. Even when the King carried out fiscal liposuction on him in 1672, the stop on the Exchequer which theoretically cost Vyner over £400,000,[21] a third of the Crown's annual income, the banker remained his affectionate friend. Special arrangements were made to protect the goldsmith's income. The very next year Vyner erected a statue of Charles on what is now the site of the Mansion House. It showed his king on horseback, crushing Cromwell. Richard Steele said that Vyner was "very fond of his sovereign",[22] and that showed in both the magnificence of the gesture and the careful economy of its execution. Picked up second-hand from the docks when its foreign customer failed to pay, it originally showed the King of Poland trampling a Turk. The faces were remodelled, but not the costumes.[23] "Cromwell" was still wearing his Turkish robe and turban. There are many ways of cynically spinning this kind of fact, but it was certainly a lot more extravagant than the option, taken by every other goldsmith in London, of not putting up a great big statue to the King.

Vyner remained wealthy enough to become Lord Mayor in November 1674. His inauguration was called "The Goldsmith's Jubilee" and was quite spectacular, his procession echoing the one Ogilby mounted for the Coronation, with almost as much extravagant display and formal street theatre.

Vyner certainly knew his way around London, and knew that the map he was validating for Ogilby was not an exact representation of the city at the time. In fact Vyner understood maps very well; he seems to have regarded the patronage of geographers as part of his global business interests. He was a supporter of Richard Blome's publications. In 1670 Blome published a set of copies of French maps of the world, the first "new" British folio atlas published in over forty-five years, and one of his Africa maps was dedicated to Vyner. Vyner was also listed as a subscriber to Blome's *Britannia* of 1673. This was the end product of the book originally commissioned by Charles in 1670; it came out in a very diminished form in 1673, two years before Ogilby's appeared. It was nothing like Ogilby's work, but was an encyclopaedia of the British Isles and colonies. It was later considered a turkey: "a most notorious piece of theft",[24] "scribbled and transcribed from Campden's Britannia and Speed's Maps",[25] and was still denigrated a hundred years later as "most notorious".[26] Its significance here is that Blome's book, which was itself dedicated to the King, did recognise the existence of Liverpool. Vyner was happy to be associated with that, and it was acceptable to Charles. But there are only two references to Liverpool in Ogilby's text, and they indicate that the road to it was removed from the book. One is the mention of it in the list of post-roads that precedes the atlas proper. The other comes in the description of the road to Carlisle further north: "Backward Turnings to be avoided … 4 Furlongs beyond Wigan, the Right to Leverpool." That road is the one drawn on Porter's map of 1668, where it is traced from York via Halifax and Rochdale.

John Ogilby had always personally avoided the road to Liverpool. In July 1662 he had travelled to Dublin with Ormond. They were taking up their posts there, the great man as Lord Lieutenant, the showman as Master of the Revels. It was a journey of great pomp, almost a Royal Progress across England, and the object was to sail from Chester. Liverpool, a Puritan stronghold, was not an inviting transit point in terms of attitude or facilities. But passengers did not take ship from Liverpool. They needed accommodation while their ship waited for wind and weather, and Liverpool had none.

So they stayed in Chester and then, if they were lucky, were taken in small craft five miles or more up the Dee to meet their vessels. In this case the weather was against them. They had to strike out at low tide on foot or horseback towards Anglesey, get themselves and any horses into a row-boat ferry over the channel, and pick up a ship from Holyhead. In *Britannia*, the elderly but cheery Ogilby describes the journey to Anglesey as "a pleasant Way over the Sands".[27] His text on Chester a few pages later must be read in the light of this journey. It proclaims that the city "Has a great Intercourse with IRELAND, This and Holyhead being the principal Places of taking Shipping for DUBLIN". This was very carefully phrased – "taking Shipping" meant embarking. Ogilby avoids mentioning that Liverpool was the port for commercial traffic. Or, indeed, that it was in business at all. And it seems pretty clear that Vyner and the King were happy for Ogilby to handle Liverpool the way he did. But why?

The rush to publish

The last advertisement for *Britannia* had appeared in the *Term Catalogue*, where publishers set out their wares, in November 1673, shortly after the Secret Treaty plot was abandoned. It said that it was being worked on with "extraordinary vigour". After that Ogilby was working on it without making any noise about it. In September 1675, after five years of work, *Britannia Vol. 1* had to be published, ready or not. It was produced in a terrible hurry, and with no effort to sell it to the public. The book was built as a weapon in the royal armoury, and the gentlemen who appear in its frontispiece are very fashionably dressed in just the way the King wanted. As we have seen, they are dressed to kill in a royal fashion that, like the whole Secret

Treaty plot that gave birth to the book, was anachronistic by 1675. Re-drawing parts of copper plates was standard practice in Ogilby's business, but of course it took time. Shallow lines could be burnished out, but for deeper ones the copper surface had to be scraped away. This was a painstaking business and there was no time in the sudden rush to publication.

That rush shows in the treatment of Warrington. Having measured the road from York as far west as Warrington it is not credible that Ogilby's work did not continue the seventeen miles to Liverpool. It is pretty clear that when *Britannia* was hurried to publication, this short road was removed from its pages and the related sections hurriedly altered. There is a catalogue of routes at the start and an index at the end, both of which of course use numbers to refer to the maps, but they were rendered useless as in the rush to publication the maps themselves were not numbered.[28]

There are also mistakes in the catalogue sequence and in the index, which reveal this desperate last-minute revision. Removing Liverpool created a muddle, which shows when the book portrays the last two of the "Cross Independants", roads leading west from York. The catalogue says that route 65 is a road from York to Chester, depicted on plates 88 and 89, and that the next route, on plate 90, is from York to Lancaster. But that is not how the book was put together. Plate 88 is the York to Lancaster road, not the road to Chester. The first part of that road turns up on plate 89. This is the road that should have continued to Liverpool, but it is now labelled York to West-Chester and ends with the falsified map of Warrington.

All that effort to produce something precise and definitive ended in this sad muddle. The evidence of haste is clear. The plates of maps are astonishing, but there are only half the number that had been promised in 1672. After the introductory material there is an "advertisement" saying that the plan was to measure over 40,000 miles of roads, but that only two-thirds of the work was done and much less than that was actually included. A rationale is offered for the selection chosen: it says the book includes only the most "considerable" roads "or such as an Orderly Distribution of the Kingdom has obliged Us to Exhibit". That is as clear as the mud some of these roads were made of. "Considerable" is an odd criterion – it suggests that a well-used road might be omitted because it was beneath consideration on some other criterion. The phrase about the "orderly distribution of the kingdom" seems to mean that roads have been included which are not of any size or commercial use, and which are not post-roads, but which may, or perhaps should, serve some greater purpose.

Why the sudden rush to publish? There was clearly a financial issue, but Ogilby had been struggling with that for years. He was still hoping for subscribers, at £34 a time, but although he had successfully undertaken other publications by this method, there seem to have been very few subscribers to this one. William Morgan, his step-grandson and heir, reported after Ogilby's death that the work done so far had cost £7,000, but only £1,900 had been promised, and that included the £1,000 promised by the King which was still awaited. Instead, the King produced a royal warrant of 5 June 1674, granting him a duty-free import of 1,000 reams of paper and 1,200 reams in 1675.[29] But the need for money does not explain the need to publish in September 1675, and the act of publication did not bring in cash. Its distribution appears to have been private, rather than advertised in booksellers. It went to the people who needed it.

The sudden re-working and publication of the book clearly indicate that in 1675 there was a sense of emergency. That emergency did involve the King planning to bring in an army from abroad to consolidate his power, but this was not a French army and as we will see, the focus of invasion interest had moved from the harbours of the south and west, to Liverpool. There was a very good reason for removing it from the book.

The edge of the precipice

Charles had abruptly closed Parliament down in February 1674, but he decided to give it one more go in April 1675, with his new chief minister, Danby. They were of course well aware that this might produce a very dangerous confrontation. In Scotland, Charles having declared that non-conformists were committed to subversion, more soldiers were raised and the whole army was paraded through the country in a programme of arrests and intimidation. He also had a brigade of the Irish army sent to Ulster ready to be shipped to Ayrshire if there was serious trouble. In England, the King tried to appease his recalled Parliament by agreeing to anti-Catholic measures and said he had no wish to rule without it. Many members did not believe him and tried to impeach a number of ministers including Arlington and Danby, and demanded the removal of Lauderdale, who was still running Scotland against their will and had even been made a Duke. They demanded the recall of English forces serving under Louis XIV, who was seen as the great example of arbitrary despotism which Charles wanted to follow.[30] Charles' delayed and evasive answers simply stoked the fire, as did his respectful references to "the most Catholic King" of France. The Commons even considered passing a bill that would make it treason to raise money except by Act of Parliament. In June the session became physically aggressive, and the House was on the edge of pitched battle, "every man's hand on his hilt".[31] Charles, despairing, closed the session down.

The mood was very powerfully expressed soon afterwards in Andrew Marvell's only political pamphlet, *An account of the growth of popery, and arbitrary government in England.* His anonymous diatribe proclaims the King to be actively working to introduce French slavery and Roman idolatry, to "assassinate the kingdom" and commit treason by making the monarchy absolute. Charging the King with high crimes took the debate straight back to 1649 and the trial of Charles I.[32]

In August 1675 Louis agreed to pay Charles £100,000 a year to enable him to govern without Parliament if necessary.[33] James urged the King to give up on the impossible task of working with Parliament and rely on France's treasure instead of taxes granted in England. Charles was not yet ready to face down the forces that would oppose him in that case. He needed to buy time, to emasculate the opposition. He was in no hurry to throw down the gauntlet.

That is when someone told Ogilby that he had to deliver the book.

On 13 October Parliament was recalled in the desperate hope that the evident crisis could be averted, but after just five weeks it was sent away again. Compromise was impossible. Heneage Finch, who had taken over as the Lord Keeper of the Great Seal (and had been one of the subscribers to *Virgil*), had opened it with an address on Charles' behalf that described the edge of the precipice, saying:

> The Matters to be treated of, deserve no less than an Assembly of the Three Estates, and a full Concourse of all the Wise and Excellent Persons who bear a Part in this great Council, and

do constitute and compleat this high and honourable Court
… And if ever there were a Time when the Gravity and the
Counsel, the Wisdom and the good Temper, of a Parliament
were necessary to support that Government which only can
support these Assemblies, certainly this is the Hour.

He enumerated the blessings that could be achieved by
co-operation, including to

enrich and adorn this Kingdom, by providing for the Extent
and Improvement of Trade … 'tis in your Power … to secure
a happy Conclusion of this Meeting, by studying to preserve
a good Correspondence, and by a careful Avoiding of all such
Questions as are apt to engender Strife.

Immediately before this speech, Ogilby's magnum opus had
been brought to birth, proclaiming that its purpose was

Reviving and Propagating the great Soul of the World,
Commerce and Correspondency, in maintaining Privileges,
encouraging Industry, and inciting the whole Kingdom to a
Noble Emulation of recovering a Pristine Splendor, establishing
a Present Greatness, or laying Foundations of a Future Glory.

The means were apparently in hand to achieve all this with
or without Parliament. The similarity of language between
Ogilby's Preface and Finch's speech suggests the reason why
there had been a desperate rush to publish. Charles needed
to be prepared to rule entirely through the royal prerogative.
He would leave Parliament in abeyance now, with the longest
prorogation in its history. It was harder now for his opponents
to confront him with a credible insurrection.

The mood was there all right. Anti-court libels appeared
on his statue. A pamphlet with powerful backing appeared in

the coffee houses which said that the court was in the hands of men who wished to introduce popery and an absolutist state. The House of Lords ordered it to be burned, and the identities of the author, printers, and distributors to be revealed. The authorities started by searching the coffee houses of London, and the King issued a proclamation closing them down.[34] He had been suspicious of them for years, as centres of what he regarded as seditious gossip in a worrying atmosphere of sobriety. He believed public grumbling was less dangerous in the alcoholic fug of taverns. But closing the coffee houses down by his own fiat was itself a demonstration of what looked like the new order that people were warning about, an evident extension of the power of the royal prerogative. Coffee house licences, which were the property and livelihoods of their holders, were issued by local licensing authorities, not by the King, so the idea that the King could decide by himself to remove them was quite shocking. His proclamation envisioned the courts punishing those who faced down his arbitrary power, with no authority to do so except his command. Marvell riposted: "Let the city drink coffee and quietly groan, – They who conquered the father won't be slaves to the son."[35]

Charles would not bring about a showdown if he could evade it. The proclamation was, it turned out, too dangerous to be pursued. He needed to avoid a physical confrontation if possible, but make it clear that he would deal with it decisively if he had to. That meant that he needed to guarantee the availability of his troops waiting in Ireland. Liverpool had to be made harmless.

Eliminating Liverpool

The approach to Liverpool

The King had taken a close interest in Liverpool from the time of his restoration. Although it was a small port with primitive facilities, it mattered because it controlled access to Dublin and was dominated by anti-Royalist non-conformists. This had been very clear in the Civil War, when its ships prevented Charles I's troops being brought from Dublin.

Liverpool's part in the Civil War had been a nasty lesson for the Stuarts. Its noble overlords, Stanley and Lord Molineux (who controlled the castle) were royalist, but most of the burgesses of the town, who were artisans and seamen, were non-conformist Parliamentarians. A rich Puritan, John More, was elected by them as MP and Mayor. More was the town's biggest landlord, and partly at his own expense, fitted out six warships which blocked shipping from Dublin until Prince Rupert advanced overland and took the town in 1644, slaughtering most Liverpudlians that had not fled. It was very clear that, large or not, Liverpool was dangerous.

Rupert left a garrison of his own there, but it soon surrendered to Parliamentary forces and when the Restoration came Liverpool's re-installed citizens were not as delighted as London's. Charles acted to establish his control over access to the port without making any overt provocation. He did it by secretly taking over Liverpool's emergency warning beacon. The town is too far upstream to have sight of the sea. The channel into the Mersey passed close inshore along the Wirral's coast, where it was under the eye of Bidston Hall, built on a rock outcrop two miles inland.[1] Bidston could be seen from the town, so whoever controlled it could warn Liverpool of attack – or let the attack proceed.

Bidston had belonged to the Earl of Derby. Once Parliament had it, they had eyes surveying ships coming from Ireland towards Liverpool. As a result, the only Royalist troops successfully shipped into the north-west had to be landed on the Welsh coast near Holywell and could not be brought into the field where they were needed.

After the Restoration, Derby had a Bill moved to recover Bidston. To his baffled anger, this was blocked by the King. Charles could not allow it because it went to the heart of the restoration settlement and the Act of Indemnity, his promise not to overthrow the property changes that had happened in the Interregnum. But Charles needed Bidston to be back in safe hands, so worked out a plan to let Derby have it by sleight of hand. He told the Earl that "he doubts not but to make a better end for the noble Earl than he would attain if the Bill had passed".[2] He had evidently arranged for Derby to buy it with a non-repayable loan from the royal banker, but Derby must have thought the idea of having to buy his own property on any terms at all quite outrageous. If Charles brought up the question of national security, Derby must have replied along the lines of "so buy it yourself". The King did, in complete secrecy, through a proxy, Lord Kingston of Roscommon.

That explains why the Attorney General expressed a belief in November 1679, that the real owner of Bidston might actually be the King.[3] A resolution was passed in February 1688 that the government should uncover the truth.[4] The King's banker, who had put up the money for Kingston's "purchase", was his very loyal friend Robert Vyner, who eventually took over legal possession of Bidston by default. Vyner regarded this manor as something he was taking care of rather than his property and did not mention it in his will.

The "Glorious Revolution" intervened later in 1688 and the Vyner family have owned Bidston manor ever since. But Bidston's importance as the eyes of Liverpool depended on the approach to the Mersey estuary remaining hidden from the town. In 1675, when political tension was at a very high pitch, and when Liverpool, still aggressively hostile to the King, was becoming rich and powerful, that changed.

Suppressing the town

The town of Liverpool was, from the Crown's point of view, a nest of vipers. The Council was a virtually closed group, sixty strong, who appointed each other. Freemen of the town voted for the mayor and bailiffs, and since men became Freemen by becoming established in trades, generally through apprenticeships, this meant the town, left to its own devices, would be a democracy of artisans and tradesmen.[5]

A Corporation Act passed in 1661 obliged every urban office holder to take an oath as a practising member of the Church of England, swearing that "it is not lawfull upon any pretence whatsoever to take Arms against the King". Almost one third of Liverpool Council refused and resigned. They were replaced with new Freemen of known loyalty who did not live or work there. These were local gentry from the countryside.

Considerable efforts were then made to weaken the town by hampering its commerce. Its trade was entirely with Ireland, mainly consisting of livestock, with small ships bringing over sheep and, especially, cheap cattle for fattening and butchery.[6] In 1663 livestock imports from Ireland were forbidden for half of each year by Act of Parliament. This had a massive financial impact on Liverpool.

Four years later animal imports from Ireland were banned completely, with a new Act of Parliament that did not expire until 1679. As Liverpool lost its trade from Ireland, it also saw Ireland's capacity to import collapse. From 1663 to 1675, English exports to Ireland fell by 90%.[7] Ogilby, Ormond's Master of the Revels, suffered as the arts always do in a financial crisis. He had gone to Dublin because the Lord Lieutenant wanted him there, and he had expected that the new regime would put the city back on its feet and encourage wealthy theatrical patronage. In fact his remarkable efforts there were in the face of tremendous unexpected financial problems which crushed the Liverpool–Dublin trade.

Instead of withering away, Liverpool's merchants found a way to prosper without Ireland. In September 1666 a small ship, the *Antelope*, had set out on a transatlantic venture.[8] She sailed for Barbados with shoes, nails, candles, butter, coal and cheese, and two miles of cotton cloth; she came back with sugar. This would be the start of a great new industry, involving more capital than the old hand-to-mouth trade with Dublin, bigger ships and financiers who could carry greater risks. London merchants set up refineries there, and by 1670 Liverpool's residents were making serious money. In 1669 they made their move to take back control of the town. A mayor was installed who had refused to take the oath denouncing insurrection that was demanded by the Corporation Act. He was Thomas Bicksteth,[9] a rope maker, popular with the town's sailors and exactly the kind of anti-Stuart non-conformist who was growing rich as shipping prospered.

The King was obviously concerned to keep control of this tiny but dangerous port. His opportunity came in 1670 with a vacancy for one of the town's two MPs. Charles decided that he wanted the new MP to be a London alderman, Bucknall, the leader of a group of brewers who had bought the right to collect and keep the spirit tax in London and the south-east. This privatised tax collecting was called "tax-farming". Bucknall had a deal, made through Charles' mistress, Barbara Villiers, to take over the farm of some 75% of all the excise revenues of the kingdom.[10] A splendidly caustic sketch of nearly 180 MPs, drawn up around 1671, probably to help manage Charles' business in Parliament, says that Bucknall paid her the staggering sum of £20,000 – several millions in modern money.[11]

In an age of untrammelled corruption, Bucknall did not find it hard to buy up the burgesses of Liverpool.[12] Their "treats" were supplied by a relative with £500 to strew around, who travelled ahead of him in an impressive coach-and-six, arriving on the road that *Britannia* would pretend did not exist. Liverpool's other MP, a non-conformist, was outraged by the direct engagement of the King in the election, complaining about installing "an Exciseman": this, he stormed, would put Parliament at the mercy of the Crown "and then good night to the liberty of the subject".[13] There were plenty of others who felt the same way. In his way, the King was one of them. That, after all, was the point of what he was doing. Once Bucknall was elected, Liverpool's American trade simply stopped. There is no explanation of this, but it certainly hit the town hard in the pocket. Its new refineries suddenly had nothing to refine.[14]

This happened shortly before the Secret Treaty of Dover. This election success came at just the right moment to secure the port for the King, in case of the French invasion anticipated in the Secret Treaty. As the town struggled to make a living, new loyalist Freemen were appointed and in 1672 the town's leading doctor, Sylvester Richmond, a country gentleman, was elected mayor. There was a tremendous row in the Council about some document listing claimed abuses, which was suppressed. The Court of Freemen then declared that if any member was strongly believed to have "discovered or disclosed any part of the acts or things here done in Council" he was liable to a fine of £20 – doubled if he was an Alderman.[15] That was enough to wipe out most townsmen and the records become hard to follow. The next mayor was a man who had been working for the Earl of Derby, trying to get Charles to issue a new charter permanently changing the balance of power.[16] There was a riot in the town hall chamber which was only ended by bringing in armed guards.[17] The record books subsequently had pages ripped out.[18]

If Liverpool was now ruined, then the non-conformists of the town would be powerless to hinder the arrival of Charles' troops from Ireland. That is certainly the picture painted in the fragmentary and rotting official records. But in fact the port revived its American trade under the radar. There are no entries in the port books to show it, but by the end of 1674 the sugar was coming, and it was making money for the town.[19] The loyalist Freemen found they were once more outnumbered and in 1675 Bicksteth, backed by artisans and sailors,[20] re-appeared as Mayor. There seems to have been a surge in transatlantic shipping.[21]

This was exactly the time when Charles was facing the impossibility of working with Parliament and was looking at how to prevent his opponents taking the country back into insurrection. In fact there was probably no appetite for a return to civil war, but the anti-Court party believed that there was a real prospect of Charles seizing absolute power and his own advisors, especially James, were sure that plots were in hand and insurrection a real possibility. That insurrection seemed much likelier if Liverpool could do again what it had done before, using its ships to stop troops being brought from Dublin. Charles wanted to demonstrate to his opponents that Liverpool had been neutralised. That would once have been the case with Vyner controlling the lookout point at Bidston, but the port's new wealth significantly altered the situation.

Liverpool built its own look-out point, in the middle of the town. In 1674 the Council authorised the construction of a new Town Hall on the highest point of the town, and the old High Cross was dismantled to make room for it. It was surmounted by a square tower, creating a viewing platform about 170 feet above sea level, significantly higher than the castle turrets near the shore. Liverpool had, for the first time, its own view of the sea right across towards Anglesey. The object appeared innocent enough – to provide commercial intelligence about approaching ships, information that could not be gleaned from a signal fire on Bidston hill. But it also meant that Liverpool would know what military movements were taking place at sea. By September 1675 the new Town Hall was up and running,[22] and Bidston had lost its strategic value.

The decision to have *Britannia* published, ready or not, must have been made that summer, when Charles had become convinced that things were desperate and Louis was offering him the finance to rule without any need of Parliament. Charles was ready to face down what might follow, using the troops he had on standby in Ireland. But suddenly his control of the approach to Liverpool was lost, thanks to the prosperity of the town and its nearly-finished town hall tower. The answer seems to have been to do whatever could be done to cut off Liverpool's trade – to renew the assault made by the Cattle Acts, but this time try to completely reduce the city to helplessness. Liverpool would, quite literally, be taken off the map.

Shipping floats on a sea of credit, and it looks as if Liverpool's credit-worthiness was now put under attack. We have no evidence of what was done. Given the systematic concealment and destruction of records, that is hardly surprising. Liverpool's disappearance from *Britannia* should be seen as part of a pattern which indicates government policy. Liverpool disappears from central government records between 1674 and 1676. Normally, the Northern Secretary of State, Williamson, recorded a few communications each year from the town: for example, in May 1672 he was advised that Liverpool had three times the tonnage of Chester and that the press gangs were corruptly taking landsmen instead of seamen to protect commercial shipping.[23] But that stops. In 1674 there are just some notices of Liverpool ships trading with France being wrecked, French warships sheltering there and the landing of an Irish Privy Councillor.[24] Of the town and its affairs, not a word. We can simply see that *Britannia* was rushed into print with the road to Liverpool hidden behind a non-existent wall of houses at Warrington, and that all the port's trade, not just the trans-Atlantic shipping, began to disappear. In 1675 the Calendar of State Papers has not a single word from Liverpool. The port books show that this year Liverpool recorded fewer ship movements than in 1674, and in 1676 the number fell again.[25] Something was strangling the trade of this particular port, and this was not just a question of ships evading the official record. It was reported in Parliament that in the last three months of 1676 not a single ship left Liverpool for Dublin, so that even the tax farmers were stranded.[26]

In 1676 a local loyalist landlord and politician, Edward More, was trying hard to draw attention to something going seriously wrong there. The Northern Secretary was warned on behalf of the Corporation that More was sending a petition which needed to be blocked. The warning was obscure, as his correspondent felt this was a matter of state about which nothing should be put in writing. He said he expected to explain in person, and in the meantime provided the names of two people who could fill things in privately. They were Sir Robert Carr (one of the strongest proponents of the Cattle Act that had so damaged Liverpool) and Sir Thomas Chicheley (Master-General of the Ordnance in England and Ireland).[27] The petition has, unsurprisingly, vanished.

The most extraordinary indication of what had happened pops up in Richard Blome's already published *Britannia*, which underwent a dramatic and very sudden revision of its description of Liverpool in 1675. The book that Blome had produced in 1673 treated Liverpool as a very minor place, "well inhabited and traded unto by Merchants and Shopkeepers, and is of late beautified with good built houses: and the more for its commodious Haven, and convenient passage to Ireland".[28] But then, despite his avowal to keep his book as concise as possible, being "confined to the narrow limits of a Twenty shillings Volume", Blome changed it to devote a massive fifty-four lines of text to this small town, six more than he gave to York, which had at least four times the population! Far from abolishing Liverpool, it was extolled at great length. This was an extensive and expensive advertising feature inserted to try to drum up business in the face of serious problems.

Blome's book is not so much an atlas as an encyclopaedia of Britain and its colonies and he made it clear that he was not the author of the text, but the compiler. In 1675, it seems he was paid to insert completely new text as a pre-emptive riposte to Ogilby and sell the town's business potential to investors who were being discouraged by the Cosmographer. It was done in such a rush that he mis-numbered the re-written page 132 as 232.

The new material can be found in the copies of the book in the British Library. You are encouraged to see a substantial community of entrepreneurs, men who under-stand the meaning of opportunity, the kind of men that you want to be among, earning their respect and their profits. These men appreciate Liverpool's low rates of duty and short passage-times:

> its situation affording in greater plenty, and at reasonabler rates then most parts of England such exported Commodities proper for the West-Indies; as likewise a quicker return for such imported Commodities, by reason of the Sugar-Bakers, and great Manufacturers of Cottons in the adjacent parts, and the rather for that it is found to be the convenient passage to Ireland, and divers considerable Counties in England with which they have intercourse of traffick.

And then this highly-polished commercial arrives at its high point as we are shown, in all innocence, the new Town Hall in the process of construction:

Here is now erecting at the public charge of the Mayor, Aldermen, &c, a famous Town-house placed on Pillars and Arches of hewen Stone; and underneath is the public Exchange for the Merchants.

That is how we can be sure that this text was inserted after the book was published in 1673. The order for the building of the "famous Town-House" was not made until 1674, and the new building was completed and the old town hall leased out in September 1675.[29]

Bound in with the revised volumes of the book, Blome displays the coats of arms of his "Benefactors & promoters". They are arranged on a strict grid, but one stands out, number 623, Edward More. It stands out because it is the only coat of arms which is drawn too large to fit into the grid. He had invested in making his presence felt in Blome's *Britannia*, and he had written the advert for his city.[30] He had not felt the need to do this when Blome's book was first published in 1673, but something very serious had happened since then. The most probable explanation is that he found that the town's existing sources of credit had suddenly disappeared. Edward, who wanted to lease out land for a sugar factory, had decided on a crash advertising campaign. It seems not to have worked. It did not reverse the steep decline in shipping.

It was at this moment that *Britannia* was published, and Liverpool's suppression threatened to be more than a paper exercise. In October 1676, Mayor Bicksteth thought a military assault was imminent and all Freemen were ordered to equip themselves with "sword, firelock, and musket" as fast as possible.[31] A few days later, as his term of office ended, he tried to ensure the succession by admitting a whole batch of his supporters as Freemen. His man was elected but

ejected and the new Freemen were thrown out.[32] The port
was paralysed. This is when the Northern Secretary was
advised to block any petition from More for reasons that the
Master of the Ordinance, of all people, could best explain.
Charles now felt his authority was sufficient to impose a new
charter of his own devising which put Liverpool in fetters.
The Freemen lost the power of appointing their own mayor
and were given a Council. The King named his own men to
it and made them permanently self-electing. If anyone was
looking for an example of royal absolutism, this was as good
as they could hope for. And they were certainly looking.

> The good old cause reviv'd, a plot requires.
> Plots, true or false, are necessary things,
> To raise up common-wealths, and ruin kings.
>   (J. Dryden, *Absalom and Achitophel*, 1681)

Fear of those plots had driven the final stages of *Britannia*. The
pre-emptive precautions Charles took to ensure his access to
the troops in Ireland seemed to have served their purpose. He
was given a new subsidy by Louis in 1678, and then sailed his
own yacht to survey the defences in Portsmouth, Plymouth
and Pendennis Castle, which had been his last refuge before
his escape across the sea in 1646. Tension grew even greater
when Parliament was finally recalled in 1679, and eventually,
in 1681, Charles dismissed it and ruled as an absolute
monarch for the rest of his life. There was no uprising, and he
did not need to bring troops from Ireland into England. He
shipped them into Scotland to pre-emptively suppress insurrection there instead.

Once Charles had Liverpool under his own control the
town was put back on its economic feet. The port book for
1677 is too badly damaged to be consulted, but the 1678 book

looks as if it belongs to a different port. It records over 900 ship movements. Only when Charles' successor James surrendered his throne in 1688, did the town's subservience end. The usurper, William of Orange, gave it a new more democratic charter which declared that Charles II's had been the product of a conspiracy.

The End of the Road

Charles triumphant

Britannia had been a little mangled by swift changes and hurried publication. That was, in its creator's view, a price worth paying to keep the natural order in its proper place. That was what it was for, a book created to assist Charles in eventualities which never came about. The early work on it was to lay down the framework for military control using French troops and managing a new Catholic kingdom. The later work was to help weaken opposition and prevent Charles' opponents from being able to resist him. That was a successful operation.

Ogilby's infirmity finally carried him off in September 1676, still far from breaking even on the project.[1] A year later his wife died; according to Aubrey, at nearly ninety years old.

Five years after Ogilby's death Britain was being ruled by the King alone, without Parliament. He was ruling by Divine Right, exercising absolute power within the law, and of course no court could decide what law he might be transgressing. The militia in England was thoroughly purged of commanders he could not trust, and non-conformists, who were identified with opposition to royal authority, were quite brutally suppressed. Any non-conformist religious gathering was deemed to be "riot", and physical abuse would be followed by large fines and often by imprisonment. Hundreds died in jail.

He was careful to avoid being seen as a tyrant, and knew he had to keep local elites on his side, but he now had the power to replicate what he had done in Liverpool and ensure that those elites were made up of the right people. *Britannia* provided an extraordinary grasp over the business and administration of the 399 communities which it identified in England and Wales, and the crown took a grip on them all. 133 were identified as electing burgesses, and between 1682 and 1687 that number of municipal corporations were given the Liverpool treatment, having their charters replaced to ensure that they were run by people amenable to the Crown.[2] There were abortive plots against him, but the possibility of armed uprising had been made remote and the Catholic succession of James had been secured. The English Parliament had been set aside thanks to a cash supply from Louis and the effective disposition of military resources.[3] Under the Triennial Act Charles should have recalled Parliament in 1684, but there was no outcry when he simply ignored that. In Scotland, which had been brought even more firmly to heel, Parliament was still in business because it now provided the King with whatever he wanted. It willingly funded armed forces to put down "rebellious commotions". Over the whole of Britain, administrative efficiency was increased and tax collection improved so that Charles' permanent ordinary revenue grew by 35% by 1684–5.

Britannia's place in this new system of government was made clear in 1682. The great map of London had been published in 20 sheets by William Morgan, now Cosmographer Royal, in the year after his step-grand-father's death.[4] At 100 feet to the inch, covering a space 8 feet 5 inches x 4 feet 7 inches (2.57 x 1.4 metres), it was intended for the Aldermen and guilds of the city. But in 1682 he re-issued it for the halls of royal government, making a statement about the takeover of local civic power. The top right showed some of the great new buildings of the City, including the Guildhall, the Royal Exchange and a speculative version of the unfinished St Paul's. It also had a huge list of leading figures of the Church and the nobility of Ireland, under a dedication to Ormond. These names had little to do with the creation of the map, but were attached to a general acknowledgement of "the LORDS Spiritual and Temporal, most of whom have Subscribed or Adventured for the Encoragment of Mr. OGILBY and the AUTHOR". The top corners now showed statues of the King on horseback, and the top left also displayed the King's gate at Whitehall "leading to Westminster", the royal complex of buildings (including the Banqueting House), banners with the names of the royal family and a pear tree whose fruits carry the names of the Privy Council.[5] Among these images of royal authority was displayed an engraving inscribed "Mr. OGILBY Presenting their MA[ties] with his Book of Subscriptions for the Survey".

The survey in question was not the map; that had no volume of subscribers. It was *Britannia*, where the King had ordered the Privy Council to create such a list and took a close interest to ensure that the work was completed. This book was the necessary handbook of the new system of rule, and the machinery by which the King had brought it into being was being celebrated as key to the process by which London became the royal metropolis and Britain was managed.

Carolus A Carolo, the vision of Britannia as a royal project to compare with France, had been achieved. Ogilby's opening

40. Ogilby presenting the subscription list for *Britannia* to the King and Queen.

address to the King at the start of *Britannia* is a statement that the alterations he made to the book, in order to strengthen the Crown, are themselves an example to other nations. No longer need Britain concede first place in the scientific representation of the world to "the Fame of *France* and *Belgium*". The teacher of the Old Measures has now

> Given such Measures to The Virtuosi of the World, as Forein Princes and States shall be Glad to Imitate. But ... Your Majesty and The World may See, how Effectually Operative Your Royal Countenance is, in Adapting such Mean Abilities to so Great Performances.

Science, and indeed geography, changes its form in the light of the royal countenance. Ogilby's *Britannia* contains the evidences of real plots, and real dangers. But it depicts a landscape transformed like the cosmos of the masque, shaped by showing each road on imaginary scrolls to magnify and glorify the transcendent monarch in ways that belong to a different kind of truth. Instead of the old maps of counties, showing the land as the territory of its lords and gentlemen, this *Britannia* shows no counties, no boundaries, and the only geographic space is defined and filled by the King's Highways. Royal authority fills *Britannia* in a measured apotheosis, not on a banqueting house ceiling but bound in finest leather.

The place of the book

Britannia was an extraordinary and beautiful creation, developed with members of the Royal Society in the service of the King. It was obviously never intended as a book for travellers, or for merchants. It was designed for the grandeur of power, and its place was in Whitehall and the libraries of statesmen.[6] Copies were placed in the palaces and offices of state and in public rooms at the Universities. It was a significant step forward not just in mapping, but in the development of science as a tool of government. It played a significant part in reshaping the power of royal government, at least until James came to the throne and lost his grip on power.

The book's guidance worked well so long as it did what it claimed. As we have seen, sometimes it did something else. In 1689 William III, the Dutch Protestant invader who replaced James II, needed to ship an army to Dublin. He evidently relied on *Britannia* as an administrator's bible and demanded ships from Chester. He had to be told that Chester had no ships, just a few barques for coasting. There was a place called

Liverpool, on the other hand, that had "60 or 70 good ships of 50 to 200 tons".[7]

Britannia could not be cannibalised for more mundane users. Ogilby produced a cheaper volume containing just the strips and sold individual map sheets to try to bring in a bit more money, but without the text these would have been very tricky to use. (A new printing twenty-two years after his death showed that the plates still had plenty of life left in them, which was not a good sign.)[8] Britannia's impressive size and cost meant that no other publisher could see any point in trying to pirate it. Roads immediately began to appear on county maps[9] and Ogilby wrote complaints about pirating, but it was not the maps that were being copied. It was the data. That was used in new editions of Speed and Saxton. There really was a market for this information, and Ogilby published it just before his death as *Mr. Ogilby's Tables of his Measur'd Roads*, sixty-four narrow pages with tables of distances without illustration. The huge master volume was deeply puzzling to commercial publishers, since they knew nothing of its real purpose:

> The charge of engraving the maps had so much enhanced the price of the book, that it came into few hands, and especially the bulk of it rendred it unfit for the use it seems to have been purposely complied, I mean the direction of travellers.

That was the view of a publisher nearly twenty-five years later, who re-cast it as *Ogilby and Morgan's The Traveller's Guide*, a pocket book of Ogilby's descriptions, without bothering with the maps.

A travellers' hand-book was certainly needed. Within two years, three other publications appeared with the strip-maps redrawn in crude small versions, inexpensive and easily carried. *Ogilby and Morgan's Book of the Roads*, a purely text version, ran to at least twenty-three editions and was still selling over a hundred years after the dancing master's death. Bizarrely, Liverpool remained missing from these books. In 1771 the *Book of the Roads* was still being re-published with the message that

> Length of time has produced great alterations by turning the roads, and the traveller by following Ogilby has often been led into the mire. Many instances may be found, where new roads are struck out, that were never known or frequented until lately.

This was certainly true: by this time there was a regular stage-coach running to Liverpool on a turnpike road. But the road to Liverpool was still missing from the book. This was not any act of anti-Liverpool plotting, simply an illustration of the indolence of publishers.

Eventually the idea that Ogilby really meant to make a map-book for travellers produced a useable version of it. In 1720 Emanuel Bowen and John Owen published *Britannia Depicta or Ogilby Improv'd*, a complete re-engraving of the maps and a mass of information about gentry families and local history. Ogilby's work had become what *Britannia* was not, a replacement for the hired guides who escorted travellers through the concealed and private lands of England and Wales. This truly was a new age. *Britannia* itself had opened a future, but was now lost in the past.

The place of the man

Ogilby himself had by now been dismantled, firstly and subtly by his younger rival Richard Blome. Blome must have been badly stung by Ogilby's statement that *"one Blome"* had simply copied out other people's work and added his own errors to theirs.[10] Three years after Ogilby's death, Blome took the trouble to show to Ogilby's noble friends that the coat of arms he used was nothing more than that of a simple clan member. One of Blome's publishing franchises was *A Display of Heraldry*, a standard work which had run through four editions since appearing in 1610, the latest in 1666. It was a scholarly guide to English heraldry, so had never included any mention of the Ogilvies or any other Scottish arms. But in 1679 Blome brought out a new edition on the pretext that he was expunging those who had been included as "Oliver's creatures" and replacing them with those given arms since the Restoration – which he could have done in the previous edition. This seems to have given him the opportunity to introduce just one purely Scottish coat of arms – the Ogilby lion. He did not show the Earl's arms, but a lion with mullet, a five pointed star. Perhaps its presence was sponsored. The 1st Earl of Airlie was dead, so was Ogilby, his usefulness was past and it was time for the House of Airlie to shut down the connection with the old scandal of his birth. The new edition said that this lion and mullet "is born by the Name of Ogilby, an honourable & spreading Family in Scotland, the chief of which are the Right Honourable James Earl of Airly".[11] There was no fixed way to spell the clan name, but this spelling was of course particularly associated by Blome with his fellow publisher. The clan chief referred to was the 2nd Earl, the man John met in the Tower of London. The book does not normally provide biographies of its arms-bearers, but in this case Blome relates the tale of how the Earl had come to be in the Tower and his heroic devotion to the Crown. Blome also lists other distinguished members of this "family", who are carefully referred to as Ogilby, not Ogilvie. A reader may look for the best known Ogilby among them, but he is not there. His name does not, apparently, signify a place in this clan.

This effort to detach John Ogilby from his escutcheon was not very well done. A clan is not quite the same as a family, and clans do not have generic arms. The one displayed as "Ogilby's" was not, because the mullet there is on the lion's shoulder. It was part of the image, not a mark of difference. It did belong to a real man, an obscure Scot called Leighton of Usan who had taken part in clan violence alongside the Earl's father a few years before John was born.[12] When this necessary fact was eventually inserted he was called "Leichstein of Uzzan". It seems to be an oddity introduced to muddy the water of John Ogilby's entitlement to arms. But it did its job, and the Airlie connection had been killed off, so far as posterity was concerned.

Three years later came a more public assault. John Dryden was a successful poet and playwright, employed by Killigrew to write for his theatre, and at the time of Ogilby's death was poet laureate and historiographer royal. He was fiercely defensive of his intellectual independence and wrote for a general public, not noble patrons. Ogilby had made his way by the necessary art of serving great men. Dryden was a combative satirist who despised Ogilby's literary pretensions and saw him as the very model of fawning pomposity. His "armigero", that bastard Latin word which Ogilby used to represent status, was surely the mark of Justice Shallow, Shakespeare's comic turn in the opening scene of *The Merry Wives of Windsor*, which of course Dryden knew very well. Shallow is sycophantically described as "A Gentleman borne ... who ... writes himselfe Armigero".[13] In 1682, Dryden wrote *MacFlecknoe*, a satire on a poet called Shadwell with whom he was feuding. It is a mock-heroic work in which Shadwell's heroic virtue is dullness, and he is heir to a kingdom of dullness in which Ogilby features as one of a number of once-prized poets whose work is now used for wrapping paper. Chapman is included in that list, so it seems that translations of Homer are especially dull, at least until Dryden made one. Ogilby's pages, along with Shirley's, were also used as toilet paper in this heroically dull kingdom, where pie shops served the same digestive purpose as our own curry takeaways:

> From dusty shops neglected authors come
> Martyrs of pies, and relics of the bum,
> Much Heywood, Shirley, Ogilby there lay,
> But loads of Sh— almost choked the way.

Dryden actually made quite extensive use of Ogilby's work in his own translation of Virgil[14] but came to bury, not to praise him. In the meantime the shrewdest bookseller in England, Thomas Guy, published a popular pocket edition of Ogilby's *Virgil* with re-drawn plates, no patrons, and no picture of Ogilby or his coat of arms. Guy, who made a fortune out of speculation and founded Guy's Hospital, had no doubts about Ogilby's saleability, at least until Dryden published his own *Virgil* in 1697. Then Pope joined in. At the end of the century, the seven-year-old Alexander Pope was sent to live with a Catholic priest who made him read Ogilby's *Iliads*, a book which the frail child could never have been able to pick up. He must have stood on a step to lean over the text. He also learned Greek, and Pope came to love the *Iliad* and to detest Ogilby. It is not hard to see why. He picked up on Dryden's satire of heroic dullness and produced a full-scale epic in four books, the *Dunciad*, to demolish his own rivals, and like Dryden threw Ogilby into the pot as a member of the dull ranks: "Here swells the shelf with Ogilby the great".[15]

So when Jove's block descended from on high
(As sings thy great forefather Ogilby),
Loud thunder to its bottom shook the bog,
And the hoarse nation croak'd, "God save King Log!"

His determination to do better eventually gave us the best-known English version of Homer – his own. Today, according to the *Encyclopaedia Britannica*, "as a poet and translator (Ogilby) is chiefly remembered for being ridiculed by Dryden in MacFlecknoe and by Pope in the Dunciad". But Ogilby's *Aesop* is not in the least dull, and his translations of Virgil and Homer, one the first complete version in English, the other the first for half a century, laid the foundation for a political aesthetic which created the elegant space that these later Augustans inhabited, and from which they ruled the fashionable world. In reality his legacy was not just a road atlas but an enterprise, of which these works were the beginning.

The new reality

But the road atlas above all was more important than the man, and the journey John Ogilby made to *Britannia* was the journey of our entire culture. This was a fundamental transformation from one cosmology to another. He grew up under heavens that circled the Earth, among people that believed these visible movements were directly revealed to human understanding and were reflected in the patterns of life, of law and government. He learned the significance of dance as an education in the harmony of a moral universe that unified nature, human society and divine law in a single order endorsed by religious revelation and classical wisdom.

We cannot recognise the sky under which he was schooled. He died under a totally different sky. That one, we know very well.

In *Britannia*, the Cosmographer Royal sets out journeys under this new sky, where nature is not revealed but hidden, where the key to understanding is not the steps of a dance and the Old Measures, but the new measures that allow nature to be dissected, analysed, computed, divided. Milton set out to justify the ways of God to man. Ogilby's great work became to demonstrate the ways of man to man – the highways that created a network of connections which would now replace all other connections. The land was once bound together by traditions, customs and obligations. They had all been shattered by the ruthless upheavals of brutal war and terrible plagues, on a scale which we can hardly grasp, and by the new philosophy which destroyed the certainty of perception and the safety of old teachings.

The ways themselves were not paved, and unless they were enclosed the precise course travelled would depend on the traveller. Until Ogilby arrived, tracks would shift from side to side according to the state of the ground and the mood of man, land and weather. Every journey was a multi-dimensional engagement with the landscape and its people, requiring guidance and co-operation between locals and travellers. *Britannia* would change that. Its ways became precise paths in the conceptual world of its pages. Those pages implied a new kind of traveller who carried his own book of knowledge about these unfamiliar ways, and his own entitlement to use them.

So the land was opened for use by those who had never had a place on it. This was part of a great shift in the way literate and thoughtful people related to the world around them. Ogilby's work is not just part of that shift but a compelling metaphor for it. It was of course propelled into being by the ambitions and secret plans of the King. The legacy of Charles' plots and Ogilby's place in them fades over time into obscurity. But the deeper object was to create a more centralised administration that could systematise its knowledge of the world in order to wield more effective power. That certainly was achieved, and Britain became the model of how to do it. The lesson of *Britannia* is that whoever controls the map controls the world – indeed, whoever makes the map makes the world. We should all be grateful that Google's code of conduct includes "Don't be Evil", and perhaps uneasy that they have dropped it as a motto. The world is sliced, diced, weighed and measured, and the old rules of cosmic harmony and unity have no meaning here. This is where our way of thinking began, and Ogilby's wheel still rolls on, in a world where nothing now counts but everything is counted:

> ... behold
> There in the moonshine, rolling up an hill,
> Steered by no fleshly hand, with spokes of light,
> The Wheel—John Ogilby's Wheel—the WHEEL hiss by,
> Measuring mileposts of eternity.
> (Kenneth Slessor, "Post-Roads")

Notes

INTRODUCTION

1 "The maske was well liked and all things passed orderly", according to a letter from Chamberlain on 9 January. Chamberlain wrote frequent accounts of affairs in London and Westminster. It was not a ringing endorsement. N.E. McClure (ed.), *The Letters of John Chamberlain*, American Philosophical Society (1939), vol. 2, p. 200.

2 The Banqueting House was 120 feet by 53 feet, the Great Hall was about 70 feet by 30 feet (*Survey of London*, vol. 13, St Margaret, Westminster, Part II: Whitehall I).

3 R. Stoyan, *Atlas of Great Comets* (Cambridge 2015); J. Doelman, "The Comet of 1618 and the British Royal Family", *Notes and Queries* (March 2007), pp. 30–5.

4 Sir Thomas Lorkin to Sir Thomas Puckering, 1 December 1618, in T. Birch, *Court and Times of James I* (London 1849), vol. II, p. 110.

5 S.J. Schechner and S.S. Genuth, *Comets, Popular Culture, and the Birth of Modern Cosmology* (Princeton 1999), p. 55.

6 The proof that Ogilby performed in this masque is set out below in "Life 2. The Dancer: the evidence deciphered". The masque itself was identified in 2007 by M. Butler, "George Chapman's Masque of the Twelve Months (1619)", *English Literary Renaissance* (Oxford), vol. 37, no. 3 (Autumn 2007), pp. 360–400. Prognostication was the only part which required a professional solo dancer, and therefore must have been Ogilby's part. The device of a character directly addressing the King and telling his fortune in a masque was used again by Buckingham two years later in *The Gypsies Metamorphised*, when he played that role himself. The description of the audience is based on Venetian Ambassador Bursino's account of the previous year's Court masque, from M. Sullivan, *Court Masques of James I: Their Influence on Shakespeare, and the Public Theatres* (London 1913).

7 The Civil Wars killed approximately 7% of the population, making them more deadly than any later conflict (G. Parker, *Global Crisis: War, Climate Change and Catastrophe in the Seventeenth Century* [New Haven 2013], p. 359). Epidemics of plague carried off some 20% of the population of London in 1603 and 1625, and about 18% in 1665 (A.L. Moote and D.C. Moote, *The Great Plague: The Story of London's Most Deadly Year* [Baltimore 2008], p. 10).

8 J. Kepler, *The Harmony of the World* (1619), book IV.

LIFE 1. BEGINNING

1 J.G.A. Pocock (ed.), *The Political Works of James Harrington* (Cambridge 1977), part 1, p. 264.

2 Ms. Aub. 8, f. 45.

3 Sir W. Gilbey, *Early Carriages and Roads* (London 1903), p. 21.

4 T. Moule, *The True Narration of the Entertainment of His Royal Majesty, from the time of his departure from Edinburgh till his receiving at London* (London 1603), p. 20.

5 He was admitted on 16 June 1606: see Guildhall Library, London, Merchant Taylors Guild Records (microfilm MF 326, f.246ʳ).

6 SP Dom. James I, v. 24, 4 December 1606.

7 T. Dekker, *Villanies Discovered* (1616), ch. XV.

8 http://www.british-history.ac.uk/survey-london/vol25/pp9–21#anchorn27, consulted 10/1/2016.

9 R.H. Helmholz, "Bonham's Case, Judicial Review, and the Law of Nature", *Journal of Legal Analysis* I, 1 (2009), pp. 326–56.

10 *The Records of the Honourable Society of Lincoln's Inn, The Black Books of Lincoln's Inn*, vol. 2 (1898), p. 131. A note by the editor suggests that it was the barristers themselves, who were called Utter Barristers, who did not dance, and that "Under Barristers" is a slip of the pen. But the antiquary William Dugdale reported the record without question in 1666 and he was in a position to know.

11 His name does not appear in the school register, a work largely compiled from the list of pupils taking an exam called "probation". The list for 1607 indicates a school population of 187 (C.J. Robinson, *A Register of the Scholars Admitted into Merchant Taylors*, vol. 1 [London 1883], p. 2), but the headmaster claimed it was at least 250 (F.W.M. Draper, *Four Centuries of Merchant Taylors School* [London 1962], p. 44), so a quarter of the pupils do not seem to be listed. Ogilby's lifelong connection with the Company, and his entitlement to education there, indicate that this is where he was – briefly – schooled. A boy of his age would normally have started school around 1608. That is when one

of his closest friends, James Shirley, was registered, though Shirley was four years his senior.

12 W.C. Hazlitt, *Schools, School-Books, and Schoolmasters* (London 1888), pp. 136–45.

13 O.L. Dick (ed.) *Aubrey's Brief Lives* (New Hampshire 1999), pp. 219–21.

14 From "Memorial XXXII: The Banquet given to James I, 1607", *Memorials of the Guild of Merchant Taylors: Of the Fraternity of St. John the Baptist in the City of London* (1875), pp. 147–81.

15 J.P. Sommerville, *King James VI and I: Political Writings* (London 1994), p. 178.

16 I. Janicka-Swiderska, "The Dance in Elizabethan and Stuart Drama", *Real: The Yearbook of Research in English and American Literature*, vol. 5 (1987), p. 65.

17 S.M. Kingsbury (ed.), *Records of the Virginia Company, 1606–26* (Washington 1906–25), vol. III, p. 54.

18 W. Hone, *The Every-Day Book and Table Book; or, Everlasting Calendar of Popular Amusements* (London 1837), p. 1410.

19 Act III, sc. 3.

20 J. Smith, *The Generall Historie of Virginia, New England & the Summer Isles* (Bedford, MA 2007), p. 91.

21 H.E. Rollins (ed.), *The Pepys Ballads* (Cambridge, MA 1929), vol. I, pp. 26–31: "London's Lotterie", first part.

22 McClure (ed.), *Chamberlain*, vol. 1, p. 367: John Chamberlain to Sir Dudley Carleton, 9 July 1612.

23 http://booty.org.uk/booty.weather/climate/1600_1649.htm, consulted 1/5/2016.

24 J. Stow and E. Howe, *Annales, or A Generall Chronicle of England* (London 1631), p. 1002.

25 L.H. Officer and S.H. Williamson, "Five Ways to Compute the Relative Value of a UK Pound Amount, 1270 to Present", http://www.measuringworth.com/ukcompare/, a website created by Lawrence H. Officer, Professor of Economics at University of Illinois at Chicago and Samuel H. Williamson, Professor of Economics, Emeritus from Miami University, consulted 7/2/2014.

26 G. Lindahl, *Dances from the Inns of Court*, http://www.pbm.com/~lindahl/dance/ioc/intro.html, consulted 6/1/2015.

27 T. Leunig, C. Minns and P. Wallis, *Work, Training, and Economic Mobility in Premodern Societies: New Evidence from English Apprenticeship Records*, http://personal.lse.ac.uk/minns/Leunig%20Minns%20 Wallis%20apprentices%2030%2011%2008%20clean.pdf, consulted 5/6/2014.

28 "The Loseley Manuscripts", *The Literary Gazette* (24 October 1835), no. 979, pp. 681–2.

LIFE 2. THE DANCER

1 "De Scoto-Britannis", Bodleian MS Rawl. Poet. 26, fol. 1r.
2 McClure (ed.), *Chamberlain*, p. 356.
3 "Yt seems the Scottishmen were bodilie afraide for we heard of above three hundred that passed through Ware towards Scotland within ten days", McClure (ed.), *Chamberlain*, p. 355.
4 John Hoskins MP, reported in M. Jansson (ed.), *Proceedings in Parliament, 1614* (House of Commons 1988), pp. 422–3.
5 The Merchant Taylors Membership Index 1530–1928, http://www.parishregister.com/merchant_taylors.asp, consulted 8/6/2013.
6 "Highgate Road and Kentish Town Road, east side", *Survey of London*: vol. 19: *The Parish of St Pancras part 2: Old St Pancras and Kentish Town* (1938), pp. 33–51, http://www.british-history.ac.uk/report.aspx?compid=64861, consulted 6/6/2013.
7 31 January 1618. G.J. Armytage (ed.), *Allegations for Marriage Licences Issued by the Bishop of London* (London 1887), vol. IV, p. 57.
8 Patent Rolls, Eliz i, memb 29–30; précis in the Calendar of Patent Rolls, Eliz i, vi, 1381. Forty shillings was a thumping great fine, but students were paying a pound for a course of lessons. See J.M. Ward, "Apropos 'The olde Measures'", *Records of Early English Drama*, vol. 18, no. 1 (1993), pp. 2–21.
9 F. Yates, *The Rosicrucian Enlightenment* (London 1972), p .9.
10 "The Suburbs without the walls", *A Survey of London*, by John Stow: reprinted from the text of 1603 (1908), pp. 69–91, http://www.british-history.ac.uk/report.aspx?compid=60055, consulted 9/6/2013.
11 Strype, *Survey of London* (1720), [online] (hriOnline, Sheffield), http://www.hrionline.ac.uk/strype/TransformServlet?page=book3_254, consulted 9/6/2013.
12 William Le Hardy (ed.), *County of Middlesex. Calendar to the Sessions Records*: new series, vol. 1: 1612–14 (1935), pp. 46–370.
13 P.J. Finkelpearl, *John Marston of the Inner Temple: An Elizabethan Dramatist in his Social Setting* (Cambridge, MA 1969), p. 5.
14 D.S. Bland (ed.), *Gesta Grayorum* (Liverpool 1968), p. 32.
15 G. Buck, *Of Orchestrice or the Art of Dancing* (1612) published with his tract *The Third Universitie of England* as an appendix to Stowe's *Annals* (London 1615), p. 905.
16 R. Pierce, *A Guide to the Inns of Court and Chancery* (London 1855), p. 334.

17 Brerewood manuscript, written c. 1635, in W.R. Prest, *The Inns of Court Under Elizabeth I and the Early Stuarts* (Longman 1972), p. 113.

18 Thomas Hedley, speech in Parliament, 28 June 1610.

19 S.F. Black, "Coram Protectore: The Judges of Westminster Hall under the Protectorate of Oliver Cromwell", *American Journal of Legal History*, vol. 20, no. 1 (January 1976), p. 48.

20 J. Daly, "Cosmic Harmony and Political Thinking in Early Stuart England", *Transactions of the American Philosophical Society*, new series, vol. 69, no. 7 (1979), pp. 1–41.

21 Extracts from *Orchestra: or, a Poem of Dancing* by Sir John Davies, transcribed by Risa S. Bear of the University of Oregon, November 2001, from the Huntington Library's copy of the 1596 edition, STC number 6360, spelling modernised, http://www.luminarium.org/renascence-editions/davies1.html, consulted 14/6/2013.

22 R. Hooker, *Of the Laws of Ecclesiastical Polity*, vol. I (1591), ii, pp. 5–6.

23 D.H. Radcliffe (ed.), *Lives of Scottish Poets* by the Society of Ancient Scots Re-Established A.D. 1770, London (1821–22), p. 22, http://scotspoets.cath.vt.edu/select.php?select=Ogilby._John#!Ogil1566V–4–4, consulted 14/6/2013.

24 M. Fortier, "Equity and Ideas: Coke, Ellesmere, and James I", *Renaissance Quarterly*, vol. 51, no. 4 (Winter, 1998), pp. 1255–81.

25 *Dictionary of National Biography*: Bedingfeild [née Draper], Anne (1560–1641), theatre landlord and benefactor, by Eva Griffith.

26 E. Griffith, *A Jacobean Company and its Playhouse: The Queen's Servants at the Red Bull Theatre* (Cambridge 2013).

27 e.g. *A Woman Killed With Kindness*, Act I, sc. 2.

28 Jean Macintyre, "Buckingham the Masquer", *Renaissance and Reformation*, new series, vol. 22, no. 3 (Summer 1998), p. 60.

29 M.B. Young, *King James and the History of Homosexuality* (New York 1999).

30 Tiens moy ce que tu m'as promis …
   On a foutu Monsieur le Grand (de Bellegarde),
   L'on fout le Compte de Tonnerre.
   Et le savant roy d'Angleterre
   Foutoit-il pas le Boukinquan
   Claire Gaudiani, *The Cabaret Poetry of Théphile de Viau: Texts and Traditions* (Études littéraires françaises, Tübingen 1945).

31 A. Clifford, *The Memoir of 1603 and the Diary of 1616–1619* (Peterborough, Ont. 2006), p. 59.

32 M.S. Steele, *Plays & Masques at Court During the Reigns of Elizabeth, James and Charles* (London 1968), p. 151.

33 J. Mackintyre, "Buckingham the Masquer", *Renaissance and Reformation/Renaissance et Réforme* vol. 34, no. 3 (1998), p. 62.

34 Account of Orazio Bosino, Chaplain to the Venetian Ambassador, quoted in M. Sullivan, *Court Masques of James I* (New York 1913), p. 114ff.

35 M. Butler, "George Chapman's *'Masque of the Twelve Months (1619)'*", *English Literary Renaissance*, vol. 37, issue 3 (2007), pp. 360–400.

36 Quoted in Butler, "Chapman's Masque", p. 372.

37 Dick (ed.), *Brief Lives*, p. 220.

38 There has been an assumption that it was probably *The Gypsies Metamorphosed*, a masque mounted by Buckingham in August 1621 to entertain James on a visit to his new house. There were always problems with this theory, as it was not "at court".

39 C.H. Josten, *Elias Ashmole (1617–1692)* (Oxford 1966), vol. II, p. 655; Nativity in Bodleian: Ashmole 332, f.35˚.

40 K. Jostens, *Ashmolii Steganographiae aliquot exemplificationes abbreviationesque speciales ex variis MSS. Ashmoleanis elicitae et collectae a Conrado Josten A.D. MCMIL*, Bodleian: Ashmole 37786.

41 T.P. Logan and D.S. Smith (eds), *The New Intellectuals: A Survey and Bibliography of Recent Studies in English Renaissance Drama* (University of Nebraska Press 1977), p. 87.

42 A. Blair, "Tycho Brahe's Critique of Copernicus and the Copernican System", *Journal of the History of Ideas*, vol. 51, no. 3 (July–September 1990), p. 364.

43 L.P. Smith, *The Life and Letters of Sir Henry Wotton* (Oxford 1907), pp. 486–7.

LIFE 3. THE SOLDIER

1 Dick (ed.), *Brief Lives*, p. 220.

2 J. Sanderson, *A Compleat History of the Lives and Reigns of Mary Queen of Scotland, and of her Son … James the Sixth* (London 1656–57), p. 481. Quoted in M.A.E. Green, *Elizabeth, Electress Palatine and Queen of Bohemia* (London 1909), p. 133.

3 Green, *Elizabeth*, p. 167.

4 *Dictionary of National Biography*: Herbert, William, 3rd Earl of Pembroke (1580–1630).

5 D. Worthington (ed.), *British and Irish Emigrants and Exiles in Europe: 1603–1688* (Leiden 2010), p. 251.

6 McClure (ed.), *Chamberlain*, vol. 2, p. 200.

7 McClure (ed.), *Chamberlain*, vol. 2, 21 December 1622.

8 H.F. Waters, *An Examination of the English Ancestry of George Washington* (Boston 1889).

9 C.H. Josten, *Ashmole*, vol. II (1967), p. 655, n. 4.

10 M.J. Dobson, "Death and Disease in the Romney Marsh Area in the 17th to 19th Centuries", in J. Eddison, M. Gardiner and A. Long (eds), *Romney Marsh: Environmental Change and Human Occupation in a Coastal Lowland*, OUCA Monograph 46 (1998), pp. 166–81.

11 Sir William MacArthur, "Malaria in England", *British Medical Bulletin* (1951) 8 (1), pp. 76–9.

12 O.S. Knottnerus, "Malaria Around the North Sea: A Survey", in G. Wefer, W.H. Berger, K. Behre and E. Jansen (eds), *Climatic Development and History of the North Atlantic Realm: Hanse Conference Report* (Berlin 2002), pp. 339–53.

13 D.R. Lawrence, *The Complete Soldier: Military Books and Military Culture in Early Stuart England, 1603–1645* (Leiden 2009).

14 W. Krüssmann, Ernst von Mansfeld (1580–1626), *Grafensohn, Söldnerführer, Kriegsunternehmer gegen Habsburg im Dreißigjährigen Krieg* (Berlin 2010). There is a long and thorough review in English by Aart Brouwer, https://crossfireamersfoort.wordpress.com/2012/07/14/book-review-ernst-von-mansfeld–1580–1626-by-walter-krussmann/ consulted 20/6/2013.

15 "Historical Collections: 1624 to the Death of James I", *Historical Collections of Private Passages of State*, vol. I: *1618–29* (1721), pp. 140–64.

16 "The Life of Mr. Arthur Wilson" V, transcribed in F. Peck, *Desiderata Curiosa* (London 1779), p. 467.

17 A. Thrush and J.P. Ferris (eds), *The History of Parliament: The House of Commons 1604–1629* (London 2010).

18 SP Dom. 16 v. 89 (46).

19 SP Dom. 16 v. 66 (63).

20 I.R. Bartlett, "Scottish Mercenaries in Europe 1570–1640: A Study in Attitudes and Policies", *International Review of Scottish Studies* 13 (2008).

21 R.B. Manning, "Styles of Command in Seventeenth Century English Armies", *Journal of Military History*, vol. 71, no. 3 (July 2007), pp. 671–99.

22 SP Dom. 16 v. 67 (78), v. 68 (62–3).

23 SP Dom. 16 v. 67 (64).

24 R. Lockyer, *Buckingham: The Life and Political Career of George Villiers, First Duke of Buckingham, 1592–1628* (London 1981), pp. 373–4.

25 SP Dom. 16 v. 91 (87) ff174v, 175 Warrant Office 55, 1682–1684.

26 G. Wishart, *Montrose Redivivus: Or The Portraicture of James Late Marquess of Montrose* (London 1652), p. 97.

27 ParishRegister.com online database, consulted 16/4/2014.

28 Dick (ed.), *Brief Lives*: John Lacy.

29 SP Dom. 16 v. 239 (69); K. van Eerde, *John Ogilby and the Taste of his Times* (Kent 1976), pp. 21–2.

30 C.V. Wedgwood, *Thomas Wentworth* (London 1961), p. 174.

31 Dick (ed.), *Brief Lives*. It is said in a modern thesis that the only evidence for him being in the Troop of Guards comes from *The Whole Works of Sir James Ware concerning Ireland* (published in 1764), and Ware must be confused as John Ogilby was not a military man. The author suggests he has muddled Ogilby with one Sir John Ogle, who was a Dublin captain. But Ware, a scrupulous record-keeper, actually knew Ogilby in Dublin: he was the University of Dublin's MP in the 1634 Parliament. Ogle was in any case not even in Ireland, and Aubrey is in fact a further source. Justine Isabella Williams, *The Irish Plays of James Shirley, 1636–1640*, PhD thesis (2010), University of Warwick, http://webcat.warwick.ac.uk/record=b2341442~S15, consulted 28/7/2013.

LIFE 4. THE IMPRESARIO

1 SP Ireland, 4, p. 178.

2 Fynes Moryson, "The Effects of Elizabethan Policy in Ireland, 1602", in John Carey (ed.), *Eyewitness to History* (Cambridge, MA Press 1987), p. 164.

3 Wentworth to Coke, 26 October 1633, W. Knowles (ed.), *The Earl of Strafforde's Letters and Dispatches* V.1 (London 1739), p. 139.

4 D. Shaw, "Thomas Wentworth and Monarchical Ritual in Early Modern Ireland", *The Historical Journal*, vol. 49, no. 2 (June 2006), pp. 331–55.

5 Knowles, *Strafford*, vol. I, p. 85.

6 I know this because I once persuaded a very celebrated sailor, Chay Blythe, to have a crack at it in a square-rigged training ship in a moderate breeze. It was impossible. Instead of turning the bow into the wind and continuing to turn past it onto our new course, the ship simply slowed, stopped and drifted backwards. Instead of tacking, we had to turn through 270°, turning away from the wind and then letting the stern swing right round so we could approach the wind from the other side. This needs plenty of space and deep water, and is not something to do in a river.

7 Richard Plumleigh, whose heroic sea action was discussed in the House of Commons on 9 June 1628. *Commons Debates 1628*, vol. 4.

8 E. Hull, *A History of Ireland and Her People* (Freeport, NY 1926) p. 444.

9 It was not referred to them until 15 July. The result is lost. SP Dom. 16, v. 239, 69.

10 Memoir of Mrs Lucy Hutchinson in D.F. Bacon, *Memoirs of Eminently Pious Women in Britain and America* (Connecticut 1833), p. 112.

11 A. Daye, "The Banqueting House, Whitehall: A Site Specific to Dance", *Historical Dance*, vol. 4, no. 1 (2004).

12 P. Palme, *Triumph of Peace* (London 1957), pp. 255–66.

13 R. Bagwell, *Ireland Under the Stuarts and During the Interregnum* (London 1909), p. 216.

14 D. Howarth, *Images of Rule: Art and Politics in the English Renaissance, 1485–1649* (London 1997), p. 205.

15 K. Sharpe, *Criticism and Compliment: The Politics of Literature in the England of Charles I* (Cambridge 1987), p. 263.

16 T. Nabbes, *Tottenham Court* (1633), Act III sc.1, quoted in T.E. Bentley, *Profession of Dramatist in Shakespeare's Time, 1590–1642* (Princeton 2015), p. 57.

17 J.S. Nye, Jr., "Public Diplomacy and Soft Power", *Annals of the American Academy of Political and Social Science*, vol. 616: *Public Diplomacy in a Changing World* (March 2008), pp. 94–109.

18 Patent for Master of the Revels for Ireland, PRO: MS C. 66/2995, mb 38 (8 May).

19 PRO: CSPI 63, vol. 345, no. 50.

20 A.J. Fletcher, *Drama, Performance, and Polity in Pre-Cromwellian Ireland* (University of Toronto Press 2000), p. 600, n. 7.

21 Rev. A.B. Grossart, *The Lismore Papers* (London 1886) vol. iv, p. 6.

22 Grossart, *Lismore Papers*, p. 146.

23 The long debate over the year of its opening seems to have been settled by A.J. Fletcher, *Drama in Ireland*, p. 601.

24 C. Morash, *A History of Irish Theatre, 1601–2000* (Cambridge 2002), p. 5.

25 M. Bayer, "The Curious Case of the Two Audiences", *Imaging the Audience in Early Modern Drama, 1558–1642*, ed. J.A. Low and N. Myhill (London 2011), p. 56.

26 PRO: C, 66/2995, mb38 ob., cited in Fletcher, *Drama in Ireland*, p. 442, n. 42.

27 T. Wilkes, *A General View of the Stage* (London 1759), quoted in Fletcher, *Drama in Ireland*, p. 488.

28 F. Hopkins, *Hidden Dublin: Deadbeats, Dossers and Decent Skin* (Cork 2007), p. 55.

29 A.H. Stevenson, "James Shirley and the Actors at the First Irish Theater", *Modern Philology*, vol. 40, no. 2 (November 1942), pp. 147–16.

30 Fletcher, *Drama in Ireland*, p. 263.

31 J. Ussher, *Annals* (London 1658), Epistle.
32 Williams, *Shirley*, pp. 70–1.
33 Williams, *Shirley*, p. 287.
34 J. Kerrigan, *Archipelagic English: Literature, History, and Politics 1603–1707* (Oxford University Press 2008), p. 181.
35 T. Wilkes, *The Stage*, quoted in Fletcher, *Drama in Ireland*, p. 488.
36 Dick (ed.), *Brief Lives*.

LIFE 5. THE LIFE REDACTED

 1 Trinity College Dublin Ms 729, f. 134v, Deposition of Mulrany Carroll of Donegal 26/4/1643.
 2 Joseph Quincy Adams, quoting a contemporary manuscript source, in H. Mifflin, *Shakespearean Playhouses: A History of English Theatres from the Beginnings to the Restoration* (Boston 1917), p. 419.
 3 Dick (ed.), *Brief Lives*.
 4 R.F. Foster, *Modern Ireland 1600–1972* (London 1988), pp. 87–8.
 5 Trinity College Dublin, 1641 Depositions Project, online transcript January 1970, http://1641.tcd.ie/deposition.php?depID<?php echo 839028r020?>, consulted 24/2/2014.
 6 J. D'Alton, *King James' Irish Army List* (Limerick 1997), pp. 442–3.
 7 J. Ogilby, *Africa: being a Description of the Regions of Ægypt, Barbary, Lybia, and Billedulgerid* (London 1670), Preface. The lost land of Billedulgerid (land of dates) was between Algiers and Tripoli, south of Tunis.
 8 The *Oxford English Dictionary* quotes this definition from W. Gouge and T. Gouge, *Learned Comm. Hebrewes* (vi. 18), 1655, II.112.
 9 J.L. Malcolm, "All the King's Men: The Impact of the Crown's Irish Soldiers on the English Civil War", *Irish Historical Studies*, vol. 22, no. 83 (March 1979), pp. 239–64; J. Lowe, "The Campaign of the Irish Royalist Army in Cheshire, November 1643–January 1644", *Transactions of the Historic Society of Lancashire and Cheshire* (1961), 113, pp. 47–76.
10 Lowe, "Irish Army".
11 R.T. Pritchard, "The History of the Post Road in Anglesey", *Transactions of the Anglesey Antiquarian Society & Field Club* (1954), pp. 18–33.
12 H. Rothwell, *The Chronicle of Walter of Guisborough*, Royal Historical Society (Camden Series, lxxxix) (1957).
13 Sir G. Fordham, "A Note on the 'Quartermaster's Map', 1644", *Geographical Journal*, vol. 70, no. 1 (July 1927), pp. 50–2.
14 M. Stoyle, *Soldiers And Strangers: An Ethnic History of the English Civil War* (London 2005), p. 210.

15 Stoyle, *Soldiers And Strangers*, p. 210.
16 R.D. Thomas, *George Digby, Hero and Villain* (AuthorHouse 2005), pp. 184–8.
17 Dick (ed.), *Brief Lives*. Aubrey gives the date as about the year 1648.
18 Bodleian: Tanner 59, ff. 640, 642, 643; *House of Commons Journal*, vol. 5, 21 January 1647.

LIFE 6. THE POET

 1 A.B. Appleby, *Famine in Tudor and Stuart England* (Stanford 1978), p. 129.
 2 "The Civil War in Somerset", http://www1.somerset.gov.uk/archives/ASH/Civilwar.htm, consulted 9/5/2014.
 3 Virgil, tr. J. Ogilby, *The Works of P.V.M.* (London 1649), Dedication.
 4 W.T. Lowndes, *The Bibliographer's Manual of English Literature* (London 1871), vol. 4, p. 2780.
 5 T.M. Caldwell, *Virgil Made English: The Decline of Classical Authority* (New York 2008), ch. 1. The arena of Classical authority has diminished but clearly survives for some. During the Chilcot Enquiry into the Iraq War, a British spy replied to a question on the failure to find WMD with a gloomy quotation from Aeneid Book I. The chairman responded with a line from Book 6 abut the yearning of the dead. www.iraqinquiry.org.uk/media/98149/XXXX-XX-XX-Transcript-SIS4-part"-declassified.pdf p.29, consulted 25/7/2016.
 6 Virgil, tr. R. Fagles, *The Aeneid* (London 2006).
 7 Anthony à Wood, *Athenae Oxonienses* (London 1817), vol. 3, pp. 739–44.
 8 Mince pies.
 9 Thomason Tracts (669. f. 10 (47)), 8 April 1646.
10 Van Eerde, *Ogilby*, p. 29.
11 A.M. Patterson, *Pastoral and Ideology: Virgil to Valéry* (Oxford 1988), pp. 169–85.
12 At the time of writing, a copy of Virgil inscribed to Mainwaring by Ogilby is being advertised for sale.
13 H. Wood, "The Offices of Secretary of State for Ireland and Keeper of the Signet or Privy Seal", *Proceedings of the Royal Irish Academy*, vol. 38 (1928/29), pp. 51–68.
14 E. Hyde, *The History of the Rebellion and Civil Wars in England, Begun in the Year 1641* (Oxford 1717), vol. 2, pp. 528–9.
15 Ward, "Olde Measures", p. 10.
16 I. Payne, *The Almain in Britain, c.1549–c.1675: A Dance Manual from Manuscript Sources* (Aldershot 2003), p. 10.
17 A.R. Ingpen, *The Middle Temple Bench Book* (London 1912), p. 24.
18 SP Dom. v. 25/65 p. 108.

19 K. Curran, *Marriage, Performance, and Politics at the Jacobean Court* (Farnham 2009), p. 161.
20 B.J. Kaplan, *Divided by Faith: Religious Conflict and the Practice of Toleration in Early Modern Europe* (London 2007), p. 52.
21 J. Bodin, *Les Six Livres de la République* (Lyons 1579), 1.8.
22 Bodin, *République*, 6.6.
23 G. Parker, *The Thirty Years' War* (New York 2006), p. 188.
24 A. McFarlane, *The Savage Wars of Peace: England, Japan and the Malthusian Trap* (Basingstoke 2003), p. 51.
25 L. Gwynn, "The Architecture of the English Domestic Library, 1600–1700", *Library & Information History*, vol. 26, no. 1 (March 2010), pp. 56–69.
26 *Clockmakers' Company Masters and their Apprentices*, transcribed from Atkins' list of 1931, compiled by Jeremy Lancelotte Evans, http:// www.clockmakers.org/museum-and-library/clockmaker-masters-and-apprentices/, consulted 11/5/2014.
27 Acc. No. 17.190.1473.
28 Ahasuerus is a startling name for this son of a Dutch Reform refugee family. It refers to the character in the biblical Book of Esther who was identified with Ataxerxes, understood as the evil Persian king who ruled the whole world. In fact "Ahasuerus" was Xerxes and did not rule the world, but arguably his namesake's pendulum clock achieved total power over mankind.
29 Ogilby, *Africa*, Preface.
30 M. Kishlansky, "Turning Frogs into Princes: Aesop's *Fables* and the Political Culture of Early Modern England", in S.D. Amussen and M.A. Kishlansky, *Political Culture and Cultural Politics in Early Modern Europe* (New York 1995), pp. 338–61.
31 www.oed.com/viewdictionaryentry/Entry/173877, consulted 28/8/13.
32 K. Acheson, "The Picture of Nature: Seventeenth-Century English Aesop's Fables", *Journal for Early Modern Cultural Studies*, vol. 9, no. 2 (Fall/Winter 2009), pp. 25–50.
33 http://en.wikipedia.org/wiki/Marcus_Gheeraerts_the_Elder, consulted 15/9/13.
34 A.L. Rowse, *The Tower of London in the History of the Nation* (London 1972), p. 183.
35 Fables iii, vi, viii, xxi, xxix, xxviii xxxii, xl, xlii, lxxii.
36 M. Pritchard, *Aesop, Fables Moral and Political*, University of Western Ontario PhD dissertation, 1976.
37 T. Hobbes, *Leviathan* (1651), ch. 21, 21.

38 C.H. Firth, "The Royalists under the Protectorate", *English Historical Review*, vol. 52, no. 208 (October 1937), pp. 634–64.

39 B. Woodford, "Developments and Debates in English Censorship during the Interregnum", *Early Modern Literary Sudies*, vol. 17 (2) (2014).

40 Ogilby, *Africa*, Preface.

LIFE 7. THE GENTLEMAN

1 Rowse, *Tower of London*, pp. 156–7.

2 M. McClain, *Beaufort: The Duke and his Duchess, 1657–1715* (New Haven 2001), pp. 7–8.

3 W. Wilson, *The House of Airlie* (London 1924), vol. 2, p. 81.

4 Wilson, *Airlie*, p. 25.

5 Dick (ed.), *Brief Lives*.

6 Katherine van Eerde says that this was "the lion of Scotland", which it was not.

7 A. Clark (ed.), *Brief Lives … with facsimiles* (Oxford 1898), vol. II, p. 104.

8 Bysshe was well known as a soak who arrived so drunk on his heraldic visitations that his genealogies became very muddled, but that does not mean he would have let this one pass if it was completely fictitious. He added this book to his large library distinguished by its many pornographic and almost-atheistic volumes. His visitations must have been memorable. R. Myers and M. Harris, *Property of a Gentleman: The Formation, Organisation and Dispersal of the Private Library 1620–1920* (St Paul's Bibliographies 1991), p. 125.

9 Act concerning the office of lyoun king of armes and his brether herauldis (1592 cap. 127).

10 M. Noble, *A History of the College of Arms* (London 1804), p. 269.

11 SP Dom. 63 v. 467, 46.

12 R. Chambers, *The Scottish Ballads: Collected and Illustrated* (Edinburgh 1829), pp. 92–4.

13 National Archive of Scotland CC20/4/8.

14 Forty-eight years later, in 1673, another testament was, rather oddly, posthumously registered for the same man, "brother german to the [interpolated – "late"] Earl of Airlie". It is an altogether peculiar document. The executor ("executive dative surrogate") is a chap called John Livingston of Balrowny. This is very strange, not just because of the passage of time but also because an executor is usually next of kin or a creditor, and Livingston seems to be neither, just a man doing a job for someone else. Who wanted this done? The first testament was recorded at St. Andrews, but this new one was in the Commissary Court of Brechin which, it has been suggested to me by an expert in

the Scottish National Archives, was a little more flexible and open to persuasion. Was there some anxiety that there was another John, who must not be regarded as a real, true brother of the late Earl?

15 J. Wormald, *Court, Kirk, and Community: Scotland, 1470–1625* (Edinburgh 1991), ch. 10.

16 Wilson, *Airlie*, vol. I, pp. 174–90.

17 Dated 11 June 1606. Copy of a letter from James, 6th Lord Ogilvy to his grandson James, 1st Earl of Airlie 1586 (notebook) / Mabell Countess of Airlie. The text is transcribed in S. Collet, *Relics of Literature* (London 1823), pp. 346–7.

18 The admission was either 3 or 16 June 1606; see van Eerde, *Ogilby*, ch. 1, n. 4.

19 His portrait was credited to Peter Lely, who had taken over Van Dyke's mantle, and the engraving was signed by the top portrait engraver, William Faithorne.

20 E. Ashmole, *The Lives of Those Eminent Antiquaries Elias Ashmole, Esquire, and Mr. William Lilly, Written by Themselves* (London 1774), p. 314.

21 E. Ashmole, *Theatrum Chemicum Britannicum* (New York 1967), Prolegomena.

22 Bodleian: Ashmole 332, f. 35v.

23 Ogilby, *Africa*, Preface.

24 S.L.C. Clapp, "The Subscription Enterprises of John Ogilby and Richard Blome", *Modern Philology*, vol. 30, no. 4 (May 1933), pp. 365–79.

25 E. Hyde, *The Life of Edward Earl of Clarendon* (Oxford 1751), vol. I, p. 339.

26 D. Underdown, *Royalist Conspiracy in England 1649–1660* (New Haven 1960), ch. 10.

27 E.H. Lechmere, *Hanley and the House of Lechmere* (London 1883), p. 22.

28 Van Eerde, *Ogilby*, p. 46.

29 J. McElligott, *Royalism, Print and Censorship in Revolutionary England* (Woodbridge 2007), p. 132; S. Morison, *Ichabod Dawks* (Cambridge 1931), p. 1.

30 McElligott, *Royalism, Print and Censorship*, pp. 137–8.

31 R. Pennington, *A Descriptive Catalogue of the Etched Work of Wenceslaus Hollar 1607–1677* (Cambridge 1982), pp. 39, 43; R. Doggett et al., *Impressions of Wenceslaus Hollar* (Washington 1996), pp. 35–9.

32 Ogilby's proposal for the *Iliad* speaks of the "Design, and graving of a Plate, which will cost the Author at least 10l." S.L.C. Clapp, "The Subscription Enterprises of John Ogilby and Richard Blome", *Modern Philology*, vol. 30, no. 4 (May 1933), p. 367.

33 Wood, *Athenae Oxonienses*, vol. 2, p. 263.

34 J. Ogilby, *Virgil* (London 1654), p. 2.

35 Patterson, *Pastoral*, pp. 169–85.

36 Ogilby, *Africa*, Preface.

37 A. Welch, "Epic Romance, Royalist Retreat, and the English Civil War", *Modern Philology*, vol. 105, no. 3 (February 2008), pp. 570–602.

38 Wood, *Athenae Oxonienses*, vol. 1, p. 264.

39 *The Tragedy of Chabot* by Chapman and Shirley was published in 1635, after Chapman's death.

40 E. Gutting, Review of A. Nicholl (ed.), *Chapman's Homer. The Iliad* in *Bryn Mawr Classical Review*, 1999.10.14, www.brynmawr. edu/1999/1999-10-14.html, consulted 22/12/2015.

41 K. Tranter, "Samuel Sheppard's 'Faerie King' and the Fragmentation of Royalist Epic", *Studies in English Literature, 1500–1900*, vol. 49, no. 1, "The English Renaissance" (Winter 2009), pp. 87–103.

42 G. Pursglove, "George Chapman", in O. Classe (ed.), *Encyclopedia of Literary Translation into English: A-L* (Abingdon 2000), p. 261.

43 J. Ogilby, *Homer His Iliads* (London 1660), Dedication.

44 Ashmole, *Diary* (Oxford 1927).

45 W. Lilly, *Christian Astrology* (London 1659), p. 77.

46 Lilly, *Christian Astrology*, p. 81.

47 Bodleian: Ashmole 243 f. 190.

48 J. Broadway. "'The honour of this Nation': William Dugdale and the History of St Paul's (1658)", *Royalists and Royalism during the Interregnum*, ed. J. McElligott and D. Smith (Manchester 2010), pp. 194–213.

49 Dunkirk was sold to France in 1662 by Charles II.

50 Ashmole, *Diary*, 21 August 1658.

51 S.L.C. Clapp, "The Subscription Enterprises of John Ogilby and Richard Blome", *Modern Philology*, vol. 30, no. 4 (May 1933), pp. 365–79.

52 Clapp, *"Subscription Enterprises"*, p. 367.

53 Ogilby, *Africa*, Preface.

54 J. Brotton, *The Sale of the Late King's Goods: Charles I and His Art Collection* (London 1970), p. 343.

55 Brotton, *Sale*, p. 338.

56 Pepys, *Diary*, 27 May 1667.

57 Van Eerde, *Ogilby*, p. 47.

58 Van Eerde, *Ogilby*, p. 62.

59 C.F. Milliet Dechales, *Les Elemens d'Euclide expliquez d'une maniere nouvelle et tres-facile* (Paris 1677), Avant-propos, quoted in A. Malet, "Euclid's Swan Song: Euclid's Elements in Early Modern Europe", in P. Olmos

(ed.), *Greek Science in the Long Run: Essays on the Greek Scientific Tradition (4th c. BCE–17th c. CE)* (Newcastle 2012). My translation.

LIFE 8. THE PAGEANT MASTER

1 N.H. Keeble, *The Restoration: England in the 1660s* (Oxford 2002), p. 52.

2 Van Eerde, *Ogilby*, pp. 48–9.

3 Keeble, *Restoration*, p. 50.

4 J. Ogilby, *The Entertainment of His Most Excellent Majestie Charles II in His Passage through the City of London to His Coronation* (London 1662).

5 Keeble, *Restoration*, p. 45.

6 Pepys, *Diary*, 23 April 1661.

7 E.M. McGirr, *Heroic Mode and Political Crisis 1660–1745* (Newark 1972).

8 J. Ogilby, *The Relation of His Majestie's Entertainment Passing Through the City of London* (London 1661), p. 39.

9 S. Harrison, *Arches of Triumph* (London 1604).

10 *The Entertainment of the High and Mighty Monarch Charles King of Great Britaine, France, and Ireland, Into his auncient and royall City of Edinburgh, the fifteenth of June 1633* (Edinburgh 1633). There are no contemporary illustrations, but Dr Giovanna Guidicini has attempted to draw them for the Recreating Early Modern Festivals project, http://www.recreatingearlymodernfestivals.com/exhibition_giovanna.htm, consulted 9/8/2014.

11 Pepys, *Diary*, 28 May 1663.

12 *Dictionary of National Biography*; Ogilby, *The Entertainment*, pp. 12–13.

13 R.C. Strong, *Art and Power: Renaissance Festivals, 1450–1650* (Berkeley 1984), p. 49.

14 A. Knaap and M. Putnam, *Art, Music and Spectacle in the Age of Rubens* (London 2013).

15 G. Reedy, S.J., "Mystical Politics: The Imagery of Charles II's Coronation", in P.J. Korshin (ed.), *Studies in Change and Revolution: Aspects of English Intellectual History 1640–1800* (Scolar Press 1972), pp. 29–39.

16 Knowles, *Strafford*, intro., p. 21.

17 Ogilby, *The Entertainment*, p. 32.

18 K. Pierce, *The Coronation Music of Charles II*, Master of Music thesis, Graduate College of Bowling Green State University (2007).

19 B.O. Hehir, *Harmony from Discords: A life of Sir John Denham* (Berkeley 1968), p. 162.

20 A.M. Ridley, *The Staging of The Siege of Rhodes at Rutland House (1656)*, MA thesis, University of New Brunswick (1980), http://www.uoguelph.ca/~mridley/documents/StagingoftheSeigeofRhodes-AMRMAThesis.pdf, consulted 16/5/2014.

21 Van Eerde, *Ogilby*, p. 63.
22 T. Carte, *An History of the Life of James, Duke of Ormonde* (London 1736), vol. II, p. 257.
23 É.Ó. Ciardha, " 'The Unkinde Deserter' and 'The Bright Duke': Contrasting Views of the Dukes of Ormonde in the Irish Royalist Tradition", *The Dukes of Ormonde 1610–1745*, ed. T. Barnard and J. Fenlon (Woodbridge 1999), p. 181.
24 T.E. Jordan, "Quality of Life in Seventeenth Century Dublin", *Dublin Historical Record*, vol. 61, no. 2 (Autumn 2008), pp. 136–54.
25 W.S. Clark, *The Early Irish Stage: From the Beginnings to 1720* (Oxford 1955).
26 S.A. Kelly, "The Theatre Royal in 1662: Smock Alley's First Season", *Dublin Historical Record*, vol. 61, no. 2 (Autumn 2008), pp. 201–18.
27 Excavation report Dublin 2009: 313, Smock Alley Theatre, Essex Street West, Dublin, Post-medieval, 315326.066 234089.974, DU018–020 06E1073 ext., http://www.excavations.ie/Pages/Details.php?Year=2009&County=Dublin&id=20724, consulted 4/6/2014.
28 Elizabeth Carey, Viscountess Falkland, published *The Tragedy of Mariam the Fair Queen of Jewry* in 1613, but it was not performed in a theatre until 1994.
29 A. Russel, "Katherine Philips as Playwright: 'The Songs Between the Acts' in Pompey", *Comparative Drama* (2010), http://www.thefreelibrary.com/2010/September/22-d3, consulted 23/9/2015.
30 P. Thomas (ed.), *The Collected Works of Katherine Philips, the Matchless Orinda* (Stump Cross 1970), vol. I, p. 80.
31 Morash, *Irish Theatre*, p. 14.
32 Van Eerde, *Ogilby*, p. 68.
33 Katherine Philips, *Printed Letters* (Farnham 2007), p. 164.
34 Philips, *Printed Letters*, p. 164.
35 W.R. Chetwood, *A General History of the Stage: From its Origin in Greece Down to the Present Time* (London 1766).
36 K.L. Lesko, "Evidence of Restoration Performances: Duke Ferdinand Albrecht's Annotated Playtexts from 1664–65", *Philological Quarterly* 79:1 (2000), p. 58.
37 J. Ogilby, *The Fables of Aesop*, 2nd ed. (London 1665), Preface.
38 V. Barbour, *Henry Bennet, Earl of Arlington* (Baltimore 1913), pp. 7–8.
39 Barbour, *Henry Bennet*, p. 73.
40 *The Works of His Grace George Villiers, Late Duke of Buckingham* (London 1715), vol. II, pp. 80–2, quoted in M.D. Lee Jr, "The Earl of Arlington and the Treaty of Dover", *Journal of British Studies*, vol. 1, no. 1 (November 1961), pp. 58–70.

41 Moote and Moote, *The Great Plague*, p. 10.

42 G.W. Bell, *The Great Plague in London in 1665* (London 1924).

43 S. Porter, *The Great Plague* (Stroud 1999), p. 49.

44 Porter, *Great Plague*, p. 64.

45 C. Ward and R. Chandler, *Magna Britannia* (London 1738), vol. 5, p. 402.

46 Grenville MS. xxv, BL. Add MS 33747 ff. 219, 300.

47 Ogilby, *Africa*, Preface.

48 Le Wright, *Yearbook*, BL MS 33747, f. 172, referring to the execution of Sir Henry Vane on 14 June 1662 at the place where Strafford had been executed. Vane had pushed for Strafford's death.

49 Le Wright, *Yearbook*, f. 219

50 W. Griswold, *Renaissance Revivals: City Comedy and Revenge Tragedy in the London Theatre, 1560–1980* (Chicago 1986), p. 218.

51 Porter, *Great Plague*, p. 66.

52 *Encyclopædia Londinensis* (London 1820) vol. 17, p. 430.

53 E. Phillips, *Theatrum poetarum anglicanorum* (London 1675).

LIFE 9. THE ATLAS MAKER

1 Pepys, *Diary*, 21 December 1663.

2 "Hearth Tax: City of London 1666, St Bride Fleet Street, Kings Head Court", in *London Hearth Tax: City of London and Middlesex, 1666* (2011), *British History Online,* http://www.british-history.ac.uk/london-hearth-tax/london-mddx/1666/st-bride-fleet-street-kings-head-court, consulted 19/3/2016.

3 "... goods laid in the Churchyarde fired through the windows those in St. Fayth's church; and those coming to the warehouses' doors fired them, and burned all the books and the pillars of the church, so as the roof falling down, broke quite down, which it did not do in the other places of the church, which is alike pillared (which I knew not before); but being not burned, they stand still. He do believe there is above; 50,000l. of books burned; all the great booksellers almost undone: not only these, but their warehouses at their Hall, and under Christchurch, and elsewhere being all burned. A great want thereof there will be of books, specially Latin books and foreign books; and, among others, the Polyglottes and new Bible, which he believes will be presently worth 40l. a-piece". (Pepys, *Diary*, 5 October 1666).

4 Ogilby, *Africa*, Preface.

5 Scraps of burned paper were driven by the wind as far as Eton and Windsor Great Park: G.P. Elliot (ed.), *Autobiography and Anecdotes by William Taswell D.D., 1651–82*, vol. 2 (London 1853). "My Lady

Carteret herself did tell us how abundance of pieces of burnt papers were cast by the wind as far as Cranborne; and among others she took up one, or had one brought her to see, which was a little bit of paper that had been printed, whereon there remained no more nor less than these words: 'Time is, it is done.'" (Pepys, *Diary*, 3 February 1667). "Little pieces of scorched silk and paper were taken up in very many places near Windsor, Henley, Beaconsfield, etc.". They continued to drift down from the sky for days after the fire (Gough MS London 14).

6 BL Add. Ms. 33747 f.253. A. Ereira, "Alone in the Ruins", *History Today* (online edition September 2016) http://www.historytoday.com/alan-ereira/alone-ruins

7 Unsigned personal letter from the Middle Temple, 29 September 1666, in J.P. Malcolm, *Londinium Redivivum*, vol. IV (1807), p. 78.

8 Ogilby, *Africa*, Preface.

9 Wood, *Athenae Oxonienses*, vol. 2, p. 166.

10 Ogilby, *Africa*.

11 It was within 50 metres, probably at what is now 8–10 Bouverie Street. M. Schuchard, *John Ogilby, 1600–1676: Lebensbild eines Gentleman mit vielen Karrieren* (Hamburg 1973).

12 *London Topographical Record Illustrated*, vol. 5 (London 1908), p. 119.

13 J.S. Loengard (ed.), "Introduction", *London Viewers and their Certificates, 1508–1558: Certificates of the Sworn Viewers of the City of London*, British History Online, http://www.british-history.ac.uk/report.aspx?compid=36052, consulted 5/1/2016.

14 R. Hyde, *The A to Z of Restoration London* (London 1992), p. x.

15 For example: "1675 Tuesday, January 26 With Ogylby at Joes. I was witness to a bond of his and Morgans to Brook, plaisterer, for £50 as he told me."

16 Ogilby, *Africa*, Preface.

17 T. Elyot, *The book named the Governor, 1531* (Menston 1970), p. 35.

18 Van Eerde, *Ogilby*, p. 83.

19 A. Semedo, *The History of that Great and Renowned Monarchy of China* (1638), translation published in London in 1655 for Ogilby's first publisher, John Crook. For an extensive discussion of the significance of Ogilby's translation, see R.K. Batchelor, *London: The Selden Map and the Making of a Global City, 1549–1689* (Chicago 2014), pp. 168–77.

20 A-M. Desaulty and F. Albarede, "Copper, Lead, and Silver Isotopes Solve a Major Economic Conundrum of Tudor and early Stuart Europe", *Geology*, 11/6/2012.

21 China experienced great inflation in the early seventeenth century. Silver was used to pay the army, and its value relative to gold fell by

over 70% between 1580 and 1650; the silver needed to pay the army increased from the late fifteenth century to the early seventeenth century by a factor of eight (J.A. Goldstone, "East and West in the Seventeenth Century: Political Crises in Stuart England, Ottoman Turkey, and Ming China", *Comparative Studies in Society and History*, vol. 30, no. 1 (January 1988), pp. 103–42). H.F. Lee and D.D. Zhang, "A Tale of Two Population Crises in Recent Chinese History", *Climatic Change* 116 (2013), pp. 285–308, published with open access at Springerlink.com, explore the role of climate in the social breakdown.

22 J. Bolt and J. L. van Zanden (2013), "The First Update of the Maddison Project; Re-Estimating Growth Before 1820", *Maddison Project Working Paper* 4, http://www.ggdc.net/maddison/maddison-project/home.htm, and A. Maddison, *Historical Statistics of the World Economy: 1–2008 AD*, www.ggdc.net/maddison/Historical_Statistics/horizontal-file_02-2010.xls, consulted 12/7/2014.

23 His coat of arms has a crest with an arm holding a war-mace, the traditional weapon of a churchman, and under it the motto Fax Mentis Honestae Gloria, which was used on the badges of Irish baronets, a creation of Charles I. Rev. Erskine was not a baronet but his wife's father was (*Journal of the Ceredigion Antiquarian Society* (1977) VIII, 2, p. 147).

24 Ogilby, *Africa*, Preface.

25 English as opposed to Dutch. The title did not mean that it was an atlas of English lands.

26 Bodleian: Wood 658, f. 792.

27 Batchelor, *Selden Map*, p. 171.

The Use of Maps

1 D. Hodson, *The Early Printed Road Books and Itineraries of England and Wales,* University of Exeter thesis for the degree of Doctor of Philosophy in Geography, 18 November 2000. I am very grateful to Dr Hodson for his generous assistance.

2 M.I. Williams, "The Port of Aberdyfi in the 18th Century", *National Library of Wales Journal* Cyf. 18, rh. 1 Haf 1973.

3 SP Dom. 29 v. 179, 21(i)S. (November 1666), quoted in Hodson, *Itineraries*, ch. 9.

4 R. Blome, *Britannia* (London 1673).

5 Alan Crosby, "The Regional Road Network and the Growth of Manchester in the Sixteenth and Seventeenth Centuries", *Manchester Region History Review* 19 (2008), p. 10.

6 W. Morgan, *Mr. Ogilby's and William Morgan's Pocket Book of the Roads*, 4th ed. (London 1689).

7 Porter, *A New Map of England and Wales*.

8 T. De Laune and J. Stow, *The Present State of London* (London 1681).

9 "Liverpool: The Castle and Development of the Town", in *A History of the County of Lancaster*, vol. 4, ed. William Farrer and J. Brownbill (London 1911), pp. 4–36. British History Online http://www.british-history.ac.uk/vch/lancs/vol4/pp4–36, consulted 22 April 2016.

10 A single sheet tracing itinerary routes, the Porter map, had appeared in 1668 and is discussed later. The Chinese had been putting measured roads on their maps for at least 1,500 years, but Europeans did not see the point of doing it.

11 M.D. Clark, "Now Through You Made Public for Everyone: John Ogilby's *Britannia* (1675), the 1598 Peutinger Map Facsimile and the Shaping of Public Space", in A. Vanhaelen and J.P. Ward (eds), *Making Space Public in Early Modern Europe: Geography, Performance, Privacy* (London 2013).

12 It was in the Cotton family library in London and known to members of the Royal Society. Catherine Delano-Smith and Roger J.P. Kain, *English Maps: A History* (London 1999), p. 170.

13 T. Campbell, *The Earliest Printed Maps 1472–1500* (British Library 1987), pp. 59–67, http://digital.bodleian.ox.ac.uk/static/records/XYL–20.html, consulted 18/11/2015.

14 *Das seyn dy lantstrassen durch das Romisch reych von einem kunigreych zw dem andern dy an Tewtsche land stossen von meilen zw meiln mit puncten verzaichnet* (The country roads through the Roman Empire from one German kingdom to another recorded from mile to mile with dots).

15 W. Lang, "The Augsberg Travel Guide of 1563 and the Erlinger Road Map of 1524", *Imago Mundi*, vol. 7, 1 (1950), pp. 85–8.

16 R. Helgerson, "Nation or Estate?: Ideological Conflict in the Early Modern Mapping of England", *Cartographica* Monograph 44, vol. 30, 1 (Spring 1993), pp. 68–74.

17 R. Thoresby, *Diary*, 17 May 1695 (London 1830).

18 De Laune and Stow, *London*, p. 346.

19 Pepys, *Diary*, 21 April 1661.

20 T. Moule, *The True Narration of the Entertainment of His Royal Majesty, from the time of his departure from Edinburgh till his receiving at London* (London 1603); J. Lavagnino, *Thomas Middleton and Early Modern Textual Culture* (Oxford 2007), p. 446.

21 J.B. Harley, *Britannia* facsimile (Amsterdam 1970), intro., fig. 2.

22 "An Acte againste newe Buyldinges", 35 Elizabeth 6 (1592–93).

23 J. Cowell, *The Interpreter: or Booke containing the Signification of Words: Wherein is set forth the true meaning of all, or the most part of such Words and Termes, as are mentioned in the Lawe Writers, or Statutes of this ... etc.* (Cambridge 1607).

24 An Act for Erecting and Establishing a Post Office (12 Car. II., cap. 35, 1660).

25 BL Maps *1175.(117.).

26 D. Gerhold, *Carriers and Coachmasters: Trade and Travel before the Turnpikes* (Chichester 2005), p. 16.

27 *New Hollstein German Engravings, Etchings and Woodcuts, 1400–1700*, vol. 7, item 1970.

28 *The Etchings of Wenceslaus Hollar in the Royal Library*, published in microform by Mindata Ltd., Bath (1982) item 650.

29 Pennington, *Hollar*, item 650.

30 W. Hollar, *A New Mappe of the Kingdome of England and Principalitie of Wales*, BM Q.6.135.

31 Van Eerde, *Ogilby*, p. 137.

32 www.measuringworth.com.

33 7.94 kg, 17.5 lb. James R. Akerman (ed.), *Cartographies of Travel and Navigation* (Chicago 2006), p. 51.

34 Akerman, *Cartographies*, pp. 53–4.

35 Ogilby, *Atlas Chinensis* (1671), 543. See Batchelor, *Selden Map*, p. 175.

THE SECRET TREATY OF DOVER

1 G. Parker, *Global Crisis* (New Haven 2013), Introduction.

2 Colbert, "Memorandum to the King on Finances, 1670", in A. Lossky, *The Seventeenth Century* (New York 1967), p. 281.

3 The story of the verse first appears in the Papers of Thomas Hearne (17 November 1706), quoted in C.E. Doble (ed.), *Remarks and Collections of Thomas Hearne*, vol. 1 (Oxford: Clarendon Press for the Oxford Historical Society 1885), p. 308. So it is apocryphal, but feels like the truth.

4 P. Riley (tr.), *Bossuet: Politics Drawn from the Very Words of Holy Scripture* (Cambridge 1990), pp. 57–8.

5 D. Defoe, *Legion's Memorial* (London 1701).

6 M.K. Mason, *The Role of Anti-Catholicism in England in the 1670s* (2008), http://www.moyak.com/researcher/resume/papers/catholic.html#N_68_, consulted 22/7/2014.

7 L. Innes and T. Innes, *James II: The Life of James the Second, King of England* (London 1816), p. 441.

8 This clause, and the rest of the treaty, were published in F.A.A. Mingnet, *Négociations relative á la Succession d'Espagne* (Paris 1835–42),

vol. III, pp. 187–99. The first translation of the text is in J. Dalrymple, *Memoirs of Great Britain and Ireland* (London 1790), vol. I, pp. 96–102.

9 R. Hutton, "The Making of the Secret Treaty of Dover, 1668–1670", *The Historical Journal* 29, 2 (1986), pp. 297–318.

10 C.H. Hartmann, *Charles II and Madame* (London 1934), p. 308.

11 "The Second Parliament of Charles II: Thirteenth Session – Begins 7/1/1674", *The History and Proceedings of the House of Commons*, vol. 1: *1660–1680* (1742), pp. 186–201, http://www.british-history.ac.uk/report.aspx?compid=37629, consulted 14/8/2014.

12 J. Miller, "The Potential for 'Absolutism' in Later Stuart England", *History*, vol. 69, no. 226 (June 1984), p. 187.

13 D. Hume, *History of England* (London 1812), vol. 8, p. 4.

14 There is a full survey of the debate in Hutton, "Making of the Secret Treaty of Dover", pp. 297–318.

15 C.H. Hartmann, *Clifford of the Cabal* (Heinemann 1937), pp. 153–4.

16 C.S. Saint-Evremond, *The Letters of Saint Evremond* (London 1930), p. 146.

17 BL Harley 7319, ff. 33v–5.

18 Hartmann, *Clifford*, p. 153.

19 "Entry Book: June 1670, 1–14", *Calendar of Treasury Books*, vol. 3: *1669–1672* (1908), *Warrants Early* XXII, p. 115; *Order Book* XXXVII, p. 355, http://www.british-history.ac.uk/report.aspx?compid=79704, consulted 18/8/2014.

20 "Entry Book: June 1670, 1–14", *Calendar of Treasury Books*, vol. 3: *1669–1672* (1908), *Order Book* XXXVII, p. 214, http://www.british-history.ac.uk/report.aspx?compid=79704, consulted 18/8/2014.

21 C. Meide, *The Development and Design of Bronze Ordnance, Sixteenth through Nineteenth Centuries* (College of William & Mary, November 2002), http://www.staugustinelighthouse.org/LAMP/Conservation/Meide2002_Bronze.pdf, consulted 18/8/2014.

22 K.A.J. McLay, "The Restoration and the Glorious Revolution, 1660–1702", in *A Military History of Scotland*, ed. E.M. Spieres, J.A. Crang, M.J. Strickland (Oxford 2012), p. 302.

23 J. Robertson (ed.), *Andrew Fletcher: Political Works* (Cambridge 1997), p. 189.

24 BL. Add MS 23132, f. 156. The Earl of Lauderdale to Charles II, Holyroodhouse, 16 November 1669.

25 BL. Add MS 23132, f. 115. The Earl of Lauderdale to Charles II, Holyroodhouse, 12 October 1669.

26 Acts of Parliament 22 & 23 Car. 2, ch. 25 (1671).

27 C.R. Boxer, "Some Second Thoughts on the Third Anglo-Dutch War, 1672–1674", *Transactions of the Royal Historical Society*, fifth series, vol. 19 (1969), pp. 67–94.

28 O. Airy, *The English Restoration and Louis XIV* (London 1888), p. 197.

29 J.W. Konvitz, *Cartography in France 1660–1848* (Chicago 1987), p. 1.

30 Broadsheet Proposals for the Britannia, http://www.mapforum. com/09/9blome.htm, consulted 9/1/2016.

31 B.J. Shapiro, *Political Communication and Political Culture in England, 1558–1688* (Stanford 2012), p. 69.

32 R. Blome, Prospectus and subscription form for "A Geographical Description of His Majesties Kingdoms and Dominions of England, Scotland and Ireland" (London 1670).

33 "Entry Book: July 1672, 16–31", in *Calendar of Treasury Books*, vol. 3: *1669–1672*, ed. William A Shaw (London 1908), pp. 1281–93. British History Online, http://www.british-history.ac.uk/cal-treasury-books/ vol3/pp1281–1293, consulted 26 April 2016.

34 E. Arbor, *Term Catalogues 1668–1709* (London 1903), vol. 1, p. 46.

35 Ms. Aub. 4, f. 220.

36 Arbor, *Catalogues*, vol. 1, p. 94.

37 Bodleian: Ashmole 92.

38 Letter from Denbigh to Ashmole, Bodleian: Ashmole 89, 17 Dec. 1671, copy dated 10 December 1671 in Warwickshire County Archives, CR 2017/C2/234.

39 Konvitz, *Cartography*, p. 4.

40 M.J. Ferrar, *The Saxton Map, 1579; An Investigation*, 2008, http://www. cartographyunchained.com/pdfs/cs1_pdf.pdf, consulted 9/1/2016; D. Bower, "Saxton's Maps of England and Wales: The Accuracy of Anglia and Britannia and Their Relationship to Each Other and to the County Maps", *Imago Mundi* (June 2011), vol. 63, issue 2, pp. 180–200.

41 BL Harley 5946.

42 T.F. Heck, *Picturing Performance: The Iconography of the Performing Arts in Concept and Practice* (Rochester, NY 1999), p. 21.

43 "Mr. Ogilby's Design For Carrying on His Britannia", Yale University Library. The proposals are reproduced and transcribed by Harley, *Britannia* facsimile, IX-X and plate 2.

44 W.J. Ashworth, "Metrology and the State: Science, Revenue, and Commerce", *Science*, new series, vol. 306, no. 5 (19 November 2004), pp. 1314–17.

45 A.M. Ogilvie, "The Rise of the English Post Office", *The Economic Journal*, vol. 3, no. 11 (September 1893), pp. 443–57.

46 K.A. Vogel, "Cosmography", *Cambridge History of Science* (Cambridge 2003), vol. III, p. 487.

47 Johannes Keuning, "The Van Langren Family", *Imago Mundi* 13 (1956), pp. 101–9.

48 J. Norden in the dedication to his *Speculum Britanniae: Cornwall* said that "Julius Cæsar … sowght for … both exquisite Cosmographers to describe the whole Worlde: as also skilfull Geographers to deliniate.. particular Countries, Kingdomes and Cities". This was written around 1610, though not published until 1728. The "worlde" was the whole universe; that is how Locke used the word in 1690, when he spoke of "The great collective Idea of all Bodies whatsoever signified by the name World", J. Locke, *Essay on Humane Understanding* ii.xxiv.149.

49 J.B. Harley, intro. to *Britannia* facsimile, p. xii.

50 Colbert to Louis XIV, 3 June 1671, noted in Hartmann, *Clifford*, p. 211.

51 A copy of this licence, dated February 1674, says that he was given "liberty to erect a printing house for the printing such volumes as he shall publish in the arts of cosmography and geography and any other volumes of his own composure and translation: to hold the said printing house to him and his assigns for the uses aforesaid and no other and during pleasure." BL. Add MS. 28075, f. 37.

52 http://www.measuringworth.com.

53 It is said to be reckoned at between $500 million and $1 billion a year. *NY Times*, Business Day, Technology, 18 June 2012, http://www.nytimes.com/2012/06/18/technology/apples-goes-head-to-head-with-google-over-mobile-maps.html?pagewanted=all&_r=0, consulted 3/8/2013.

54 J. Keith Horsefield, "The 'Stop of the Exchequer' Revisited", *Economic History Review*, new series, vol. 35, no. 4 (November 1982), pp. 511–28.

55 SP Ireland, Car. II. 331, No. 151.

56 Hartmann, *Clifford*, p. 219.

57 BL Harley 5946.

58 F.R. Harris, *The Life of Edward Montagu, First Earl of Sandwich (1625–1672)* (London 1912), vol. 2, pp. 249–51.

59 Horatio Nelson was a Vice Admiral.

60 SP Dom., Entry Book 36, p. 93.

61 Hartmann, *Clifford*, p. 253.

62 Correspondance Angleterre, 103, Colbert to Louis XIV, 9 May 1672.

63 Dick (ed.), *Brief Lives*, letter from Aubrey to Anthony Wood, 12 August 1672.

WHAT'S IN THE BOOK

1 Saxton had created a map in 1583 called *Britannia Insularum in Oceano Maximo* – the Island of Britain in the Great Ocean – which left out Scotland and Ireland but he would have included them if he could have surveyed them.

2 Arbor, *Catalogues,* Michaelmas 1671, vol. 1, p. 93.

3 Yale University Library. The proposals are reproduced and transcribed by Harley, *Britannia* facsimile: IX–X and plate 2.

4 K. Eustace, "Britannia: Some High Points in the History of the Iconography on British Coinage", *British Numismatic Journal* (2006), p. 328.

5 J. Toynbee, "Britannia on Roman Coins of the Second Century AD", *Journal of Roman Studies,* vol. 14 (1924), pp. 142–57.

6 This odd expression is taken from French references to the succession to Charlemagne. See M. Bouquet, *Recuil des Histoiriens des Gaules et de la France* (Paris 1870), vol. 6, p. 724.

7 Ogilby, *Homer His Iliads.*

8 R.J. Mayhew, *Enlightenment Geography: The Political Languages of British Geography, 1650–1850* (Basingstoke 2000), p. 79.

9 N. Flis, "Francis Barlow: The Decoy Decoded", *History Today,* vol. 61 no. 7 (2011), pp. 6–7.

10 M.D. Clark, "Now Through You Made Public for Everyone: John Ogilby's *Britannia* (1675), the 1598 Peutinger Map Facsimile and the Shaping of Public Space", in A. Vanhaelen and J.P. Ward (ed.), *Making Space Public in Early Modern Europe: Geography, Performance, Privacy* (London 2013).

11 I am grateful to Prof. Charles Withers for this suggestion.

12 For example the execution in 1663 of John Twyn, in T.B. Howell, *State Trials* (London 1816), vol. 6, p. 522 seq.

13 The incomplete engraving is in the Royal Library, Windsor. It is listed in R. Pennington, *A Descriptive Catalogue of the Etched Work of Wenceslaus Hollar 1607–1677* (Cambridge 1982), no. 2681.

14 T. Harris, *Restoration: Charles II and his Kingdoms 1660–1685* (London 2006), p. 121.

15 N. Deakin (tr.), *Count Gramont at the Court of Charles II* (London 1965), p. 45.

16 "Of the ninety-four Fellows concerning whom we have evidence … sixty-eight were royalists in their political attitudes or actions, while only twelve were Parliamentarians": L.S. Feuer, *The Scientific Intellectual: The Psychological & Sociological Origins of Modern Science* (London 1963), p. 75.

17 D. Stevenson (ed.), *Letters of Sir Robert Moray to the Earl of Kincardine, 1657–73* (Aldershot 2007), p. 39.

18 C. Spenser, *Prince Rupert, the Last Cavalier* (London 2007), ch. 24.

19 E.G.R. Taylor, "Robert Hooke and the Cartographical Projects of the Late Seventeenth Century (1666–1696)", *Geographical Journal*, vol. 90, no. 6 (December 1937), pp. 529–40.

20 "Mr. Ogilby's Design For Carrying on His Britannia", Yale University Library, probably February 1672. The proposals are reproduced and transcribed by Harley: IX–X

21 Ogilby, *Britannia*, Preface.

22 Ogilby, *Britannia*, Preface.

23 Ms. Aub. 4, ff. 243–4.

24 J. Ogilby, *QUERIES In Order to the Description of BRITANNIA* (1673), http://name.umdl.umich.edu/A53238.0001.001, consulted 17/5/2015.

25 "Mr. Ogilby's Design For Carrying on His Britannia", Yale University Library.

26 Pepys, *Diary*, 24 February 1659/60.

27 "Charles II, 1663: An Act for repairing the Highwayes within the Countyes of Hertford Cambridge and Huntington", in *Statutes of the Realm*, vol. 5, 1628–80, ed. John Raithby (s. l, 1819), pp. 436–40, http://www.british-history.ac.uk/statutes-realm/vol5/pp436-440, consulted 7/2/2015.

28 C. Cochrane, *The Lost Roads of Wessex* (London 1969), pp. 123–9.

29 *Itinerarium Angliae*, Preface.

30 Harley, *Britannia* facsimile, XVII.

31 Rev. G. Eyre Evans, "The Royal Mint, Aberystwyth", *Transactions of the Cardiganshire Antiquarian Society*, vol. 2, no. 1 (1915), p. 71.

32 T. Richards, "The Religious Census of 1676: An Inquiry into its Historical Value, Mainly in Reference to Wales", *Transactions of the Honourable Society of Cymmrodorion* 1925–1926 (1927), p. 102; information from Father Seamus Cunnane, September 2007.

33 I am grateful to the local map expert Mike Parker for his guidance through the area.

34 *The Life and Death of That Matchless Mirror of Magnanimity and Heroique Vertues, Henrietta Maria De Bourbon etc.* (London 1671).

35 Chaucer, *Canterbury Tales*, 3229–33.

36 W. White, *History … of the Borough of Sheffield, and the Town and Parish of Rotherham* (Sheffield 1833), p. 48.

The King's *Britannia*

1 An undated advertisement announcing completion of a new map of Middlesex (van Eerde, *Ogilby*, p. 129). Hooke purchased a copy of the map in Spring 1673 (Harley, introduction to facsimile of *Britannia*).

2 D. Kutcha, *The Three-Piece Suit and Modern Masculinity* (London 2002), p. 80.

3 Kutcha, *The Three-Piece Suit*, p. 88; E. Settle, *Pastor Fido* (London 1677), Epilogue.

4 Hartmann, *Clifford*, pp. 258–60.

5 Hutton, *Charles II*, ch. 11.

6 Sir W. Coventry, "Englands appeal from the private cabal at White-Hall to the great council of the nation, the Lords and Commons in Parliament assembled by a true lover of his country" (1673); J. Miller, *Popery and Politics in England 1660–1688* (Cambridge University Press 1973), pp. 127–8. The effectiveness of this in causing anti-war feeling has been challenged by C.J. Ekberg, *The Failure of Louis XIV's Dutch War* (Chapel Hill 2011) pp. 85–9.

7 J. Evelyn, *Memoirs of John Evelyn … Comprising his Diary, from 1641 to 1705–6* (London 1827), vol. 2, 18 August 1673.

8 *London Gazette*, 12–15 May 1673.

9 On the social tensions between gentlemen of the Royal Society and technical artisans, and the place of the coffee-houses, see L. Stewart, "Other Centres of Calculation, or, Where the Royal Society Didn't Count: Commerce, Coffee-Houses and Natural Philosophy in Early Modern London", *British Journal for the History of Science*, vol. 32, no. 2 (June 1999), pp. 133–53.

10 E.G.R. Taylor, "Robert Hooke and the Cartographical Projects of the Late Seventeenth Century (1666–1696)", *Geographical Journal*, vol. 90, no. 6 (December 1937) p. 532.

11 J. Miller, "A Moderate in the First Age of Party: The Dilemmas of Sir John Holland, 1675–85", *English Historical Review*, vol. 114, no. 458 (September 1999), pp. 844–74.

12 Quoted in van Eerde, *Ogilby*, p. 133.

13 R. Hutton, *Charles II* (London 1989), p. 317.

14 D.T. Witcombe, *Charles II and the Cavalier House of Commons, 1663–1674* (Manchester 1966), p. 164.

15 J. Childs, *The Army of Charles II* (London 2013), p. 204.

16 J. Norden, *Survey of Prince Charles' Manors*, quoted in J. Edwards, *Writing, Geometry and Space in Seventeenth-century England and America: Circles in the Sand* (Psychology Press 2006), p. 79. See also B. Kle, *Maps and the Writing of Space in Early Modern England* (New York 2001), ch. 2.

17 W. Dugdale and G. King, *Heraldic Miscellanies* (London 1783), p. 31.

18 H. Johns, "Introduction to the Maps", in M.D. Lobel and W.H. Johns, *The City of London: From Prehistoric Times to c. 1520* (Historic Towns Trust 1989).

19 L. Hollis, *The Phoenix: St Paul's Cathedral and the Men who Made Modern London* (London 2008), p. 193.

20 D.I. Bower, "Further Light on Ogilby and Morgan's Map of London (1676)", *Imago Mundi* 65:2 (2013), pp. 280–7.

21 J. K. Horsefield, "The 'Stop of the Exchequer' Revisited", *Economic History Review*, new series, vol. 35, no. 4 (November 1982), pp. 511–28.

22 *The Spectator*, no. 462, 20 August 1712.

23 B.W. Palmer, "More Vestigial Remnants in the Law: The Splendid Forbears of the Alderman", *American Bar Association Journal* (February 1950), vol. 36, p. 102.

24 Bishop William Nicholson, 1696, quoted by R.A. Skelton, *County Atlases of the British Isles* (reprint edition, Folkestone, William Dawson & Son, 1970), p. 142.

25 Anthony à Wood, quoted by R.A. Skelton, *County Atlases*, p. 142.

26 Richard Gough, 1780, quoted by D. Kingsley, *Printed Maps of Sussex 1575–1900* (Lewes 1917), p. 39.

27 Ogilby, *Britannia*, p. 41.

28 BL 192.f.1. See Fordham, *Britannia* (Facsimile), xxvii. There were two further impressions of the book within the year, correcting some of the mis-numberings, and the final version had plate numbers inserted. BL Maps C.6.d.8.

29 BL. Add MS 28077 f. 59r.

30 A. Patterson, *The Long Parliament of Charles II* (New Haven 2008), p. 169.

31 Patterson, *Long Parliament*, p. 175.

32 D.M. Schmitter, "The Occasion for Marvell's Growth of Popery", *Journal of the History of Ideas*, vol. 21, no. 4 (October–December 1960), pp. 568–70.

33 Hutton, *Charles II*, p. 330.

34 *A Proclamation for the Suppression of Coffee-Houses*, London, 29 December 1675; B. Cowan, "The Rise of the Coffeehouse Reconsidered", *Historical Journal*, vol. 47, issue 1 (March 2004), pp. 21–46.

35 H. Rogers (ed.), *The Poetical Works of Andrew Marvell* (London 1870), p. 174.

Eliminating Liverpool

1 Capt. G. Collins, *Great Britain's Coasting Pilot* (London 1693).

2 B. Coward, *The Stanleys* (Manchester 1983), p. 76.

3 William A Shaw (ed.), *Calendar of Treasury Books*, vol. 6, 1679–1680 (London 1913), pp. 242–57.

4 *Calendar of Treasury Books*, vol. 8, 1685–1689 (London 1923), pp. 1767–88.

5 M. Power, "Councillors and Commerce in Liverpool, 1650–1750", *Urban History*, vol. 24 (3 December 1997).

6 D. Woodward, "The Anglo-Irish Livestock Trade of the Seventeenth Century", *Irish Historical Studies*, vol. 18, no. 72 (September 1973), pp. 489–523.

7 W. Petty, *Political Anatomy* (Shannon 1970), p. 64.

8 Rev. T.E. Gibson (ed.), *A Cavalier's Notebook* (London 1880), p. 247.

9 Lease and Release or Conveyance of a messuage or dwelling-house in Moor Street, two other messuages and a warehouse in Phenwick Street, with a spinning place or rope yard near Dry Bridge, all in Liverpool, National Archives, Lancashire DDK/471/127 & 128.

10 ww.historyofparliamentonline.org/volume/1660–1690/member/bucknall-sir-william-1633-76, consulted 16/2/2015.

11 Anon., *Flagellum Parliamentarium* (London 1827), p. 12.

12 E.B. Saxton, "Fresh Light on the Liverpool Election of 1640", *Transactions of the Historic Society of Lancashire and Cheshire* (1941), pp. 54–68.

13 B. Henning (ed.), *The House of Commons, 1660–1690*, vol. 1 (London 1983), pp. 288–90.

14 C. Northcote Parkinson, *The Rise of the Port of Liverpool* (Liverpool 1953).

15 E.M. Platt and R. Muir, *A History of Municipal Government in Liverpool to 1835* (Liverpool 1906), vol. I, pp. 102–5.

16 J.A. Picton, (ed.), *City of Liverpool. Selections From the Municipal Archives and Records, From the 13th to the 17th Century Inclusive* (Liverpool 1883), p. 244.

17 Liverpool Corporation records v. 6 ff. 19–21.

18 J. Wallace, *A General and Descriptive History of the Ancient and Present State of the Town of Liverpool* (Liverpool 1797), p. 264.

19 It is not unusual for a port to handle cargoes which do not appear in the records, especially when the port officials dislike the policy they are evading. In 1980, during the European Union ban on herring fishing in the North Sea, I found an entire illicit fleet unloading and selling herring before dawn in Antwerp.

20 Rev. A. Hume, "Some Account of the Liverpool Election of 1670", *Historic Society of Lancashire and Cheshire* (1853–4), p. 17.

21 R. Blome, *Britannia* (London 1673) says that Liverpool "exported Commodities proper for the West-Indies; as likewise a quicker return for such imported Commodities, by reason of the Sugar-Bakers". This is in a volume dated 1673, but was inserted later, probably 1675; see below.

22 A. Black, *The Changing Face of Liverpool 1207–1727* (Merseyside Archaeological Society 1981), p. 33.

23 SP Dom. Car. II, 1671–2, May 1.

24 SP Dom. Car. II, 1674.

25 Liverpool port books National Archives: 1675 E 190/1339/21, 1676 E 190/1347/3.

26 SP Dom. Car. II. v. 378, 25.

27 SP Dom. Car. II, 16 November 1676.

28 Facsimile with stamp "Eigenthum der Stadt Augsburg" on play.google. com/books p. 134, consulted 18/8/2015.

29 Liverpool Corporation records v. 6 ff. 23, 27.

30 Black, *Liverpool*, p. 6.

31 Liverpool Corporation records v. 6 f. 32.

32 Liverpool Corporation records v. 6 ff. 32–3.

THE END OF THE ROAD

1 Van Eerde, *Ogilby*, pp. 137–9. See also Delano-Smith, "Milieus of Mobility: Itineraries, Route Maps, and Road Maps", in Akerman, *Cartographies*, p. 53.

2 T. Harris, *Restoration* (2006), pp. 290–346.

3 G. Tapsell, *The Personal Rule of Charles II, 1681–85* (London 2007).

4 http://www.bl.uk/onlinegallery/onlineex/crace/1/007000000000002u00061000.html, consulted 27/01/2016.

5 http://www.british-history.ac.uk/no-series/london-map-morgan/1682, consulted 27/01/2016.

6 Van Eerde, *Ogilby*, p. 141.

7 R. Muir, *A History of Liverpool* (Liverpool 1907), p. 138.

8 J. Ogilby, *Britannia*, Printed for Abel Swell and Robert Morden (London 1698).

9 J.R. Wadsworth, "John Ogilby: His Influence on English Itineraries", *Manchester Review* 9 (1961), pp. 109–19.

10 "Mr. Ogiby's Design For Carrying on His Britannia", Yale University Library.

11 J. Guillim, J. Barkham and J. Logan, *A Display of Heraldry*, 6th edition (London 1679), p. 135.

12 *Domestic Annals of Scotland, Reign of James VI, 1591–1603* Part A, http://www.electricscotland.com/history/domestic/vol1ch8a.htm, consulted 1/10/2015.

13 *Merry Wives of Windsor* i.i.8.

14 W. Frost and V.A. Dearing (eds), *The Works of John Dryden*, vol. 5: *Poems; The Works of Virgil in English;1697* (Berkeley 1987), pp. 862–5.

15 A. Pope, *The Dunciad*, I, 141.

Bibliography

WORKS BY JOHN OGILBY

The works of P.V.M., translation, 1649.

The Fables of Æsop paraphras'd in verse, 1651.

The works of P.V.M., translation, 1654.

Publii Virgilii Maronis Opera, 1658.

Homer His Iliads, translation, 1660.

The Holy Bible, 1660.

The Relation of his Majestie's Entertainment passing through the City of London to his Coronation, 1661.

The Entertainment of His Most Excellent Majestie Charles II, 1662.

The Fables of Æsop paraphras'd in verse, 1665.

Aesop's Fables, Androcleus, The Ephesian Matron, 1665.

Homer His Odysses, translation, 1665.

Esopics: or, a Second collection of fables, Androcleus: or, the Roman slave, The Ephesian Matron: or Widows tears, 1668.

An embassy from the East India Company of the United Provinces to the Grand Tartar Cham, Emperor of China., translated, 1669.

Africa, 1670.

Atlas Japannensis, translated, 1670.

America, 1671.

Atlas Chinensis, translated, 1671.

Asia, The First Part. 1673.

Britannia Vol. 1, 1675.

Itinerarium Angliae, 1675.

A Large And Accurate Map Of The City Of London, 1677.

PRIMARY SOURCES

Anon. *Memoirs of the Life and Death of Prince Rupert* (1683).

Arbor, E., *Term Catalogues 1668–1709* (London 1903).

Ashmole, E., *Theatrum Chemicum Britannicum* (New York, 1967).

Ashmole, E., *The Lives of Those Eminent Antiquaries Elias Ashmole, Esquire, and Mr. William Lilly, Written by Themselves* (London 1774).

Aubrey, John, ed. Andrew Clark, *"Brief Lives", Chiefly of Contemporaries, Set down by John Aubrey, between the Years 1669 & 1696* (Oxford 1898).

Aubrey, John, ed. Oliver Lawson Dick, *Aubrey's Brief Lives* (Boston 1996).

Bacon, F., *The Essays Or Counsels, Civil And Moral, Of Francis Ld. Verulam Viscount St. Albans* (London 1625).

Baildon, W. Paley, and J. Douglas Walker, *The Records of the Honorable Society of Lincoln's Inn* (Abingdon 1897).

Black, A., *The Changing face of Liverpool 1207–1727* (Liverpool 1981).

Blome, R., *Britannia, Or, A Geographical Description of England* (1673).

Blundell, William, and Thomas Ellison Gibson, *Crosby Records. A Cavalier's Note Book* (London 1880).

Bodin, Jean, *Les six livres de la republique* (Lyons 1580).

Chamberlain, John, and N.E. McClure (ed.), *The Letters of John Chamberlain*, American Philosophical Society (1939), 2 vols.

Chambers, Robert, *The Scottish Ballads* (New York 1974).

Clarendon, Edward Hyde, *The History of the Rebellion* (Oxford 1717).

Clarendon, Edward Hyde, *The Life of Edward Earl of Clarendon* (Oxford 1760).

Clifford, Anne, and Katherine O. Acheson, *The Memoir of 1603 and the Diary of 1616–1619* (Peterborough, Ont. 2007).

Clode, Charles M., *Memorials of the Guild of Merchant Taylors* (London 1875).

Collins, Greenville, *Great Britain's Coasting-Pilot ...* (London 1693).

Cork, Richard Boyle, and Alexander Balloch Grosart, *The Lismore Papers. First [and Second] Series ...* (London 1886).

D'Alton, John, *Illustrations, Historical and Genealogical of King James's Irish Army List (1689)* (Limerick 1997).

Dalrymple, John, *Memoirs* (London 1790).

Davies, John, and E.M.W Tillyard, *Orchestra; Or, A Poem of Dancing* (London 1945).

De Laune, Thomas, and John Stow, *The Present State of London* (1681).

Defoe, Daniel, *Legion's Memorial* (London 1701).

Dekker, Thomas, *English Villanies* (London 1638).

Dryden, John, Vinton A. Dearing, and Edward Niles Hooker, *Poems: The Works of Virgil in English 1697* (Berkeley 1987).

Euclid, ed. Claude François Milliet de Chales, *Les élémens d'Euclide* (Paris 1632).

Evelyn, John, and William Bray, *Memoirs* (London 1827).

Folger Shakespeare Library et al., *Impressions of Wenceslaus Hollar* (Washington, DC 1996).

Griffith, E., *A Jacobean Company and its Playhouse: The Queen's Servants at the Red Bull Theatre (c. 1605–1619)* (Cambridge 2013).

Guillim, John, John Barkham, and John Logan, *A Display of Heraldry* (London 1679).

Harrington, James, and J.G.A Pocock, *The Political Works of James Harrington* (Cambridge 1977).

Harrison, Stephen, *The Archs of Triumph* (London 1604).

Hearne, Thomas et al., *Remarks and Collections of Thomas Hearne* (Oxford 1885).

Hemingford, Walter, *Chronicle of Walter of Guisborough* (Royal Historical Society 1957).

Hobbes, Thomas, and Richard Tuck, *Leviathan* (Cambridge 2014).

Hone, William, *The Every-Day Book and Table Book* (London 1830).

Hooker, Richard, *Of the Lawes of Ecclesiasticall Politie: Four Bookes* (London 1591).

Hyde, Ralph, John Fisher, and Roger Cline, *The A to Z of Restoration London (the City of London, 1676)* (London Topographical Society 1992).

Innes, Lewis, and T. Innes, *The Life of James the Second, King of England, &c., Collected out of Memoirs Writ of His Own Hand* (London 1816).

Kepler, Johannes et al., *The Harmony of the World* (American Philosophical Society 1997).

Le Wright, Robert, *Year-book*, Grenville Mss. xxv BL Add. Ms. 33747.

Marvell, Andrew, Henry Rogers, and James Russell Lowell, *The Poetical Works of Andrew Marvell* (Cincinnati 1870).

Middle Temple, and Arthur Robert Ingpen, *The Middle Temple Bench Book* (London 1912).

Mignet, M., *Négociations Relatives à la Succession D'Espagne* (Paris 1842).

Moore, Edward, *The Moore Rental* (Chetham Society 1847).

Moray, Robert, *Letters of Sir Robert Moray to the Earl of Kincardine, 1657–73*, ed. David Stevenson (Aldershot 2007).

Ogilby, John, William Morgan, and J. Moxon, *Mr. Ogilby's and William Morgan's Pocket Book of the Roads* (London and Westminster 1689).

Payne, Ian, *The Almain in Britain, c.1549–c.1675: A Dance Manual from Manuscript Sources* (Farnham 2003).

Pearce, Robert R., *A Guide to the Inns of Court and Chancery* (London 1855).

Peck, Francis et al., *Desiderata Curiosa* (London 1732).

Pennington, Richard, *A Descriptive Catalogue of the Etched Work of Wenceslaus Hollar, 1607–1677* (Cambridge 1982).

Pepys, Samuel, ed. Robert Latham and William Matthews, *The Diary of Samuel Pepys* (London 1971).

Pepys, Samuel, and Hyder Edward Rollins, *The Pepys Ballads* (Cambridge, MA 1929).

Petty, William, *The Political Anatomy of Ireland* (Dublin 1970).

Phillips, Edward, Egerton Brydges, and Thordarson Collection, *Theatrum Poetarum Anglicanorum: Containing Brief Characters of the English Poets, down to the Year 1675* (Geneva 1824).

Philips, Katherine, ed. Patrick Thomas, *The Collected Works of Katherine Philips: The Matchless Orinda* (Stump Cross 1990).

Philips, Katherine, *Printed Letters* (Farnham 2007).

Saint-Evremond, *The Letters of Saint Evremond* (Freeport, NY 1971).

Sanderson, William, *A Compleat History of the Lives and Reigns of, Mary Queen of Scotland, and ... James the Sixth, King of Scotland.* (London 1656).

Settle, Elkanah et al., *Pastor Fido* (London 1677).

Smith, John, *The Generall Historie of Virginia, New England & the Summer Isles* (Bedford, MA 2007).

Smith, Logan Pearsall, and Henry Wotton, *The Life and Letters of Sir Henry Wotton* (Oxford 1907).

Sommerville, Johann P., *King James VI and I Political Writings* (Cambridge 1995).

Stow, John et al., *Annales, Or, A Generall Chronicle of England* (London 1631).

Stow, John, and Charles Lethbridge Kingsford, *A Survey of London: Reprinted from the Text of 1603* (1908).

Stow, John, and John Strype, *A Survey of the Cities of London and Westminster* (London 1720).

Strafford, Thomas Wentworth, *The Earl of Strafforde's Letters and Dispatches* (London 1739).

Virgil, tr. Robert Fagles, *The Aeneid* (London 2006).

Wallace, James, *A General and Descriptive History of the Ancient and Present State of the Town of Liverpool ... Second Edition* (Liverpool 1797).

Wishart, George, *Montrose Redivivus* (London 1652).

Wood, Anthony à, ed. Philip Bliss, *Athenae Oxonienses* (London 1813).

Wotton, H. and Smith, L.P., *The Life and Letters of Sir Henry Wotton* (Oxford 1907).

Secondary sources

Acheson, Katherine, "The Picture of Nature: Seventeenth-Century English Aesop's Fables", *Journal for Early Modern Cultural Studies* 9.2 (2009): 25–50.

Adams, Joseph Quincy, *Shakespearean Playhouses: A History of English Theatres from the Beginnings to the Restoration* (Boston 1917).

Airy, Osmund, *The English Restoration and Louis XIV: From the Peace of Westphalia to the Peace of Nimwegen* (London 1888).

Akerman, James R. (ed.), *Cartographies of Travel and Navigation* (Chicago 2006).

Altman, Ida, and James P.P. Horn (eds), *"To Make America": European Emigration in the Early Modern Period* (Berkeley 1991).

Andrews, John Harwood, and K.J. Rankin, "William Petty, Topographer", in *At the Anvil: Essays in Honour of William J. Smyth*, ed. Patrick J. Duffy and William Nolan (Dublin 2012), 241–69.

Anon., *History … of the Borough of Sheffield, and the Town and Parish of Rotherham* (Sheffield 1833).

Appleby, Andrew B., *Famine in Tudor and Stuart England* (Stanford 1978).

Ascott, Diana E., Fiona Lewis, and Michael Power, *Liverpool 1660–1750: People, Prosperity and Power* (Liverpool 2006).

Ashworth, W.J., "Metrology and the State: Science, Revenue, and Commerce", *Science* 306.5700 (2004), 1314–17.

Aylmer, G.E., *The Crown's Servants: Government and Civil Service under Charles II, 1660–1685* (Oxford 2002).

Bacon, D.F., *Memoirs of Eminently Pious Women in Britain and America* (Connecticut 1833).

Bagwell, R., *Ireland under the Stuarts and During the Interregnum* (London 1909).

Baines, E., *History of the Cotton Manufacture in Great Britain* (London 1835).

Barbour, V., *Henry Bennet, Earl of Arlington* (Baltimore 1913).

Barnard, John, and D.F. McKenzie (eds), *The Cambridge History of the Book in Britain*, vol. 4: *1557–1695* (Cambridge 2009).

Barnard, T.C., and Jane Fenlon (eds), *The Dukes of Ormonde, 1610–1745* (Woodbridge 2000).

Barnard, T.C., "Restoration or Initiation?" in *The Seventeenth Century*, ed. Jenny Wormald (Oxford 2008), 117–48.

Bartlett, I.R., "Scottish Mercenaries in Europe 1570–1640: A Study in Attitudes and Policies", *International Review of Scottish Studies* 13 (2008).

Batchelor, Robert K., *London: The Selden Map and the Making of a Global City, 1549–1689* (Chicago 2014).

Beckett, J.C., *The Cavalier Duke: A Life of James Butler, 1st Duke of Ormond, 1610–1688* (Belfast 1990).

Belchem, John, "A City Apart: Liverpool, Merseyside and the North West Region", *An Agenda for Regional History*, ed. Bill Lancaster, Diana Newton, and Natasha Vall (Newcastle upon Tyne 2007), 217–32.

Bell, Walter George, *The Great Plague in London in 1665, Etc.*, revised ed. (London 1951).

Bennett, James Arthur, "Robert Hooke as Mechanic and Natural Philosopher", *Notes & Records of the Royal Society (of London)* 35 (1980), 33–48.

Beresford, E., *The Annals of Fleet Street: Its Traditions & Associations* (London 1912).

Birch, Thomas, and Robert Folkestone Williams, *The Court and Times of James the First* (New York 1973).

Black, Stephen F., "Coram Protectore: The Judges of Westminster Hall under the Protectorate of Oliver Cromwell", *American Journal of Legal History* 20.1 (1976), 32.

Blair, Ann, "Tycho Brahe's Critique of Copernicus and the Copernican System", *Journal of the History of Ideas* 51.3 (1990), 355.

Bower, David I., "Further Light on Ogilby and Morgan's Map of London (1676)", *Imago Mundi* 65.2 (2013), 280–7.

Bower, David I., "Saxton's Maps of England and Wales: The Accuracy of *Anglia* and *Britannia* and their Relationship to Each Other and to the County Maps", *Imago Mundi* 63.2 (2011), 180–200.

Boxer, C.R., "Some Second Thoughts on the Third Anglo-Dutch War, 1672–1674", *Transactions of the Royal Historical Society* 19 (1969), 67.

Brand, Desmond, *Gesta Grayorum* (Liverpool 1968).

Brotton, Jerry, *The Sale of the Late King's Goods: Charles I and His Art Collection* (London 2006).

Burner, Sandra A., *James Shirley: A Study of Literary Coteries and Patronage in Seventeenth-Century England* (Stony Brook, NY 1988).

Butler, M., "George Chapman's Masque of the Twelve Months (1619) [With Text]", *English Literary Renaissance* 37.3 (2007), 360–400.

Butler, Todd Wayne, "The Rhetoric of Early Modern Cartography: Politics, Theology, and Inspiration", *Explorations in Renaissance Culture* 26.1 (2000), 45–71.

Caldwell, Tanya, *Virgil Made English: The Decline of Classical Authority* (New York 2008).

Camden Society (Great Britain) et al., *The Camden Miscellany Volume 2* (London 1853).

Campbell, Tony et al., *The Earliest Printed Maps, 1472–1500* (Berkeley 1987).

Carey, John, *Eyewitness to History* (Cambridge, MA 1987).

Carlton, Charles, *Charles I, the Personal Monarch* (London 1983).

Carte, Thomas et al., *An History of the Life of James, Duke of Ormonde* (London 1735).

Champion, Justin, *London's Dreaded Visitation: The Social Geography of the Great Plague in 1665* (London 1995).

Charters, J.A., "Road Carrying in England in the Seventeenth Century: Myth and Reality", *Economic History Review* 30, 2nd series (1977), 73–94.

Chetwood, W.R et al., *A General History of the Stage* (London 1749).

Childs, John, *The Army of Charles II* (London 1976).

Ciano, Cesare, "La Registrazione Navale in Inghilterra e le Matricole di Liverpool", *Economia e storia* 16 (1969), 38–54.

Clapp, S.L.C., "The Subscription Enterprises of John Ogilby and Richard Blome", *Modern Philology* 30.4 (1933), 365–79.

Clark, William Smith, *The Early Irish Stage, the Beginnings to 1720* (Oxford 1955).

Classe, O., *Encyclopedia of Literary Translation into English* (London 2000).

Cochrane, Cyril, *The Lost Roads of Wessex* (Newton Abbot 1969).

Cooper, Michael Alan Ralph, "The Civic Virtue of Robert Hooke", *Robert Hooke and the English Renaissance*, ed. Allan Chapman and Paul Welberry Kent (Leominster 2005), 161–86.

Cooper, Michael, and Michael Cyril William Hunter, *Robert Hooke: Tercentennial Studies* (Aldershot 2005).

Coote, Stephen, *Royal Survivor: A Life of Charles II* (New York 2000).

Cowan, Brian, "The Rise of the Coffeehouse Reconsidered", *The Historical Journal* 47.1 (2004), 21–46.

Coward, Barry, *The Stanleys, Lords Stanley, and Earls of Derby, 1385–1672: The Origins, Wealth, and Power of a Landowning Family* (Manchester 1983).

Crofts, J.E.V., *Pack-Horse Waggon and Post: Land Carriage and Communications under the Tudors and Stuarts* (London 1967).

Crosby, Alan, "The Regional Road Network and the Growth of Manchester in the Sixteenth and Seventeenth Centuries", *Manchester Region History Review* 19 (2008), 1–16.

Cumming, Valerie, "The Fashionable Merchant: A Case Study", *City Merchants and the Arts, 1670–1720*, ed. Mireille Galinou (Wetherby 2004), 120–31.

Cummins, Neil et al., *Living Standards and Plague in London, 1560–1665* (Dublin 2013).

Curran, Kevin, *Marriage, Performance, and Politics at the Jacobean Court* (Farnham 2009).

Daly, James, "Cosmic Harmony and Political Thinking in Early Stuart England", *Transactions of the American Philosophical Society* 69.7 (1979), 1.

Davies, M.P, and Saunders, A., *The History of the Merchant Taylors Company* (Leeds 2004).

Daye, A., "The Banqueting House, Whitehall: A Site Specific to Dance", *Historical Dance* 4.1 (2004).

Daye, A., *Restoration and Revolution in Britain: A Political History of the Era of Charles II and the Glorious Revolution* (Basingstoke 2007).

De Krey, Gary Stuart, *London and the Restoration, 1659–1683* (Cambridge 2005).

Delano-Smith, Catherine, and Roger J.P. Kain, *English Maps: A History* (London 1999).

Desaulty, A.-M., and Albarede, F., "Copper, Lead, and Silver Isotopes Solve a Major Economic Conundrum of Tudor and Early Stuart Europe", *Geology* 41.2 (2013), 135–8.

Dew, Nicholas, "The Hive and the Pendulum: Universal Metrology and Baroque-Science", *International Archives of the History of Ideas* 208 (2013), 239–56.

Dickinson, Gordon C., "Britain's First Road Maps: The Strip-Maps of John Ogilby's 'Britannia', 1675", *Landscapes* 4.1 (2003), 79–98.

Doelman, J., "The Comet of 1618 and the British Royal Family", *Notes and Queries* 54.1 (2007), 30–5.

Donaldson, Ian, *Ben Jonson: A Life* (Oxford 2011).

Draper, Frederick William Marsden, *Four Centuries of Merchant Taylors School, 1561–1961* (London 1962).

Dunan-Page, Anne, and Beth Lynch (eds), *Roger L'Estrange and the Making of Restoration Culture* (Aldershot 2008).

Eddison, Jill et al., *Romney Marsh: Environmental Change and Human Occupation in a Coastal Lowland* (Oxford 1998).

Edgar, F.T.R., *Sir Ralph Hopton: The King's Man in the West (1642–1652): A Study in Character and Command* (Oxford 1968).

Edwards, Jess, *Writing, Geometry and Space in Seventeenth-Century England and America: Circles in the Sand* (London 2006).

Ekberg, Carl J., *The Failure of Louis XIV's Dutch War* (Chapel Hill 2011).

Eustace, K., "Britannia: Some High Points in the History of the Iconography on British Coinage", *British Numismatic Journal* (2006), 328.

Evans, G.E., "The Royal Mint, Aberystwyth", *Transactions of the Cardiganshire Antiquarian Society* 2.1 (1915), 71.

Feiling, Keith, *British Foreign Policy 1660–1672* (London 1968).

Feuer, Lewis S., *The Scientific Intellectual: the Psychological & Sociological Origins of Modern Science* (New York 1963).

Finkelpearl, Philip J., *John Marston of the Middle Temple: An Elizabethan Dramatist in His Social Setting* (Cambridge, MA 1969).

Finlay, Roger, *Population and Metropolis: The Demography of London, 1580–1650* (Cambridge 1981).

Firth, C.H., "The Royalists Under the Protectorate", *English Historical Review* LII.CCVIII (1937), 634–48.

FitzRoy, Charles, *Return of the King: The Restoration of Charles II* (Stroud 2007).

Fletcher, Alan J., *Drama, Performance, and Polity in Pre-Cromwellian Ireland* (Toronto 2000).

Fletcher, Andrew, and John Robertson, *Political Works* (Cambridge 1997).

Flis, N., "Francis Barlow: The Decoy Decoded", *History Today* 61.7 (2011), 6–7.

Fordham, George, "A Note on the 'Quartermaster's Map', 1644", *Geographical Journal* 70.1 (1927), 50.

Fortier, Mark, "Equity and Ideas: Coke, Ellesmere, and James I", *Renaissance Quarterly* 51.4 (1998), 1255.

Foster, Robert F., *Modern Ireland 1600–1972* (London 2011).

Geneva, Ann, *Astrology and the Seventeenth Century Mind: William Lilly and the Language of the Stars* (Manchester 1995).

Gerhold, Dorian, "The Development of Stage Coaching and the Impact of Turnpike Roads, 1653–1840", *Economic History Review* 67.3 (2014), 818–45.

Gerhold, Dorian, *Carriers and Coachmasters: Trade and Travel before the Turnpikes* (Chichester 2005).

Gilbey, Walter, *Early Carriages and Roads* (London 1903).

Glennie, Paul, and N.J. Thrift, "Revolutions in the Times: Clocks and the Temporal Structures of Everyday Life", *Geography and Revolution*, ed. David N. Livingstone and Charles W.J. Withers (Chicago 2005), 160–98.

Green, Mary Anne Everett, and S.C Lomas, *Elizabeth, Electress Palatine and Queen of Bohemia* (London 1909).

Griffiths, Antony, and Robert A. Gerard, *The Print in Stuart Britain, 1603–1689* (London 1998).

Griswold, Wendy, *Renaissance Revivals: City Comedy and Revenge Tragedy in the London Theatre, 1576–1980* (Chicago 1986).

Gwynn, Lucy, "The Architecture of the English Domestic Library, 1600–1700", *Library & Information History* 26.1 (2010), 56–69.

Hammond, Paul, *The Making of Restoration Poetry* (Cambridge 2006).

Hanrahan, David C., *Charles II and the Duke of Buckingham the Merry Monarch and the Aristocratic Rogue* (Stroud 2006).

Hanse Conference on Climate and History, and G Wefer (eds), *Climate Development and History of the North Atlantic Realm* (Berlin and New York 2002).

Harbage, Alfred, *Sir William Davenant, Poet Venturer, 1606–1668* (New York 1971).

Harley, J.B., "Ogilby and Collins: Cheshire by Road and Sea", *Cheshire Round* 1.7 (1967), 210–25.

Harris, F.R., *The Life of Edward Mountagu* (London 1912).

Harris, Frances, "'Alchemy and Monstrous Love': Sir Robert Moray and the Representation of Early Modern Lives", *Writing Lives: Biography and Textuality, Identity and Representation in Early Modern England*, ed. Kevin M. Sharpe and Steven N. Zwicker (Oxford 2008), 275–92.

Harris, Tim, *London Crowds in the Reign of Charles II: Propaganda and Politics from the Restoration until the Exclusion Crisis* (Cambridge 1987).

Harris, Tim, *Restoration: Charles II and His Kingdoms, 1660–1685* (London 2005).

Hartmann, Cyril Hughes, *Charles II and Madame* (London 1934).

Hartmann, Cyril Hughes, *Clifford of the Cabal: A Life of Thomas, First Lord Clifford of Chudleigh, Lord High Treasurer of England (1630–1673)* (London 1937).

Harwood, J.T., "Rhetoric and Graphics in 'Micrographia'", in *Robert Hooke: New Studies*, ed. Michael Cyril William Hunter and Simon Schaffer (Woodbridge 1989), 119–47.

Hazlitt, William Carew, *Schools, School-Books and Schoolmasters: A Contribution to the History of Educational Development in Great Britain* (London 1888).

Heck, Thomas F., and R.L. Erenstein, *Picturing Performance: The Iconography of the Performing Arts in Concept and Practice* (Rochester 1999).

Helgerson, Richard, "'Nation or Estate?': Ideological Conflict in the Early Modern Mapping of England", *Cartographica: The International Journal for Geographic Information and Geovisualization* 30.1 (1993), 68–74.

Helmholz, R.H., "Bonham's Case, Judicial Review, and the Law of Nature", *Journal of Legal Analysis* 1.1 (2009), 325–54.

Henning, Basil Duke, *The House of Commons 1660–1690* (London 1983).

Hey, David, *Packmen, Carriers, and Packhorse Roads: Trade and Communications in North Derbyshire and South Yorkshire* (Leicester 1980).

Hodson, D. *The Early Printed Road Books and Itineraries of England and Wales*, DPhil thesis (Exeter 2000).

Hollis, Leo, *The Phoenix: St. Paul's Cathedral and the Men Who Made Modern London* (London 2008).

Hopkins, Frank, *Hidden Dublin Deadbeats, Dossers and Decent Skins* (Cork 2008).

Horsefield, J. Keith. "The 'Stop of the Exchequer' Revisited", *Economic History Review* 35.4 (1982), 511.

Howarth, David, *Images of Rule: Art and Politics in the English Renaissance, 1485–1649* (Berkeley 1997).

Hull, Eleanor, *A History of Ireland and Her People* (Freeport, NY 1972).

Hume, A. "Some Account of the Liverpool Election of 1670", *Historic Society of Lancashire and Cheshire* (1853), 17.

Hutton, R., *The Restoration: A Political and Religious History of England and Wales, 1658–1667* (Oxford 1985).

Hutton, R., "The Making of the Secret Treaty of Dover, 1668–1670", *Historical Journal* 29.02 (1986), 297.

Hutton, R., *Charles the Second, King of England, Scotland, and Ireland* (Oxford 1989).

Hutton, R., *The British Republic, 1649–1660* (New York 2000).

Janes, Andrew, "Maps as a Recordkeeping Technology", *Journal of the Society of Archivists* 32.1 (2011), 119–34.

Janicka-Swiderska, I., "The Dance in Elizabethan and Stuart Drama", *Real: The Yearbook of Research in English and American Literature* 5 (1987), 65.

Jardine, Lisa, *The Curious Life of Robert Hooke: The Man Who Measured London* (London 2003).

Jenkinson, Matthew, *Culture and Politics at the Court of Charles II, 1660–1685* (Woodbridge 2010).

Johnston, Warren, *Revelation Restored: The Apocalypse in Later Seventeenth-Century England* (Woodbridge 2011).

Jones, James Rees, "Booth's Rising of 1659", *Bulletin of the John Rylands Library, Manchester* 39.2 (1957), 416–33.

Jones, James Rees, *The Restored Monarchy, 1660–1688* (London 1979).

Jones, Terry, and Alan Ereira, "Terry Jones's Great Map Mystery", *Transactions of the Radnorshire Society* 77 (2007), 68–82.

Jordan, T.E., "Quality of Life in Seventeenth Century Dublin", *Dublin Historical Record* 61.2 (2008), 136–54.

Josten, Conrad Hermann, *Elias Ashmole, F.R.S. (1617–1692)* (Oxford 1978).

Kaplan, Benjamin J., *Divided by Faith: Religious Conflict and the Practice of Toleration in Early Modern Europe* (Cambridge, MA 2010).

Kearney, Hugh F., *Strafford in Ireland, 1633–41: A Study in Absolutism* (Manchester 1960).

Keeble, Neil Howard, *The Restoration: England in the 1660s* (Oxford 2002).

Kelly, S.A., "The Theatre Royal in 1662: Smock Alley's First Season", *Dublin Historical Record* 61.2 (2008), 201–18.

Kennerley, Peter, *Liverpool: The Making of the City on the Mersey* (Lancaster 2010).

Kermode, Jennifer I., Janet E. Hollinshead, and J.M. Gratton, "Small Beginnings: Liverpool 1207–1680", in *Liverpool 800: Culture, Character & History*, ed. John Belchem (Liverpool 2006), 59–111, 489.

Kerrigan, John, *Archipelagic English Literature, History, and Politics, 1603–1707* (Oxford 2008).

Keuning, Johannes, "The van Langren Family", *Imago Mundi* 13.1 (1956), 101–9.

Kingsley, David, *Printed Maps of Sussex, 1575–1900* (Lewes 1982).

Kirsten Tranter, "Samuel Sheppard's 'Faerie King' and the Fragmentation of Royalist Epic", *SEL Studies in English Literature 1500–1900* 49.1 (2008), 87–103.

Kitchin, George, *Sir Roger L'Estrange: A Contribution to the History of the Press in the Seventeenth Century* (London 1913).

Klein, Bernhard, "Constructing the Space of the Nation: Geography,

Maps, and the Discovery of Britain in the Early Modern Period", *Journal for the Study of British Cultures* 4.1–2 (1997), 11–29.

Klein, Bernhard, *Maps and the Writing of Space in Early Modern England and Ireland* (Basingstoke 2001).

Knaap, Anna C., and Michael C.J. Putnam (eds), *Art, Music, and Spectacle in the Age of Rubens: The Pompa Introitus Ferdinandi* (London 2013).

Knellwolf, Christa, "Robert Hooke's Micrographia and the Aesthetics of Empiricism", *Seventeenth Century* 16.1 (2001), 177–20.

Konvitz, Josef W., *Cartography in France, 1660–1848: Science, Engineering, and Statecraft* (Chicago 1987).

Korshin, Paul J., *Studies in Change and Revolution: Aspects of English Intellectual History, 1640–1800* (Menston 1972).

Krüssmann, Walter, *Ernst von Mansfeld (1580–1626)* (Berlin 2010).

Kuchta, David, *The Three-Piece Suit and Modern Masculinity: England, 1550–1850* (Berkeley 2002).

Landrum, Robert, "The Plague and the Fire, 1665–1666", *Events That Changed Great Britain, from 1066–1714*, ed. John E. Findling and Frank W. Thackeray (London 2004), 147–64.

Lang, Wilhelm, "The Augsburg Travel Guide of 1563 and the Erlinger Road Map of 1524", *Imago Mundi* 7.1 (1950), 85–8.

Lawrence, David R., *The Complete Soldier Military Books and Military Culture in Early Stuart England, 1603–1645* (Leiden 2009).

Leasor, Thomas James, *The Plague and the Fire* (London 1962).

Lee, Harry F., and David D. Zhang, "A Tale of Two Population Crises in Recent Chinese History", *Climatic Change* 116.2 (2013), 285–308.

Lee, Maurice D., Jr., "The Earl of Arlington and the Treaty of Dover", *Journal of British Studies* 1.1 (1961), 58.

Lesko, Kathleen Menzie, "Evidence of Restoration Performances: Duke Ferdinand Albrecht's Annotated Playtexts from 1664–65", *Philological Quarterly* 79:1 (2000), 45–68.

Lindberg, David C., Ronald L. Numbers, and Roy Porter (eds), *Cambridge History of Science*, vol. 3: *Early Modern Science* (Cambridge 2003).

Livingstone, David N., and Charles W.J. Withers, *Geography and Revolution* (Chicago 2005).

Lobel, M.D. and W.H. Johns, *The City of London from Prehistoric Times to c. 1520* (Oxford 1989).

Lockyer, Roger, *Buckingham: The Life and Political Career of George Villiers, First Duke of Buckingham, 1592–1628* (London 1981).

Logan, T.P., and D.S. Smith, "The New Intellectuals: A Survey and Bibliography of Recent Studies in English", *Renaissance Drama* (1977), 87.

Logan, T.P., and D.S. Smith, *A Survey and Bibliography of Recent Studies in English Renaissance Drama* (Lincoln 1973).

Lord, Evelyn, *The Great Plague: A People's History* (New Haven 2014).

Lossky, Andrew, *The Seventeenth Century* (New York 1967).

Low, Jennifer A., and Nova Myhill, *Imagining the Audience in Early Modern Drama, 1558–1642* (New York 2011).

Lowe, J., "The Campaign of the Irish Royalist Army in Cheshire, November 1643–January 1644", *Transactions of the Historical Society of Lancashire and Cheshire* 113 (1961), 47–76.

Lowndes, W. Thomas, *The Bibliographer's Manual of English Literature, Containing an Account of Rare, Curious, and Useful Books, Published in or Relating to Great Britain and Ireland, from the Invention of Printing: with bibliographical and critical notices, collations of the rarer articles, and the prices at which they have been sold …* (London 1871), vol. 4.

Loxley, James, *Royalism and Poetry in the English Civil Wars: The Drawn Sword* (New York 1997).

Macarthur, W.P., "A Brief Story of English Malaria", *British Medical Bulletin* 8.1 (1951), 76–9.

Macfarlane, Alan, *The Savage Wars of Peace: England, Japan and the Malthusian Trap* (Oxford 1997).

Macintyre, J., "Buckingham the Masquer", *Renaissance and Reformation*, new series, vol. 22.3 (1998), 60.

Malcolm, Joyce Lee, "All the King's Men: The Impact of the Crown's Irish Soldiers on the English Civil War", *Irish Historical Studies* 22.83 (1979), 239–64.

Manning, Roger B., "Styles of Command in Seventeenth-Century English Armies", *Journal of Military History* 71.3 (2007), 671–99.

Marshall, Alan, *Intelligence and Espionage in the Reign of Charles II, 1660–1685* (Cambridge 1994).

Mayhew, Robert John, *Enlightenment Geography: The Political Languages of British Geography, 1650–1850* (Basingstoke 2000).

McClain, Molly, *Beaufort: The Duke and His Duchess, 1657–1715* (New Haven 2001).

McElligott, Jason, and David L. Smith (eds). *Royalists and Royalism during the English Civil Wars* (Cambridge 2007).

McElligott, Jason, *Royalism, Print and Censorship in Revolutionary England* (Woodbridge 2007).

McElligott, Jason, *Royalists and Royalism during the Interregnum* (Manchester 2010).

McGirr, Elaine M., *Heroic Mode and Political Crisis, 1660–1745* (Newark 2009).

McMillan, Norman, "William Petty, 1623–1687", *Physicists of Ireland: Passion and Precision*, ed. Mark McCartney and Andrew Whitaker (Bristol 2003), 1–7.

Merritt, J.F., *The Political World of Thomas Wentworth, Earl of Strafford, 1621–1641* (Cambridge 1996).

Miller, J., "A Moderate in the First Age of Party: The Dilemmas of Sir John Holland, 1675–85", *English Historical Review* 114.458 (1999), 844–74.

Miller, J., *Charles II* (London 1991).

Miller, J., "Politics in Restoration Britain", *A Companion to Stuart Britain*, ed. Barry Coward (Oxford 2003), 399–415.

Miller, J., *Popery and Politics in England 1660–1688* (Cambridge 1973).

Miller, J., "The Potential For 'Absolutism' in Later Stuart England", *History* 69.226 (1984), 187–207.

Mitchell, A.A., "Charles II and the Treaty of Dover, 1670", *History Today* 17 (1967), 674–82.

Molloy, J. Fitzgerald, *Royalty Restored; Or, London under Charles II* (London 1897).

Moore, J.H., "Notes on the History of Navan", *Journal of the Royal Society of Antiquaries of Ireland* 4.1 (1894), 47–53.

Moote, A. Lloyd, and Dorothy C. Moote, *The Great Plague: The Story of London's Most Deadly Year* (Baltimore 2004).

Morash, Chris, *A History of Irish Theatre, 1601–2000* (Cambridge 2002).

Morrill, John Stephen, *Revolution and Restoration: England in the 1650s* (London 1992).

Muir, Ramsay, *A History of Liverpool* (East Ardsley 1970).

Muir, Ramsay, *A History of Municipal Government in Liverpool from the Earliest Times to the Municipal Reform Act of 1835* (London 1906).

Myers, Robin, and Michael Harris, *Property of a Gentleman: The Formation, Organisation and Dispersal of the Private Library 1620–1920* (Winchester 1991).

Nichols, Richard, *Robert Hooke and the Royal Society* (Lewes 1999).

Nicholson, Susan, *The Changing Face of Liverpool 1207–1727: Archaeological Survey of Merseyside* (Liverpool 1982).

Noble, M., *A History of the College of Arms* (London 1805).

Nye, J.S., "Public Diplomacy and Soft Power", *Annals of the American Academy of Political and Social Science* 616.1 (2008), 94–109.

O'Hehir, Brendan, *Harmony from Discords: A Life of Sir John Denham* (Berkeley 1968).

Ogilby, John, and Harley, J.B., *Britannia*, facsimile with foreword (Amsterdam 1970).

Ogilvie, A.M., "The Rise of the English Post Office", *Economic Journal* 3.11 (1893), 443.

Ollard, Richard Lawrence, *Cromwell's Earl: A Life of Edward Mountagu* (London 1994).

Olmos, Paula, *Greek Science in the Long Run: Essays on the Greek Scientific Tradition (4th C. BCE–17th C. CE)* (Newcastle 2012).

Palme, Per, *Triumph of Peace: A Study of the Whitehall Banqueting House* (Stockholm 1956).

Palmer, Ben W., "More Vestigial Remnants in the Law: The Splendid Forebears of the Alderman", *American Bar Association Journal* 36.2 (1950), 101–4.

Parker, Geoffrey, and Simon Adams (eds), *The Thirty Years' War* (London 1984).

Parker, Geoffrey, *Global Crisis: War, Climate Change and Catastrophe in the Seventeenth Century* (New Haven 2013).

Parker, Mike, *Mapping the Roads: Building Modern Britain* (Basingstoke 2013).

Parkes, J., *Travel in England in the Seventeenth Century* (Oxford 1968).

Parkinson, C. Northcote, *The Rise of the Port of Liverpool* (Liverpool 1952).

Paterson, Raymond Campbell, "'King of Scotland': Lauderdale and the Restoration North of the Border", *History Today* 53.1 (2003), 21–7.

Patrick, Derek J., "Restoration to Revolution: 1660–1690", *Scotland: The Making and Unmaking of the Nation c. 1100–1707*, vol. 2: *Early Modern Scotland c. 1500–1707*, ed. Bob Harris and Alan R. MacDonald (Dundee 2006), 56–73.

Patterson, Annabel M., *Fables of Power: Aesopian Writing and Political History* (Durham 1991).

Patterson, Annabel M., *Pastoral and Ideology: Virgil to Valéry* (Berkeley 1987).

Patterson, Annabel M., *The Long Parliament of Charles II* (New Haven 2008).

Pettegree, A., Review of John Barnard and D.F. McKenzie (eds), *Cambridge History of the Book in Britain*, vol. 4: 1557–1695, in *Journal of Modern History* 77.2 (2005), 418–19.

Picard, Liza, *Restoration London: Everyday Life in London, 1660–1670* (London 2004).

Picton, James A., *City of Liverpool: Selections from the Municipal Archives and Records, from the 13th to the 17th Century Inclusive* (Salt Lake City 1992).

Pierce, K., *The Coronation Music of Charles II*, Master of Music thesis (Graduate College of Bowling Green State University 2007).

Porter, S., *The Great Plague* (Stroud 1999).

Porter, S., *Lord Have Mercy upon Us: London's Plague Years* (Stroud 2005).

Porter, S., *The Plagues of London* (Stroud 2008).

Power, Michael, "Councillors and Commerce in Liverpool, 1650–1750", *Urban History* 24.03 (1997), 301.

Power, Michael, "Politics and Progress in Liverpool, 1660–1740", *Northern History* 35 (1999), 119–38.

Prest, Wilfrid R., *The Inns of Court under Elizabeth I and the Early Stuarts, 1590–1640* (Totowa, NJ 1972).

Pritchard, M., *Aesop, Fables Moral and Political*, PhD dissertation (University of Western Ontario 1976).

Pritchard, R.T., "The History of the Post Road in Anglesey", *Transactions of the Anglesey Antiquarian Society & Field Club* (1954), 18–33.

Ravelhofer, B., *The Early Stuart Masque Dance, Costume, and Music* (Oxford 2006).

Read, Gordon, "Liverpool – an Irish Port", *Aspects of Irish Genealogy 3: A Selection of Papers from the Third Genealogical Congress*, ed. Christopher Ryan (Dublin 1999), 145–90.

Reese, Peter, *The Life of General George Monck: For King and Cromwell* (Barnsley 2008).

Richeson, A.W., *English Land Measuring to 1800: Instruments and Practices* (London 1966).

Ridley, A.M., *The Staging of the Siege of Rhodes at Rutland House (1656)*, MA thesis (New Brunswick 1980).

Robertson, Barry, *Royalists at War in Scotland and Ireland, 1638–1650* (Farnham 2013).

Robertson, Joseph, *Lives of Scottish Poets* (London 1821).

Ross, Sutherland, *The Plague and the Fire of London* (London 1965).

Rowse, A.L., *The Tower of London in the History of the Nation* (London 1972).

Royle, Trevor, *Civil War: The Wars of the Three Kingdoms, 1638–1660* (London 2004).

Russell, Ann, "Katherine Philips as Political Playwright: 'The Songs Between the Acts' in 'Pompey'", *Comparative Drama* 44.3 (2010), 299–323.

Saxton, E.B., "Fresh Light on the Liverpool Election of 1640", *Transactions of the Historic Society of Lancashire and Cheshire* (1941), 54–68.

Schechner, Sara, *Comets, Popular Culture, and the Birth of Modern Cosmology* (Princeton 1997).

Schmitter, Dean Morgan, "The Occasion for Marvell's Growth of Popery", *Journal of the History of Ideas* 21.4 (1960), 568.

Schuchard, Margret, *A Descriptive Bibliography of the Works of John Ogilby and William Morgan* (Bern 1975).

Schuchard, Margret, *John Ogilby, 1600–1676; Lebensbild eines Gentleman mit vielen Karrieren* (Hamburg 1973).

Seaward, Paul, *The Cavalier Parliament and the Reconstruction of the Old Regime, 1661–1667* (Cambridge 1989).

Seaward, Paul, *The Restoration, 1660–1688* (Basingstoke 1991).

Shapiro, Barbara J., *Political Communication and Political Culture in England, 1558–1688* (Stanford 2012).

Sharpe, Kevin M., "Restoration and Reconstitution: Politics, Society and Culture in the England of Charles II", *Reading Authority and Representing Rule in Early Modern England*, ed. Kevin M. Sharpe (London 2013).

Sharpe, Kevin M., *Criticism and Compliment: The Politics of Literature in the England of Charles I* (Cambridge 1987).

Sharpe, Kevin M., "Van Dyck, the Royal Image and the Caroline Court", *Reading Authority and Representing Rule in Early Modern England*, ed. Kevin M. Sharpe (London 2013).

Shaw, Dougal, "Thomas Wentworth and Monarchical Ritual in Early Modern Ireland", *Historical Journal* 49.02 (2006), 331.

Shirley, Evelyn Philip, *Hanley and the House of Lechmere* (London 1883).

Simpson, Linzi, *Smock Alley Theatre: The Evolution of a Building* (Dublin 1996).

Skelton, R.A, and Thomas Chubb, *County Atlases of the British Isles, 1579–1850: A Bibliography* (London 1970).

Slauter, Will, "Write up Your Dead: The Bills of Mortality and the London Plague of 1665", *Media History* 17.1 (2011), 1–15.

Smith, Geoffrey, *Royalist Agents, Conspirators and Spies Their Role in the British Civil Wars, 1640–1660* (Farnham 2011).

Spencer, Charles, *Prince Rupert: The Last Cavalier* (London 2007).

Spiers, Edward M., Jeremy A. Crang, and Matthew Strickland (eds), *A Military History of Scotland* (Edinburgh 2012).

Stammers, Michael, "Ships and Port Management at Liverpool before the Opening of the First Dock in 1715", *Transactions of the Historic Society of Lancashire & Cheshire* 156 (2007), 27–50.

Steele, Mary Susan, *Plays & Masques at Court during the Reigns of Elizabeth, James and Charles* (London 1968).

Stevenson, Allan H., "James Shirley and the Actors at the First Irish Theater", *Modern Philology* 40.2 (1942), 147–60.

Stevenson, Christine, "Occasional Architecture in Seventeenth-Century London", *Architectural History* 49 (2006), 35–74.

Stewart, Larry, "Other Centres of Calculation, Or, Where the Royal Society Didn't Count: Commerce, Coffee-Houses and Natural Philosophy in Early Modern London", *British Journal for the History of Science* 32.2 (1999), 133–53.

Stewart, Larry, "Science, Instruments, and Guilds in Early-Modern Britain", *Early Science and Medicine* 10.3 (2005), 392–410.

Stoyan, Ronald, and Storm Dunlop, *Atlas of Great Comets* (Cambridge 2015).

Stoyle, Mark, *Soldiers and Strangers: An Ethnic History of the English Civil War* (London 2005).

Strong, Roy C., *Art and Power: Renaissance Festivals, 1450–1650* (Berkeley 1984).

Sullivan, Mary, *Court Masques of James I: Their Influence on Shakespeare and the Public Theatres* (New York 1973).

Tapsell, Grant, *The Personal Rule of Charles II, 1681–85* (Woodbridge 2007).

Taylor, E.G.R., "Robert Hooke and the Cartographical Projects of the Late Seventeenth Century (1666–1696)", *Geographical Journal* 90.6 (1937), 529.

Taylor, Gary, and John Lavagnino, *Thomas Middleton and Early Modern Textual Culture: A Companion to the Collected Works* (Oxford 2007).

Thomas, Keith Vivian, *Religion and the Decline of Magic: Studies in Popular Beliefs in Sixteenth- and Seventeenth-Century England* (London 1991).

Thomas, Roy Digby, *George Digby: Hero and Villain* (Bloomington 2005).

Thrush, A.D, and John P. Ferris, *The House of Commons, 1604–1629* (Cambridge 2010).

Toynbee, Jocelyn, "Britannia on Roman Coins of the Second Century A.D.", *Journal of Roman Studies* 14.1–2 (1924), 142–57.

Tulloch, Alexander R., *The Story of Liverpool* (Stroud 2008).

Turner, Henry S., "Literature and Mapping in Early Modern England, 1520–1688", *Cartography in the European Renaissance*, ed. David Woodward, vol. 1 (London 2007), 412–26.

Uglow, Jennifer S., *A Gambling Man: Charles II and the Restoration 1660–1670* (London 2009).

Underdown, David, *Royalist Conspiracy in England, 1649–1660* (New Haven 1960).

Van Eerde, Katherine S., *John Ogilby and the Taste of His Times* (Folkestone 1976).

Vanhaelen, Angela, and Joseph P. Ward, *Making Space Public in Early Modern Europe: Performance, Geography, Privacy* (London 2013).

Varanka, Dalia, "The Manly Map: The English Construction of Gender in Early Modern Cartograph", *Gender and Landscape: Renegotiating Morality and Space*, ed. Josephine Carubia, Lorraine Dowler, and Bonj Szczygiel (London 2005), 223–39.

Vernier, Veronika, "Maps for Intelligence Gathering? Rediscovered Seventeenth-Century Manuscript Maps from The Queen's College, Oxford", *Imago Mundi* 63.1 (2011), 76–87.

Viau, Théophile de, and Claire Gaudiani, *The Cabaret Poetry of Théphile de Viau: Texts and Traditions* (Tübingen 1981).

Wadsworth, J.R., "John Ogilby: His Influence on English Itineraries", *Manchester Review* 9 (1961), 109–19.

Wall, Cynthia, *A Concise Companion to the Restoration and Eighteenth Century* (Oxford 2005).

Wall, Cynthia, *The Literary and Cultural Spaces of Restoration London* (Cambridge 1998).

Ward, John M., "Apropos 'The Olde Measures'", *Records of Early English Drama* 18.1 (1993), 2–21.

Waters, Henry F., *An Examination of the English Ancestry of George Washington* (Boston 1889).

Watts, R.D., *The Moore Family of Bank Hall Liverpool: Progress and Decline 1606–1730*, PhD thesis (Bangor 2004).

Wedgwood, C.V., *Thomas Wentworth, First Earl of Strafford, 1593–1641* (New York 1962).

Welch, Anthony, "Epic Romance, Royalist Retreat, and the English Civil War", *Modern Philology* 105.3 (2008), 570–602.

Wilkes, Thomas, and Samuel Derrick, *A General View of the Stage* (London 1759).

Williams, J.I., *The Irish Plays of James Shirley, 1636–1640*, PhD thesis (Warwick 2010).

Williams, Moelwyn I., "The Port of Aberdyfi in the 18th Century", *National Library of Wales Journal* Cyf. 18, rh. 1 Haf 1973 (1973), 98.

Wilson, William, *The House of Airlie* (London 1924).

Witcombe, Dennis Trevor, *Charles II and the Cavalier House of Commons, 1663–1674* (Manchester 1966).

Wood, Herbert, "The Offices of Secretary of State for Ireland and Keeper of the Signet or Privy Seal", *Proceedings of the Royal Irish Academy. Section C: Archaeology, Celtic Studies, History, Linguistics, Literature* 38 (1928), 51–68.

Woodford, Benjamin, "Developments and Debates in English Censorship during the Interregnum", *Early Modern Literary Studies* 17.2 (2014).

Woodward, Donald, "The Anglo-Irish Livestock Trade of the Seventeenth Century", *Irish Historical Studies* 18.72 (1973), 489–523.

Woolrych, A.H., *Penruddock's Rising, 1655* (London 1955).

Wormald, Jenny, *Court, Kirk and Community: Scotland, 1470–1625* (Toronto 1981).

Worms, Laurence, "Maps, Prints, Presses and the Merchant Taylors in the Seventeenth Century", *London Topographical Record* 28 (2001), 153–66.

Worthington, David, *British and Irish Emigrants and Exiles in Europe, 1603–1688* (Leiden 2010).

Yates, Frances A., *The Rosicrucian Enlightenment* (London 1972).

Yould, G.M., "The Duke of Lauderdale's Religious Policy in Scotland, 1668–79: The Failure of Conciliation and the Return to Coercion", *Journal of Religious History* 11 (1980), 248–68.

Young, Michael B., *King James and the History of Homosexuality* (New York 2000).

WEB DOCUMENTS

Ferrar, M.J., *The Saxton Map, 1579; An Investigation*, 2008, http://www. cartographyunchained.com/pdfs/cs1_pdf.pdf.

Leunig, T., C. Minns, and P. Wallis, *Work, training, and economic mobility in premodern societies: new evidence from English apprenticeship records*, http://personal.lse.ac.uk/minns/Leunig%20Minns%20Wallis%20 apprentices%2030%2011%2008%20clean.pdf.

Lindahl, G., *Dances From The Inns Of Court* http://www.pbm. com/~lindahl/dance/ioc/intro.html.

Loengard, J.S. (ed.), *London viewers and their certificates, 1508–1558: Certificates of the sworn viewers of the City of London*, British History Online, http:// www.british-history.ac.uk/report.aspx?compid=36052.

Mason, M.K., *The Role of Anti-Catholicism in England in the 1670s* (2008), http://www.moyak.com/researcher/resume/papers/catholic. html#N_68_.

Meide, C., *The Development and Design of Bronze Ordnance, Sixteenth through Nineteenth Centuries*, College of William & Mary November 2002, http:// www.staugustinelighthouse.org/LAMP/Conservation/Meide2002_ Bronze.pdf.

Officer, L.H. and S.H. Williamson, *Five Ways to Compute the Relative Value of a UK Pound Amount, 1270 to Present*, MeasuringWorth, www. measuringworth.com/ukcompare/

Picture Credits

41. Charles II, by Philippe de Champagne (1653), unaltered.

Acknowledgements

This book emerged from a BBC Wales TV series which I produced and directed in 2008, in which my old friend Terry Jones (an Ogilby enthusiast) walked four of the seventeenth-century roads in Wales while I became increasingly puzzled about them. It was a very wet summer, but everyone was game and we had a wonderful time. So I begin with a huge debt to Terry, and to Simon Mansfield the executive producer.

We were helped on the journey by many remarkable people, among them Philip Burden, Derek Bissel, the Beaumaris Lifeboat and the Maritime Coastguard Agency, Peter Conradi, Ellis Lewis, Wynn Evans, Dean of St Davids, and Nona Rees the Sub-Librarian there, Dave Evans of Memorymap, Anders Leijerstam, John Rogers (the boatman at Ferryside) and John Philpotts, Barrister. And then there were the many historians who gave freely of their rich and entertaining stores of knowledge: Professors John Davies and Richard Moore-Colyer, Drs Lloyd Bowen, Felicity Henderson, Madeleine Gray and Mike Roberts, as well as Terry Breverton, Mike Parker and Les Jones.

It was Professor Ronald Hutton who suggested that I write an article about my conclusions, and then with remarkable generosity stuck with it while I produced an entire book which he rescued from a series of errors of great magnitude (others, of course, remain, but that's not his fault). Then I fell into the remarkable hands of Professor Charles W.J. Withers, who read the text like a publishing editor and pointed me in the direction of a great deal of geographical scholarship that I had never come across at all. By now I had the benefit of an Honorary Fellowship from Lampeter College, of the University of Wales, Trinity St Davids, which opened up facilities and workspace to me and for which I am very grateful.

The list of friends who have supported me by critical listening as I tried out ideas and material, and who made important and insightful critical contributions is now, after eight years of intermittent effort, so large that I cannot list them, but I do owe each of them a great debt. And of course my wife Sarah, who has produced another of her impressive indexes, has managed to push me away from my worst ideas about how to tell this story, and has patiently endured my endlessly tedious enthusiasm for it.

Finally I would like to thank everyone who works at the British Library, that fabulous jewel in the heart of London, who do all they possibly can to support their readers and preserve their astounding collection while making it readily accessible with no fuss and great charm.

Index

Page numbers in *italics* refer to pages with illustrations.